AFTER HITLER

AFTER HITLER

◐◍◐

THE LAST TEN DAYS
OF WORLD WAR II IN EUROPE

MICHAEL JONES

NAL
CALIBER

NAL CALIBER
Published by New American Library,
an imprint of Penguin Random House LLC
375 Hudson Street, New York, New York 10014

This book is a publication of New American Library.
Previously published in a John Murray (Publishers) edition.

First NAL Caliber Printing, October 2015

For more information about Penguin Random House, visit penguinrandomhouse.com.

LIBRARY OF CONGRESS CATALOGING-IN-PUBLICATION DATA

Jones, Michael K.
After Hitler: the last ten days of World War II in Europe/Michael Jones.
p. cm.
Originally published: London : John Murray, 2015.
ISBN 978-0-451-47701-9 (hardback)
1. World War, 1939–1945—Europe—End.   2. World War, 1939–1945—Diplomatic history.
3. World War, 1939–1945—Peace.   I. Title.
D755.7.J66 2015
940.53'4—dc23   2015018149

Printed in the United States of America
1   3   5   7   9   10   8   6   4   2

Set in Adobe Caslon Pro   •   Designed by Elke Sigal

PUBLISHER'S NOTE
While the author has made every effort to provide accurate telephone numbers and Internet addresses at the time of publication, neither the publisher nor the author assumes any responsibility for errors, or for changes that occur after publication. Further, publisher does not have any control over and does not assume any responsibility for author or third-party Web sites or their content.

Penguin
Random
House

To all those—
from East and West—
who fought to rid Europe of fascism

CONTENTS

LIST OF ILLUSTRATIONS

1. The spell breaks: the Nazi eagle and swastika above the damaged grandstand of their rally site at Nuremberg.
2. East meets West: Lieutenants William Robertson and Alexander Sylvashko embrace at Torgau on the Elbe (April 25, 1945).
3. US infantrymen move down a street in Waldenburg, south-central Germany, April 1945.
4. Berlin falls to the Red Army: Marshal Georgi Zhukov on the steps of the Reichstag, May 2.
5. British tanks race toward Lübeck, May 2.
6. The horror: a sign erected by British forces outside Bergen-Belsen concentration camp, May 1945.
7. The British arrive at Hamburg: a Cromwell tank guards the bridge over the Elbe.
8. German soldiers—some using horse-drawn transport—make their way toward British forces to surrender.
9. British and Russian troops meet at Wismar, May 3.
10. A Russian tanker and British sapper drink to victory.
11. Monty's triumph: the British field marshal receives the German delegation at Lüneburg Heath, May 3.
12. A day later the formal surrender of Denmark, Holland and northwestern Germany is signed in Montgomery's tent.
13. The American field command—seated (*left to right*) are Generals William Simpson, George Patton, Carl Spaatz, Dwight Eisenhower, Omar Bradley, Courtney Hodges and Leonard Gerow. Standing (*center*) is Eisenhower's chief of staff, General Walter Bedell Smith.
14. High-ranking American and Russian officers meet on the Elbe, May 5 (from the Soviet 3rd Guards Tank Corps and the US Third Army).

ILLUSTRATION CREDITS

LIST OF MAPS

PREFACE

M ay 2015 is the seventieth anniversary of VE-Day in Europe. For many, in the Allied armed forces and among the civilians who supported the war effort, it is a last opportunity to connect with a vitally important achievement—the overthrow of Hitler and the Nazi regime. We remember those who sacrificed their lives so that we might see this day. All of us are in their debt.

This book tells the story of the last ten days of the war, from the death of Hitler on April 30 to the celebration of VE-Day in Moscow on May 9, a day after it is held in the West.

In its structure, it follows a countdown formula from day to day—but within this framework it also takes a thematic approach, bringing out the complex international politics and diplomacy that underlay these military events. It also addresses a wider concern—the humanitarian catastrophe that was engulfing Europe and the psychological impact this had on those caught up in it.

Its central aim is to show why we celebrate two VE-Days—May 8 in the West, May 9 in the East (although the Channel Islands also celebrate their liberation on May 9): how this came about and what its real significance is.

These separate days tell a story of the common cause between allies, but also of the divisions that nearly caused a rift between them in the days after Hitler's death. It was a crisis largely hidden from public view and in the event it was successfully mastered. All those involved in the behind-the-scenes diplomacy deserve credit for that.

I have tried to present a view that is fair to all the members of the Grand Alliance, and in particular the Soviet Union—whose motives in May 1945 (and indeed throughout the war) were sometimes viewed with considerable suspicion in the West—recognizing its major contribution to the victory against Nazi Germany and that it had legitimate concerns of its own. In a final reckoning, we will never know whether the descent into the Cold War was inevitable. I look at the pernicious influence of the administration of Hitler's successor, Admiral Dönitz, whose shadowy role in the days after the Führer's death is often underestimated—and the fears of both sides as the post-war map of Europe began to unfold. In such circumstances, I believe it was a real achievement that the Alliance held firm at the war's very end.

I also try to acknowledge those issues that were not resolved as this terrible war drew to its close. I counterpoint the victory celebrations in the West with the course of the little-known but important uprising in Prague in the East. On May 8, 1945, while London was *en fête* with all the joys of VE-Day, the Czech capital was fighting for its very life. By a quite miraculous series of events Prague was saved—but the Russian Liberation Army, which played a crucial part in rescuing the city, would be less lucky. Amid the euphoria, the war's end involved awkward and sometimes unjust political compromises. But in the final defeat of the Third Reich and all that it stood for there was also real reason for hope.

In the summer of 2008 I visited Berlin with the instructions of two veterans fresh in my mind. One, Armin Lehmann, had been a member of the Hitler Youth and a courier to the Führer in the last terrible days of fighting in the city, as the war drew to its close. He had been in the Führer Bunker on the morning of Hitler's death, on April 30, 1945. A day later, Armin had made a hellish breakout through the burning rubble of Berlin—eventually reaching the safety of American lines on the River Elbe. The other, Red Army lieutenant Vasily Ustyugov, had on the same day—April 30—been only a few hundred meters away from Armin, fighting inside the Reichstag—which, despite lying in ruins for most of Hitler's rule, became a symbol for the Russians of the hated Nazi regime. For Armin, the beginning of May 1945 was the collapse of everything he believed in; for Vasily, it was a triumphant vindication of a patriotic cause. As I visited some of the places seared in their memories and powerfully recounted in their stories, the genesis of this book emerged—the story of the last days of the Second World War, the days after Hitler's death.

The concept grew the following autumn when I embarked on a cruise of the Black Sea under the banner of the BBC History Magazine Team, alongside fellow lecturers Greg Neale and Martin Folly. It was a powerful experience to visit Yalta and the site of the great summit in February 1945 that decisively shaped post-war Europe, and to hear Dr. Folly's ideas on the three-power diplomacy between Britain, America and the Soviet Union that was its anvil. Since then, many have helped in this book's evolution. Alongside Martin, I would like to thank Professor Geoffrey Roberts of the University of Cork, Dr. Elke Scherstjanoi of Berlin's Institut für Zeitgeschichte, and particularly Richard Hargreaves—who shared his knowledge of the siege of Breslau and German archives in general—and Tomas Jakl of Prague's Military Institute, who guided my work on the uprising of May 1945.

Many veterans have given generously of their time. I would especially like to thank Antonin Sticha of the Czech House of Veterans in Prague for sharing his own memories of the uprising there and facilitating other interviews. Alexander Ivanov of the Russian Council of War Veterans in Moscow also arranged a number of important meetings. And Julie Chervinsky of the Blavatnik Foundation Archive has drawn my attention to a number of moving veteran accounts. Further acknowledgments are to be found in the endnotes.

I am grateful to the staff of the collections of the Imperial War Museum and the Liddell Hart Centre for Military Archives at King's College London, the National Archives at Kew, the Churchill Archive Center at Churchill College, Cambridge, the East Sussex Record Office (where the Mass Observation Archive is now housed) and the Second World War Experience Centre near Leeds. Foreign documentary material has also been drawn from the Prague City Archives, the Bundesarchiv at Freiburg, the Russian Ministry of

Defense Archive at Podolsk and the National Archives and Records Administration (NARA), Washington. Ralph Gibson of RIA Novosti kindly helped me with some of the illustrative material and also located some eyewitness accounts of Moscow on May 9, 1945.

I am grateful to Amanda Helm for giving me access to the unpublished memoir of her father, Captain Derek Thomas, and to Russell Porter for sharing the reminiscences of his father, Lance-Corporal Ray Porter, both of the British 6th Airborne Division, and to the Airborne Forces website for additional veteran information. I would like to thank the BBC for permission to cite from their "People's War" online archive (those involved are individually acknowledged in the endnotes). I have also benefited enormously from the material on the numerous US divisional websites. Soviet material has been provided by the Russian Veterans' Association, Moscow, the Blavatnik Foundation Archive, New York, and Artem Drabkin's "I remember" link at www.russianbattlefield.com. On the German side, the Courland Pocket website, www.kurland-kessel.de, has been of particular value. Place names have been modernized—except in those instances (as with Breslau instead of Wroclaw) where the original allows the narrative to be clearer. All Soviet source references—in the Endnotes and Bibliography—have been translated from the Russian.

It has been a privilege to assemble such moving material—and to tell the story of the last days of the Second World War in Europe.

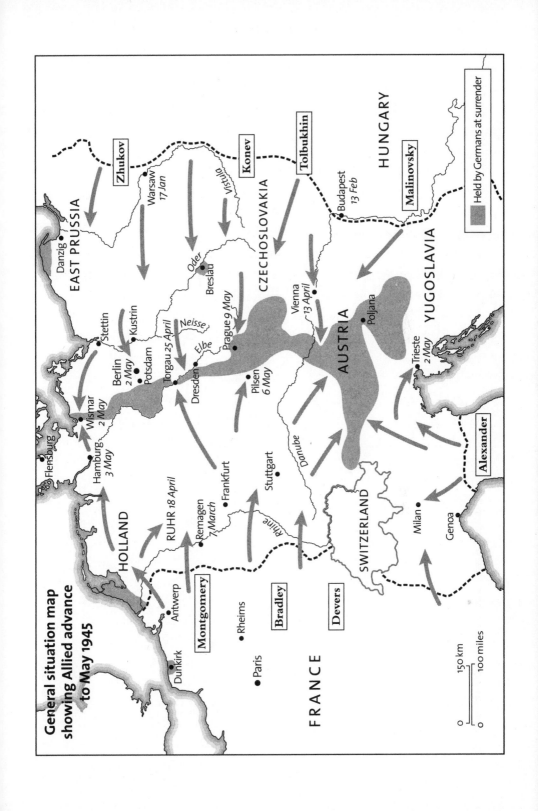

General situation map showing Allied advance to May 1945

Held by Germans at surrender

Zhukov

Konev

Tolbukhin

Malinovsky

HUNGARY

EAST PRUSSIA

Warsaw
17 Jan

Danzig

Oder

Vistula

Breslau

CZECHOSLOVAKIA

Budapest
13 Feb

YUGOSLAVIA

Stettin

Kustrin

Neisse

Prague 9 May

Vienna
13 April

Poljana

AUSTRIA

Berlin
2 May

Potsdam

Torgau 25 April

Elbe

Dresden

Pilsen
6 May

Trieste
2 May

Wismar
2 May

Flensburg

Hamburg
3 May

HOLLAND

RUHR 18 April

Remagen
7 March

Frankfurt

Stuttgart

Danube

Rhine

SWITZERLAND

Milan

Genoa

Alexander

Antwerp

Montgomery

Bradley

Devers

Rheims

Paris

FRANCE

Dunkirk

150 km

100 miles

0

0

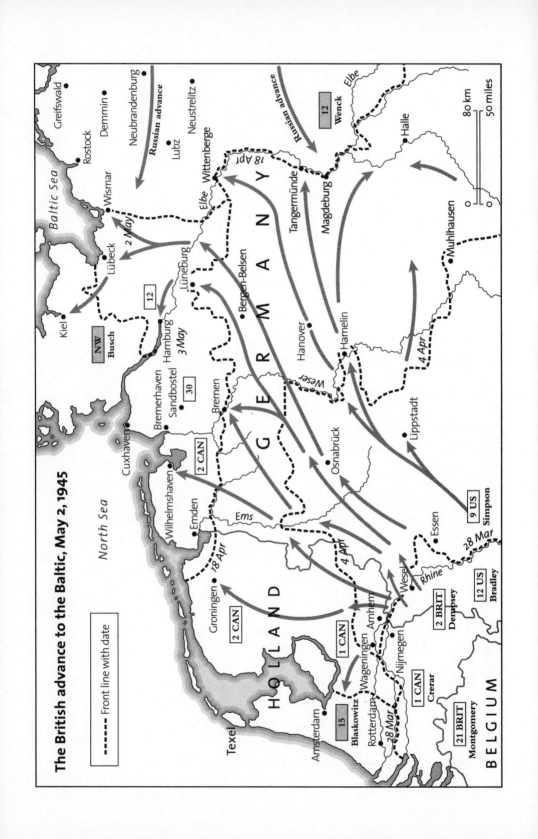

The British advance to the Baltic, May 2, 1945

- - - - - Front line with date

Baltic Sea

Greifswald
Rostock
Demmin
Neubrandenburg
Lubz
Neustrelitz
Wismar
Lübeck
Kiel

Russian advance

Wittenberge
Elbe
Tangermünde
Magdeburg
Halle
Muhlhausen

Russian advance

12 Wenck

Elbe
18 Apr

NW Busch

12

Hamburg
3 May

Lüneburg
Bergen-Belsen

2 May

Sandbostel
Bremerhaven
30
Bremen

Hanover
Weser
Hamelin

4 Apr

Cuxhaven

2 CAN

Wilhelmshaven
Emden

Osnabrück
Lippstadt

North Sea

Ems

9 US Simpson

Essen

28 Mar

Groningen
18 Apr

2 CAN

Wesel
Rhine
4 Apr

12 US Bradley

HOLLAND

Texel

Amsterdam
Rotterdam

15 Blaskowitz
Wageningen
Arnhem
Nijmegen

28 Mar

1 CAN

2 BRIT Dempsey

1 CAN Crerar

21 BRIT Montgomery

BELGIUM

GERMANY

80 km
50 miles

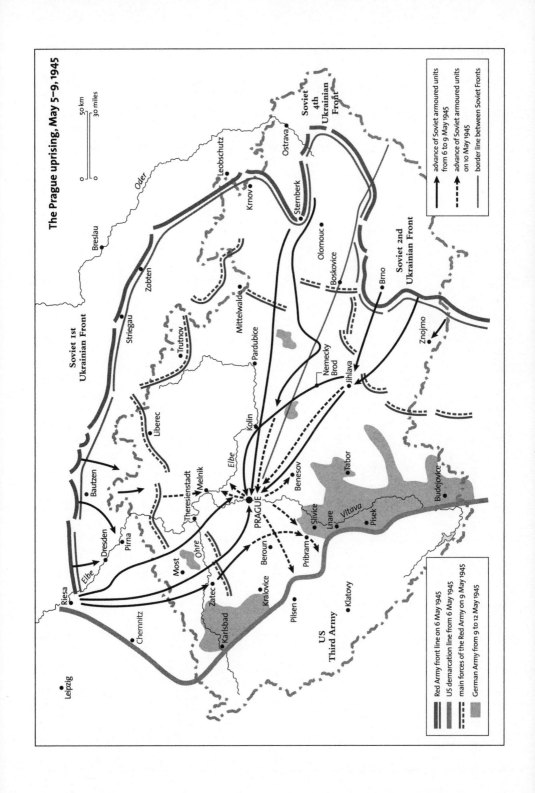

The Prague uprising, May 5–9, 1945

50 km
30 miles

advance of Soviet armoured units
from 6 to 9 May 1945
advance of Soviet armoured units
on 10 May 1945
border line between Soviet Fronts

Red Army front line on 6 May 1945
US demarcation line from 6 May 1945
main forces of the Red Army on 9 May 1945
German Army from 9 to 12 May 1945

Soviet 1st
Ukrainian Front

Soviet 4th
Ukrainian Front

Soviet 2nd
Ukrainian Front

US
Third Army

Leipzig
Chemnitz
Riesa
Breslau
Dresden
Pirna
Bautzen
Zobten
Striegau
Trutnov
Liberec
Theresienstadt
Melnik
Most
Ohre
Zatec
Karlsbad
Kralovice
Pilsen
Klatovy
Beroun
Pribram
PRAGUE
Kolin
Elbe
Mittelwalde
Pardubice
Leobschutz
Krnov
Ostrava
Sternberk
Olomouc
Boskovice
Brno
Znojmo
Jihlava
Nemecky
Brod
Benesov
Lnare
Vltava
Pisek
Tabor
Slivice
Budejovice
Oder
Elbe

TIMELINE

Hitler draws up his last will in the bunker by the Reich Chancellery. Later that day he marries his former mistress, Eva Braun. The Red Army has now captured most of Berlin except for the central government quarter (the area around the Reich Chancellery, the Reichstag and the Brandenburg Gate).

Russian forces continue to push forward in Austria and Czechoslovakia. In Vienna, the Soviet Union sets up a provisional government.

The British 2nd Army crosses the Elbe at Lauenburg, 20 miles east of Hamburg, and advances toward Schwerin and Wismar in Mecklenburg.

French forces liberate the last part of their country still held by the Germans, on the Alpine frontier.

The 30,000 surviving inmates of Dachau are freed by the US Third Army. The American advance continues toward Munich.

Arctic convoy RA 66, leaving Murmansk, becomes involved in the last convoy battle of the war.

In western Holland, still held by the Germans, a truce is agreed to enable the Allies to drop food on the starving population. Over the next ten days, in Operation Manna, British Bomber Command drops over 6,000 tons of food; the US Air Force joins in (Operation Chowhound), supplying another 4,000 tons.

Venice is liberated by the British 8th Army. The US 1st Armored Division enters Milan.

The German garrison in Italy prepares to surrender unconditionally. Terms are signed at Caserta—to come into effect on May 2. Once they are ratified twenty-two German divisions in Austria and Italy will lay down their arms.

APRIL 30

Red Army forces break into the Reichstag (although fighting within the building will continue for another two days). Russian troops are now within 400 meters of the Reich Chancellery and Führer Bunker. Hitler and Eva Braun commit suicide at around 3:45 p.m. Under the terms of Hitler's will, the new German leader will be the head of the navy, Admiral Karl Dönitz.

In northern Germany, soldiers of Marshal Rokossovsky's 2nd Belorussian Front advance toward Straslund. In Czechoslovakia, the Red Army occupies Ostrava. German forces continue to hold parts of Moravia and most of Bohemia.

The French 1st Army enters Austria near Lake Constance. The British 2nd Army advances toward the Baltic coast. The US 7th Army enters Munich.

In northern Germany, British troops free over 21,500 prisoners at Sandbostel camp. The Red Army liberates Ravensbrück concentration camp.

MAY I

General Krebs begins surrender negotiations in Berlin with Russian general Chuikov. They are suspended when Goebbels refuses to accept unconditional surrender. Early that evening Goebbels and his wife decide to kill their six children and then commit suicide. Later, in a breakout from the bunker, Martin Bormann is also killed. Dönitz announces the death of Hitler to the German nation.

In the north, the British continue their advance toward Lübeck and Hamburg. The US First and Ninth Armies are firmly established along the Elbe and Mulde rivers, but have been forbidden to advance any farther into the zone designated for Soviet occupation. The US Seventh Army continues to advance into Austria.

The Americans capture three German field marshals, von Rundstedt, von Leeb and List.

MAY 2

German forces in northern Italy and parts of Austria surrender to Field Marshal Alexander. Montgomery's 21st Army Group seizes Lübeck and Wismar, the latter only hours ahead of the Russians. Alexander sends troops into Trieste—although the city is already occupied by Tito's Yugoslav partisans.

German rocket scientist Wernher von Braun is captured by troops of US 12th Division in southern Bavaria, after he and his team of scientists flee from their rocket research base at Peenemünde.

MAY 3

Admiral Dönitz moves the seat of his government to Flensburg.

The German delegation begins surrender negotiations with Montgomery on Lüneburg Heath. Hamburg surrenders to British forces.

The *Cap Arcona* is sunk in the Bay of Lübeck.

MAY 4

Montgomery receives the unconditional surrender of German forces in Schleswig-Holstein, western Holland and Denmark (to be effective from 8:00 a.m. on May 5). It is estimated that more than half a million German troops are involved, who will join another half-million who have surrendered in the last forty-eight hours.

German forces in northern Germany, Czechoslovakia and Austria conduct rearguard actions against the Red Army, as they attempt to break away and reach the Anglo-American lines. Fighting continues in besieged Breslau, Moravia, the Vistula Delta and the Courland Pocket in Latvia.

US troops enter the Berchtesgaden, Hitler's Bavarian stronghold.

During negotiations for the formation of the United Nations in San Francisco, Soviet foreign minister Molotov informs US secretary of state Stettinius that the Red Army had arrested sixteen Polish peace negotiators (an event that actually took place in March).

MAY 5

German Army Group G surrenders unconditionally to US forces at Haar in Bavaria. US 11th Armored Division liberates Mauthausen concentration camp.

On the Baltic coast, Russian troops capture the German rocket research centers at Swinemünde and Peenemünde.

At Wageningen in Holland, General Blaskowitz surrenders the German 25th Army to Canadian general Charles Foulkes.

British paratroopers land in Copenhagen.

The beginning of the civilian uprising in Prague. General Patton's US Third Army invades western Czechoslovakia.

MAY 6

Dönitz sacks Himmler from all official positions within the Third Reich.

The US 97th Division occupies Pilsen in Czechoslovakia. The US 12th Corps advances toward Prague, but is then halted on the orders of Eisenhower—to allow the Soviet forces to occupy the rest of the country, as had originally been agreed.

The Soviet Union publishes a full report on the death camp at Auschwitz.

That evening, the 1st Division of the Russian Liberation (Vlasov) Army enters Prague in support of the rebels and Breslau surrenders after an eighty-two-day siege.

MAY 7

General Jodl signs the instrument of unconditional surrender between Germany and the Allies in a schoolroom at Rheims at 2:41 a.m. The Soviet Union refuses to accept this, and asks that a revised treaty be signed in Berlin the following day.

In western Czechoslovakia, a platoon from the US Army's 803rd Tank Destroyer Battalion is ambushed by the Germans, and one of the unit is killed. GI Charles Havlat will be the last American soldier killed in Europe.

US troops arrest Göring.

After a day of fierce fighting in defense of the Prague uprising, General Bunyachenko, commander of the 1st Division of the Russian Liberation Army, is told the city will soon be occupied by the Red Army, and his forces must leave the following morning.

MAY 8

VE (Victory-in-Europe) Day for the Western Allies. The German surrender is ratified in a second signing at Karlshorst, a suburb of Berlin.

The Red Army occupies Dresden. German forces on the Courland Peninsula in Latvia—undefeated in more than six months of fighting against the Red Army—agree to surrender the following morning.

The "day of death" in Prague as SS and regular Wehrmacht units come close to obliterating the uprising. But the approach of the Red Army forces General Toussaint to negotiate. The German garrison leaves the city that evening, although some SS units keep fighting. The Russian Liberation Army's 1st Division retreats westward through Czechoslovakia toward American lines.

MAY 9

VE-Day for the Soviet Union. The Courland Pocket and final German outposts on the Vistula Delta surrender. So do the remaining garrisons at Dunkirk, Saint-Nazaire, La Rochelle and the Channel Islands.

The Red Army occupies the Danish island of Bornholm. In Operation Doomsday, British troops prepare to fly to Norway to accept a German surrender there.

MAY 11–12

Battle of Slivice in western Czechoslovakia.

MAY 13–14

Battle of Poljana in northern Yugoslavia.

MAY 15

Final cessation of hostilities on the Eastern Front.

MAY 20

Ceasefire enforced on the Dutch island of Texel.

MAY 23

Arrest of the Dönitz government at Flensburg. Heinrich Himmler commits suicide.

1

THE FUNERAL PYRE

A t 6:00 a.m. on April 30, 1945 Major General Wilhelm Mohnke was summoned to attend Adolf Hitler in the Reich Chancellery Bunker in the center of Berlin. Mohnke's forces were responsible for defending the government quarter of the city. "I was taken to meet the Führer in his own bedroom," Mohnke recalled.

> He sat on a chair beside his bed. Over his pajamas he was wearing a black military greatcoat . . . His left hand shook incessantly and yet he exuded a strange sense of calm, as if his thoughts were collected and he had slept well—which of course he had not.
>
> Hitler was precise. He began: "Mohnke, how long can we hold out?" I answered "24 hours my Führer, no longer than that." I then described the military situation. The Russians had reached the Wilhelmstrasse and advanced through the U-Bahn tunnel under the Friedrichstrasse. Most of the Tiergarten was in their hands, and they had fought right up to the Potsdamer Platz, only 300 meters from the bunker. Hitler digested this calmly.
>
> With military matters concluded, he began to talk to me about

politics. It struck me that this might be his last discourse of any length on this subject. The basic theme was the future fate of Europe. The western democracies were decadent, and the powerful momentum of the peoples of the east—successfully channeled by the Communist system—could not be opposed by them. The west would fall under their domination. His tone of voice, as this argument was developed, was subdued and distant. Shortly after 7:00 a.m. I left and returned to my command post.

Hitler's dark yet compelling personality, which had held millions under its dominion, was now a mere shadow of its former self. Wolf Heisendorf, a personal assistant to propaganda minister Joseph Goebbels, who remained with his master in the Führer Bunker, observed:

By April 30 it was obvious to everyone that further defense of Berlin was hopeless. Germany was split into several parts by Anglo-American and Russian armies—the hoped-for clash between them had never in fact materialized. Our Army High Command no longer existed as a meaningful force—its resources were scattered in all directions by the rapid advance of our opponents. The machinery of government had virtually collapsed. Our last resort had been to pull out one of our armies [General Walther Wenck's 12th] from its defense of the Elbe (turning its back on the American troops on the far side of the river) and instead push it toward Berlin. But by the 30th it was clear that these men were unable to reach the capital. In such circumstances, to try to hold out any longer against the well-equipped Russian forces of Marshal Zhukov was utterly pointless.

Heisendorf recalled the chaotic attempts to evacuate government ministries from the threatened city.

As the Red Army neared Berlin there was utter panic. Those heads of departments who could flee did so, scattering in all directions, and leaving their staff largely to fend for themselves. Hitler's own orders were disregarded. One head of the Propaganda Ministry jammed the boot of his car so full of secret documents that the catch would not close properly. As his car accelerated a mass of paper flew up in the air behind him. As the bureaucratic vestiges of our Ministry disintegrated it all seemed like a bad farce.

At Rheims in northern France, the headquarters of the Western Allies, the fate of Hitler's capital was followed with somber expectation. "Berlin is near the end," SHAEF (Supreme Headquarters of the Allied Expeditionary Force) liaison officer Colonel Richard Wilberforce wrote simply in his diary on April 30.

Berlin—the capital of Hitler's Third Reich—was indeed tottering. The Red Army had fought its way to the center of the city and the Führer's domain had shrunk to a few square miles of government buildings. But for some in the wider Third Reich, even at this late, desperate stage of the war, the Nazi doctrine remained intact. On the same day Hildegard Holzwark, a German from the Sudetenland who had welcomed Hitler as a liberator after he annexed that part of Czechoslovakia in 1938, wrote in her diary:

Tomorrow is the first of May—workers' day, a national holiday for the German people. Will there be anyone celebrating it this year?—I doubt it. It is heartbreakingly sad to face such a bitter end to our war. For six long years we held out. And there was real value to our struggle, despite our defeat. It is hard to sum up all these war experiences.

Artillery fire from the front line draws closer and closer. And yet, for the time being, I feel insulated from the fighting. A while ago I was afflicted by such fear. I just hold out for the chance that in the Sudetenland the Americans will come before the Russians. And I can only clutch on to one hope, that the western powers will not let Europe fall completely under the sway of Bolshevism. We Germans were for a long time the bulwark against this threat. But we cannot maintain it any longer—everything is now in a state of collapse.

It seems that our remaining troops lack the resolve to maintain the struggle. Discipline has broken down and everything is chaotic—such is the effect of the losses we have borne. Our people's will to resist has been broken; we have lost our self-belief. In Berlin there is bitter street fighting. The Führer stands there, virtually alone. I fear for his life.

But in truth, little had been epic in the decision to defend Berlin to the last. Rather than being the product of cold-blooded calculation, or fanatical belief, it had come about through the German leader's utter collapse in a military briefing some eight days earlier.

At 3:30 p.m. on April 22 the day's situation conference had begun with bad news: the Russians had reached Berlin's northern suburbs. Hitler looked haggard and agitated and he twice left the room to go to his own private quarters. Then the Führer was told that a counterattack from SS general Felix Steiner that he had waited all morning for had not in fact taken place. At this point something snapped. Hitler ordered everyone out of the briefing room except Field Marshal Wilhelm Keitel (the head of the German armed forces), General Alfred Jodl (the chief of staff), General Hans Krebs (chief of staff of the German army), Lieutenant General Wilhelm Burgdorf (Hitler's adjutant), Martin Bormann (secretary of the Nazi Party) and the stenographer Gerhard Herrgeswell. There followed a violent tirade, clearly audible to all those outside the room, in which he screamed that he had been betrayed by those he most trusted. And then he slumped back in his chair.

Hitler had always resolutely claimed that the war was not lost and the fight would continue until the very end. Now he decided that he would die in Berlin. Stenographer Gerhard Herrgeswell was dumbfounded by this—the Führer had never previously acknowledged the possibility of failure, always closing matters with the resolute phrase: "We will fight to the end of the Third Reich." Struggling to find an explanation for this about-turn, he believed Hitler had suffered a form of breakdown: "He said that he had lost his faith—and that he wanted to end it all, that he would die in the German capital," Herrgeswell recalled. "He repeated this fatalistic lament between ten and twenty times, with slight variations: 'I die here,' 'I die at the Chancellery' or 'I have to die here in Berlin.'"

Others concurred. When General Burgdorf left the room, he also told his staff officer, Bernd Freytag von Loringhoven, that Hitler had suffered a breakdown. According to one report, "Hitler's face went purple, and he could not put his left foot on the ground properly. Throughout that night he suffered a nervous collapse and kept raving that he would meet his end in Berlin." Learning that SS units northeast of the city (at Eberswalde on the Finow Canal, 15 miles from Berlin's center), the so-called Steiner group, had not responded to his orders to attack the Russians threw him over the edge. He realized that the will to resist was no longer there.

Those around him were astonished. Before this extraordinary outburst no decision to stay in Berlin had been made; indeed, his closest supporters believed Hitler's plan was to leave the German capital and fly to his Bavarian retreat, the Berchtesgaden, and first Field Marshal Keitel and then Party Secretary Martin Bormann attempted to get the Führer to change his mind. They failed.

Their leader had suffered some form of psychological collapse. He could now offer little beyond the despairing utterance—"You will have to go to south Germany and form a government. Göring will be my successor. He will negotiate." Whether this was an order or a prophetic utterance was totally unclear to those around him.

If the military briefing was a complete shock to those who witnessed it, Hitler's physical and mental decline had begun months earlier. Wolf Heisendorf, personal assistant to Propaganda Minister Goebbels, observed:

It was clear to all of us that the Führer's days were numbered. He seemed broken, physically and emotionally—some even speculated that he had suffered a stroke. But whatever had occurred, he now appeared a sick, broken old man. In such a state, he was unable to broadcast live on the radio and the few speeches that he did deliver had to be prerecorded and then re-edited. His voice changed completely—its range and depth replaced by a dull monotone. And the content of the speeches, which no-one was allowed to alter (even Goebbels could only make minor adjustments), caused consternation within the Propaganda Ministry. Their historical analogies—the

Carthaginians at Cannae, or Frederick the Great and the Seven Years War—seemed increasingly absurd with the Russians at the gates of Berlin.

And yet, however much Hitler's condition had deteriorated, he remained the central reason why the Grand Alliance had been formed. The British prime minister, Winston Churchill, detested Nazism and his rivalry with the Führer was very much a personal one. The leader of the Third Reich was the symbol of a system that Churchill loathed, even before its worst excesses were widely known. On June 22, 1941, the day that Germany invaded the Soviet Union, Churchill broadcast to the nation, declaiming: "Hitler is a monster of wickedness, insatiable in his lust for blood and plunder." In a war cabinet meeting of July 6, 1942, he was scarcely less vehement, denouncing him as "the mainspring of evil," and adding that if he fell into British hands "we shall certainly put him to death." Among the three great powers of the Alliance, Churchill's struggle had been the longest, as a minister in the cabinet of Neville Chamberlain from the declaration of war against Germany in September 1939 and as prime minister from May 1940, when the United Kingdom stood alone against the Nazi hegemony in Europe.

As Britain resisted the might of Germany in the dark days of 1940, the Soviet Union had established a non-aggression pact with Hitler and was supplying the Nazi war machine with vital industrial equipment. This pact, formalized between the two foreign ministers, Molotov and Ribbentrop, allowed both powers to extend their areas of influence. Germany overwhelmed western Europe in a lightning campaign; Russia occupied the Baltic states, defeated Finland and seized territory from her, and also grabbed land from Romania. The two countries had invaded hapless Poland together—Germany from the west, the Soviet Union from the east—and divided the country between them.

On June 22, 1941, Hitler breached the non-aggression pact, ordering a surprise invasion of his former ally. The onslaught required months of preparation and yet it caught the Soviet leader, Joseph Stalin, completely off guard. He could not believe that Germany would attack him while Britain still resisted to the west. The colonization of the east was part of the Führer's personal vision—set out in his book *Mein Kampf*—which showed his detestation of the Slavs, whom he regarded as an inferior people. Hitler wanted to create *Lebensraum*—living space—for the German master race by subjugating most of European Russia. He also loathed Bolshevism, but while his attack on Russia was proclaimed as a crusade against communism, at heart it was a brutal race war. Neither side had signed up to the Geneva Convention of 1929 and the German onslaught unleashed one of the most destructive conflagrations in human history.

The Soviet leader was politically astute but also chronically suspicious. He had gambled on more time—to re-equip and retrain the Red Army and relocate Russian industries to the east, and when he received warnings from British intelligence that a German invasion was imminent, he imagined it a Western plot to embroil him in a war. Stalin's failure to anticipate a breach of the pact was the greatest blunder of his entire leadership, and in the dark days of 1941, as Hitler's Wehrmacht surged hundreds of miles into Russia, winning a series of devastating victories against a reeling Red Army, his country was brought to the brink of defeat.

But Stalin and the Soviet Union held firm—and despite sustaining losses that no Western democracy could ever have contemplated, turned the tables on the German war machine. The Führer's previously invincible forces were repulsed from Moscow, destroyed at Stalingrad, and defeated once again at Kursk—the last major offensive they would launch in the east. In the summer of 1944 the Red Army launched Operation Bagration—their most complete military success against the German army—and that autumn finally liberated all of their territories that had fallen under the sway of the Nazis. The Red Army—now consisting of a colossal 8 million men—fought its way into eastern Europe, dispatching Hitler's former allies Romania and Hungary, liberating much of Yugoslavia, and occupying Poland and eastern Germany. In sheer numerical strength, Russia was the strongest military power in the Alliance, and its armies dominated central and eastern Europe.

These events had been initiated by Hitler and always held a grave risk. At the height of his power and influence, the Führer had carried most of his party with him and many of his generals too (although a considerable number still held strong reservations), but it was highly unlikely that anyone else in

Nazi Germany would have embarked upon such a hazardous course. By opening up a war on two fronts, Hitler was gambling on defeating the Soviet Union quickly. Were he to fail, he was dooming Germany to a battle of attrition against a country of vastly superior manpower and resources.

Hitler created the war in the east—and as a result brought the Soviet Union into a most unlikely alliance with the two Western imperialist and capitalist powers—Britain and America—that were its ideological enemies. It was common hatred of Hitler—and his brutal Nazi state—which overrode their enormous differences.

In the summer of 1941 Britain stood alone. Hitler's invasion of the Soviet Union was a remarkable opportunity and it was to Churchill's considerable credit that he seized it, despite his loathing of Bolshevism. It was a mark of great statesmanship that he formed an alliance with a country whose political system he so distrusted. Britain had entered the war in partnership with France, but France had been defeated and occupied and most of Europe was now under Nazi sway. With America not yet willing to commit itself to a European war, Churchill saw it was vital that Russia and Britain join forces if the Third Reich was ever to be defeated. In the short term, the most that Britain could do was offer the Soviets material aid, through the Arctic convoy route to Murmansk and Archangel. The Arctic convoys—menaced by German U-boats and the Luftwaffe—suffered considerable losses, but Churchill insisted that they be maintained, despite the objections of the Admiralty, because they gave substance and succor to the Anglo-Soviet alliance. Churchill's courageous and powerful rhetoric after the evacuation from Dunkirk and during the Battle of Britain inspired the nation, and will always rank as one of his greatest achievements, but his embrace of the Soviet Union in 1941 matched it. In a desperate situation, there was hope once more.

And yet it was hope bought at a price. The Anglo-Soviet alliance was a partnership of expediency. Britain entered the war in September 1939 to protect Poland in the same month the Soviet Union stabbed that country in the back. Between 1939 and 1941 Stalin administered eastern Poland with a brutal ruthlessness that rivaled, and at times surpassed, the atrocities of the Nazis in the other half of the country. In the longer term, as the German war machine was rolled back, Poland would be a source of friction between the

United Kingdom and Russia. And in April 1945 Britain's diplomatic options were limited—the entire country was now occupied by a resurgent Red Army.

Then there was the United States of America. American involvement in the Grand Alliance was once again a product of Hitler's foreign policy. On December 7, 1941, the Japanese launched a surprise attack on the American fleet at Pearl Harbor—drawing the United States into a long Pacific conflict. Faced with such a prospect, President Franklin Roosevelt was unlikely to persuade the nation to enter a European war against Nazi Germany as well. Remarkably, Hitler forced his hand. Five days after Pearl Harbor, with his armies in retreat from Moscow in terrible winter weather, the Führer declared war on America.

This quite incredible decision doomed Germany to eventual defeat in the war. It is hard to find an explanation for it other than as the product of Hitler's growing megalomania. Four days later he appointed himself leader of the German army, although his military experience in the First World War had not taken him beyond the rank of corporal.

Hitler thereby brought the Grand Alliance into being. As the war continued and he demanded fanatical obedience from the German people and utterly refused to compromise or negotiate with his foes, he ensured that the Alliance held firm. Now, a wreck of his former self, entombed in Berlin and surrounded by his Russian enemies, a simple yet paramount question was forming—what would happen to the Alliance after Hitler's death?

Hitler's oratory, his sway over an audience, was always one of his greatest strengths. Its wane in the twilight of his rule—and the pathos of his terrible outburst in the bunker—was disconcerting to those accustomed to it. But even at the end, Hitler retained remnants of his political instinct and charisma. SS general Felix Steiner's failure to obey the Führer's command on April 22 to attack numerically superior Red Army forces had precipitated the Nazi leader's dramatic collapse. Steiner's army group—depleted and outnumbered by the Russians—was unable to perform the military role Hitler demanded.

This may well have been recognition from Steiner of practical reality—that the resources of men, equipment and resolve necessary to carry out this order were no longer available. But it may also have carried the vestiges of treachery, as the Führer had claimed. Earlier that month, Steiner held secret discussions in Berlin with SS comrades Richard Hildebrandt and Otto Ohlendorf. Their intention was to create a new German government and procure a separate peace with the Western Allies. Steiner hoped it would be led by Himmler and that Hitler would simply be pushed aside. Steiner wanted to encourage the Anglo-American forces to advance to the River Elbe without opposition in return for a tacit agreement that they would halt there, allowing Germany to continue its struggle against the Russians in the east. The chances of such a deal were slight, but the Nazi position was desperate enough to risk exploring it. Accordingly, Heinrich Himmler, the head of the SS, left Hitler on April 20, headed to northern Germany and within a matter of days, on his own initiative, attempted to open talks with Britain and America. With Hitler remaining in Berlin, it probably suited Steiner to simply abandon him there. His inaction did not stem from military weakness alone, but was an act of deliberate disobedience. The Führer—always the political bloodhound even at this critically late stage of the war—may well have sensed it.

As Germany's military fortunes declined, members of the SS hierarchy— a bastion of Nazi ideology—began to contemplate different policies from those of their leader. The warning signs had been there for months. One of them was Himmler's decision, without Hitler's authorization, to train an army of anti-Bolshevik Russians, led by General Andrei Vlasov. Hitler, who loathed the Slavs and was hidebound by his racism, could not countenance ever using Russians, even those who renounced Stalin's regime, in any military capacity whatsoever. Yet Himmler—once his devoted disciple in such prejudice—now struck out on a path of his own. By February 1945 two full-strength divisions had been formed; the first of these was subsequently thrown into combat against the Red Army—Russian against Russian—on the Oder front in the east.

It is unclear whether reports of such recruitment were deliberately concealed from Hitler, or that he chose instead to ignore them and act as if such formations did not exist. The soldiers of the 1st Vlasov Division remained on active service, and would play a remarkable role at the war's very end. The existence of this force showed the beginnings of Himmler's estrangement from Hitler's war policy, which in the last days of the Reich would lead him to undermine the authority of his political master.

On April 22, 1945, Hitler and his immediate entourage retreated into the massive bunker complex by the Reich Chancellery, where they commenced a bizarre underground existence. The complex had two levels: the ante-bunker, and—connected to it by a circular staircase—the deeper Führer Bunker. The Führer Bunker consisted of about twenty small, sparsely furnished rooms. The corridor in front of Hitler's private apartment boasted an upholstered bench and a few old armchairs. Next to it was the conference room—where military or situation conferences took place, and where up to twenty people would crowd around the map table in a small space measuring 3.5 x 3 meters. Hitler was the only person able to sit.

Hitler's two private rooms, a study and a bedroom, were also sparsely furnished. A Dutch still-life hung over the sofa in his study, and above his desk, in an oval frame, was a picture of Frederick the Great. At the end of the Seven Years War Frederick—exhausted and on the verge of defeat—had been saved by a miracle when, in 1762, the death of the tsarina Elizabeth had changed the course of the conflict. Hearing of the death of the American president Franklin Roosevelt on April 12, 1945, the Führer hoped for a similar miracle to rescue him from his own predicament. In each of the rooms, naked lightbulbs hung from the ceilings. The harsh light, the constantly humming diesel engines that powered the ventilation system, the cramped quarters and inlaid concrete created an oppressive and disorientating atmosphere, which the rapidly worsening events only accentuated.

Hitler's Germany had been invaded by an Allied coalition, but Russian soldiers were now poised to encircle and take Berlin. At the Big Three conference at Yalta in February 1945 the Allied powers had drawn up a political map for post-war Europe. Germany was to be divided into four zones: three for the Western Allies, including newly liberated France, whose armies were fighting with the Americans, and the fourth for the Soviet Union. The Soviet zone of eastern Germany included Berlin. The city itself would be split into four separate administrative areas—British, American, French and Russian—but it rested within territory entirely controlled by the Soviet Union. At the time these arrangements were drawn up, Russian armies were already on the Oder, only 50 miles from Berlin. At the conference, it seemed likely that the German capital would be taken by the Russians.

Allied policy was to fight first and make the necessary political realignments afterward. Hitler's propaganda minister, Joseph Goebbels, clung to the belief that even at this late stage the Allies might fall out as the Western powers realized the Soviet danger as Stalin's forces spread Bolshevism over eastern Europe. "It is well-known that Russians invariably call everything that isn't 'communist,' 'fascist,'" Goebbels wrote after the conclusion of Yalta—well aware, from his own experience, that any dictatorship muzzled its political opponents. He noted that the Russians "under the guise of 'a struggle against fascism' would exterminate all forces opposing bolshevization in any country [over which] they held influence." Goebbels hoped that such heartless realpolitik would repel the Western democracies. He was particularly drawn to Poland.

Goebbels felt not a shred of sympathy for that country, callously remarking that the suffering of the Poles was the result of failing to accept Germany's "extremely reasonable terms" in 1939—but he believed it a likely cause of rupture between the Allies. He recalled how in April 1943 German forces had uncovered the Katyn grave site near Smolensk and found more than 14,000 Polish officers murdered there. The Soviet Union claimed that this atrocity had been carried out by the Germans, but the evidence pointed elsewhere. It seemed likely that the killings were the work of Russia in the spring of 1940 and Goebbels had a propaganda field day—inviting a host of neutral observers to view the site. Stalin remained exceptionally sensitive over the issue, and when the Polish government-in-exile in London grew skeptical of his version of events, he broke off diplomatic relations with them. The Western Allies discouraged press speculation about the massacre and expressed solidarity with the Soviet view, but in private questioned their ally's version of events.

Goebbels' Nazi regime was capable of plenty of killing of its own. In August 1944 the Polish uprising in Warsaw was crushed by the SS with savage force. Stalin—well aware that the rising was led by opponents of his own puppet regime, the Lublin Poles—ordered his advancing armies to halt outside the city. The Red Army waited until the revolt was utterly destroyed before resuming its advance. Stalin denied American and British planes access to his airfields to drop supplies to assist the insurgents. The Soviet leader's cynical indifference to the suffering within the city did not bode well for the Yalta accord.

In February 1945 the Grand Alliance put an optimistic gloss on their joint communication over Poland's future. In reality it was an uneasy compromise and President Roosevelt, ill and tired, had left the proceedings early, before its provisions were fully hammered out. The devil was in the detail, and loose wording allowed each power to interpret matters differently. Roosevelt and Churchill believed they had secured a reasonable settlement over the form of the Polish government. Goebbels doubted that. He saw such aspirations—that the Soviet leader would set up a fair and representative government within the country—as utterly naive: "Stalin is firmly determined . . . to negotiate with no-one over the Polish question," Goebbels observed bluntly, but with a degree of insight. "The only choice for the Poles is either to be exterminated by force or bow to the Kremlin."

Once the Western Allies realized this, tensions with the Soviet Union would inevitably rise and Goebbels clung to this hope in his retreat to the depths of the Führer Bunker. His assistant, Wolf Heisendorf, recalled frankly:

> After the Russians broke into Berlin Goebbels fell into deep depression. He realized that death was inevitable, and yet—amidst the wreckage of all his dreams—remnants of his former policy were fleetingly grasped. Each day Goebbels gathered what material he could from foreign press and radio reports. There was one theme— that a conflict between the Soviet Union and Britain and America might suddenly erupt.

Heisendorf, seeking insight into his master's attempts to maintain a grasp of the situation, continued:

> I read these résumés many times. For Goebbels, the first touchstone would be Poland; the second, the meeting on the Elbe of Russian and American troops. The possibility that the Grand Alliance opposing him might disintegrate did after all have some basis. With keen political instincts alert to the seeds of any dissension, Goebbels

could only desperately hope it might appear in time to save Germany's fortunes.

In March 1945 the Alliance did indeed fall under strain. On March 7 American troops seized the bridge over the Rhine at Remagen in a daring *coup de main*. Four days later, they began preliminary negotiations in Switzerland with the SS leader Karl Wolf about a possible German surrender in Italy. It was uncertain whether Wolf had Hitler's backing—although Himmler had given his cautious support—and discussions were held in strict secrecy. The Western Allies correctly informed the Russians that they were taking place, but then unwisely, and tactlessly, refused a Soviet request to send a representative to them.

This played to Stalin's suspicion that the West was engineering a secret peace with Germany, to enable the Nazis to continue the fight in the east. Over the next month the telegrams between Roosevelt, Churchill and Stalin saw some of the most unhappy and mistrustful exchanges of the war. On April 3 the Soviet leader stated that either the American president was lying or he was being deliberately deceived by his advisers. Stalin himself had played a part in the sudden frosting of relations, for in response to the perceived slight of the Swiss negotiations with Wolf he began discussions of his own with a Polish nationalist group—offering them the chance to join an enlarged pro-communist government—and then promptly arrested them on charges of sabotage, a sequence of events acknowledged by Russia only in early May. All the Western powers knew in mid-March was that this group of sixteen Poles had suddenly and mysteriously disappeared.

As suspicions grew, the possibility arose that Anglo-American and Russian armies would make a dash for Berlin at the same time. The military situation gave Stalin the initiative. Two Russian fronts (the Soviet equivalent of an American or British army group)—the 1st Belorussian and the 1st Ukrainian—were on the Oder river, only 50 miles from the German capital. In fierce fighting, Red Army troops were also moving into Czechoslovakia and eastern Austria, and it was clear that the Russians would soon capture Vienna. In the west, British and American armies had crossed the Rhine on a broad front, and were advancing into Germany at speed. The Anglo-American forces were farther from Berlin than their Russian allies, but Germans might offer less resistance to them. Churchill and his commander in northwest Europe, Field Marshal Montgomery, urged that an attempt on Berlin be made.

General Dwight Eisenhower—Supreme Commander of the Allied Expeditionary Force—now took a crucial decision. He decided that Anglo-American forces would halt on the River Elbe. An exception was made for Montgomery's 21st Army Group to the north, which would cross the river and strike at the Baltic ports of Lübeck and Wismar. Denmark could then be secured by the Western Allies, ahead of the Russians. In the center, American armies would halt at the river boundary; in the south, they would push on into Bavaria and western Austria.

Eisenhower's decision to halt on the Elbe minimized the chances of American and Russian forces colliding. However, the military intelligence behind it was faulty—a concern over the so-called National Redoubt, an Alpine fortress guarded by elite SS divisions where it was believed Hitler and his followers would make a final stand. The evidence for such a mountain fastness was largely illusory, but once Goebbels realized the American preoccupation with it he delightedly arranged for a mass of false documentation to fall into their hands—most of it concocted within his Propaganda Ministry. General Omar Bradley, commander of the 12th Army Group and a close personal friend of Eisenhower, would later confess ruefully that "it was amazing how we fell for this in the way we did."

United States forces were racing southward to secure a fairy-tale fortress complex that in reality was non-existent, and the decision to halt at the Elbe left Berlin to the Russians. Eisenhower had conferred with General Bradley about the likely cost in American lives of reaching the German capital. Bradley reckoned about 100,000 men—"a lot for a prestige objective"—and General George Marshall, the army chief of staff, concurred. Eisenhower allowed the Red Army the honor of storming Hitler's capital, knowing that Soviet troops would also pay the price in casualties to take the city. He communicated directly with Stalin, saying that Berlin was no longer a major objective for him—he would be halting his armies on the Elbe and pushing southeast instead.

Stalin was taken aback. Bluffing, he said that Berlin was no longer of particular importance to him either, and then summoned his military commanders Zhukov and Konev and ordered them to take the city as soon as possible. The assault would take place on April 16, 1945. Zhukov launched the main Russian offensive directly against the last German defense line, the Seelow Heights on the western bank of the Oder, and headed straight for Berlin.

On the same day Konev's 1st Ukrainian Front crossed the Oder farther south and wheeled round the German capital. By April 23 the city was encircled and no further supplies or reinforcements would reach its defenders. Stalin—who knew Churchill was still lobbying for an attack—wanted to block any last-ditch attempt by the Western Allies to reach Berlin. But Eisenhower kept his promise to the Soviet leader and Roosevelt's successor, President Harry Truman, was content to let him do so. Even when General Wenck's 12th Army pulled out of the German battle line on the Elbe, on the same day, and marched east in an attempt to save Berlin, American troops kept to their agreed position on the far side of the river. The Grand Alliance held firm.

Within the German capital, hasty defense measures were put in place when it was realized Hitler intended to make a stand there. But there were so few troops available. On April 23 General Helmuth Weidling, commander of the LVI Panzer Corps, was appointed commander of the city. A day earlier the Führer had ordered Weidling to be executed by firing squad for having retreated in the face of the enemy. The charge was then dropped, but Weidling was unenthusiastic about his new post. "I'd rather be shot than have this honor," he exclaimed.

Weidling organized the defenses into eight sectors. He had about 45,000 regular troops available, supported by the Berlin police force, the Hitler Youth, and about 40,000 men of the Home Guard (*Volkssturm*). Soviet forces outnumbered them by eight to one. The soldiers of the LVI Panzer Corps were known to the Russians already, for in the spring of 1944 they had been responsible for the worst atrocity ever committed by the German army in the Soviet Union, the creation of typhus camps where more than 50,000 civilians in the region of Parichi were deliberately infected, and then left in the path of the advancing Red Army, with the hope of causing a major typhoid epidemic among the Russian soldiers. In the words of General Pavel Batov, commander of the Soviet 65th Army, "This atrocity we would neither forgive nor forget." The fight for Berlin would always have been bitter, but the presence of LVI Panzer Corps in the city, which quickly became known to the Russians, ensured the battle was particularly savage.

Over the next few days German troops mounted a desperate defense, but the Russians closed inexorably on Berlin's center. On April 27 General Weidling wrote in his diary:

At 5:00 a.m., after a violent bombardment and with very strong air support, the Russians attacked on both sides of the Hohenzollerndamm. Defense Zone Headquarters is under heavy fire. The account for the sins of past years has arrived.

The Potsdamer Platz is also under heavy artillery bombardment. Brick and stone dust hangs in the air like a thick fog. The car in which I am driving can only make slow progress—shells are bursting on all sides and we are showered with their fragments.

Everywhere the roads are full of craters and broken brickwork, and streets and squares lie desolate. To take cover from a Russian heavy mortar bombardment we took shelter in an Underground Station. In the two-level building many civilians had taken refuge— a mass of scared people, standing packed together. It is a shattering sight.

In my afternoon situation report, I spoke of the sufferings of the population and the wounded, about everything I had seen with my own eyes during the day. Hitler seemed in a disjointed state of mind, unable to properly comprehend what I was saying.

Time was now running out. On April 28 Admiral Karl Dönitz flew a battalion of naval cadets into stricken Berlin as a gesture of solidarity with his Führer. The commander, Lieutenant Franz Kuhlmann, remembered his nightmarish arrival: "Toward the end of our flight we recognized the capital, burning from a recent bombing raid. It was a truly apocalyptic picture.

Despite the lack of contact from the radio tower, our pilot immediately attempted a landing and the plane careered wildly all over the runway."

In the circumstances, a rough landing was hardly surprising. On April 27 both Tempelhof and Gatow airports had been lost to the Russians. An emergency landing strip was then prepared in the grounds of Berlin's zoo. This was where Kuhlmann had arrived. By the evening of April 28 this landing strip could not be used either, because of the deep shell holes.

Kuhlmann continued:

When we came to a juddering halt there was a sharp command—"To the shelters—at the double!"—and we raced toward an enormous concrete silo, where military stores and equipment were kept.

In a while, an SS officer appeared, and told us we had been ordered to the Zoo Bunker [a key defense point in the center of Berlin]. When I objected, and said we had been instructed to go immediately to the Reich Chancellery, to defend Hitler's own quarters, he looked completely bewildered. Eventually we set off in an easterly direction, toward this seemingly prestige objective—along a bombed-out military road. Time and time again we were forced to dive for cover, as Russian planes swept down, strafing the route ahead.

The SS officer accompanied me to Mohnke's command post— in one of the underground shelters of the Reich Chancellery— announced my arrival to the general, and then disappeared. SS General Mohnke, the commander of Citadelle [the government district of Berlin, with Hitler's bunker at its heart], was surprised and delighted to see us, showing a degree of interest that was flattering in view of our relatively insignificant combat strength.

General Mohnke had about 2,000 men under his command—including 800 soldiers from the elite Leibstandarte SS Guard Battalion. These formed the last bulwark against the Russians. Kuhlmann continued:

Mohnke inquired carefully about the number of men I had brought, their weaponry and combat experience—quickly grasping that most were cadets, and neither properly equipped or trained for this kind of fighting. His manner was well-disposed and friendly, until I perhaps unwisely told him that I was under orders to announce myself to Hitler personally. Then his tone changed. He told me bluntly that it was hardly practicable for every junior officer to request an audience with the Führer.

Kuhlmann accommodated his men in the cellars of the nearby Foreign Office and awaited further orders. The artillery fire raining down on the Reich Chancellery became ever more violent, as groups of Red Army soldiers began to approach Citadelle's defenses.

Despite the command to stay put, Kuhlmann was summoned into the labyrinth of the Führer Bunker. Dönitz, keen to curry favor with his master, asked—through his representative in the bunker, Admiral Hans-Erich Voss—that the marine battalion's commander formally present himself. The Führer assented—and Kuhlmann descended into this subterranean world. A shock awaited him. He arrived at the lower section of the bunker as Hitler was holding a situation conference. Voss was presiding, with General Hans Krebs, Joseph Goebbels and Artur Axmann (the head of the Hitler Youth) also present.

Kuhlmann recalled:

Hitler's body had completely shrunk in on itself. His left arm and leg shook uncontrollably. Much of what he said was incomprehensible to me—it was as if, in a state of delirium, he had discovered a completely made-up language. Odd fragments of it lodged in my mind. An oft-repeated refrain: "Oh those citizens of Berlin! Those citizens of Berlin!" or "One can never do without a Hanna Reitsch [the woman pilot who had just then audaciously landed a plane on the Unter den Linden, Berlin's main thoroughfare]!" Knowing nothing of what had happened to him in this vault, I was unable to make any coherent sense of such disjointed outpourings.

The reference to a "made-up language" is striking. It may have been partly the result of extreme stress and disorientation, but it strongly suggests that the Führer had never fully recovered from his breakdown of April 22. "Hitler then dismissed me," Kuhlmann continued, "by offering his steadier right hand, and I climbed with Voss back up the bunker stairs. Although I was deeply shaken, I said nothing of my impression to Voss—and he also avoided saying any word about the state Hitler was in. But I noticed that he was aware of my embarrassment, and probably guessing the reason for it, talked about plans to bring more naval troops into Berlin instead."

When General Weidling found that much of the last defense line was "manned" by the Hitler Youth (teenage boys aged between fourteen and eighteen), he ordered Axmann to disband such combat formations within the city. The order was never carried out. On April 29 Hitler Youth courier Armin Lehmann and three of his comrades tried to carry an urgent message to a command post across the Wilhelmstrasse—now being pulverized by Russian shells. Lehmann was the only survivor. Later, he sat in the Führer Bunker in a state of shock. A woman came out of one of the rooms and poured him a glass of water. "It's terrible out there," she said. It was Eva Braun—Hitler's long-term mistress, whom he had married only hours earlier.

Within the bunker, fatalistic despair reigned. Hearing that his deputy Hermann Göring, in Obersalzberg in Bavaria, was attempting to take control of the leadership, Hitler had him arrested. On April 28 Hitler also learned that Heinrich Himmler was putting out peace feelers to the Western Allies. Himmler's representative in Berlin, Hermann Fegelein, was rounded up and shot. The Führer then began putting his own affairs in order. He married Eva Braun early on the morning of April 29—less an occasion of celebration, more of a suicide pact—and drew up his private and public wills. Göring and Himmler were both expelled from the party for their treachery. Impressed by the loyalty of Admiral Dönitz, and recently reminded of it by Kuhlmann's visit, Hitler designated him as his successor. He hoped that Dönitz's government—to be set up in Schleswig-Holstein in northern Germany—would also be joined by Bormann and Goebbels.

Hitler's secretary, Traudl Junge, typed out the copies of Hitler's will. "I worked as fast as I could," Junge recalled. "My fingers moved mechanically and I was amazed to see I made hardly any typing errors. Bormann, Goebbels and the Führer himself kept coming in to see if I'd finished yet. They made me nervous and only delayed matters. Finally they almost tore the last sheet out of the typewriter, went back into the conference room, signed the three copies and sent them out by courier." One was sent to Dönitz in northern Germany. Another went to Field Marshal Ferdinand Schörner in Czechoslovakia. Impressed by his fanatical loyalty to the Nazi cause, the Führer had appointed Schörner as the new head of the German armed forces. "With that, Hitler's life was really over," Junge continued. "Now he was hoping for confirmation that at least one of these documents had reached its intended destination. At any moment now, we expected the Russians to storm our bunker, so close the sounds of war seemed to be . . . We were trapped there and just sat waiting."

Early on April 30 news came through that General Wenck's 12th Army was unable to make further progress and no relief of Berlin was possible. Hitler and Eva Braun both decided to commit suicide. The Führer's preoccupation that morning was that enough gasoline be found to completely burn his corpse. The previous day he had learned of the death of his ally, Benito Mussolini, who had been executed by Italian partisans. Mussolini's body—and that of his mistress, Clara Petrucci—was then strung up by its heels. Hitler resolved that his own corpse would not be made a spectacle of.

"The 30th April began like the days before it," Junge recalled. "The hours dragged slowly by . . . We ate lunch with Hitler. The same conversation as yesterday, the day before yesterday, for many days past: a banquet of death under the mask of cheerful composure." After lunch, Junge went to smoke a cigarette in the servants' room. She was told the Führer wanted to say good-bye.

> I went out into the corridor. I vaguely realized there were other people there too. But all I saw was the figure of Hitler. He came very slowly out of his room, stooping more than ever and stood at the open doorway shaking hands with everyone. I felt his right hand in mine. He was looking at me, but not seeing me. He seemed to be very far away. He said something to me but I didn't hear it. I didn't take in his last words. The moment we had been waiting for had come—but I was frozen and scarcely knew what was going on around me.

Eva Braun came over to Junge and embraced her. "Try to get out," she said. "You may get through." Shortly before 3:00 p.m. they both retired to Hitler's living room and its heavy door closed behind them. Eva Braun took cyanide. Hitler either took cyanide or shot himself. Fifteen minutes later the two bodies were carried up the bunker stairs, laid in a bomb crater in the Reich Chancellery garden and doused in petrol. The flames rose quickly and a last Nazi salute was delivered by the small group of onlookers. Hitler's rule over the German people had ended.

The Führer's legacy was one of death, destruction and terrible suffering. It was a legacy brought to Europe as a whole, and increasingly visited on his own people. Allied bombing had killed more than 400,000 German civilians and injured another 800,000. Nearly 2 million homes had been destroyed and another 5 million people had been forced to evacuate. Most of the casualties had occurred in the last months of the war. The Soviet invasion of eastern Germany in January 1945 resulted in another 500,000 civilian deaths and untold misery, with hundreds of thousands fleeing westward, away from the Red Army.

Major General Erich Dethleffsen, a former head of operations in the German Army High Command, and then a prisoner of war, began a memoir in the last weeks of the war:

> Only slowly, in shock, and with reluctance are we awakening from the agony of the last years and recognizing ourselves and our situation. We search for exoneration, to escape responsibility for all that led to the war, its terrible sacrifices and dreadful consequences. We believe ourselves to have been fooled, led astray or misused. We plead that we knew little or nothing of all the terrible crimes . . . But we are also ashamed that we let ourselves be led astray . . . Shame mainly finds expression at first in defiance or self-denigration, only gradually in regret. That is how it is among our people.

And as the war reached its terrible climax, Allied soldiers tried to make sense of what the Third Reich represented. British sergeant Trevor Greenwood of the 9th Battalion Royal Tank Regiment was in a force occupying the German town of Schüttorf. At the end of April he wrote to his wife:

> The war is developing so rapidly that I hate to miss a single news broadcast . . . The Nazis obviously know the game is up, but it is by no means certain that fighting will cease in the immediate future. It would appear that they cannot stomach unconditional surrender to the Russians. But they may think again, and then peace in Europe would be imminent. It is the awful uncertainty which is so upsetting . . .

Greenwood struggled to comprehend the mentality of his opponents. "For our sergeants' mess we have a large house, fully furnished, and including a well-stocked library of books," he related.

> And that means literature by the ton eulogizing the Nazi party and its leaders . . . Hitler, Göring, Goebbels, Streicher and Ley. To see the lavishness of these works makes one gasp. I never realized propaganda could be formed on such a colossal scale . . . They have undertaken enormous construction schemes, from road-building to gun-making. And every industry which has assisted in the creation of this "new Germany" seems to have had a staff of resident photographers on hand, recording each stage of it. These volumes have one purpose—to carefully and systematically convince the reader of the glory of the Führer and the power of his party. There is something sickeningly repetitive about them . . . Their owners must have become intoxicated with the sheer weight of propaganda.
>
> As I looked through these pages I saw how the army of the Third Reich was formed . . . how the youth of the country was regimented through "working parties" at a time when Germany was forbidden to have arms or an army. How they were taught elaborate parade discipline and "rifle drill" with spades. Of enormous roads being built . . . the Autobahn . . . Of gliding schools where future pilots were trained

under the guise of an innocuous "sport" . . . And then I lifted my eyes and glanced through the window of my temporary home, and this book-world of achievement vanished. Instead, I saw a war-damaged German town—with only a few civilians about, some wheeling hand-carts or bicycles, all carrying the pitiful remnants of their worldly possessions.

Beyond them was a seemingly endless procession of British army lorries, each packed solid with German prisoners. All were heading triumphantly westward.

Amid the debris, British troops pondered how to respond to the defeated civilians. "These people would now like to be friendly with us," Greenwood mused. "They don't like 'non-fraternization' [the official policy of minimal contact] . . . It is a stern necessity." In France, Belgium and Holland the British troops had been welcomed as "liberators." In Germany they were "conquerors." Greenwood continued:

Once across the border we cease to regard civilians as normal human beings; we have to behave toward them more as automatons than men. And that change-over, the rigid suppression of one's normal instincts, is not easy—to ignore a friendly greeting from a child, or to refuse a cigarette to a destitute tramp, or withhold assistance to an old lady, painfully pushing a handcart overladen with personal property. But we have to face these things . . . It is a horrible business having to behave in this manner, but it is hardly our fault. We cannot differentiate between "good" Germans and "bad" ones, so we have to regard them all as potential evil-doers.

Such views were widespread among British troops. In theory, there was a distinction between "Nazis" on the one hand and ordinary Germans on the other. In practice, Greenwood was not so sure. Could the Nazis alone have unleashed so much evil upon the world? "The German people had fought and worked for Hitler," he continued. "They knew what was going on—the persecution of the Jews, the horrors of Belsen . . ." Greenwood himself had not seen any of the Nazi concentration camps, but many of his fellows had. And he was struck by something in the room they now used as an officers' mess—previously the home of a prosperous German. It was a painting, and at first glance it seemed innocuous, pleasing even. "This painting is of a moorland scene—with two or three silver birches in the foreground and a background of heather in full bloom," Greenwood noted.

It is quite an attractive picture really, but when examined closely there is a sinister irregularity about the skyline, and when you draw close to this, you find that this irregularity is nothing but a complete concentration camp. Clearly visible are the watch-towers for machine guns, the searchlight towers for night use, the barbed-wire compound enclosing the squat wooden huts for prisoners. And set apart, are more imposing brick buildings for the staff. The meaning of the picture is puzzling. Is it a scenic work, with an incidental background, or was the artist inspired to paint the camp from the nearest vantage point he could find? The picture, an original, has now been ceremoniously destroyed by our officers.

On April 30 US troops from the 40th Combat Engineer Regiment took possession of Dachau concentration camp. Soldiers from the US 42nd and 45th Divisions had liberated it the previous day. These men had been spearheading the US 7th Army's drive on Munich—aware that the German army might still attempt to make a stand outside the city. They were totally unprepared for what they found at Dachau. Outside the camp were thirty-nine carriages of an abandoned freight train. Inside them were hundreds of corpses. Lieutenant Colonel Felix Sparks of the 45th Division recalled:

"Battle hardened veterans became extremely distraught. Some thirty minutes passed before I could restore order and discipline. During this time, the over 30,000 camp prisoners still alive began to grasp the significance of the events taking place. They streamed from their crowded barracks and soon were pressing up against the confining barbed wire fence. They began to shout in unison, a shout that became a chilling roar."

Now the camp had to be cleared of the dead. Engineer Donald Jackson said: "We used wagons to pile up the bodies—and forced German civilians to do the loading."

Horrors such as this made the talks in San Francisco, which had begun on April 25, over the formation of a new world body—the United Nations—all the more important. The Soviet Union had initially been suspicious, but after the death of Roosevelt had given them their backing as a mark of respect to the late US president.

Amid a world of shifting loyalties, upheaval and displacement were those who held no clear place in either the Allied camp or that of its foe. There were those in the Baltic states who had hoped to preserve their national independence and instead had been occupied, first by the Soviet Union and then by Nazi Germany. There were those in the Ukraine who also longed for independence, and had waged war against Germans who occupied their country in 1941 and the Soviets who liberated it in 1944. There were those in Poland who detested the occupation of their country—whether by Germans or Russians. And there were those Russians who were repulsed by Stalin's regime and hoped for a different future for their country.

In February 1945 Himmler had created an anti-Bolshevik army without the formal approval of Hitler. It was named the Vlasov Army, after the Soviet general Andrei Vlasov who commanded it. Vlasov had been one of Stalin's most brilliant commanders, but after his capture by the Germans in the summer of 1942 he had renounced communism and offered to recruit a force of Russians opposed to the Soviet leader. At this late stage of the war this force had finally come into being—but what its fate would now be was entirely unclear. These soldiers, whatever their motivation, had joined in common cause with the arch-enemy of their state, the Wehrmacht.

On April 30, 1945, one of the recently formed Vlasov divisions was in Austria, the other in western Czechoslovakia. The future for both seemed bleak. German liaison officer Captain Arthur Mongrovius wrote that day from Linz in Austria (Hitler's childhood home): "I have got to know a Russian general, Mikhail Meandrov, a well-educated and cultivated man. In the presence of an interpreter I have enjoyed with him many wide-ranging discussions about God and the world. These leave me in no doubt that many of the officers who join the Vlasov Army do so not out of opportunism or self-interest, but a real conviction that Stalin's rule has inflicted great damage on the Russian people."

General Meandrov was the commander of the 2nd Division of the Vlasov Army. Mongrovius was fascinated by him—and curious too. He wondered whether Meandrov was a genuine Russian patriot. At the conclusion of such a terrible war, it was difficult to gauge men's motivations. Mongrovius related one incident:

> This general shows himself as a man of compassion. When a daily transport of prisoners arrived where we were staying, Meandrov persuaded the SS guards to release the unfortunates. Half-starved, still in their convict garb, they scattered in all directions. In their pitiful state they posed a risk to others, and the fact that all passed off peacefully was due to the presence of mind of the general, who persuaded the local villagers to provide food for these hungry creatures.

This vignette, superficially pleasing, was ambiguous. A show of clemency, whether by Meandrov himself or the SS guards he apparently persuaded, could easily have been motivated by the very opportunism Mongrovius decried, in an attempt to ingratiate oneself with the Western Allies. The Vlasov Army was simply trying to survive.

And yet, some measure of patriotism was clearly there. In a different time and place, an anti-Bolshevik army of Russians would have been welcomed by the Anglo-Americans. But at the end of April 1945, with the Grand Alliance still holding firm, these ideological fellow travelers were regarded as outcasts. Mongrovius' attention turned back to the Vlasov Army itself—loathed by Stalin and the Soviet state and a political embarrassment to the Western powers:

"It has set all its hopes on the first, informal contacts it is making with the Americans," the German continued, "as it believes it impossible that the United States could hand over the Vlasov Army, which is wholeheartedly against Stalin's regime, to the Soviets." Mongrovius paused uneasily, before concluding: "If it did so, the inevitable end of such a force would be to be strung up on the Kremlin Wall in Moscow's Red Square."

The Vlasov Army had allied itself with the Germans in the desperate hope of forging a future for its people that was different from that of a communist state. However, the power of the Wehrmacht was now collapsing. North of Berlin, makeshift German defense lines buckled as Soviet marshal Konstantin Rokossovsky's 2nd Belorussian Front swung toward the Baltic. Rokossovsky's offensive had been launched on April 26, and was advancing rapidly through northern Germany. Major Erich Mende of the Wehrmacht's 102nd Infantry Division had been awarded the Knight's Cross in January 1945 for making a stand in East Prussia that allowed more than 10,000 civilians to escape the clutches of the Red Army. Now there were simply not enough troops to hold the enemy.

"Everything came apart on April 30," Mende remembered. "A Soviet tank push from the southeast overtook our forces and reached the outskirts of Rostock. The main exit route was now closed to us and a mass of our infantrymen clambered aboard our remaining trucks and jeeps, as we tried to find another way out."

Eventually Mende and his exhausted fellow soldiers reached the port of Warnemünde, only to find the remaining ships crammed full of refugees. The men stood on the quayside. And then they were joined by a sudden influx. "Some 500 or so emaciated people appeared, all in convict clothes. We realized that they were escapees from a nearby concentration camp." The two groups watched each other in uneasy silence.

In Berlin, the Red Army front line was now a mere 400 meters from the Führer Bunker. Yet early on the evening of April 30 Joseph Goebbels briefly rekindled the flame of National Socialism that had departed with his master. Lieutenant Franz Kuhlmann recalled:

I was with a group of my soldiers defending the northern flank of the Reich Chancellery. We were protecting the main shelter and the Führer Bunker, and the yard in front of it, when a sergeant relayed an order that I was to go immediately to the Green Hall of the Reich Chancellery. I followed him, and came across a farewell ceremony Goebbels had organized for the Hitler Youth defenders. Participating in it were Magda Goebbels and her children, the secretaries from the Führer Bunker and some civilian officials and young cadets. I was immediately invited to join a long table, a dish of pea soup was pushed toward me and I found myself opposite Goebbels himself, in animated conversation with some of the Hitler Youth.

My sergeant sat down next to Frau Goebbels, my cadets in between the Goebbels children. After eating, a naval cadet took to the piano and the Hitler Youth and Goebbels sang together the old National Socialist martial songs. Then Goebbels said some words, with the Hitler Youth drawn up in formation around him. As these boys had come directly from the Chancellery complex they were carrying their Panzerfausts [bazookas], which had already destroyed a number of Russian tanks. Iron Crosses were presented to these young defenders.

I was able to observe Goebbels closely and saw how completely immersed he was in the old rhetoric of defiant resistance. It had now completely taken on a life of its own, a life totally divorced from reality. In the present situation his words were nonsensical, yet they cast a spell from which none of the Hitler Youth seemed able to break free.

Outside, there was a strong, incessant bombardment, one that had left many dead with more soon to follow. Here, inside, was singing and a mass of young faces, all mesmerized by the power of Goebbels' terrible oratory, the Goebbels children, innocently playing, creating an atmosphere that was utterly unreal.

I got the feeling that a whole world was sinking here, a world for which millions of Germans had fought and died—and their blood sacrifice had been utterly futile.

2

MAY DAY IN BERLIN

Berlin was the focal point of the Russian war effort. Its capture would show its people and the wider world that Hitler's regime was finished. And German resistance was now in its death throes.

Soviet lieutenant Alexei Kalinin wrote to his wife on May Day:

I greet you from Berlin! Yes, we have reached Berlin—we fought our way from the suburbs to the center of the city, and the Fritzes have been vanquished. And here, for the first time, we are meeting German civilians face-to-face. All have the same gaunt appearance, thin and white-faced—many are clearly suffering from starvation.

When we first see them they are overwhelmed with terror, and try to hide, but after a few minutes—when they see we are not demons—they reappear, come up to us and ask for a little bread. Then they stand by the road, asking passing soldiers for food. As soon as we set up our field kitchens German civilians, old men, women, cluster round, with cups at the ready . . .

Marshal Georgi Zhukov had appointed one of his commanders, Colonel General Nikolai Berzarin, to take charge of the administration of Berlin and draw up plans to feed its population—even while the fighting was still going on. The opening up of field kitchens provided some immediate relief to the starving inhabitants of the city and this help was received with surprise and gratitude. But German civilians had differing experiences of the Red Army:

"We huddled together in the central part of the basement, shaking with fear," Dorothea von Schwanenflügel wrote on May 1.

> The last days of savage house-to-house fighting and street battles had been a human slaughter, with no prisoners being taken on either side . . . We were a city in ruins; almost no house remained intact. There was no radio or newspaper, so vans with loudspeakers drove through the streets ordering us to cease all resistance. That night a horde of Soviet troops stormed into a nearby house. Then we heard what seemed to be a terrible orgy, with women screaming for help, many shrieking at the same time . . . Gripped by terror, we sat in stunned silence.

At the beginning of May, the chief military prosecutor of Marshal Zhukov's 1st Belorussian Front, Major General Yachenin, drew up a report noting:

"Positive changes are taking place in the attitude of Red Army personnel toward German civilians. Violent crime against the native population has fallen considerably. And yet, the amount of looting and rape still presents a real problem for us."

The prosecutor cited a number of examples. A Lieutenant Enchivatov had been apprehended drunk, going from house to house in Berlin's suburbs, raping women. The investigation was now complete and Enchivatov would be brought before a military tribunal. Two Russian soldiers—Ivanov and Manankov—had been caught raping a series of women. One of these—very ill—was recovering from attempting suicide after an earlier gang rape by

Soviet troops. Again, the case was due before the tribunal. A Sergeant Do-rohin used a pistol to threaten the parents of a fifteen-year-old girl, whom he raped in front of them. A Lieutenant Kursakov tried to rape a German woman in front of her husband and children. Yachenin admitted frankly: "There are many more such cases."

Major General Yachenin acknowledged the confusion felt by many Russian soldiers. They had witnessed the terrible atrocities of the enemy and the suffering wrought on their country. They had advanced on Berlin with hatred in their hearts, determined to wreak vengeance on the Germans. But crimes against civilians were damaging the discipline and reputation of their army. Lieutenant Nikolai Inozemtsev wrote simply: "Each rape debases our army and every soldier in it." Some no longer cared; others struggled with their conscience. But military regulations were clear—harming the German population would no longer be tolerated. It remained to be seen how effectively they would be enforced.

Among the front-line troops, relief that the war was finally coming to an end was all-pervasive. Red Army soldier Petr Seveljov wrote to his parents:

We stumbled upon exhausted, bedraggled German troops, sitting by the roadside, weapons thrown down, waiting to be led into captivity by our troops. I saw two of their officers, without weapons, and carrying a white flag, go from the Tiergarten Park to the Brandenburg Gate. Alongside it more Germans were gathering, flinging their weapons into a huge pile. White flags are hanging from the surrounding houses.

Many of us have picked up a little German, and some of our opponents can manage a bit of Russian. All of this will seem quite incredible to you, but as I write this letter I can see through the window one of our men and a German soldier sharing a bottle of Schnapps, gesticulating and striking up a conversation. Amazing! It is hard to describe to you our triumph—the way it looks now in Berlin.

Near the Tiergarten, Lieutenant General Vasily Chuikov's 8th Guards Army was setting up its HQ. Captain Anatoly Mereshko recalled:

We were like a band of gypsies during the battle for Berlin, constantly moving from place to place in a city shrouded in dust and smoke.

Chuikov's last HQ was a five-story residential house at the east end of the Tiergarten Park—his office was on the first floor, up a big staircase. It had previously been a reception room—and it was an imposing place, with a heavy, dark oak ceiling.

At the beginning of May 1 I was on duty in the house next to it. The owners seemed to have left it hurriedly. I poured myself some cognac to celebrate our holiday. Then I heard a spluttering sound. I was alone—so I took my pistol and went to investigate. I found a German in a bath tub—filled up with water and blood. He had slit his wrists. His uniform had been neatly arranged next to the bath— he was a colonel. After that, my celebratory mood evaporated.

The 8th Guards Army occupied a special position within the Red Army. Re-formed in May 1943, it was originally the 62nd Army, the force that had bravely defended the center of Stalingrad against the might of Hitler's offensive a year earlier. Vasily Chuikov and his men had clung on to the Volga shoreline, beating off incessant enemy attacks. Their heroism bought time for the Russians to launch a massive counterattack, trapping the Germans and their allies the Romanians and destroying them all within the city they had hoped to conquer.

The 62nd Army had been badly battered during that titanic encounter— then re-formed around a core of officers and soldiers who had survived the battle. It fought its way through the Ukraine and Poland—winning a string of battle honors—and its advance units were now less than 300 meters from the Reichstag. Chuikov was forty-five years old when he reached Berlin. He had been a professional soldier all his life. And yet it seemed hard to envisage a future beyond the collapse of Hitler's Third Reich. "Maybe the end of Nazi Germany will put me out of a job!" he confided to his wife, Valentina.

Chuikov's pride in the success at Stalingrad was tempered with frustration that after doing so much, his army did not receive the surrender of the German commander there, the recently promoted Field Marshal Paulus.

Paulus was captured by the neighboring 64th Army and this fact still rankled with Chuikov and his men more than two years later. As Chuikov and his fighters encamped in the center of Berlin, there was a tacit agreement within the Red Army that if the Germans opened surrender negotiations the 8th Guards Army would be given the honor of hosting them.

At 3:30 a.m. on May 1 news came through that an emissary from the Führer Bunker, General Hans Krebs, wished to speak with the Russians. After some discussion it was decided that a young Soviet lieutenant, Andrei Eshpai, who was fluent in German, would escort Krebs to Chuikov's HQ from an agreed rendezvous point. When the two met, they exchanged names and ranks. Krebs was polite, but appeared surprised to be escorted by a mere lieutenant. Eshpai was more concerned to guide them both safely through Berlin's ruined streets. But before they began their journey Krebs paused and looked around at the mass of Soviet military equipment. "What incredible weaponry you have here," he said to no one in particular. Eshpai wanted to get moving, but sensed that etiquette demanded a compliment in return. "Your Panzerfausts are causing us a lot of trouble," he responded. Krebs appeared to be somewhere else. And then he suddenly snapped out of his reverie and looked directly at Eshpai, only too aware of the course the war had taken. "This is not Moscow," the general said. "It is Berlin."

Krebs arrived at Chuikov's HQ accompanied by a lone German soldier with a white flag attached to his bayonet. The soldier stood to attention as General Krebs strode into the room. "We asked Krebs if he was frightened of us and wanted protection," Mereshko remembered. "A little flustered, our visitor then addressed Chuikov as Marshal rather than Lieutenant General, so we corrected him on that." Then Krebs announced that Hitler had committed suicide the day before.

The Russians were the first people outside the Führer Bunker to learn of this. The room went completely silent. Eventually Chuikov responded, "We know." "It was pretty obvious that we did not," Mark Slavin—editor of the 8th Guards newspaper—recalled, "because as Chuikov said this all non-essential personnel were promptly ordered out of the room." The Russians had not even been sure whether Hitler had remained in the capital. The news was a bombshell.

Chuikov left the room and phoned Zhukov—who in turn phoned Stalin. The Soviet leader was told Hitler was dead and Krebs had come on the authority of Goebbels to negotiate a ceasefire. Stalin's reply was to the point: "There can be no negotiations—we will only accept unconditional surrender."

The discussion quickly reached an impasse. Krebs insisted that a truce was essential to swear in the Dönitz government under the terms of Hitler's will. Chuikov repeated that no truce could be considered—only the total capitulation of the Berlin garrison. A telephone cable was laid to the Reich Chancellery to allow direct communication with Goebbels. It yielded no result. At 1:00 p.m. Krebs was ordered to return to German lines. The general left the HQ and then returned again—claiming that he had mislaid his gloves. He looked around the room. "It was so obvious," Mereshko said, "that we could not help but laugh. We asked: 'Are your gloves so important to you?' We could tell that Krebs did not want to return to the Führer Bunker. He was clinging to each moment of life."

Then Chuikov drew Krebs to one side. Eshpai heard their brief conversation. The Soviet general spoke softly: "So what are you going to do now?" Krebs looked at him. He had been a military attaché in Moscow before the war—and he now responded in Russian: "To fulfill my duty—to the end." It was clear that Krebs was intending to commit suicide. Chuikov paused, and then said simply, "Spoken like a true soldier." He offered his adversary his hand. Krebs clasped it—then left the building for good.

Zhukov submitted a report to Stalin. "I believe the main purpose of Krebs' mission was to explore the possibility of negotiating a separate peace with us," he stated, "thereby splitting the Grand Alliance." The Soviet leader would not contemplate it. And as Chuikov and Krebs concluded their meeting, the fight for the Reichstag continued. By the end of May 1 the building was firmly in Russian hands. Red Army soldier Ilya Krichevsky wrote in his diary:

The battle for Berlin has come to an end. Our army has taken the Reichstag. The joy and exhilaration is extraordinary—everyone knows that the capture of this bastion of Fascism marks the final victory over Nazi Germany.

It was no simple matter to take it. Groups of diehard SS troops resisted desperately. The building had been transformed into a fortress. And yet, finally it was achieved. The news of its capture spread like wildfire throughout the army—and everyone wanted to know who had been the first into the building, and who had planted the Victory Banner.

The Reichstag had been chosen as the symbol of the Russian victory. The imposing building had lain empty since the 1933 fire—a fire that the Nazis had blamed on a left-wing agitator and used as a pretext for a round-up of communists within the German state. The Reich Chancellery was the administrative center of the Third Reich, but the Reichstag had lodged itself in the Russian imagination—perhaps because of the sheer size of the building. It was imposing enough—standing apart from others in the government quarter of the city. Lieutenant Vasily Ustyugov of the Soviet 150th Rifle Division, one of those who stormed the Reichstag, never forgot his first sight of it: "It was dawn and I was about 400 meters away from it. As the light grew, I saw a massive dark gray building rising above me, pock-marked with shell-fire." When it became clear how important its capture was to the Red Army, SS troops defended it fanatically.

The investigation over who first planted the victory banner was conducted by the Red Army. The results were then vetted by political officers. A Georgian, Meliton Kantaria, was chosen—although his banner was planted later than others—to flatter Stalin, who came from Georgia himself.

By May 1, 1945, Stalin had emerged from the savage fight against Germany with considerable credit. The start of his war had been disastrous. He had failed to anticipate the German invasion on June 22, 1941, and for days afterward was unable to respond to its threat. That autumn he made a catastrophic misjudgment, rejecting the advice of his military advisers and forbidding retreat from the Ukrainian capital, Kiev, a blunder that led to the encirclement and capture of nearly 650,000 Red Army soldiers. But in mid-October 1941, with Russia reeling from a succession of defeats and the fate of Moscow hanging in the balance, he decided to stay in the Russian capital rather than evacuate his government. This was both a genuinely brave decision and a politically astute one—for if the Soviet leader had left the city, Moscow would almost certainly have fallen to the Germans. Instead, Stalin summoned his best commander, Georgi Zhukov, brought up fresh divisions from Siberia and stood firm against Hitler's Wehrmacht. German forces were repulsed from Moscow in bitter winter fighting in temperatures below minus 30 degrees Celsius. It was the Führer's first significant defeat—and Stalin's first major victory.

The following year the tide of war turned at Stalingrad, the Soviet leader's namesake city on the Volga. Stalin's "Not a Step Back!" order—in the summer of 1942—galvanized his people just as Churchill's defiant rhetoric had inspired the British after Dunkirk in May 1940. The Soviet leader made it clear there could be no further retreat—too much of the country's land, people and economic resources were already lost to the enemy. Stalin, however, was no Churchillian orator and his order was backed by steely ruthlessness—"blocking detachments" of security police were placed behind army units to prevent soldiers deserting. Nevertheless, he had caught the prevailing political mood with instinctive shrewdness.

The country had begun to lose faith in its army, but at Stalingrad all this would change, for Stalin resolved to hold the city whatever the cost. He showed a characteristic and ruthless disregard for the civilians trapped within it, but the decision to make a stand was the right one. The Germans were drawn into ferocious street fighting that bled away their strength. The raw courage of the defenders, in what increasingly became a prestige battle between Hitler and Stalin, bought the Soviet Union precious time. The Red Army built up its strength, counterattacked and then surrounded its foe. On February 2, 1943, the broken remnants of the German 6th Army surrendered. It was the psychological turning-point of the war.

As that brutal war progressed, Stalin became more flexible in his thinking—willing to properly listen to his generals and in some measure to trust them. In stark contrast Hitler became increasingly dogmatic, unwilling to listen to any advice at all. At Kursk in July 1943 Stalin's commanders Zhukov and Vasilevsky argued that they should let the Germans attack first—using up their precious reserves of tanks and armor—and only then move on to the counterattack. Although the Soviet leader wanted to strike immediately, he listened to his military advisers and followed the course they recommended. The result was a stunning success that forced their opponent on to the defensive. Germany would never launch another major offensive in the east.

That autumn the Red Army regained much of the Ukraine, recapturing Kiev on November 6, but allowing the news to be relayed only a day later—on the anniversary of the Bolshevik revolution. On January 27, 1944, the 900-day siege of Leningrad was finally ended. And in the summer of 1944 came the greatest triumph of them all, Operation Bagration, which destroyed all the German forces in Belorussia. In its aftermath, captured German generals and officers were paraded through the streets of Moscow. Again, Stalin had shown the confidence to listen to his commanders, in this case Konstantin Rokossovsky, who had proposed a significant alteration to the original plan of attack—one that proved to be fundamentally correct. Stalin, impressed by the way Rokossovsky argued his case, agreed to the revised plan, at a time when Hitler had decreed a "fortress" policy in the east that gave his commanders little or no freedom of maneuver. It was a striking calibration of this war that as the Soviet leader trusted his generals more, the Führer trusted his less.

By the autumn of 1944 Stalin's Red Army had recaptured nearly all of the Soviet Union lost to Hitler's Wehrmacht at the war's onset. It had imposed terms on Finland—regaining the territory fought for in 1939–40—and reoccupied the Baltic states, as it had done in 1940 before the German invasion. Only in Courland (in Latvia) were German and Latvian troops still holding out against Russian forces. In August 1944 Red Army troops moved into Romania, toppling the pro-German regime, and another of Hitler's allies, Bulgaria, quickly came to terms with the Soviet Union. Russian troops then joined Tito's communist partisans in Yugoslavia and recaptured Belgrade; by November 1944 the Hungarian capital, Budapest, was also under siege. In January 1945 a huge new offensive across the Vistula river brought Soviet troops surging into Poland. Stalin held hegemony in eastern Europe—one based on sheer military might.

On May 1, 1945, Berlin—and the fight for the Reichstag—was its apogee, the culmination of a stream of victories that expunged the shame of the beginning of the war and gave the Soviet leader heroic status—among his own people and also with many in the West. It was a remarkable triumph and the result of an astonishing military turn-around and a complete economic reorganization on the part of Stalin.

Under his supervision, much of the heavy industry threatened by the German advance had been evacuated and relocated beyond the Ural mountains. The Soviet leader's single-minded determination and an astonishing effort from the Soviet people—for whom the slogan "Everything for the Front!" became a patriotic imperative—quickly brought it into production again. By the summer of 1943 Russia was producing considerably more planes, tanks and guns than its German opponent. It was also benefiting from significant industrial aid from Britain and America—America's Lend-Lease program (the economic program through which the United States provided military aid to the Allies) being particularly valuable. Although the Red Army bore the brunt of the fighting, after D-Day the increasing economic aid and military support from the West brought the Allies closer together. As a result, the Big Three conference at Yalta in February 1945 was more outwardly harmonious than that of Teheran in November 1943—the first time Britain, America and Russia had all met.

As Stalin had fought for survival, so he realized that communist ideology alone would not save his state. Astutely he had broadened the scope of the war, appealing to Russian patriotism and his people's love of their Motherland. He heralded this in his speech to the nation on Red Square, on November 7, 1941, and again in his "Not a Step Back!" order on July 28, 1942. Although the Bolshevik revolution derided the Tsarist history that had preceded it, now military orders and medals evoking Russia's heroes of the past—Alexander Nevsky, Mikhail Kutuzov, men who had repelled foreign invaders—were revived. However, Stalin was never willing to relinquish any shred of control, and with the military crisis past and Red Army soldiers now fighting in eastern Europe, communist ideology was fully restored and security stepped up. Stalin feared his soldiers experiencing life outside the Soviet Union.

From his perspective, this was reasonable: a different world was opening up for Soviet troops, most of whom had never before traveled beyond their own country. Lieutenant Boris Martschenko wrote to his wife on May Day that he was inspired by the beauty of Vienna:

> I spent yesterday visiting the city. I drove around it, and saw a lot, but much has still not sunk in yet. This is not just a city—it is an architectural fantasy. Budapest is a dirt-heap compared to Vienna.
>
> I visited the Opera House. The back of it had burned down—but it remains a remarkable building. Who would have thought that I ever would have had a chance to see it. And, it is amusing to say, Vienna now resembles one of our own cities in holiday mood! From the windows of the houses red flags can be seen, hanging everywhere!
>
> The civilians are cautious—they wait until they are in groups of 5–10 people before they approach us. But when they find I can speak some German, and make myself understood in conversation with them, they vie with each other in helpfulness!

As Red Army soldiers were sharing their impressions of life outside Russia, Westerners were trying to make sense of the riddle of the Soviet Union. Stalin the man had impressed many Western observers at the Big Three conferences at Teheran and Yalta. On occasions he could be personable and charming and he was a strong and effective negotiator—always on top of his brief. Roosevelt had struck up a measure of empathy with Stalin and there was grudging yet real respect between the Soviet leader and Churchill. Yet fundamentally these two men did not trust each other.

Churchill understood the ruthlessness of the Bolshevik state—and when Stalin made an apparent joke at the Teheran Conference about the need to purge the German officer corps after the end of the war, a comment that Roosevelt found innocuous, Churchill—with the massacre of Polish army officers at Katyn in his mind—left the room. Hugh Lunghi, a translator for Churchill at Teheran and Yalta, said the British prime minister was always aware of the secrecy of the Soviet state and its cruelty to those who stood in its way. "Whereas Hitler killed by categories," Lunghi remarked, "Stalin dispatched by numbers." Stalin's decision to halt his armies outside Warsaw in

August 1944—which allowed the Germans to crush the Polish resistance (opposed to Stalin's puppet regime)—was seen by the British as clear evidence of both. "We were shocked by his callous refusal to let Allied planes use Soviet air bases to drop aid to the Poles," Lunghi stated. "He seemed indifferent to the suffering of the insurgents."

Underneath Stalin's restraint and self-control—the face he showed to the West—Hugh Lunghi remembered moments when the mask seemed to slip. Once, during a presentation by the Soviet Union's foreign minister, the ice-cold Vyacheslav Molotov—whose impenetrable demeanor and immovable resolution during negotiations earned him (among the Western Allies) the nickname "Old Stone Ass"—Stalin suddenly walked into the room. Lunghi noticed how Molotov began to stutter. On another occasion, when Churchill presented Stalin with the Sword of Stalingrad at Teheran, the Soviet leader passed it to Kliment Voroshilov, who clumsily grasped the wrong end and let it fall from the scabbard. Stalin said nothing—but Lunghi noticed his clenched fists, white to the knuckle. After the ceremony was concluded, a mortified Voroshilov ran after Churchill and enlisted Lunghi's help in making a fulsome apology. The British prime minister took it in good part and a hugely relieved Voroshilov (a long-standing but incompetent crony of Stalin's) then wished him "Happy Birthday!" Voroshilov was in fact a day early. "The old fool can't even get that right!" Churchill growled. Underneath the humor, Lunghi was struck by the raw fear that the Soviet leader instilled—even among his closest associates.

But even such ideological opponents as Stalin and Churchill could work together. The two had first met in Moscow in August 1942. Many of the discussions were difficult. The Germans had begun a new attack in the south, breaking through Russian defenses and driving toward Stalingrad. The Soviet Union feared that Turkey and even Japan might enter the war in support of Hitler, who had already enlisted Hungarian, Italian and Romanian armies for his new offensive. Russia felt isolated and alone—and Churchill had to relay the difficult news that there would be no second font that year and the Arctic convoys had been suspended. At a banquet, Stalin taunted the British prime minister about his lack of resolve and made a slighting remark about his support for the White Russians in the civil war of

1918–20, a war that had ended in a communist victory. Churchill was not intimidated—and did not seek to appease Stalin: "I make no secret of my detestation of Bolshevism," was his frank rejoinder. Stalin was impressed by Churchill's candor. "Better an honest enemy than a duplicitous friend," he observed to those around him.

At this first, August meeting, Stalin had insinuated that the British Royal Navy lacked courage. Churchill—well aware of the heroism shown by those in the Arctic convoys—was having none of this and abruptly ended the proceedings. Stalin realized that he had gone too far—and in a gesture of reconciliation invited the British prime minister to an impromptu supper in his private apartments in the Kremlin. It is hard to imagine a more unusual banquet. The Soviet and British delegations were simply abandoned as Stalin led Churchill through a succession of darkened rooms, struggling with a large bunch of keys, with one British interpreter in tow. A bewildered Churchill was then introduced to Stalin's housekeeper and daughter Svetlana, a meat dish prepared and drinks poured. Later Molotov made an appearance, accompanied by a Soviet interpreter. The two leaders talked, joked and struck up a rapport. At the end of the evening Churchill said to his interpreter, Arthur Birse: "I can do business with this man."

In October 1944 Stalin and Churchill met up again in Moscow and drew up the so-called percentages agreement (a jotted note drafted by Churchill and approved by Stalin) roughly delineating areas of influence in Europe. Even if the two men did not fully trust each other, there was enough mutual respect for them to work through issues informally. And when Stalin allowed Britain greater influence in determining the future of Greece, he kept his promise even when Churchill sent in troops to crush the communist partisans' attempt to form a government there.

But on the issue of Berlin, Stalin became uneasy. Eisenhower had given him an assurance that the Americans would not take the city. Stalin trusted Roosevelt to honor this agreement, but the American president was ill. The Soviet leader speculated that Churchill might pressure Eisenhower to change his mind. He summoned his generals Zhukov and Konev on April 1, 1945. He wanted a firm assurance from them that Berlin would be taken rapidly. An offensive was planned for April 16 and Stalin reverted to an old, bad habit of toying with his commanders—saying that Berlin could be captured either by Zhukov or Konev: whoever got there first would take it. Unfortunately, both forces arrived in the city's suburbs at the same time. As late as April 28, Konev's men were still trying to force their way through to the Reichstag ahead of Zhukov. This confusion could have been avoided if Stalin had delineated a clear battle strategy.

Stalin was nervous. He did not want the prize of Berlin snatched from his grasp by the Western Allies. And the death of President Roosevelt on April 12, 1945, had left him shaken. US ambassador Averell Harriman recalled that Stalin was genuinely saddened and moved by Roosevelt's death. Stalin's telegram to Churchill conveyed an unusual degree of emotion:

"In President Franklin Roosevelt the Soviet people saw a distinguished statesman and an unswerving champion of close cooperation between our three countries," Stalin wrote on April 15. "The friendly attitude of President Roosevelt will always be remembered and highly valued by our nation. As far as I am personally concerned, I feel exceptionally deeply the burden of the loss of this great man, who was our mutual friend."

The new American president, Harry Truman, was not known to the Soviet leader—and he could not easily anticipate what stance he might take. And the role of an arbiter of power within Europe was something neither Stalin nor his recently forged Bolshevik state had any experience of. Although his position appeared strong, his people were exhausted by the war and his country's economy—for all its wartime production—needed to be completely rebuilt. The United States had a new president and Britain and America remained his ideological opponents. And yet, as the war drew to its close, Stalin felt that some form of accommodation with both countries might be possible, if Russia's security was not in any way compromised.

Anatoly Smriga, on the staff of Lieutenant General Chuikov's Soviet 8th Guards Army, recalled:

At the time of Berlin's surrender, in political meetings, we were warned: "The war has not only been caused by Hitler and the Germans, but by the imperialist system." And of course the representatives of this system included our allies—Britain, America and

France. It was not said directly, but an idea was being planted: yesterday's allies might become tomorrow's enemies—be vigilant. But we were also aware that Britain and America were sending us arms and equipment, and of the importance of lend-lease. This seemed a guarantor that in the immediate future at least these countries would remain our friends—for they would not keep sending us weapons if they intended to fight us.

The Soviet leader remained pragmatic. The one issue he would not compromise on was Poland: he believed it vital to install and maintain a regime there friendly to the Soviet government. Britain and America wanted a Polish government to be formed after free and fair elections. Stalin did not. He already had a communist administration in place at Lublin to run the country and did not want to jeopardize it. The Soviet leader now demonstrated renewed solidarity with the Lublin government, invoking powerful ritual to bind both Poles and Russians to his cause.

Stalin knew Polish soldiers representing the rival London government had fought with great courage in Italy. Polish troops had stormed the German stronghold at Monte Cassino and planted their flag atop the summit of the ruined monastery—an event which was photographed and became famous throughout the world. The Soviet leader wished to create a rival photo opportunity, showing Poles and Russians as comrades-in-arms in the capital of the Third Reich. In the last days of the battle for Berlin, Stalin decided that Polish soldiers representing his client regime at Lublin would share battle honors with the Red Army.

Early on April 30, after consultation with the Lublin government, Stalin phoned Marshal Zhukov and asked that units from the 1st Polish Army—which had taken a supporting role in the attack on the German capital—be brought urgently to the center of Berlin. Regiments and artillery units from the 1st (Warsaw) Infantry Division were hurriedly mobilized. The 2nd Infantry Regiment was transported to the front line, arriving at 7:00 a.m. that morning, where it stormed the Berlin Technical College and advanced through the Zoological Gardens. The 3rd Infantry Regiment went into action around the Tiergarten railway station on the same day. The division's combat journal referred to it being involved in heavy street fighting, capturing the station building and taking over 450 German soldiers prisoner. It then pushed westward across Tiergarten Park on May Day, and after further fighting reached the Brandenburg Gate at 6:55 a.m. on May 2, where it joined forces with Chuikov's 8th Guards Army. The Polish red and white flag was raised over Berlin's Victory Monument and jointly with Red Army banners on the Brandenburg Gate. Russian photographers and film crews recorded these events.

Polish artilleryman Antonin Jablonski spoke of the emotional impact of seeing his national flag raised over Berlin. Jablonski had been recruited to the 1st Polish Army in 1944. "We fought hard to free our native land from the Germans," he said. "Our countrymen had greeted us joyfully as we advanced westward." The 1st Polish Army was fighting with Marshal Zhukov's 1st Belorussian Front—and many Poles were in fact less than enthusiastic as Russian troops reoccupied their country. But Jablonski spoke with unmistakable pride about his regiment's arrival in the German capital: "At Berlin, my five-man unit climbed to the top of the 70 meter high Victory Column, erected to commemorate German success in the Franco-Prussian War. We used a wooden pole we had cut from a nearby forest and draped our flag around it. Then we unfurled it over the city. It was an unforgettable moment."

These Polish troops well knew the cruelties inflicted by the Germans upon their country. As they were now fighting with the Russians, they had to turn a blind eye to the suffering meted out by Stalin in 1939–40. For some—flushed with victory—the Germans became convenient scapegoats for all that they had endured. Poles looted, raped and killed German civilians with as much vehemence as the Russians. Shortly before the battle for Berlin, the 1st Polish Army was forced to draw up a disciplinary ordinance to curb the wilder excesses of its soldiers—although attempts to do so began in inflammatory fashion:

"The Germans started this war—and have murdered hundreds of thousands of innocent civilians in Poland. They tried to systematically exterminate our nation. The German Army and the Nazi Party are not the only culprits—it is clear that the whole German people supported this policy."

However, its tone then changed: "The Polish soldier is nonetheless obliged to maintain his discipline, follow the orders of his High Command and not mete out punishment to German civilians. We only bring shame upon us by attacking the weak and the unprotected. Such lawlessness undermines our army and the moral cause for which we fight. Any transgressions will be dealt with severely by the military courts."

The Red Army—advancing alongside these Polish forces—was struggling with much the same issue. In a private conversation with Yugoslav partisan Milovan Djilas, Stalin had shown scant concern for the suffering of Germany's civilians:

"You have, of course, read Dostoevsky," he began.

Do you see what a complicated thing is a man's soul, a man's psyche? Well then, imagine a man who has fought from Stalingrad to Belgrade, over thousands of kilometers of his own devastated land, across the dead bodies of his comrades and dearest ones. How can such a man react normally? And what is so awful in his having fun with a woman after such horrors? You have imagined the Red Army to be ideal. And it is not ideal—and never can be. The important thing is it is fighting the Germans—and it is fighting them well. The rest doesn't matter.

But Stalin also had a change of heart. On April 20, 1945, he sent out a decree to Red Army officers and soldiers demanding that their behavior toward German civilians be improved. Soviet lieutenant Nikolai Inozemtsev saw a flurry of orders prohibiting arson, robbery and harm to the native population. But he also recognized the power of war correspondent Ilya Ehrenburg's "revenge" articles, which for years had permeated the consciousness of ordinary Russian soldiers. Now *Pravda* was accusing him of presenting an oversimplified view of the war. But Russian troops loved the man—"Our Ilya," they called him—and were intoxicated by his writing. "Kill the German and jump on his woman!" Ehrenburg had enjoined. Lieutenant Inozemtsev observed in his diary: "It will require much effort from our commanders and officers to erase the effect of this."

On May 2 Lieutenant General Chuikov finally received the surrender that had eluded him at Stalingrad. General Helmuth Weidling, the commander of the Berlin garrison, now arrived at 8th Guards Army HQ and agreed on the unconditional surrender of all troops in the capital. It was to come into effect at noon. Many German soldiers had given up already. There was a last hiatus. At 1:00 p.m. Dönitz came on the radio, countermanding Weidling's order and instructing the Wehrmacht to continue fighting in Berlin. Some isolated strongholds continued to resist—but by the evening all were in Russian hands.

For ordinary Russian civilians, now far away from the brutality of frontline fighting, there was an extraordinary sense of relief and joy as the war drew to a close. Nina Koshova wrote from Moscow to a friend on May 1, 1945:

I send my best wishes for the holiday! For the first time in years everyone in Moscow is truly happy. Joy is everywhere—we know the downfall of the German fascists is so close. Our troops have met up with those of our Allies. And most important of all—our army is in the center of Berlin! The most longed-for dream has come to pass— our army has taken Berlin. Now we can truly celebrate!

Yesterday all black-out restrictions were lifted in Moscow. Now the city is bathed in light. Already it is the second evening I do not have to lower the black net curtains. The room seems different— bright and cozy.

And there has been more good news today. There has been a salute [gun salvo] for the Ukrainian Front for capturing Ostrava [in Czechoslovakia]. And another one, for Rokossovsky, who has taken a whole procession of German towns. It is only 11:00 p.m. It is possible that at midnight we may hear another—that is the way things are going.

Now our people can draw a deep breath. War may soon become a thing of the past.

Marshal Konstantin Rokossovsky's troops—praised in Koshova's letter— were pushing forward hard. Rokossovsky's 2nd Belorussian Front had launched its offensive later than Konev and Zhukov but on April 26, 1945, it smashed flimsy enemy defenses at Stettin on the Oder and raced across northern Germany. On April 29, the German front opposing it disintegrated completely. General Hasso von Manteuffel's 3rd Panzer Army was now fleeing toward the Anglo-American forces, desperate to surrender to them rather than the Russians.

Rokossovsky's troops had committed terrible atrocities against the civilian population when they entered Germany in January 1945. Soviet private Efraim Genkin witnessed the destruction of the town of Gumbinnen: "It answers for the torment of thousands of our Russian brethren, turned into ashes by the Germans in 1941," he said. Lieutenant Yuri Uspensky added: "This is revenge for all they have done to us." Genkin and Uspensky initially felt that harsh treatment of German civilians was justified. Both men were then increasingly dismayed by the robbery and rape that came in their army's wake. "This picture provokes repulsion and horror in me," Genkin confessed.

Rokossovsky demanded that "exemplary order and iron discipline be imposed an all units," stressing that officers of all ranks were expected "to eradicate all activities shameful to the Red Army with the force of a red-hot iron." A measure of order had indeed been restored, but killing, looting and rape were still occurring with worrying regularity. Events would now put his army's discipline to the test.

At Greifswald, townspeople and the local commander took matters into their own hands. Colonel Rudolf Hagen gathered emissaries and negotiated directly with the approaching Russians. University rector Karl Engel was one of the intermediaries. His diary entry for April 30, 1945, recorded a capitulation offer to the Red Army. "We are making preparations to meet with the Russian divisional commander General Bortschev to discuss the surrender of Greifswald," Engel noted. Hagen, Engel and an interpreter met with Bortschev at 3:00 a.m. The meeting was successful. At 11:00 a.m. the first Russian tanks entered the town and an orderly surrender was enacted. On May 1 Engel's diary revealed that isolated cases of robbery, theft and rape were occurring. Again, a meeting with the Russian commander was arranged and police constables were put in place, with the agreement of both sides, to preserve public order. Greifswald had been spared the full horror of war.

At Demmin matters were rather different. On April 30 a Red Army advance column of troops from the Soviet 65th Army and 1st Guards Tank

Corps approached the town at noon. A white flag was hoisted on the church tower and three Soviet negotiators approached the anti-tank ditch on its outskirts, promising to spare the civilian population from looting and robbery if Demmin surrendered without a fight.

General Mikhail Panov, Soviet commander of the 38th Tank Brigade, wanted to take the town in quick and orderly fashion. That morning he sent out a command to all his officers:

"We have found during our advance that some of our soldiers are still preoccupied with plundering—and such cases of profiteering show an incorrect attitude to the German population. Those involved in such breaches of discipline prevent the proper fulfillment of our combat orders. I require unreserved adherence to this directive and the improvement of discipline and orderly behavior in all our units."

However, Panov's exhortation proved to be a pious hope. An SS detachment opened fire on the negotiators, killing all three, and then retreated through the town, blowing up the bridges behind it. Demmin—enclosed by the Peene river to the north and west and the Tollensee river to the south—now became a noose for the civilians (some 30,000 of them) trapped inside it. More white flags were hoisted, but as Soviet troops entered, members of the Hitler Youth opened fire on them. In retaliation, Russian soldiers doused buildings with gasoline and set part of the town alight.

Terrified civilians—inculcated with Nazi propaganda about Bolshevik atrocities—now succumbed to mass panic. A wave of suicides had begun even before the Red Army reached the town. Entire families committed suicide together, some using guns, razor blades or poison, others drowning themselves in the rivers. As Demmin began to burn, some Russian soldiers lost all control and began raping the remaining female inhabitants—provoking another spate of suicides. Others—appalled by what was happening—tried to stop the people killing themselves. By May 1 more than 900 had died in this terrible fashion.

In the aftermath, the NKVD and Soviet military police were brought in to restore order. Demmin further tarnished the Red Army's reputation. But the Russians had been provoked, and the Wehrmacht was deliberately putting its own civilians at risk. To aid its flight to the British and American lines farther west, the 3rd Panzer Army employed delaying tactics—leaving behind diehard groups of SS fanatics or Hitler Youth, who would sacrifice themselves, buying time for their comrades to make good their escape. German inhabitants would approach the Red Army with a white flag, wanting to surrender their town without further resistance, unaware that these groups were now installing themselves in strongholds within it, ready to fight to the last.

Late on April 30 the men of Lieutenant Ivan Vasilenko's 121st Rifle Division—part of the Soviet 70th Army—heard that the small town of Neustrelitz wished to give up peacefully. Vasilenko's tanks led the way and as the Russian troops moved forward they saw its civilians holding out white flags, signaling a straightforward surrender. Then something else happened.

"On the approaches to Neustrelitz we came under attack from a railway embankment," Vasilenko recollected. "We returned fire and I ordered my tanks to converge on this place of resistance. But we ran into an ambush. Two Tiger tanks were dug in at the town's outskirts—and anti-tank guns opened up on us from a nearby fortified building. Then Hitler Youth began firing on us with their Panzerfausts. Soon one of my tanks was burning, then another . . ." Vasilenko quickly ordered his remaining armor into the town center—only to run into another German stronghold set up around the marketplace. "Here my own tank went up in flames," said Vasilenko. "I was carried out, wounded." There would be no surrender at Neustrelitz. The combat journal of the 121st Rifle Division recorded that 128 Red Army soldiers were killed taking the town.

The situation in northern Germany remained highly volatile. US Airborne chaplain Father Francis Sampson—captured by the Germans near Bastogne—was now in a POW camp outside Neubrandenburg.

"The mere reputation of Rokossovsky's army was enough to panic the Germans," Sampson related. "The roads were soon jammed with wagons loaded with cherished family possessions, children and old people. The Germans headed west, hoping to escape the Russians and preferring anything to falling into their hands."

The Neubrandenburg camp guards fled and the prisoners waited cautiously for the arrival of Soviet forces. The first Red Amy troops were a model of correct behavior, striding through the gates, all smiles, expressing sorrow for the death of President Roosevelt and thanking American POWs for equipment they had received through Lend-Lease.

But by April 30 Neubrandenburg was burning. The following day Sampson attempted to visit the town:

"Just a few yards into the woods by the camp we came across a sight that I shall never forget. Several German girls had been raped and killed; some of them had been strung up by their feet and their throats slit."

In Neubrandenburg itself the streets were piled with debris and most of the buildings were still burning. Bodies lay everywhere—ignored unless they were blocking the traffic.

Sampson believed this to be a failure of Red Army discipline—with Russian soldiers using arson as a weapon of retribution against the civilian population. The picture was more confused and complex. A German rear-guard unit had made a last stand in the town center and then blown up its remaining ammunition store. The destruction that Sampson witnessed was in fact caused by tank fire and artillery shelling.

Sampson and his fellow POWs had simply walked free of their camp. Others—in different camps close to the front line—were force-marched by the SS to new locations. And then there were the slave laborers. Nina Romanova had been forcibly transported from her country and made to work on a farm just outside Greifswald. She recalled:

We, the Russian laborers, were kept in three barracks, alongside Poles and Ukrainians. Each day, whatever the weather, we had to work in the surrounding fields. On April 30 we were putting in potatoes—I was carrying a large basket of them. It was warm and sunny outside. And then we saw white sheets being hung out from the landowner's house. Suddenly some soldiers on horseback appeared. It was a reconnaissance patrol of Red Army soldiers.

"Where are the German troops?" they asked. We told them they had pulled back. My God! We surrounded them, kissed their boots, stirrups, stroked their horses—we were overwhelmed with relief. It was the happiest moment of my life. After this first encounter, more and more of our troops appeared: tanks, lorries, horse-drawn wagons, all rolling westward. We stood at the edge of the road, waving to our soldiers—and cried for joy.

Australian war correspondent Omar White wrote:

A procession of liberated slaves was commonplace on every country road in Germany. They came in knots and files through the spring rain, marching in the long grass or on the shoulders of the roads. One often saw their mutilated bodies where they had trodden on mines at the approaches to culverts and bridges. But they did not delay—they were free, so they marched.

The first-comers were the farm workers. They wore the rags of all the uniforms of Europe. Some had boots, some clogs, some the gaping wrecks of shoes. Some went barefoot, even in the frost, others wrapped their feet in blanket strips and sacking. As the armies went deeper into Germany the character of the marchers began to change. Some limped and were obviously ill and half-starved. Women and children were among them.

White was struck by the German attitude toward the Slavs.

They scarcely regarded them as people at all, more as convenient farm animals. I vividly recall one old woman who came out to the commander of an American reconnaissance column and begged him to stop her Russian slave laborer from running away. Her son and husband had been taken by the Wehrmacht, she said, and without her Russian there would be no-one to do the heavy work on the farm. The Russian was carrying a bundle of clothes, and understandably, seemed fully intent on flight. The old woman had been following him along the road, remonstrating with him. The commander said something unprintable and moved the column on. When I last glimpsed this unusual pair, the woman was sitting in the ditch with her head in her hands, the Russian striding purposefully away.

The war in the east had indeed been a race war. Hitler believed the Slav to be subhuman and so did many of his followers. These views had filtered down to the German population as a whole. Countless atrocities were committed against the Russian people, and as Red Army soldiers advanced through the Ukraine and Belorussia they uncovered ghastly evidence of the Holocaust and genocide. Soviet troops liberated the first functioning extermination camp at Majdanek in Poland in July 1944 and many Red Army soldiers had subsequently toured the camp. And on January 27, 1945, the Russians had discovered Auschwitz.

Rape and robbery were committed by the Western Allies as well. It was the scale and sheer brutality of what was happening between Russian and German which defied easy comparison. War correspondent Omar White had been with General George Patton's Third US Army as it moved through southern Germany in April 1945. He said frankly:

Even before American troops reached the big concentration camps in which death squads specialized in the murder of Jews and Slavs, and the world learned the meaning of Hitler's promise to arrive at a "final solution," the fighting men who stormed into Germany were angry and in a vengeful mood. They had found out in France and Belgium, at first hand, about Nazi atrocities. Few wavered in the conviction that the Germans they killed deserved their fate, or that the survivors had little right to human consideration. At first, the treatment of German civilians was harsh. General Eisenhower's broadcast proclamation—"We come as conquerors"—implied the right of military commanders to requisition whatever accommodation remained intact in half demolished towns. The aged, the sick, the very young, were often driven out into the ruins to fend for themselves.

I heard one idea expressed again and again: "The only way to teach these krauts that war doesn't pay is to kick them about the way they kicked other people about." And conquest tacitly implied the right to booty. The victorious troops appropriated whatever portable enemy property they fancied: liquor and cigars, cameras, binoculars, shotguns and sporting rifles, ceremonial swords and daggers, silver ornaments and plate and fur garments. This sort of petty looting was known as "liberating" or "souvenir-ing." Military police looked the other way. The men felt that they were handing out rough justice—morally valid retribution—to a race whose armies had plundered Europe for nearly five years.

But after the fighting moved onto German soil there was also a good deal of rape by combat troops and those immediately following them. The incidence varied between unit and unit according to the attitude of the commanding officer. In some cases offenders were identified, tried by court martial and punished. The army legal branch was reticent, but admitted that for brutal or perverted sexual offenses against German women, some soldiers had been shot. Yet I know for a fact that many women were raped by American troops and no action was taken against the culprits. In one sector a report went round that a certain very distinguished army commander had made the wisecrack: "Copulation without conversation does not constitute fraternization."

The Reverend Cecil Cullingford wrote of British troops stationed near Bremen:

Our soldiers, who have now seen or know about the unspeakable horrors of Belsen and similar camps, have found hospitals of POW camps full of our own men. These are the survivors of those who were force-marched from Poland to the North Sea, in the depth of winter and without food—all who fell out of line, for whatever reason, being immediately shot. Most are without hands or feet as a result of frostbite from the march. Those who have witnessed this are not inclined to feel sentimental about the Germans.

Cullingford added starkly: "There is a good deal of rape going on—and those who suffer have probably well deserved it."

"Do you see what a complicated thing is a man's soul?" Stalin had remarked. It was a time of upheaval, and for some, a moral breakdown was taking place within it. Ideas and beliefs became confused. Some descended into raw anger and aggression; others maintained honor and high standards. Many were no longer in control of themselves and their commanders were in quite a few cases no longer consistent in their maintenance of discipline. When a Soviet military prosecutor observed at the beginning of May that some officers were still ignoring regulations for better treatment of civilians, Marshal Zhukov added a note to his report: "Anyone found behaving in this fashion must be dismissed immediately . . . the Red Army will suffer no further dishonor."

Lieutenant Andrei Filin, moving through East Prussia with Marshal Rokossovsky's 2nd Belorussian Front, recalled the sunshine of May 1 and the trees in blossom. The troops were marching westward—but soon something disturbed them. "I saw a German woman," Filin continued, "who ran suddenly from her house—about half a kilometer away—across a field toward us. She was crying out 'Help, please help! Red Cross, Red Cross!' As far as we were able to understand, she was trying to get help for her father, whom a Russian soldier had shot and badly wounded." Filin and his comrades were not slow to imagine the likely scenario in which the wounding had taken place. Filin continued:

Our regimental commander had always strongly opposed any attempt to rape German women. He told us:

"This war has lasted a long time. It would have finished much sooner if we had not behaved like wild animals in East Prussia. Now each German soldier is no longer simply defending his Führer and fatherland, but his mother and his sisters as well. And for that cause he will fight to the very last cartridge. By losing our own discipline and self-control, we are creating an enemy who will resist us to the very end."

Our commander sent an officer from my own battalion—a Colonel Pjatov—to investigate, and as I knew a little German he asked me to come with him as an interpreter. We ran toward the house. Unfortunately, when we reached it we found that the old man was already dead. It turned out that the Russian soldier had entered their home looking for alcohol. He was given some schnapps, but then he saw a young girl in the house and wanted to rape her. The old man stepped forward in an attempt to protect his granddaughter—and got shot in the stomach.

A short distance away from the house we found an NKVD soldier, completely drunk, lying fast asleep in a meadow. These units followed behind the frontline fighting—and we were well aware of their reputation.

The woman identified him as the murderer and the two men kicked him awake. Filin covered him with a sub-machine gun. The colonel took out his pistol, removed all the bullets except one and said quietly:

"I give you a minute. At least end your life with some self-respect. At the end of the minute I will help you finish it as a coward."

"The shot rang out after a few seconds. We reported it as a suicide."

On April 30, 1945, troops of Rokossovsky's 49th Army occupied the small German town of Fürstenburg, about 50 miles north of Berlin. Captain Boris Makarov's 385th Rifle Division was leading the way. Makarov had been ordered to set up an advance HQ. It was a picturesque location—the town was bordered by three lakes. "Everything was very peaceful," Makarov recalled. "There was nothing to hear and nothing to see—all was calm and still. And then a woman appeared who spoke Russian, who told us about a nearby camp at Ravensbrück. There were many women there—and they were all sick."

Makarov and his soldiers accompanied her to the camp. At its gates they were met by Nina Nikiforov, the senior Russian prison doctor, who was now in charge of the Infirmary. She showed Makarov and his men round, explaining the dire situation. There was no electricity, no water, and around forty women were dying every day. Soviet soldier Yakov Drabkin was one of the liberators: "We found about 3,000 sick women there—and adolescent girls at an ancillary camp at Uckermark," he remembered. "The most horrifying thing was finding out about the 'medical experiments' performed on these poor women." These had included amputations and a sterilization program. Many Russians had been in the camp, including female Red Army POWs.

Ravensbrück was built in 1938—and was Nazi Germany's largest women's camp. Shortly before the Russians arrived the SS took more than 20,000 of these women on a "death march," leaving in the camp those too sick to move. The following day a Russian medical unit headed by Major Bulanov arrived and set up a hospital for all those who had been left behind.

All seemed in a ghastly state of flux. Amid these horrors, political matters proceeded inexorably. To safeguard Russia's future relations with Poland, Stalin had proposed that territory in the eastern part of the country should be given to the Soviet Union and Poland recompensed in the west with land taken from Germany. At Yalta, Britain and America had consented to this arrangement. Stalin now envisaged that the Silesian city of Breslau and the lands around it would be ceremonially handed over to the Polish army. Under the Yalta agreement, these lands would form part of the new Poland and its German inhabitants would then be expelled. But the Red Army had to capture the city first.

Breslau was Hitler's "fortress city." It had endured a siege of over three months under the fanatical defense of Karl Hanke, the Nazi Party leader in Silesia. Soviet planes bombed the city and Red Army artillery shelled it constantly. German and Russian soldiers fought ferociously for every street, every house. On May 1 Breslau was still holding out against the Soviet 6th Army. On that day the city's Nazi broadsheet, the *Schlesische Tageszeitung*, opined: "We want to celebrate May 1st in our way—as a German spring festival. We do not want to be slaves of Bolshevism, far from our homes and families, living a life of little or no value, losing everything which we have created . . . We must come through this struggle at all costs."

Walter Lassman observed: "Today is the so-called national holiday of the German people. Here, in besieged Breslau, people 'celebrate' in different ways. Our doctor, Dr. Franz, is plastered and unable to work. Many soldiers also stagger drunkenly through the streets of the fortress. The constant tension briefly evaporates—and the harsh reality is turned on its head."

That evening, news of Hitler's death—now recast as a heroic stand at the head of his troops outside Berlin's Reich Chancellery—was announced on the German radio. A Wehrmacht officer from Army Group Center, stationed at Rawenitz, near Prague, jotted down his thoughts:

"The Führer has died in Berlin. Deep impression. Long silence. Appeal: resistance goes on. The troops see the death of the Führer as a heroic gesture—or at least the majority do."

In Breslau, German soldier Hans Gottwald observed mixed reactions: "Many seem initially paralyzed by shock or horror," he noted, "but some comrades openly show relief and even delight."

In London's Downing Street news of Hitler's death was brought in midway through Winston Churchill's dinner with press baron Lord Beaverbrook. "He was perfectly right to die in such a fashion," the British prime minister responded. "Except that it almost certainly didn't happen like that," Beaverbrook responded more carefully. A Nazi mythology was already being created.

Beneath it lay a harsh reality. As the month of May began, the first day after the death of Hitler, it was hard to comprehend all that was being uncovered. In Breslau, Walter Lassman was struck by a reluctance to engage with it all. He continued: "We hear shouting in the streets, an accordion playing somewhere. Soldiers in uniform waltz with each other. I saw one who pranced around like a horse, barefooted and wearing a top-hat. It all gives the impression of a *danse macabre*."

3

EAST MEETS WEST

"The 2nd May was one of the most astounding days I have ever experienced," remembered Major Jerry McFadden of the 1st Canadian Parachute Battalion, fighting as part of the British 6th Airborne Division.

> We ran out of Germans and ran into the Russians. The German Army gave up by the thousands. We rode on tanks and in trucks from 5:00 a.m. to 4:00 p.m.—sometimes driving at 40 mph. At one point, in a heavily wooded area, we drove through what seemed to be a German tank corps, all lined up facing the road, officers and crew standing at attention, saluting as we went by. We saluted back and got the hell out of there. Our tail gunners stopped and chatted, discovering that they were surrendering. They were out of fuel.
>
> As we drove toward Wismar at dusk, we saw Russian Army tanks at the crossroads. All Germans, civilians and soldiers, are terribly afraid of the Russians—and I don't blame them. They are exceptional fighters—and just as tough as they look.

Captain Derek Thomas, manning an advance observation post on 6th Airborne's flank, formed a similar impression. He recalled:

> We were in an isolated and vulnerable position, in a near-deserted village. We set up our forward HQ in a large house. And then we encountered a foot patrol of Russians—on reconnaissance—led by a senior officer. They were surprised to see us but greeted us with great exuberance. The Soviet commander insisted on showing me his equipment, with some pride. He had an automatic pistol, a compass and a map case—all attached to him by a fine chain.

The meetings between troops of the Western Allies and the Soviet Union were—for many who participated in them—unforgettable experiences. Not all of those impressions were favorable, but for the majority they were powerful and moving, despite the language difficulties. As soldiers from both sides met each other their encounters made the Grand Alliance tangible. Meetings took place against a political and military backdrop that was sometimes carefully planned and choreographed; on other occasions spontaneous and even dangerous. Suspicion existed on both sides. And yet there was also a strong reservoir of goodwill. The fighting men recognized that they had achieved a joint victory and one worth celebrating.

On May 2, 1945, Field Marshal Montgomery's 21st Army Group was crossing the Elbe and making a dash for the Baltic ports of Lübeck and Wismar. The Western Allies knew Marshal Rokossovsky's Soviet forces were pushing fast along the Baltic from the opposite direction. By linking up with the Red Army they would cut off retreating German forces, including the 3rd Panzer Army. Several hundred thousand Wehrmacht troops would not then be able to regroup in Schleswig-Holstein and bolster the new Dönitz regime which was based there.

This bold plan, which had been approved by the Supreme Allied Commander, General Dwight Eisenhower, gave Montgomery—Britain's chief commander in northwest Europe—a final attacking role in the war's last stages. The objective was to secure the quick surrender of a mass of German troops and hasten the end of hostilities. Eisenhower trusted the Russians—

saw the link-up with them positively—and was looking to finish off the Wehrmacht. He spelled out these plans in a directive at the end of April 1945:

"By a thrust to the Baltic we should cut off from the main enemy armies [those in central Germany, Austria and Czechoslovakia] those elements located in Denmark, Norway, northwest Germany and [western] Holland . . . Furthermore we should gain the north German ports and thus deny the enemy the use of his naval bases and ship-building yards. Finally, we should link hands with the Russian forces sweeping across Pomerania to the north of Berlin."

The British—Prime Minister Winston Churchill and his chief of staff, General Sir Alan Brooke—saw things differently. They were less concerned about the Germans and more about the Russians. They did not want the Red Army to advance too far into Europe. And they particularly did not want Russian troops moving into Denmark. At Yalta, no one had foreseen that Denmark might be in a Soviet zone of influence. On April 19, 1945, Churchill had telegraphed his foreign secretary, Anthony Eden, stating:

It is thought most important that Montgomery should take Lübeck [the Baltic port halfway between Hamburg and Wismar] as soon as possible—and he has an additional American Army Corps to strengthen his movements if he requires it. Our arrival at Lübeck before our Russian friends from Stettin would save a lot of argument later on. There is no reason why the Russians should occupy Denmark, which is a country to be liberated and to have its sovereignty restored. Our position at Lübeck, if we get it, would be decisive in this matter.

Churchill was always aware of the course of history. He would have remembered the importance of Nelson's gaining a sea victory at Copenhagen over the Russian fleet, which prevented them gaining an outlet on the Baltic. And he keenly felt the symbolism of the last stages of the war. The Red Army was liberating all the major capitals of central and eastern Europe. He felt rebuffed that an Anglo-American attempt on Berlin had not been given serious consideration—and by the fact that Eisenhower had communicated this decision directly to Stalin without consulting the British chiefs of staff first.

Relations between Britain and Russia had deteriorated after Yalta. As early as March 8, 1945, Churchill apprised the war cabinet of recent events in Romania, saying that the Groza government had been put in power by violence—and that this had been orchestrated by the Russians. He added that while he felt no sympathy for the Romanians, he detested these "murderous methods." Churchill then remarked that Russia was behaving badly—not only in Romania but also in Poland. On April 3 he was much more emphatic, saying that there had been "a change of atmosphere" since Yalta and wondering whether Stalin's power was being challenged by others. Events in April would further fuel his suspicions of the Soviet Union.

Churchill was concerned that the Russians had liberated Vienna and installed a pro-Soviet government there, and excluded Western observers from visiting the city. He remained deeply pained by the deterioration of the situation in Poland. On April 24 he made an outright condemnation of the Soviet Union in a meeting of the war cabinet:

"The Polish issue has now become the crux of Russian good faith—or the lack of it," Churchill declared. "At the Yalta conference no-one could have envisaged things would become as bad as this."

He was also saddened by the perhaps inevitable decline in Britain's influence within the Grand Alliance. In terms of manpower and industrial might, America and Russia were now the main players—with Britain reduced to a supporting role.

Churchill's military schemes had grown increasingly erratic in the last months of the war. His insistence on conquering the Greek island of Rhodes—held by an isolated German garrison—was the nadir: the eastern Mediterranean theater of war had little relevance now to anyone but Churchill, and his preoccupation with this arena was greeted with bafflement by America, disdain by the Soviet Union and exasperation even within Churchill's own circle of supporters. But at the very end, Churchill recovered his military instinct. There was real wisdom in securing Denmark and some of the Baltic ports. And the situation in northern Italy was now working to the advantage of the Western Allies.

Italy had always exercised a strong magnetism over Churchill. He had persuaded America to work with him in expelling the Germans from North Africa. Then first Sicily and subsequently Italy proper were invaded by Anglo-American forces. Churchill had regarded Italy as the "soft underbelly" of Europe. It proved anything but. The invasion brought down Mussolini's fascist government, but the Germans moved in in force, using the mountain spine of the country to their advantage and constructing a series of strong defense lines. As they were dislodged from one, they fell back in good order to the next. This was the remarkable achievement of Field Marshal Albert Kesselring, who managed his ground troops with the same organizational skill that he had deployed with the Luftwaffe.

Fighting in Italy became bogged down, and the priority became the establishment of a second front in northwest Europe. This was the objective of President Roosevelt, his army chief of staff General George Marshall and the brilliant operational planner General Eisenhower, who would be chosen to enact it as Supreme Allied Commander. It was absolutely the right course of action—one that began to rebuild trust with the Soviet Union, and was pushed through over the objections of Churchill, who never had much enthusiasm for it.

In matters of broader strategy, British influence progressively waned after the D-Day landings in France in June 1944. America was now the major contributor to the war effort—in manpower and material—and it was only right that it should drive forward the direction of the war. But this situation was made worse by the behavior of Britain's chief commander in northern Europe, Field Marshal Bernard Montgomery.

Montgomery, who had been appointed overall commander of the Allied ground forces in Normandy—a post he exercised until Eisenhower arrived in person—never really accepted the American as his boss. In November 1944 matters between the two men had come to a head and Montgomery very nearly lost his job—only the tireless diplomacy of Freddie de Guingand, his chief of staff, saved the day. In January 1945—during the Battle of the Bulge, the German Ardennes offensive—Montgomery gave a disastrous press conference in which his manner came across as so patronizing that many American officers became completely alienated from him. General Omar Bradley, the commander of the 12th Army Group, never forgave Montgomery for it. The effect of this was to further reduce the influence of Churchill and his advisers.

And yet, at the end of April 1945 the military situation in Italy changed dramatically. A well-planned Allied assault across the Po valley broke the German position and pushed their generals to the negotiating table. At Caserta on April 29 an unconditional surrender was signed—pending ratification from Kesselring, who had been appointed by Hitler overall commander of all German forces in southern Europe. The Soviet Union was fully informed of proceedings and invited to send a representative. Kesselring hesitated, but after the death of the Führer was confirmed and he had informed Dönitz of the agreement, he approved it on May 2.

The German surrender in Italy was accepted by the overall Allied commander there, British field marshal Harold Alexander—and Alexander's military and diplomatic success allowed Churchill to re-establish a measure of influence in this region, bringing British troops into Austria to counter the presence of the Russians. Surveying the scene from the map room, Churchill felt this was a necessary precaution against an unpredictable ally. But the encounters between the two sides took place with real cordiality. "I will always remember our meeting with our British allies in Austria," said Soviet sergeant Yuri Eltekov of the 40th Guards Artillery Regiment (part of the 57th Army). "We swapped gifts—we took the stars off our uniform; British soldiers gave us pens and cigarettes. Our allies spoke little German or Russian so we largely communicated by sign language. However, there was a tremendous sense of friendship nonetheless—and relief that the war would soon be over."

Eltekov's Red Army unit enjoyed a joke as they approached their British allies in Austria—that they were renewing the abortive marriage negotiations between the Russian tsar Ivan the Terrible and the English queen Elizabeth I. The image of two thwarted lovers—separated by great geographical and cultural distance, and trying to consummate a union nonetheless—appealed to the humor of the Russian troops. Churchill had professed himself delighted with Alexander's success at Caserta—telling the war cabinet that it was "a magnificent achievement"—but sadly the Soviet government was less romantically inclined than its soldiers. When Hugh Lunghi (serving with the

British Military Mission in Moscow) relayed news of the German surrender in Italy to the Soviet Ministry of Defense, he was greeted with "a surly, couldn't-care-less attitude." The Russians—forever focused on the need for a "second front" in France—had always treated the Allied campaign in Italy as a sideshow.

But Churchill was not in the wooing mood either. He also ordered Alexander to occupy Trieste, in order to block the advance of Tito's Yugoslav communist army. Tito's partisans had been allies against the Germans and Churchill had recognized their government as legitimate, but now began to fear that they would secure this port on the Adriatic. Alexander moved his New Zealand troops into Trieste, only to find that Tito's men were already in the town. An uneasy standoff took place. Tito was unwilling to renounce his claim on Trieste as part of a greater Yugoslavia. In the interim, the soldiers carried out guard duties together.

A strategy of restraining communist ambition was being put in place and the race toward the Baltic ports formed an important part of it. On April 30, in a meeting of the British war cabinet, General Sir Alan Brooke outlined the situation: "Bremen has been taken. We have crossed the Elbe and are advancing on Hamburg. The Second Army will now go direct to Lübeck—and we plan to push on to Wismar and Schwerin. We should get there before the Russians do."

Churchill realized that a military advance—which would precede any political settlement—gave both sides (the Soviet Union and the Western Alliance) useful bargaining chips. He did not want too many of these chips in the hands of the Russians. Churchill's policy was based on a lack of trust of his Russian allies. From that position, it made sense to be cautious. But since the Soviet Union also mistrusted him, it risked creating an impasse rather than allowing real engagement.

Field Marshal Montgomery understood Churchill's political objectives and he also felt it important to secure Denmark. But Montgomery was concerned that he did not have the military means to bring about this dash to the Baltic—and that he was exposing his men to an undue level of risk. His army group had been stripped of American support after it had crossed the Rhine in March—and with the Germans still resisting in western Holland, was fully extended. Eisenhower's transfer of the US Ninth Army to General Bradley's 12th Army Group on March 29, 1945, still rankled. Montgomery wrote in his diary: "With victory in sight, the violent pro-American element at SHAEF is pressing for a set-up which will clip the wings of the British group of armies and relegate it to [an] unimportant role on the flank; the Americans then finish off the business alone."

The British chief of general staff, General Sir Alan Brooke, was sympathetic to Montgomery: "Most of the changes are due to national aspiration and to ensure that the USA effort will not be lost under British command. It is a pity and the straightforward strategy is being affected by the nationalistic outlook of the allies."

It was not in fact unreasonable—with America shouldering the greatest burden in prosecuting the war (both in manpower and resources)—for SHAEF to want American divisions under American command. Both Montgomery and Brooke underestimated how much Montgomery's arrogance and aloofness rankled with the United States command—many American generals no longer wanted to serve under him for any length of time.

However, Montgomery—always a far-sighted and clear planner in military affairs, whatever his lack of personal diplomacy—was concerned by the chaos on the eastern side of the Elbe and the risk of sustaining casualties for a part of Germany that would probably then be returned to Russia anyway. As his army had pushed up toward the Elbe, his men were increasingly unsure whether the German troops facing them would fight with determination or not.

One British lieutenant, Geoffrey Picot, wrote of the fighting in Germany that spring: "Our advance was much easier than it had been in Normandy [the previous summer]. But danger attended us at every stage."

Lieutenant Sydney Jary of the 4th Somerset Light Infantry gave an example of what that danger might be—foolhardy bravado from an enemy on the verge of military collapse. He was briefing one of his messengers when the alarm was raised:

"I heard the cry: 'Sir, they are charging at us!' Sure enough, from about one hundred and fifty yards ahead, a well spread out line of Germans were putting in a bayonet charge. Brave lads, but they didn't stand a chance. No-one got within seventy yards of us."

Sometimes, as British troops pushed ahead of or bypassed German units, they would then surrender to forces coming up behind. On other occasions, they did not. Advance formations would sweep past straggling German groups, which would then lie low and later re-emerge and attack British transport and supply lines. Outnumbered and surrounded Wehrmacht defenders would on occasion refuse to submit—whether out of a sense of battle honor or sheer stubbornness. In mid-April 1945 the British 43rd Division had isolated a small group of German soldiers on the River Lethe. And yet, with only 200 soldiers and two tanks, they went on to the attack, which they continued—despite heavy losses—until the whole force disintegrated. One of the British officers wrote:

"Later in the day, when our advance was resumed, old men and women emerged from the woods and neighboring villages to carry away their dead, who lay in long rows in front of our position. Many were young boys; others were old men who had been hurriedly pressed into uniform. It was a somber scene, pathetic in its utter futility—even to the battle-hardened troops of the Division."

British soldiers were advancing into a landscape of destruction and chaos. William Lawrenson of the 7th Armored Division noted:

"The German towns that we have passed through have been terribly knocked about . . . Most of the German civilians we have seen have been women, many of them wheeling handcarts which carry their only remaining belongings . . ."

And Lieutenant Bill Bellamy said on witnessing the destruction at one town, Osnabrück:

"I was stunned at the totality of it all and, despite my anger, horrified at the suffering which it had brought in its wake. Whatever the German people had done, I couldn't gloat over their anguish, or get satisfaction from a feeling of revenge."

British soldier Ronald Mallabar said: "Stories of SS atrocities made our men angry—but when you see a person face-to-face and he is helpless, unarmed and wants to surrender you lose that wildness." Others felt that desire for revenge and acted upon it. In mid-April 1945 three German women were raped by British troops in the town of Neustadt-am-Rübenberge.

However unacceptable, for some, vengeance came into play when they gained a fuller understanding of what Hitler's Germany stood for. On April 11, 1945, the British 11th Armored Division had uncovered the death camp at Belsen. Within the camp, more than 60,000 inmates were suffering from disease, malnourishment and appalling mistreatment—a further 10,000 corpses of murdered victims lay about the camp and in open pits. British soldiers had little idea of the scale of the horror awaiting them. Although some information was already available about the death camps liberated by the Red Army in Poland—at Majdanek in July 1944 and Auschwitz in January 1945—not a great deal had filtered through to the West, and virtually nothing to the British Army in northwest Europe.

"I was not prepared for the horrific sights, even in the first few hundred yards of the camp," wrote Major Bill Close. "The huts were full of almost naked inmates, some dead, some only just alive and pitifully thin. There were bodies everywhere—lying in the ditches surrounding the huts; the stench was indescribable." Lieutenant Lawrence Aslen added: "The sheer scale of the horror just overwhelmed us—the SS guards seemed to us utterly evil, depraved murderers who should all be hanged."

On April 15 the medical services of the British 2nd Army had arrived at the camp to assess the situation. At first, they struggled to get to grips with it—nothing comparable to Belsen had ever been encountered before—and tragically, the standard army food and supplies rushed into the camp were highly unsuitable for inmates in such a terrible condition. In the immediate aftermath of liberation, more than 600 of these unfortunates died each day. In time, greater understanding and better facilities brought the situation under control. But at the beginning of May 1945 the shadow of Belsen still strongly affected British soldiers in Germany.

It was hard to contain the emotions thrown up by such a terrible experience. "Some of the camp guards at Belsen who refused to help bury the bodies were shot for mutiny," Lieutenant Aslen acknowledged, "others succumbed to typhus through being forced to do so. And two of the guards were badly beaten up by our soldiers, thrown into a burial trench and left to die."

Belsen—horrific though it was—was a piece in a broader mosaic of upheaval. As the British 2nd Army moved across Germany it had to house and feed an increasing number of displaced persons (DPs)—those slave laborers transported to the Reich from all over Europe. Montgomery communicated these difficulties bluntly to Eisenhower on April 16, in the immediate aftermath of the medical inspection at Belsen: "I cannot possibly push up toward Denmark and also place under military governorship the large area of Germany that we now occupy." Eisenhower took Montgomery's point—and released two American divisions to support his army group.

Displaced persons, and the increasing number of Germans wishing to surrender, placed a heavy logistical burden on the Allied armies, and made it hard for their forward units to maintain the speed of their advance. War correspondent Wynford Vaughan-Thomas reported:

Our 11th Armored Division, with the 6th Airborne on its southern flank, has raced down the main roads from Osnabrück toward the River Weser . . . The airborne boys travel in the most varied collection of transport I've yet seen . . . lorry-borne or tank-borne, motorbike-borne, even cart-borne infantry. The Germans have little to stop our racing columns—they rushed some units up . . . a regiment from Denmark, on its way to defend Osnabrück, oblivious to the fact that it had already fallen days before . . . But speed brings with it its own problems. Apart from that ever-present nightmare of supply, how to get the petrol and food up to our leading tanks, there are other headaches for our army—the problem of prisoners for example. What on earth are you to do with the thousands upon thousands of these survivors of warfare, cluttering up the roads and offering to surrender to the first of our troops that appear?

It's difficult for an armored division to begin to cope with them. Our tanks have got to get on and our lorries are wanted to bring up supplies. The only thing to do with these prisoners is to disarm them and send them off to the rear. And with an advance as fast as ours, the rear may be 60 miles away. These are just the ordinary spectacles—miles behind the lines, long columns of prisoners, sometimes led by their officers, quietly tramping along in the middle of our back areas. Nobody pays the slightest attention to them. And none of them make the slightest effort to escape.

Despite the run of successes, by April 1945 it had become increasingly hard to motivate British troops to fight. They knew the end of the war was close at hand—and no officer wanted to see men unnecessarily killed at the conflict's close. And yet, when the objectives of the Baltic ports of Lübeck and Wismar were announced, the 21st Army Group galvanized itself. General Miles Dempsey, commander of the British 2nd Army, believed that a rapid strike at Lübeck would stop the Soviets from reaching Denmark and push Germany into a final capitulation, and on May 2 ordered the 11th Armored Division to reach the port with all speed. Striking farther northeast, toward Wismar, would hasten that process.

Then news of Hitler's death, which had been publicly announced for the first time on Hamburg radio at 10:30 p.m. on May 1 and was then relayed to Anglo-American troops the following morning, had an electrifying effect.

Montgomery brought up the 6th Airborne Division for the advance to Wismar. The twin objectives of Lübeck and Wismar would allow British and American troops to carve a land corridor across northwest Germany and seal off Denmark from the Russians.

Moving across the Elbe and into the plain of Mecklenburg was certainly hazardous, for as many as 250,000 German troops were caught there between the British and Russians. If they surrendered to the British all well and good—but Montgomery certainly didn't have the resources to deal with them if they decided to fight. Only after Eisenhower promised two supporting US divisions—the 7th Armored and 82nd Airborne—did he commit himself to the advance to the Baltic, on April 29—and even then with considerable reluctance. General Eric Bols' 6th Airborne Division would lead the attack; the American divisions would advance on his right flank. Bols needed eighteen hours to ready his troops: the operation would start at first light on May 2.

The window of opportunity was narrow. Montgomery did not exactly know where the Russians were, but his reconnaissance—and he had the best reconnaissance system of all the Allied army groups—warned him that they were moving up fast and the roads in between were increasingly clogged with

German soldiers and civilians. All of these were fleeing westward, so they would be an obstacle for the British, not the Russians. There was little time to spare. Montgomery's troops would ride on top of tanks and armored vehicles. There was no time to take the surrender of German units. The men would have to keep pushing forward, for if Wismar was not reached by nightfall on May 2 the operation would probably fail.

At the forefront of Bols' deployment was Lieutenant Colonel Fraser Eadie's 1st Canadian Parachute Battalion. At 4:00 a.m. the entire battalion moved forward, sitting astride the tanks of the Royal Scots Greys. Their orders were to press forward as fast as possible and run over or around anything that got in their way—advancing around 60 miles if possible. If all went well, they were to capture Wismar on the Baltic Sea.

Sergeant Andy Anderson recalled on the morning of May 2:

It is expected that at some point we may run up against the Soviet Army, who are advancing in the opposite direction. We have no clear idea of where the Russians are, or how fast they are coming—and there is real concern that we do not end up shooting at one another by accident.

As we moved off, we attempted to remember the briefings we had had about the Red Army, their tanks and vehicles, how they were marked, what the uniformed soldier looked like and the weapons he carried. I picked up two Polish Americans from other platoons who claimed they could speak some Russian . . .

By noon we were moving at a great rate, through towns and villages—it was impossible to recall any of the names. The strangeness of the situation was that we were passing complete units of the German Army, lying by the roadside, some with vehicles, even horse-drawn artillery, but no shots were exchanged, no white flags shown and we could not stop to disarm them. The advance was incredible to experience. We pushed through division after division of the enemy—completely out on a limb as we dashed onward. It was almost like an unofficial surrender.

As we continued this mad dash, the roadside became more and

more clogged. Fully armed German troops mixed with civilians, prisoners of war, in fact just about everything. The Germans looked tired, downcast and dirty. We passed many POW cages—some of the prisoners were visibly overcome, others had a wild look about them. We were not able to stop—and could only throw chocolate or rations to them.

Anderson was feeling a powerful mixture of exhilaration and apprehension. He knew his small force was dangerously overextended, its communications stretched—and thousands of Germans were now behind it. He could only hope that someone in the rear was taking charge of the situation and disarming them all. The adrenaline surge kept him going. He had a dawning realization that this might be the end of the war—an experience he would never forget.

The leading tanks reached the outskirts of Wismar. Anderson continued:

"We dismounted and moved forward on foot, cautiously, through the town. It seemed untouched by the war, a very pretty place and some civilians were moving about with white flags. We got to the far end and I received orders to stop. I set up an HQ in the last house on the main highway and sent one of my sergeants and a platoon to establish a roadblock about 100 yards down the main road, reinforced by a machine gun crew."

The 11th Armored Division had now reached Lübeck and occupied the town. There had been little organized resistance from the Wehrmacht. Farther east, Anderson settled in to the new HQ at Wismar—a pleasant house, two stories high with a stucco finish. It was beautifully furnished—and its occupants seemed to have fled only hours earlier. Field telephones were installed—and then he decided to check on the roadblock. A remarkable sight met his eyes. Thousands of Germans were coming down the road—fully armed—yet looking scared and wanting to surrender. They began to gather by the roadblock. Amid the confused milling-about Anderson could see German ranking officers—and even two generals. He radioed for assistance, telling his men to stack the Germans' weapons and send them on into the town. He could only hope someone would take charge of the situation. And yet, watching it all, Anderson said:

"It began to dawn on me that this was the end of the war—at least as far as the German army was concerned. They seemed to be extremely pleased to be surrendering to us. Things settled down into an orderly process. The pile of weapons stood about ten feet high, and twenty-five at the base and was growing rapidly."

The way was now barred for the Russians to continue along the Baltic coast and occupy Denmark. Hugh Lunghi remembered the moment that the British Military Mission in Moscow received an urgent signal from London that Montgomery's Army Group had reached the Baltic. "It had been suspected for some time that Red Army forces might make an attempt on Denmark," Lunghi said. "As I remember, we did not pass on the news of the capture of Lübeck and Wismar to the Soviet Ministry of Defense." The Russians would come across Anderson's wooden barricade entirely by chance.

As interrogations of some of the Germans began, it became clear that their entire army was in full flight from the Red Army, which was only a few miles up the road. There were many tales of brutality and atrocities. "We could not verify this," Anderson said, "but from the fright on some of their faces it seemed it might be true."

Shortly after 11:00 p.m. Anderson went to bed. He was quickly woken up again. A Russian patrol had now arrived at the roadblock. They were demanding entry into the town. They were very belligerent—and also quite drunk. Anderson arrived at the roadblock. He had no interpreter. "My first impression of them was that they were the hardest-looking bunch of toughs I had ever seen."

General Eric Bols had now established a forward divisional HQ and got in contact with his opposite number, Soviet general Panfilov. At first Panfilov warned Bols that his orders were to move on to Lübeck and if the British commander did not immediately move his men out of the way, he would use his armor to blast a way through. Bols replied that he had substantial air support—and was quite happy to bomb the advancing Russian tank column in return. After this exchange of pleasantries was concluded, a demarcation line was set up for the night—and then, in a sudden change of mood, Anderson found himself invited to an impromptu reception to celebrate the Allied meeting:

"We were escorted to the Soviet divisional headquarters," Anderson recalled. "We were greeted by a Russian general in full dress uniform, with rows of medals, attended by many aides—including several young women soldiers. A full banquet table had been prepared, loaded with caviar, a multitude of other dishes and bottles of vodka. Once seated, there began a series of toasts—to Churchill, Stalin and just about everything else." By departure time, Anderson's interpreter had passed out and he and his companions could hardly see. Later—safely back in British lines—he reflected: "I was conscious of the fact that we had been party to an historic meeting. My regret was that I had no memory of who or what we had linked up with."

The Western Allies and the Russians had already met at the central section of the front, on the Elbe river at Torgau in Germany. The first contact had been made on April 25—an auspicious day, as it coincided with the opening session of the San Francisco talks that aimed to create a new world body, the United Nations. Subsequently more meetings were held, and contact established at a higher level of army command on both sides. They took place under the remit of US general Courtney Hodges' First Army. Dialogue between the two sides was not always easy.

On May 2 General Hodges noted that General Bill Kean—his army chief of staff—had left for a conference with the Russians over the transfer of displaced persons and liberated Russian POWs. Hodges stated bluntly:

"For some reason—the most charitable being that the local commanders require orders from Moscow before they can proceed—the Russians do not appear either interested or concerned to facilitate the return of these many thousands of people, and likewise have not been too cooperative as yet on the return of the many American POWs liberated by their advance. However, with patience on our side, the problem will work itself out."

The issue of returning POWs had become a thorny one for both sides. The Russians would overrun German camps with American prisoners held within them; the Americans and British would now liberate increasing numbers of Russian POWs. The Russian system of dealing with United States and British servicemen was byzantine in its complexity—they were relocated to camps in Odessa in the Ukraine, and only then, after long delays and in piecemeal fashion, allowed to return home. This understandably led to bad feeling and suspicion between the Western Allies and the Soviet Union. But Russia had complaints of its own—that when camps were liberated the British and American forces had not adequately protected Russians within them.

Russian POWs could certainly create problems. An American army doctor with the 438th Anti-Aircraft Artillery Battalion had participated in the liberation of the slave labor camp at Nordhausen near Leipzig, and was subsequently stationed there. He wrote home on May 2:

> Meanwhile, I come back here to find the French [POWs] moving out and a mob of Russians moving in. Boy—are they a wild bunch, and completely uncivilized! They really run us wild. They have no discipline and have never really soldiered. With most of them it was a question of being given a uniform, a rifle and being told to go out and kill Germans—which they did. I have a heck of a time with them on sick-call—but if I stay here long enough I will learn a little Russian. It's a sure bet they won't learn a little English. I've had a few suture jobs—cuts about the face. Usually the story is the same—someone's friend bashed him with a bottle. But they don't seem to mind. They're tough and I use the so-called Bulgarian anesthetic, which is no anesthetic at all. To date, I've had no complaints.

Two days later, the doctor wrote again from Nordhausen:

> Here the work continues—and I'm learning a little Russian. They're a tough people and damned hard to handle, from an administrative point of view. They just won't be disciplined and they run wild all over the place—and this camp is going to be all-Russian! They get hold of liquor somewhere or other—and the first thing they do after drinking it is to start a brawl. Someone always gets beat up badly.

But both sides were trying to improve the situation. The Russians began to keep a better check of how many Allied prisoners were being returned and when, and started to allow local commanders to transfer prisoners direct, if and when it was feasible. And in return, more Russian POWs were kept in properly secure camps until they could be transported back to the Soviet Union. Despite the problems and mutual suspicion, the goodwill was there.

At Hodges' First Army HQ on May 2 there were plenty of grounds for optimism. He noted the "biggest news," the unconditional surrender of all enemy forces in northern Italy and western Austria. There were the "tremendous gains" by the British 2nd Army, "which has almost cut off the Danish Peninsula by advancing 20 miles to reach Lübeck." The US 36th Division had just captured First Army's greatest opponent, Field Marshal von Rundstedt, who was found at a castle in Bad Tolz with his wife and son. Hodges believed that the whole front opposing him would collapse soon. Amid all this, the behavior of the Russians remained an enigma.

Ten days earlier, with a link-up between American and Russian forces imminent, Hodges had spent the better part of the day on the phone trying to ascertain from SHAEF instructions for the army group on procedures for making contact with their allies fast approaching from the east. He commented:

"Although SHAEF must surely have envisioned such a meeting in the near future, they were apparently caught completely off-base. When instructions were finally received, they consisted of 'treat them nicely.' Information on mutual recognition signals will follow, General Bradley stated, if we can get the Russians to agree to a satisfactory procedure."

Hodges had followed news of the link-up at Torgau with much interest, noting: "Contact was extremely friendly but military information was difficult to obtain because of language difficulties and general merriment." On April 30 he had gone to Torgau himself to meet with the Russians. He was met at the river's edge by a Russian major general, who promptly put Hodges in his car, a captured German black sedan, and without further delay whisked him across the bridge, where a banner proclaimed welcome "to our victorious allies." He sped at 50 mph past Red Army soldiers standing to attention, before turning into a beautiful estate—commandeered for the occasion—which he learned had been one of the largest stud farms in Germany. Here he met General Zhadov of the Russian 5th Guards Army, "a 50-year-old, heavy-set, handsome man." The national anthems were played, short speeches were made praising Truman, Roosevelt and the American army, and then everyone retired to the dining room where the festivities started in earnest. Tables were laden with vodka, cognac, large loaves of black Russian bread, whole roasted pigs, geese, caviar—and a clear broth with a whole fish floating in it, which the bemused Americans were told "was considered a great delicacy." After a long round of toasts, concerns about the fish receded into the background.

If the Americans were caught somewhat by surprise, the Russians were better prepared. On April 18 a report was passed back on a series of political meetings held to "popularize the successful operations of our allies in Germany." Maps were used to show to soldiers the likely area where the link-up would take place and the position of the respective armies. There was a uniformly positive reaction to the progress of British and American forces, and the fact that it was achieved by rapid progress across a broad front. Sergeant Nikolai Churkin of the 169th Rifle Division said: "Now everyone can see that the decisions taken at the Crimean [Yalta] Conference are actually being implemented. Nazi Germany—caught in the vise-like grip of two fronts—is now tottering to its defeat and all of us are now convinced that the next concerted blows will bring the war to an end." "Once it was a dream—now it is a reality," added Lieutenant Sergei Odintsov of the 250th Rifle Division. "Our army has crossed the Oder; our allies the Rhine—now we know for sure that the Nazis are finished."

While the speed of the Western advance was now a cause of great satisfaction—"Our allies have now truly learned to beat the Germans" was a comment made again and again—it also gave rise to concern. A uniform reaction of Red Army officers and soldiers was that if there was any risk British and American armies might be tempted to advance on Berlin, Russia must take Hitler's capital on its own and as fast as possible. "Our allies are sometimes moving 60 kilometers a day, with little or no opposition," said one officer. "If they were to launch a sudden strike and take Berlin before us, they could claim the major role in ending the war. We must speed things up, and redouble our efforts to get into the city first." Another added: "We must never let our allies get to Berlin. For us to take the city will demonstrate to the world everything our forces have achieved." The Red Army had kept to its timetable.

Amid awareness of the symbolic importance of Berlin was much discussion of the ceremonies that should be arranged when Russian troops linked up with those from the West. Time and time again it was stressed that the Red Army must not lose face. The remarks of Lieutenant Ivan Sokolov of the 250th Rifle Division were typical: "The world will be watching our link-up. We need to act in a way that will bring honor to the Red Army. Discipline needs to be tightened up."

Although the Russians had prepared carefully for the link-up and wanted to be positive, it was hard for them to put their distrust of the West completely aside. Time and time again they were reminded by their political officers that no military secrets must be disclosed to British or American troops. The excitement remained. And now—on April 25, 1945, at Torgau, on the Elbe in central Germany—that link-up had happened. One of the best-known depictions of it was a photo taken by American Signal Corps photographer Bill Poulson of a Soviet and an American lieutenant—Alexander Silvashko and William Robertson—embracing each other in front of the sign "East meets West."

The two divisions involved in that link-up were the US 69th and the Soviet 58th Guards. At the beginning of May the US 69th Division had pulled back from the Elbe to the vicinity of Colditz. It was there that the 271st Infantry Regiment's anti-tank company met a young Russian POW, Rotefan Marcosovitch, who had been freed from a labor camp at Saalfeld several weeks earlier. No provision had been made for him—POWs like him, if strong enough to be able to walk, were now on the move all over Germany looking for food and shelter. Marcosovitch was willing to work for them. The anti-tank company needed extra help, and let him stay with their unit for a few weeks.

The American troops took an immediate liking to Marcosovitch, although communication was not easy: his English was limited, although his German—learned during his time in the camp—was much more fluent. It took time to understand him, but the nineteen-year-old Russian was spirited and lively and he had a remarkable story to tell. British and American troops, on first meeting Russian soldiers, often described them as "tough." But Marcosovitch offered a window for US soldiers to see what that "toughness" might actually mean.

He had joined the Red Army in the autumn of 1941, even though he was only fifteen years old. Officially, the age of conscription was eighteen, but Moscow was in deadly peril in October 1941 and volunteer units were being formed from those who would not normally be eligible to fight. He was not forced to join up—he was a young patriot and wanted to do something for his country. Marcosovitch joined a volunteer regiment in the 140th Rifle Division with his older brother. Within weeks most of the regiment—including his brother—was wiped out in a battle with the Germans at Vyazma; Marcosovitch was wounded by a shell splinter in his thigh and taken prisoner, and spent the next three and a half years in the labor camp at Saalfeld.

Conditions inside the camp were harsh. In the summer of 1943 seventeen-year-old Marcosovitch organized an escape attempt—but he was recaptured and publicly beaten before all the camp inmates, after which he was unable to move for two weeks. Subsequently, he began to organize attempts to sabotage factory output. He was caught on one occasion and beaten with a bull-whip until he lost consciousness.

In a work accident in early 1944, Marcosovitch suffered a deep muscle cut and fractured his left arm in two places. While recovering in hospital, and able to acquire a pencil and some paper, he wrote a short piece in German entitled "All nations are equal," and, having struck up a rapport with one of the nurses who had helped him recover, and who treated him with a measure of humanity, he gave it to her on leaving the hospital. In it, he said that Germany was wrong to believe it was a master race, superior to the Slavs. Marcosovitch believed that no one country should place itself above another. His work was discovered by the hospital doctor, who reported him to the camp police: the result was another beating with a rubber truncheon, causing him to fall and refracture his left arm.

In the autumn of 1944 Saalfeld was visited by the senior Nazi labor minister, Robert Ley, who ordered everyone to work harder. Marcosovitch responded to this exhortation with a further campaign of sabotage within the camp. The frequent beatings he received, and a daily work ration of 300 grams of soup, with a little bread and potatoes, never broke his spirit or his patriotism.

In January 1945 Saalfeld had another important visitor, a representative of the Russian general Andrei Vlasov, now actively recruiting men for his anti-Bolshevik army (one that would fight with the Germans on the Oder front against Soviet forces three months later). This high-ranking officer had been given permission by the camp authorities to address all the Russian prisoners. Those who wished to enlist in the new army would be immediately released.

The Vlasov Amy was described by this representative as a force of patriots—stressing that Bolshevism was their enemy, not Russia. There may have been truth in this, but Marcosovitch was suspicious. After Vlasov's man had spoken to the Russian POWs he stood up and challenged him—asking for his credentials, demanding to know who had awarded him his medals, and who he really took his orders from. In a heated exchange, he then denounced Vlasov as an opportunist who was trying to save his skin and described his whole endeavor as a folly. Few POWs joined up.

On April 13, 1945, Saalfeld was liberated. Marcosovitch met the anti-tank company a little more than two weeks later—and worked as an auxiliary with the American unit for two months, before arranging for his return to the Soviet Union. His exceptional courage and perseverance—though demonstrated in a labor camp, not on a battlefield—told the US soldiers much about how Russia was able to win the war against the German invader. There were many Marcosovitches in the Red Army.

The Allied link-up at Torgau continued to be commemorated. Lieutenant William Robertson and his patrol were taken back to SHAEF HQ at Rheims on May 2, where they met American Supreme Commander General Eisenhower. All the men were promoted on the spot. And Eisenhower would be the crucial guarantor of that link-up's success.

General Eisenhower wrote of the Soviets: "The Russians are generous. They like to give presents and hold parties, as almost every American who has served with them can testify. In his generous instincts, in his love of laughter, in his devotion to a comrade, and in his healthy, direct outlook on the affairs of workaday life, the ordinary Russian seems to me to bear a remarkable similarity to what we call an 'average American.'"

This response showed Eisenhower's own generosity. He was not naive, and he knew that some Red Army troops behaved atrociously—but he did not want to tar all Russian soldiers with the same brush. He also knew first hand of the incidents and conflicts that had arisen between the Allies. And above all, he was aware how easily misunderstandings could arise, commenting: "Because of the difference in languages, no-one had available the instrument of direct and personal conversation to alleviate the ensuing arguments." In such a situation, Eisenhower resolved on an approach very different from Churchill's:

"We insisted that every firm commitment of our government should be properly and promptly executed. We felt that for us to be guilty of bad faith in any detail of operation would defeat whatever hope we had of assisting in the development of a broad basis of international cooperation." In essence, Eisenhower's policy toward Russia was one of "firm adherence to the pledged word."

The main obstacle that Eisenhower faced in his dealings with the Soviets was their inherent suspicion. The Soviet regime could never entirely rid itself of its fear of Western capitalist powers and its recollection that allies could suddenly become enemies. Throughout the war they were unwilling to entrust the Western Allies with much information concerning the Red Army's activities. "We were struck by their incredible secrecy," Hugh Lunghi said. "During the battle of Kursk—the major tank battle in the summer of 1943— they told us [the British Military Mission in Moscow] virtually nothing of what was going on."

Eisenhower took the initiative. Shortly after the Normandy landings, an arrangement was made whereby SHAEF furnished the Soviet government with outlines of all Anglo-American operations and, when necessary, its plans for the future. The Soviet response was rather more modest. They promised to give the Allied military missions in Moscow copies of Red Army communiqués a short time before their release to the press. But for any serious attempt to coordinate military activities, Eisenhower had to transmit his wishes to the military missions themselves, who would then pass them on to the Red Army chief of staff. Then the whole laborious process was repeated in reverse. As the war neared its end, this lack of speedy and effective liaison was both exasperating and potentially dangerous, and would considerably impact on the final negotiations for an unconditional surrender with Germany.

Yet Eisenhower was not alone in seeing in the Russian character something of the American. US doctor Henry Swan wrote home about a visit to them on May 2:

> I took two of my men in a new car and went to see the Russkis! It was some trip, as contact in this army is still strictly tenuous. We saw Magdeburg . . . the two spires of the cathedral remain untouched, watching over the crumbled ruins of the city. For blocks on end, no house remains standing—only walls, chimneys and piles of brick and masonry. It seems like a sort of symbol, or judgment, to see these stately spires standing amidst the ruins.
>
> Then, well on the east side of the river, we found these great big beautiful Russians! They are more like carefree, wild-western style cowboys on a spree than anything else I can think of. Hearty—rough and tough—full of the devil and friendly. They seem to be as American as possible, only more so. Of course, these are strictly their frontline fighting men, on a victorious campaign.
>
> We had some schnapps with a captain—a large, powerful man with close-cut hair, a chest-full of medals and red ribbons, a booming laugh and a crushing handshake. And a major—a quieter man with a keen level eye and a crisp, decisive manner. Our visit was short. I had a color picture taken of myself with them—then we had to get back, while we could. We couldn't speak a word they understood, and vice-versa. But it was a friendly, exciting meeting and a fitting finale to our work here. When one thinks back and visualizes the situation as it was at Stalingrad, then one realizes that we have come a long way over a rough road. Yes, it was satisfying to stand in the heart of Germany and shake hands with the Russians.

Such instinctive rapport was not shared by the new American president. President Truman was very different from Roosevelt. He had not been briefed by his predecessor on foreign policy and was best known to the Russians for his 1941 statement that the Nazis and the Bolsheviks should be allowed to kill each other off. The Soviet Union had been very suspicious of the Western Allies in the first half of the war. They had seen Churchill and Roosevelt's friendship, their conferences on military strategy at Quebec, Casablanca and New York, from which the Russians were excluded, repeated postponements of the Second Front and the suspension of supply convoys at the height of the Nazi onslaught in the summer of 1942. By the spring of 1943 relations between Russia and the West had reached a low point. The Soviets did not trust Churchill—and believed that the US and Britain were ganging up against them. Teheran in November 1943 had marked a turning-point: Roosevelt and Stalin forged a good personal relationship.

President Roosevelt's instinctive approach was not shared by Truman. Roosevelt had once remarked that the Russians had a habit of sending him a friendly note on Monday, spitting in his eye on Tuesday and then being nice again on Wednesday. The first time it had happened, he was "sore," and "came back at them," but this only made things worse. Since then he had learned that if he ignored them, the Soviets "straightened out" by themselves. In contrast, Truman believed in scolding the Russians every time they were belligerent or uncooperative. He compared the Russians to people "from the wrong side of the tracks."

To convince the Soviets that the US would keep its promises, Roosevelt had ordered that all Lend-Lease contracts must be fulfilled, even at the expense of US defense needs. In this, Roosevelt shared the view of Eisenhower that the way to build trust was to keep one's word. Truman ended the protocol system and allowed Russian supplies to be diverted to western Europe. Roosevelt insisted that Lend-Lease should never be used as a lever on Soviet foreign policy; Truman shared Churchill's view of bargaining chips—and he tried to use Lend-Lease as a bargaining chip with the Russians.

Roosevelt had tried hard to win Stalin's friendship. Truman was willing to meet with his Soviet counterpart—but let Stalin make the first move. To preserve good relations with Stalin, Roosevelt tried to avoid quibbling with the Russians over details (leaving such matters to the State Department). He would not get involved personally unless he felt the Alliance itself was at risk. Truman got drawn in to a series of cables with Stalin over more minor issues.

Roosevelt—from his first meeting with Stalin at the Teheran summit—attempted to play the role of mediator between Britain and the Soviet Union. Truman, since coming into office, had sided with the British on a whole range of issues: opposing the Soviet recognition of a provisional government in Austria; demanding that Allied representatives be admitted to Vienna and joining with Churchill in opposing the recognition of the Lublin Poles.

Journalists began to perceive this shift in direction. *New York Times* columnist C. L. Sulzberger wrote at the beginning of May 1945:

"The discussions at San Francisco and some of our reactions to the Soviets have given to Russian as well as American sources the impression of an Anglo-American front against Moscow. Such a 'front'—diplomatic, political or military—can only serve to heighten and justify the super-suspicions that are the product of the Communist mind and convince the Soviet Union of the necessity of unilateral action and reliance on its own strength."

Joseph Davies, a former ambassador to Moscow, warned Truman at this time: "I have found that when approached with generosity and friendliness, the Soviets respond with even greater generosity. The 'tough' approach induces a sharp rejoinder—that 'out-toughs' anyone they consider hostile." But Davies' view was disliked by other Soviet experts in the State Department, who felt that he was politically naive and was rationalizing Soviet cruelty and atrocities. They nicknamed his 1941 book *Mission to Moscow* "Submission to Moscow."

Before Truman's first, confrontational meeting with Soviet foreign minister Molotov on April 23, 1945, there had been a discussion of what approach to adopt. Admiral Leahy said that he had left Yalta with the impression that the Soviet government had no intention of permitting a free government to operate in Poland, and that he would have been surprised had the Soviets behaved any differently. In his opinion the Yalta agreement—over Poland—was susceptible to two interpretations. He added that he felt it was a serious matter to break with the Russians, but that the US should tell them that it stood for a free and independent Poland. But others believed the Soviet Union was reneging on its agreements and should be challenged.

This change of approach had already raised concerns in Moscow by the beginning of May 1945, but its effect was softened by the more conciliatory stance taken by Eisenhower. Truman held army chief of staff General George Marshall in considerable respect, and Marshall in return completely trusted Eisenhower. As a result, the Supreme Allied Commander could make the important decisions about military relations with the Russians without interference from above.

These were confused and turbulent times, and in the circumstances it was remarkable that things on the ground worked out as well as they did. Field Marshal Montgomery had been rightly concerned over the risk in pushing forward to Wismar. Proof was found in the experience of the lead elements of the US 7th Armored Division, advancing on Montgomery's right flank.

Captain William Knowlton's 87th Cavalry Reconnaissance Squadron was leading the way. He was told to push on through any retreating Germans and keep going until he made contact with the Russians. These were quite remarkable orders—but their simplicity was deceptive. Knowlton's situation was to become more and more surreal.

On the morning of May 2 Knowlton's tanks sped toward their first objective, the town of Neustadt-Glewe. They passed German troops marching westward, who shouted out to the Americans and threw down their guns. Knowlton's men simply went faster. They passed fresh groups of the Wehrmacht, who did the same. Occasionally, German gunners aimed at the lead tanks and then stopped in puzzlement as the Americans remained seated atop their turrets and made no move toward their own weaponry. They concluded there must be a huge US force following up to justify such confidence—and abandoned their artillery.

Neustadt-Glewe was awash with German soldiers and civilians. One of the Americans jumped down and helped one of Neustadt's military police direct the traffic. On Knowlton's men raced, through the town of Parchim. The Germans had been alerted that Knowlton's force was on its way. They reckoned the faster it could continue eastward the more of their soldiers would escape captivity at the hands of the Russians. When the Americans arrived they found German police on each corner to direct them through.

The SS kept the crowds off the streets and German soldiers lined the roads six deep, cheering loudly. They seemed to think Knowlton's small force was off to fight the Russians. General Hasso von Manteuffel's 3rd Panzer Army had been heading westward in an effort to escape the Red Army. The rapid advance of Knowlton's tiny force was triggering a mass surrender. So many German soldiers were throwing down their weapons that the US troops following the 87th Reconnaissance Squadron were overwhelmed by the sheer press of numbers. They were falling farther and farther behind. As the Americans reached Lübz, the fairy tale dissolved into a harsh reality.

"I got as scared as I ever had been in my life," Knowlton confessed. The Americans had tried to reach their HQ on the radio and found they were out of contact. They were 40 miles inside enemy lines—about sixty-five men, in the center of the German 3rd Panzer Army. "Here in Lübz we encountered some of the real fighting men of the Wehrmacht," Knowlton recalled. "They sat on mammoth tanks and field artillery pieces, their faces were grim, dirty and bearded, and they kept their guns leveled on us. They were a tough collection—and they did not like us."

Knowlton was engaged in a desperate game of bluff. The Germans were holding back because they still imagined that many more Americans were following behind, that a line of demarcation with the Russians would then be made and their Wehrmacht units would be on the right side of it. But as Knowlton moved into their command post—surrounded by hostile faces— and attempted to keep control of the situation, he remained completely cut off from other American units. There was still no radio contact with HQ and no US troops were following up behind. And the Germans were starting to realize this.

A panzer captain who had been fighting the Russians came up close to Knowlton. "You are not in touch with your HQ," he said. All eyes were on the American. Knowlton said: "In the silence that followed, outside sounds suddenly became louder. I heard the clashing of tank tracks, the splutter of trucks starting up, the songs of the SS carrying in the cold, bitter wind, the crack of hobnailed boots, the loud commands of German officers." Knowlton had one thought—that he had led his men into a death trap.

But he tried a last act of bravado. He looked the panzer officer straight in the eye and said loudly, so that all could hear: "Don't be stupid! Do you think I'd be dumb enough to come all the way here, take three towns and disarm thousands of your soldiers unless I had a large force following up behind." The German paused, scratched his head—and agreed with Knowlton. Instead of being shot or arrested, he was appointed garrison commander of Lübz with three surrendered German divisions under his control. The entire room clicked their heels, gave him the Hitler salute and said in unison: "*Gute nacht, Herr Kommandant.*"

Knowlton and his men were able to snatch a little sleep. But they awoke to find things even more critical. The German High Command—now based at Flensburg with the Dönitz government—had discovered that a handful of Americans seemed to be disarming most of their army, with the Russians fast approaching. Orders were sent through that all their units should now stand and fight the Red Army. The US 7th Armored Division's After Action Report put it succinctly:

"Situation critical: The German High Command have correctly guessed that there are no more American troops within 50 kilometers of Captain Knowlton's position—and General Fronhein has ordered all German troops to retrieve their weapons immediately and go forward to meet the Russian onslaught. If our American soldiers object they will also be attacked."

Lübz was about to become a battleground.

Knowlton's only hope was to reach the Russians first. He formed up a reconnaissance group and moved eastward out of the town, looking for the Red Army:

"At 9:25 a.m. I saw on the skyline—from east to west—the longest column of horses, horse-drawn wagons and marching men I had ever seen."

Knowlton had found the Soviet 191st Rifle Division. He managed to reach the commanding officer. When the Russian realized Knowlton was an American, the two shook hands and slapped each other on the back. Once more East had met West.

"Everybody grinned, saluted us and yelled unintelligible gibberish—and we grinned, saluted and yelled back."

A simple command—to make contact with the Russians—had led to an exhilarating, dangerous and utterly unreal journey. For a wonderful moment, Captain Knowlton and his men completely forgot about the war.

4

A SHADOW REALM

"We arrived at Flensburg and it was utterly peaceful," remembered adjutant Karl Böhm-Tettelbach. "The weather was nice. It was the beginning of May and the navy had posted sailors in white outside the Naval Academy at Mürwik where we were quartered. They presented arms whenever Admiral Dönitz (whom Hitler had nominated as Head of State) entered the building. All was quiet around us—it was almost unreal."

At the very end of the war, the government chosen by Hitler to replace him gathered in Germany's most northerly town, close to the Danish border in Schleswig-Holstein. It was a place largely unmarked by conflict.

At its head was Admiral Karl Dönitz. In his last days in the Führer Bunker, Hitler had chosen Dönitz to replace him. Böhm-Tettelbach said of Dönitz: "He was a total devotee of Hitler—if the Führer set out a course of action, he followed it without hesitation." Hitler had now instructed him—in his last will and testament—to be his successor.

The decision was relayed to Dönitz, who was based in northern Germany, by Martin Bormann on April 30. Bormann then delayed informing him of Hitler's suicide until the late afternoon of May 1, some twenty-four hours after the Führer had killed himself. It is unclear what his motives were for this—but possibly he wanted to enlarge his own influence within the new regime. He attempted to break out from the bunker and travel north to join Dönitz, but died in the streets of Berlin. Neither he, nor Goebbels—who chose to commit suicide early on the evening of May 1—would be joining Dönitz's new government, as Hitler had hoped. Once he learned that the Führer was dead, Admiral Dönitz broadcast news of this to the German people and announced his own assumption of power.

Dönitz's supporters believed or chose to believe this was done out of duty. U-boat captain Otto Kreschner said: "He was a total patriot—he saw himself as a servant of his people and Fatherland." War correspondent Lothar-Günther Bucheim was less impressed by the admiral's motives: "Toward the end, I could only see him as a harbinger of death—a party lackey, who could not have been more contemptible."

Admiral Karl Dönitz presided over a shadowy regime that lasted a little over three weeks—from the moment he accepted his appointment as German leader on May 1 to the arrest of his entire government at Flensburg by British troops twenty-three days later. The Dönitz administration was never formally recognized by the Allies. Its existence seems a mere footnote to history and its influence on the last days of the war negligible. And yet, the very fact it existed at all would create real problems—and sow distrust between Britain and America and the Soviet Union.

On May 3 the outside world was still absorbing the news of Hitler's death. The fact that Göring and Himmler had apparently been cast out of the party, in disgrace, in the last days of the Führer's rule, was beginning to be realized by the Allies. It seemed at first glance that Hitler's following had dissolved around him—and that Admiral Dönitz was simply a military man stepping into the breach and a job he probably did not want.

For many, Dönitz was not regarded as either a political figure or a Nazi ideologue. Rather, the Allies knew him as the head of the Third Reich's navy. America and Britain associated him with the U-boat campaign in the Atlantic; Russia with the activities of the Kriegsmarine in the Baltic, particularly in the last months of the war, when the German fortress outpost on the Courland Peninsula in Latvia was supplied and maintained by the German fleet. No one had anticipated he was about to take over the tottering

Reich. For most people, his appointment as Hitler's successor was a complete surprise.

And yet, in the last period of Hitler's rule, Admiral Dönitz had assumed a more and more important role within his leader's entourage. He was in regular contact with the Führer—inspired by his presence and slavishly loyal to his wishes. Fellow naval commander Admiral Friedrich Ruge was struck by how often Dönitz sought out his master—noting that afterward, however desperate the war situation, he was filled with new hope:

> Hitler possessed a kind of mesmerism that acted on different people in different ways. Susceptibility to this influence seemed to be dependent on a kind of resonance, an ability which some leaders possess and are able to manipulate. Its effect was particularly striking on Dönitz, to a slightly lesser extent with Kesselring. The situation might be darker than ever, and his spirits at a low ebb when he went into Hitler's headquarters, but he returned radiating an optimism not at all warranted by the general conditions. A similar case was Vice Admiral Voss, Dönitz's representative in Hitler's headquarters, who was completely under this spell as late as April 1945.

Dönitz certainly seemed to be under Hitler's spell. After a meeting with him in August 1943 he sang his praises in the most fulsome fashion:

"The immense power the Führer radiated, his unswerving confidence, his far-sighted evaluation of the situation . . . has made it very clear that in comparison to him, we are all very wretched pip-squeaks . . . Anyone who believes he could do better than the Führer is plain stupid."

This was a remarkably subservient comment for a leading military figure to make. His obedience never wavered—in fact, as Germany's situation grew ever more perilous, Dönitz's appreciation of his master waxed ever more lyrical, until it seemed to lose contact with all reality. In a radio speech of February 20, 1945, at a time when the Third Reich was suffering catastrophic losses to Allied bombing and the Red Army had invaded East Prussia, inflicting untold hardship on the civilian population there, Dönitz announced to Germany's youth:

"You have been very fortunate as to be placed by destiny in the greatest era of our people . . . You must be attached body and soul and with all the forces of your heart and character to the Führer. You must regard yourselves as his children, whom nothing on earth could make waver in their unconditional loyalty. This is the greatest and finest thing in a man's life—unconditional and loyal devotion to the great man who is his leader."

In pursuit of his overarching loyalty, Dönitz had become a steadfast advocate of all of Hitler's principles—military and political—strongly believing in the Führer's "fortress policy," of holding out to the very end, whatever the cost, in a fanatical defense of the Nazi cause. He saw a kind of glorious martyrdom in this. In March 1945 he urged Germans to follow the example of the Japanese at Iwo Jima, where American troops killed over 14,000 of the island's defenders, but captured only 180 of them. There was certain nobility, Dönitz felt, in dying on behalf of Hitler.

And the admiral warmed to this dark theme, warning in a decree of April 11 that only slavery awaited Germans found in the Soviet zone of occupation, and those "intellectual weaklings" who considered surrender would be the first to perish under such conditions. Astonishingly, in such a disastrous military situation, Dönitz stressed time and time again that Germany's only hope lay in continuing to fight.

In his public speeches, Dönitz was going far beyond his military mandate—and he was doing so quite deliberately. He once revealed: "I am a strong supporter of ideological indoctrination . . . It is nonsense to say that soldiers or officers must be non-political." Such exhortations would have met with Hitler's heartfelt approval.

Dönitz last met with Hitler on his birthday, on April 20, 1945, when the Führer granted him the honor of a personal audience. Two days later, on April 22, Dönitz left Berlin and traveled to Plön in northern Germany. The Führer had realized that the Grand Alliance—shortly to join forces on the River Elbe at Torgau—was about to carve the Third Reich in two. In a response to this threat, Hitler decided that Field Marshal Kesselring would command German troops in the south and Admiral Dönitz would lead a "northern" military region consisting of northwest Germany, Denmark and Norway. At this late stage of the war, Dönitz was rising rapidly in the Führer's favor.

In his new command, Dönitz maintained a rigid adherence to Hitler's by now utterly pointless war strategy. At a meeting with Nazi Party representatives in the area on April 25 the issue arose of ending the war to save lives. Dönitz would have none of it. He made it clear that this was a matter for Hitler alone to decide—and that no one had the right to challenge him over this. "The Führer's actions," he declared emphatically, "are solely inspired by his concern for the German people. And since capitulation must mean the destruction of the German people's ideology and faith, it is only right that we fight on."

Dönitz backed up his words with actions. On April 27 the military situation in Berlin was hopeless. He nevertheless ordered that several hundred naval cadets be flown into the city to help defend the capital—to be sacrificed on the pyre of Dönitz's devotion to the Nazi cause. The gesture impressed Hitler—although the naval cadets had no training in street fighting and suffered heavy casualties for little result.

Soviet lieutenant Vasily Ustyugov was surprised by the introduction of such troops late in the battle. He remembered encountering some of the cadets in the fighting near the Reich Chancellery: "We learned that a German marine battalion—young naval trainees—had been brought in to defend the center of Berlin," he said. "We found this inexplicable, for they were completely inexperienced soldiers—little more than kids—and most of them died very quickly."

Ustyugov remembered one instance.

I was in the city center—and it was a night-time operation. There was an arch-way to my right leading down to a basement. Some light came up from it and I went to take shelter there to look at my map. Suddenly, a couple of Germans—who must have heard me moving about—ran up the stairs and straight into me. I opened fire—a pure reflex action—and hit them both. Their naval berets flew up into the air and one fell back down the stairs—I remember he had blond hair—and the other crumpled in front of me.

Street fighting is all about instinct—and they clearly had not acquired any of it. As I stepped into the arch-way my silhouette was framed by the light, making me a clear target. Experienced soldiers would have shot first. But instead they panicked, ran out to see what was happening and collided with me.

It was all a pointless sacrifice of young lives. And yet the Führer was delighted:

"Grand Admiral Dönitz has sent navy soldiers for my personal protection," he remarked. "They are the bravest men he has. He wants to make a certain number available to me. This offer comes from Dönitz himself—he'll bring them in at any cost . . . The moment could come when extreme steadfastness is everything . . ."

Dönitz readied more naval troops—but at this stage of the battle for Berlin it was no longer possible to fly them in.

Unswerving dedication to the cause chimed well with the sentiments Hitler expressed in his will: "I request that commanders of the army, navy and air force strengthen our soldiers' will to resist and imbue them with the National Socialist spirit to the utmost," he enjoined. Dönitz was showing himself a worthy disciple. And he did not remain passive in his master's presence. He understood what Hitler wanted to hear and learned to anticipate it.

Dönitz knew that the Führer was fascinated by new technology. To sustain morale as the stream of military defeats swept ever closer to Berlin, Hitler came to believe more and more in "miracle weapons," astonishing triumphs of technology that would turn the war in his favor.

Realizing this, at the end of February 1945 Dönitz submitted to the Führer a massively over-optimistic assessment of the U-boat war. Dönitz looked to the future—and the possibilities offered by a new model of submarine that could remain completely submerged, without ever needing to resurface. The head of the navy claimed that Britain and America would have no means of detecting or combating this force, and that the imminent arrival of these "miracle weapons" completely justified hopes of a major transformation of the war "in the nick of time." Dönitz agreed that the goal in the last period of the war should be to hold out at all costs, to allow these weapons to become operational. Hitler was enthralled and encouraged by this report—which undoubtedly sustained his own fanaticism.

By such means Dönitz won his way into Hitler's closest confidence. All his political views now mirrored those of his master. He had become a member of the National Socialist Party in 1944 and was firmly committed to its principles. A number of his speeches showed a strong anti-Semitism. When the Swedes closed their waters to German shipping, Dönitz claimed their action was a result of "fear and dependence on international Jewish capital." In a speech of March 1944 he warned against "degenerate Jewish enslavement," declaring:

"What would have happened to our country today if our Führer had not united us under National Socialism? A divided government, infected with the spreading poison of Jewry and at its mercy because we lacked the shield of our present uncompromising ideology, we would have collapsed under the burden of this war long ago."

In August 1944, Dönitz proclaimed his advocacy of this "uncompromising ideology" to his commanders in blunt terms, admitting: "I would rather eat dirt than see my children grow up in the filthy, poisonous atmosphere of Jewry."

Dönitz was also strongly anti-Bolshevik, emphasizing time and time again the importance of holding on to every scrap of ground in the war against the Soviet Union. "I am an adherent of not giving up anything in the east unless we have absolutely no other choice," he declared resolutely. He had supported and encouraged Hitler in retaining a foothold in Latvia—the Courland Pocket—long after the war had reached Germany's own borders. Courland's defenders continued to be supplied by sea by the Kriegsmarine— an immense operation, personally supervised by Dönitz. As the Red Army was fighting its way into Berlin, more than 200,000 soldiers of the Wehrmacht were still holding out in this remote fastness, alongside a Latvian SS division. The point of such a stand was lost to all except its fanatical devotees.

In the last days in the bunker, Hitler became increasingly fond of Dönitz—and admiring of his loyalty. The Führer's valet, Heinz Linge, recalled his master frequently exclaiming how Dönitz was the only one who had not deceived him. Hitler's air force adjutant added that in the war's final weeks the Führer displayed great confidence in Dönitz, but not in Göring or Himmler—emphasizing that Dönitz now held a great authority, not just among military men but also within the Nazi Party itself. In Goebbels' diaries several entries praised Dönitz for his ideological attitude and determination to continue the struggle. Revealingly, when Hitler drew up his will, he instructed Bormann and Goebbels to break out of Berlin and join Dönitz's government—but he did not intend them to lead it.

There was nothing accidental about Hitler nominating Dönitz as his successor or forming an administration around him. Admiral Wilhelm Meisel—a man close to Dönitz—believed that at the end of the war the navy leader was engaged in a power struggle with Göring, provoked by Dönitz's "unbridled ambition" to become "the second man in the state" after the Führer himself.

Although Hitler wanted Dönitz to be his successor, he appointed him as Reich President rather than Führer, clearly believing his own power and authority within the Reich—even in the last days in the bunker—were unique. Nevertheless, he saw Dönitz as the custodian of his legacy. And as Reich President, Dönitz did not break with Nazi policies and he made no attempt to ban or dissolve the party. Pictures of Hitler were prominently displayed on the walls of the Naval Academy where his administration took up residence— and diehard Nazis were included in his fledgling government.

The most unsavory of these new recruits was SS leader Otto Ohlendorf. During the war in Russia Ohlendorf had commanded an extermination squad—Einsatzgruppe D—that had butchered thousands of Jews and Slavs in southern Russia and the Ukraine. Dönitz was either unconcerned or secretly approving of such fanaticism, and he appointed Ohlendorf his senior adviser on economic affairs. This appointment alone should have provoked an immediate Allied intervention, the forcible dissolution of this so-called government and the arrest of all its members. But such a response was delayed— with unfortunate consequences.

On May 3 Dönitz installed his government in the Naval Academy at Mürwik, in the suburbs of Flensburg. The red-brick complex had been built by Kaiser Wilhelm II in 1910. Its striking Gothic architecture imitated the castle of Marienburg, the headquarters of the Teutonic Knights (a medieval military order which had launched a series of bloody crusades against the Slav peoples of the East) and a site of enduring fascination to the Nazis. Known as the "red castle by the sea," the Naval Academy was certainly imposing—rising from a small hill, overlooking the Flensburg Fjord. For a few weeks it would contain a shrine that held the unsteady flame of the dying Nazi movement.

Within it was a fastidious commemoration of Hitler's memory. One of Dönitz's first actions—on May 4—was to approve the death sentence for a sailor who had made critical remarks about the Führer (on May 9, after the war had ended, the Naval High Command checked to ensure this execution had been carried out). Three more sailors, who deserted on May 5, were recaptured—and again, Dönitz decided to impose the death penalty. These men had sworn an oath of loyalty to Hitler and in Dönitz's eyes that oath still held a moral force, even after the Führer's death.

In forming his government, Dönitz gave the post of Minister of Industry and Production to Hitler's devoted follower Albert Speer. He toyed with the idea of appointing Heinrich Himmler as Minister of the Interior, keeping the post open for several days. It was only on May 6 that Dönitz decided that such an appointment was too risky—and might provoke the Allies to dissolve his government in the midst of its surrender negotiations with General Eisenhower. So Wilhelm Stuckhart, Minister of Culture, was moved into the position instead, although Himmler still retained a behind-the-scenes influence. But the most important appointment would be Count Schwerin von Krosigk as Foreign Minister.

Von Krosigk—a finance minister in Hitler's regime—was clever and duplicitous. Descended from an old German aristocratic family, he had studied law and politics at Lausanne and then as a Rhodes Scholar, at Oriel College, Oxford. He had received the Iron Cross award for bravery in the First World War and then risen high in the German Civil Service. On the evening of May 2 Dönitz and Von Krosigk traveled together to Flensburg, and the following morning Von Krosigk formally accepted the post of Foreign Minister in Dönitz's government.

Together the two men formulated a strategy, one based on their mutual loathing of Bolshevism. They would attempt to end the war by piecemeal surrenders to the Western Allies, postponing a full and unconditional surrender to all parties for as long as possible, in an attempt to buy time for

German soldiers and civilians fleeing the Red Army to reach British and American lines. A military high command was in place to support this, for Field Marshal Wilhelm Keitel (head of the German armed forces) and General Alfred Jodl (his chief of staff) had now arrived at Flensburg, and both men—close associates of Hitler—were kept in their posts.

The mettle of the fledgling regime was quickly shown by its public statements. On May 1, 1945, Dönitz broadcast the news of Hitler's death to the German people, delivering a eulogy to his departed leader:

"Our Führer Adolf Hitler has fallen," he intoned. "The German people bow their heads in deepest mourning and respect. At an early stage he had recognized the terrible menace of Bolshevism and dedicated his life to opposing it. At the end of his struggle and unerring straight path, he died a hero in the capital of the German Reich. His life was a unique service for Germany. His war against the Bolshevik flood was fought for Europe and the whole civilized world."

Dönitz then informed the German people of his own appointment as leader:

"The Führer appointed me as his successor," he continued. "Conscious of the responsibility, I accepted this position in this fateful hour. It is my first duty to save the German people from annihilation by the advancing Bolshevik enemy. We fight on simply for this reason."

Dönitz had begun his rule with a lie—insinuating that Hitler had died in combat, fighting at the head of his troops. The reality, that he had committed suicide in the bunker, was seen as shabby and uninspiring—and simply ignored. In his first statement to the world, Dönitz showed himself as slippery and untrustworthy.

The new leader followed up this announcement with an Order of the Day to the Wehrmacht. He repeated the fiction that Hitler had "died a hero's death," adding: "We have lost one of the greatest heroes in German history."

He then made it clear that as new head of state and supreme commander, his overriding objective was: "To continue the war against the Bolsheviks until our fighting troops and hundreds of thousands of families from the east of Germany have been saved from annihilation or enslavement."

Dönitz demanded unconditional obedience and loyalty from all fighting men. Thus Hitler's race ideology, and his loathing of communism and the Slavic people that underlay it, was perpetuated.

On May 2 Von Krosigk, who had now decided to accept the post of Foreign Minister within Dönitz's government, also broadcast to the German people. The nation's suffering at the hands of the Red Army was his constant theme, fashioned through clever oratory into the form of a mantra. Germany's fight, Von Krosigk emphasized, had been a noble one. He warned: "A stream of desperate, starving people is heading westward . . . fleeing from unspeakable horror, from murder and rape."

Bolshevik terror, mass starvation and famine were all invoked in an apocalyptic vision that prophesied the inexorable march of Soviet communism. Nazi Germany had tried with all its might to repel this threat. "The world can only find peace if the Bolshevik tide does not flood Europe," Von Krosigk said. "In a heroic struggle without parallel, for four years Germany fought to its last reserves of strength as Europe's bulwark, and that of the world, against the Red menace."

This was an extraordinary distortion of history. Nazi Germany had first invaded most of western Europe and imposed its rule by force. Hitler had then launched an unprovoked war upon the Soviet Union, his armies driving deep into her territory, inflicting death and destruction upon millions of her citizens. The extermination squads that followed behind his troops inflicted mass annihilation on the Jews and the civilian population of Belorussia and the Ukraine. This was one of the most brutal wars in human history. And yet the "blood guilt" that Germany had on its hands as a result of Hitler's quest for *Lebensraum*, "living space" in the east, was now portrayed as a noble mission of sacrifice on Europe's behalf.

Von Krosigk's speech was delusional—but dangerously delusional, resonating with the race propaganda the German people had been inculcated with and expressed in language that was powerful and beguiling. And Von Krosigk employed a most striking metaphor to bring his point across. "In the east," he warned, "an Iron Curtain is advancing, and behind it, hidden from the eyes of the world, the work of exterminating those who have fallen into Bolshevik hands goes on."

The phrase "iron curtain"—*ein eiserner Vorhang*—was a Nazi slogan first used by Goebbels in a leader article in *Das Reich* on February 25, 1945. Writing about the recent Allied conference at Yalta, Goebbels warned the German people:

"If the German people lay down their weapons, the Soviets, according to the agreement between Roosevelt, Churchill and Stalin, would occupy all of East and Southeast Europe along with the greater part of the Reich. An iron curtain would fall over this enormous territory controlled by the Soviet Union, behind which nations would be slaughtered."

The powerful phrase had immediate impact, and a few days later it was used by the Nazi paper, the *Völkischer Beobachter*, in its main front-page headline: "An Iron Curtain is falling over Europe."

Now Von Krosigk had popularized it further. This metaphor—striking, but deeply tainted by Nazi propaganda—should never have subsequently been used by a Western leader. Events would turn out differently.

The public speeches of Dönitz and Von Krosigk were broadcast across Germany from the radio transmitter at Flensburg—and monitored by all the members of the Grand Alliance. The warning was already clear. This was not a transitional, caretaker regime—as claimed—but a rump of partisan, anti-Russian Nazi sycophants, bent on promulgating Hitler's legacy. And yet, reactions to it within the Alliance were very different.

At the beginning of May 1945, the Americans were the least interested in the prospective Dönitz government. They believed the priority was to apprehend Göring and Himmler—whom they saw as the most dangerous members of the Nazi hierarchy at large. Initially, they did not take the Dönitz regime seriously.

The British had by now established their 21st Army Group at Lüneburg Heath, 30 miles southeast of Hamburg. The British 7th Armored Division was on the city's outskirts and Flensburg was less than a hundred miles farther north. They had the military power to remove or arrest the regime within a matter of days. But Churchill saw practical advantages in allowing some form of German government to exist, and without inquiring too deeply about that government's composition said to Foreign Office staff "Let it rip"—allow it to stay in being for a while.

Realizing this, and anxious to prove their usefulness, the Dönitz regime made an offer to surrender the city of Hamburg to the British on May 3. The reason given for this was: "in order to spare the city and its population from total destruction." It then initiated broader negotiations, headed by Admiral Georg von Friedeburg (Dönitz's replacement as head of the German navy), with the 21st Army Group. British lieutenant colonel Henry Crozier recorded: "After a fantastic day of negotiations with high-ranking German officers Hamburg formally surrendered at 1800 hours. We are going in at first light tomorrow."

While Hamburg was offered to the Western Allies, the city of Breslau—under siege by the Red Army—was ordered to keep resisting the Soviets. The total destruction of this city and its population would carry on. Surrender was the policy in the west; in the east, the war was to be continued for as long as possible.

The Soviet Union was deeply suspicious of the new regime—and for good reason. The Russians had monitored Dönitz's radio transmissions—and were struck by the vehemence of his declaration that the war against Bolshevism would continue. As their troops entered the Reich Chancellery and the Führer Bunker on May 2 they had captured Dönitz's personal representative, Admiral Hans-Erich Voss, and a portfolio of documents about the hoped-for government, including a copy of Hitler's will. As they were digesting this information, Dönitz made a personal intervention by radio, countermanding the unconditional surrender of Berlin agreed by the garrison commander General Helmuth Weidling and ordering the troops to fight on. The following day, Russian surrender offers to the garrisons at Courland and Breslau were also rejected after Dönitz instructed both strongholds to continue their fight against the Red Army. By now it was clear that this was a regime implacably opposed to the Soviet Union. Russia saw it as a deeply corrupt, if not criminal, gathering—and believing it had no authority or mandate outside the Nazi hierarchy, wanted nothing to do with it whatsoever.

The capacity of this administration to cause mischief among the Allies was beginning to emerge. But for its policies to have any real impact they needed to command support from German forces still resisting the Grand Alliance. On May 3, 1945, the situation across Europe was confused. In France, German garrisons continued to hold out at La Rochelle and Dunkirk.

The Channel Islands also remained under Nazi occupation. In central Europe, German forces had recently surrendered in northern Italy, and the Wehrmacht's Army Group G, defending southwest Germany, had also begun negotiations with the Americans. These two surrenders would bring British and American troops into Austria and marked the effective dissolution of Field Marshal Kesselring's southern military district. The only force remaining in this region was General Alexander Lohr's Army Group E. Here some 30,000 German troops and their Croatian and Slovenian allies were cut off in northern Yugoslavia and surrounded by Tito's partisans.

The German commander responsible for protecting Flensburg itself was Field Marshal Ernst Busch. Busch commanded the garrison at Hamburg and an assortment of troops defending Schleswig-Holstein. Under his overall authority were Generals Joseph Blaskowitz—holding western Holland—and Georg Lindemann, in charge of Denmark.

There were also the German forces retreating from the Russians in northern Germany, the remnants of Army Group Vistula, the 3rd Panzer Army and, farther south, the 9th and 12th Armies and the ill-fated Steiner Group. The majority of these troops were falling back through Mecklenburg—hoping to avoid capture by the Russians and to surrender to the British or Americans instead.

Four major Wehrmacht formations formally swore loyalty to the Dönitz regime on May 2. In Norway, General Fritz Böhme gave Dönitz his allegiance—along with the eleven divisions and five brigades under his command, totaling some 380,000 men. These were fresh and properly equipped troops, capable of putting up a considerable fight against the Western Allies. On the same day, Army Group Courland also offered its oath of loyalty to Dönitz. More than 200,000 German troops were still holding out in this corner of Latvia, along with a Latvian SS division of some 15,000 men. General Dietrich von Saucken's Army Group of East Prussia, the battered remnants of the German 2nd and 4th Armies, holding out along the Bay of Danzig and the Hela Peninsula—a gathering of around 100,000 Wehrmacht troops—did the same. And finally, and most importantly, Field Marshal Ferdinand Schörner's Army Group Center—stationed in eastern Czechoslovakia—also confirmed its allegiance. Schörner's army group totaled some 580,000 men.

Ferdinand Schörner was a fanatical Nazi who, like Dönitz, soared high in Hitler's favor in the last months of the war. His rise had been meteoric. In the summer of 1939 he had been a mere lieutenant colonel and regimental commander. By the end of the war he was commanding entire army groups, first as colonel general and then as field marshal. The Führer said of him in April 1945:

"On the entire front, only one man has proven himself to be a real field strategist—Schörner. Schörner had to endure the worst attacks, but he has maintained the most orderly front. When Schörner had terrible equipment he put it in order again. He has achieved excellent results from every task given to him: he can take over a chaotic situation and imbue its defenders with fresh spirit and determination."

Hitler specially honored Field Marshal Schörner in his will, sending him a copy of his last testament and appointing him commander of the German army (a post Schörner was never able to take up). In fact, Schörner's successes, such as they were, were founded on excessive brutality and fanaticism. He executed more soldiers for cowardice than any other German commander. He sacked divisional, corps and army commanders he did not consider tough enough and established squads of military police to round up stragglers behind the front. His unflattering nicknames included "Wild Ferdinand," "the Bloodhound" and "the Legend of a Thousand Gallows."

Schörner's motto was that a soldier's fear of his commander should be greater than his fear of the enemy. His fanaticism knew no bounds. While fighting in northern Norway against the Russians, he received reports that the bitter conditions there were causing a decline in morale. He responded by issuing his most famous battle order: "The Arctic does not exist!"

Yet Field Marshal Schörner was also a clever and effective propagandist. In the winter of 1944 he and Dönitz had worked together to create a "fortress mentality" in the Courland Pocket. This remote Latvian stronghold was now entirely cut off from the rest of the fighting. But Schörner issued a series of clever orders, emphasizing how Courland was a breakwater, drawing off Soviet forces that otherwise would be free to attack Germany. There was little truth in this assertion—the Courland Pocket had been securely blockaded by the Red Army and these troops would have been much better deployed in the Reich itself. But it appealed to the imagination of his soldiers.

Conditions in Courland were harsh: troops had to beat off frequent enemy attacks, the weather was miserable, trenches often filled with icy water and men in front-line positions rarely received any warm food. And yet soldiers retained their morale, hanging placards in their bunkers declaiming: "We relieve pressure on East Prussia" and "In Courland too we fight for the Reich."

Soviet leader Joseph Stalin was bewildered that the Courland Pocket was still holding out and had not been evacuated. Its resistance seemed to make no sense, and Stalin began to imagine some ulterior purpose. At the end of the Russian civil war the Western powers had briefly intervened in the Baltic states—and he wondered whether history might be going to repeat itself. German intelligence played on this fear—sending him false information that the British navy had been in contact with the Latvian SS defenders. Courland preyed on Stalin's mind in the same way that the fate of Denmark did on Churchill's.

German resistance here continued. Schörner was able to weave illusion into fanatical belief—and it was a tribute to his dark skill that the resolve of the Courland defenders did not diminish after he left the pocket. Indeed, in April 1945 soldiers' letters revealed a remarkable conviction that it was worth defending this isolated redoubt and they might yet see a turning-point in the war.

Sergeant Walter Kaese of the German 126th Infantry Division wrote: "Life is very hard at the moment, but we hope to be able to get through this and see the war turn once again in our favor . . . We must persevere—and victory will still be ours."

Lieutenant Fritz Willbrand of the 300th Infantry Division echoed these sentiments: "Whatever the conditions here, it does not matter as long as we tie down the Russians. For as long as the Red Army is here these men cannot menace our homeland. Hopefully, soon the war will reach a turning-point."

And Sergeant Joseph Meyer of the 263rd Infantry Division added: "The news we hear is anything but encouraging—but we cannot allow ourselves to become despondent, for we can never give up this fight until we have achieved victory: peace with honor and our nation secure in its existence and future."

Meyer was a soldier and an artist—and in one of his letters home he asked to be sent fresh oil paints, brushes and palette. As Berlin was stormed by the Red Army—and their soldiers joined with the Americans at Torgau, cutting Germany in two—Meyer was photographed next to one of his pictures. In it, a resolute German infantryman stood guard—with grenade at the ready. A fortress lay in the background. It was Ventspils castle, overlooking one of the Courland Pocket's main ports—where the Kriegsmarine delivered vital supplies to the army group. Ventspils was a medieval stronghold built by the Livonian Order—a branch of the Teutonic Knights—when the crusaders were on the defensive, resisting the threat of the Russian kingdom of Novgorod.

In Meyer's depiction its stark silhouette seemed to belong to an enchanted fantasy rather than recent history. Hitler believed that the finished picture in contemporary art should be heroic and never show anguish, distress or pain. It should display "the true German spirit." Here, the remnants of that Nazi mythology were fading but still alive.

But propaganda cannot exist in a vacuum. The resolve of the Courland defenders fed off the atrocity stories reaching them about Red Army soldiers' behavior toward the civilian populations of East Prussia and Upper Silesia—the looting, shooting and rapes. At the end of January 1945 a Red Army soldier wrote to his family: "I once again have sworn before my Motherland and the Party to avenge the death of my brother. Hundreds of Germans will have to atone for his life. Not one who falls into my hands will survive." Soviet lieutenant Nikolai Inozemstev, advancing into East Prussia and shocked by the cruelty of his compatriots, had confided to his diary: "Lines of carts full of refugees, the gang-rape of women, abandoned villages, these are the 'battle scenes' of our army of avengers."

General Dietrich von Saucken's Army Group of East Prussia held on to bridgeheads on the Bay of Danzig, the Hela Peninsula and the western end of the Frisches Haff. Its defenses extended along the Samland coast, along the coastal plain of the Vistula delta and miles of sand dunes. And yet it showed remarkable ingenuity in clinging to this foothold. Engineers from the Kriegsmarine, supplying the army group by sea, had brought in raw materials to this isolated German force and helped create a network of underground bunkers and tunnels around well-camouflaged concrete towers and pillboxes, linked to anti-aircraft gun positions. Wehrmacht soldiers nicknamed their position "the sandbox." The defenders were holding out against Marshal Rokossovsky's 2nd Belorussian Front and their resolve had only grown when they saw the suffering of German civilians.

Many thousands of old men, women and children had died fleeing westward along the narrow spit of land—with the Baltic on one side and a lagoon on the other—known as the Frisches Haff. Soviet pilot Yuri Khukhrikov said candidly and without a shred of remorse:

"We really worked that strip. We flew in a group of six planes over the Frisches Haff, west of Königsberg. We turned so many people into mincemeat—only God knows how many. Thousands upon thousands died. Tens of thousands of people were on that road—you just couldn't miss. Only the start and the end of it had any kind of air defense—a few German flak guns. The rest was entirely in our hands."

Panzer lieutenant Leopold Rothkirch of the German 4th Army had now joined General von Saucken's army group: "Witnessing these atrocities had a very powerful effect on us," he said. "We grew extremely angry and resolved to hold out for as long as possible, to help our people evade the Russians."

As long as the Army Group of East Prussia remained in existence, fleeing civilians could be evacuated from its territory. Von Saucken's resistance had a purpose—but this only fed the race prejudice of the new German regime. For Dönitz and Schörner were united in their devotion to Hitler's memory and by an implacable hatred of the Russians. On May 3 they ordered Breslau to maintain its resistance against the Red Army. They saw it as another redoubtable outpost, holding firm against the Bolshevik threat. And yet these civilians were not escaping from Breslau—they were dying by the thousand to maintain its defense, a struggle that after the fall of the German capital on May 2 had no strategic point whatsoever.

The city—185 miles southeast of Berlin—had been under siege for over three months. It had been designated by Hitler as a fortress—although it possessed no natural fortifications worthy of the name—and it had been transformed into a stronghold at enormous cost to the civilian population. Field Marshal Schörner, welding a defense line against the advancing Red Army, wanted Breslau to be held by a ferocious act of will. "Almost four years of an Asiatic war have transformed our front-line troops," he exclaimed. "They have become hardened and fanaticized by the struggle with the Bolsheviks."

There was little doubt that Schörner himself had become hardened and fanaticized. Most of Breslau's inhabitants were forced to evacuate their homes in the freezing cold January of 1945 and march westward. Many died en route. The city was then garrisoned with SS detachments, regular German troops, the *Volkssturm* people's militia and Hitler Youth units. A force of some 45,000, and the remaining civilian population—which amounted to another 20,000—were exhorted to make Breslau a bastion of National Socialism by the equally fanatical *Gauleiter* (local party leader) Karl Hanke.

Hanke's disciplinary measures—inspired by Schörner's policy of "strength through fear"—were terrible. He terrorized defenders and civilians alike—there were more than 11,000 executions for desertion during the siege—much to the delight of Hitler and Goebbels, who were inspired by Hanke's devotion to the Nazi Party. Even ten-year-old children were put to work under Soviet artillery attack to clear an airstrip within the city. Attempts to avoid such work were met with the death sentence.

Fighting was brutal as the Soviets flung tanks and troops into the city—and the conflict descended into savage street fighting, causing untold suffering. Now, at the beginning of May, with Berlin captured, and Hitler and Goebbels dead, its continued resistance made little sense. And yet both Dönitz and Field Marshal Schörner urged it to hold out, regardless.

Troops of the 2nd Polish Army were fighting with the Russians at Breslau. They knew that at the war's end Breslau would be granted to them, for Stalin—annexing lands in the eastern part of Poland—intended to recompense them with lands seized from Germany in the west. Lieutenant Waldemar Kotowicz wrote:

> In our imagination, Breslau was a panorama of church steeples, white buildings and pleasing squares—with the River Oder running through it. In reality, we saw a huge cloud of dust and smoke hanging over the entire city, a swirl of raging chaos that completely obscured the sun. There were no lofty Gothic towers or green parks, only a

gigantic sea of flames where houses or churches had once stood. It was a scene whose scale and impression bordered on madness.

German firefighter Walter Lassman recalled: "It was hard to believe it was not a dream . . . I was amazed, bewildered, shaken, as if I had seen a canvas of Hell. Behind me the cathedral towers were in flames, next to them, the archbishop's palace—all around me, the city burned. Five-story buildings were on fire, every window lit up . . ."

Fifteen-year-old Max Besselt, fighting with the Hitler Youth, added: "Wherever we looked there were smoking ruins and burned-out houses. It was enough to leave even the most hardened person at a loss for words."

The pulverized city was entirely surrounded by the Soviet 6th Army and its Polish allies. There was now no prospect of it being relieved—and its continued defense served no useful purpose. It was at the mercy of heavy artillery shelling and frequent aerial bombardment. One of the city's inhabitants, Thea Seifert, wrote:

About this dark time of horror it is almost impossible to speak and even writing about it is hard. One of the worst things is the terrible shelling we constantly endure. Each bombardment lasts for hours and causes a high number of casualties. One searches in vain for a lost loved one. The corpses are loaded onto lorries and then flung—without coffins—into the mass graves which have been dug close to the churches in the city center. Here lie soldiers and civilians alike. One cannot recover any of their personal belongings—in most cases no records are kept and if they are, they are soon lost again. It is possible that some of the evacuees from Breslau, who left the city when it was still beautiful, fondly remember their former homes and imagine returning to them after the war is over. But nothing is left here but ruins.

Max Besselt wrote in his diary on May 3:

No-one knows how things will turn out. There are fourteen of us left—manning two medium 8mm mortars. We used to be classmates at one of Breslau's schools—now we are a gun team. Our position lies between two partially standing houses amidst a landscape of ruins in southern Breslau. The oldest of our group has just turned sixteen. For the last five weeks none of us have had any rest. We slowly retreat, repelling a constant stream of Russian attacks. We fight in the wreckage of these burning buildings—waiting for an end to it all.

Hugo Hartnung was fighting in one of the *Volkssturm* units, formed of men too old to be conscripted, some with health problems, all with utterly inadequate military training and equipment. These men struggled to see the point of continued resistance—and yet military discipline remained severe.

"They bring a deserter in," Hartnung wrote in his diary. "He is a craftsman, father of several children, who committed the 'crime' of trying to save his family and get them out of the city, seeing that its defense is now utterly pointless. The man is of good character and bearing." The man's responses in his interrogation were matter-of-fact—there was no special pleading: he knew that his fate was sealed. The cross-examination took a turn for the worse when a young lieutenant appeared, berating the man for his cowardice. "He repeatedly insults him," Hartnung noted, "tells him that he is a disgrace to the Fatherland who does not even deserve to have one bullet wasted upon him. The craftsman is shot nonetheless. His body is flung into a trench latrine and covered in chlorinated lime. Later that evening the lieutenant reappears to check that the court martial judgment against this deserter has been duly enforced."

On May 3 Dönitz extolled Breslau's continued resistance. The nearest German troops were at Zobten, over 20 miles to the west, and these lacked the strength to break through the besieging Soviet forces. Field Marshal Schörner telephoned the garrison commander and demanded that the city be held "in Hitler's memory." He told General Hermann Niehoff: "Fight to the last round and to the last man." Karl Hanke could brook no thought of surrender either. Hitler had appointed him to oversee the "fortress," and although the Führer was now dead, he told the defenders to carry on resisting anyway. "We must do everything in our power to save as many people as possible from Bolshevism," he enjoined. A lengthy order was issued to the troops making it clear Breslau must still be defended.

Horst Gleiss wrote in his diary that day:

After a lull, the heavy aerial bombardment of our fortress city resumed today at the end of the heroic struggle for Berlin. The Soviet Air Force can now be committed in all its might against the remaining sectors of the eastern front still holding out—and complete its destructive work here. From about 9:30 a.m., numerous twin-engined bombers appeared in the sky with fighter escorts. As a result of their surprise attack, in the Benderplatz, where I am stationed, there have already been ten killed and many more wounded. Three soldiers were killed as they sat at the roadside by the air pressure from the blasts—one was decapitated. In front of them a woman lay dead. At 16 Benderplatz we found an old man dead, and another person badly injured—we carried them by stretcher to the hospital. There are many wounded among the soldiers.

In the afternoon the Ivans [the Russians] sent three negotiators to our lines, in an attempt to persuade the fortress commander to surrender. However, General Niehoff has decided to continue the struggle and rejected the Soviet offer, after a three hour ceasefire.

This was the invocation Dönitz and Schörner made in Hitler's memory. German soldier Heinz Liedtke wrote to his brother:

We sit in Breslau like rats in a trap, we are just waiting for the end. I've already lost hope I'll ever get out of this shit-hole. We fight, drink out of despair (if we manage to organize something to drink) and lead a debauched life with whores of various nationalities— there's no shortage of them here. Yesterday I received a pass for a couple of hours and went to find Aunt Trude. All that's left of her house in Königsplatz is a burned wall. No-one knows what happened to our aunt and the rest of the tenants but it seems to me we will never see her again. I'll probably meet the same fate in this damned place.

Liedtke concluded: "If you can, pray for me—the heroic defender of the infamous fortress Breslau."

Russian forces were bewildered that Breslau continued to fight. They dropped leaflets over the city, appealing to its inhabitants to surrender. They could not understand—with Berlin captured—why it was still resisting. A dark joke began to circulate among the besieging Soviet 6th Army. Victorious Red Army troops are on their way from Berlin to Moscow for the Victory Parade. Suddenly, they hear explosions and machine-gun fire. "Is that our welcoming salute?" asks one soldier. "No," his comrade replies, "it's just the 6th Army—it's still busy conquering Breslau."

Beneath the mask of Nazi ideology lay unbelievable cruelty. On the afternoon of May 3 Captain John MacAuslan, an intelligence officer with the British 5th Reconnaissance Regiment, was advancing along the Bay of Lübeck when he saw a stricken German vessel—some 2 miles out to sea— being bombed by a squadron of RAF Torpedoes. The ship was the *Cap Arcona*. As MacAuslan took in the terrible scene, an escaped slave laborer appeared, waving down the British column. "That ship is full of prisoners from a concentration camp," he told the horrified troops. "They are locked away in the hold—and there are no lifeboats."

The *Cap Arcona* was originally a large German luxury liner. In 1940 she had been taken over by the German navy and used in the Baltic Sea. Briefly— in 1942—her military service was interrupted, as she was used to portray the doomed *Titanic* in a propaganda film commissioned by Joseph Goebbels. In early 1945 she was employed by the Kriegsmarine to evacuate German soldiers and civilians from East Prussia. By April her turbines were completely worn out and could only be partially repaired. No longer seaworthy, she was decommissioned—only to be acquired by Himmler's SS at the end of the month and turned into a prison ship.

On May 3 the *Cap Arcona* was loaded with thousands of prisoners from the Neuengamme concentration camp. It was later claimed that the ship was taking these prisoners to Sweden. But SS officers from Himmler's head-quarters, which had transferred to Flensburg with its master, testified that the real purpose of the voyage was to scuttle the *Cap Arcona*, with all the prisoners still on board. There were no Red Cross markings—and all these unfortunates were locked away in the hold. The RAF pilots thought they were attacking an SS ship trying to make an escape to Scandinavia.

RAF intelligence had received reports that the Germans were assembling ships in the Bay of Lübeck to make a retreat across the Baltic to Norway: "The ships are gathering in the area around Lübeck and Kiel," it was stated. "At SHAEF it is believed that important Nazis who have escaped from Berlin to Flensburg are on board and are fleeing to Norway or neutral countries."

Among the Western Allies there remained the fear that the Flensburg government could be a front, and that the important Nazis—Himmler and Bormann (whose death in Berlin had not yet been confirmed)—might still evade their clutches.

"The Navy are unable to reach the area because of the minefields in the Kattegat," the intelligence report continued, "so an all-out air effort is being planned to block this last escape hole." The 2nd Tactical Air Force called out four of its squadrons. On May 3 Warrant Officer Derek Lovell of 197 Squadron recalled: "We were told to go up to the Baltic and attack shipping. On our way up we passed some of our planes coming back. They'd set the *Cap Arcona* on fire. It was red hot from head to stern."

The ship was already burning extensively and soon began to capsize. MacAuslan's men—realizing that thousands of prisoners were trapped inside it—tried desperately to establish radio contact with their HQ, to pass the information on. It was too late. A massive explosion ripped open the *Cap Arcona*'s hull. She turned on her port side and sank. More than 4,250 of the prisoners perished.

The slave laborer warned the 5th Reconnaissance Regiment there was something else that they had to see—a short drive away, on the beach at Neustadt. It was from this beach—earlier in the morning—that the prisoners had been put in barges and taken out to the *Cap Arcona*. But there had not been room in the ship for all of them and this news had been relayed back to the SS and German marines supervising the loading.

Captain MacAuslan's regiment pushed on into Neustadt, 23 miles north-west of Lübeck. There they found concentration camp prisoners who had not received any food for eight days. "They were totally dehydrated," MacAuslan said, "and when they walked, those that could walk, they were like mario-nettes in those dreadful costumes they had to wear, pajamas with a bluish thick stripe and white in between . . . None of the Germans would help at all. The hospital refused point blank to take in any of the prisoners until we made them do it at gun point." And then the British soldiers reached the beach.

MacAuslan related:

The beach at Neustadt was the most horrifying place I have ever seen. The Germans had barges into which they had packed prisoners. But some were not able to set sail. So the guards took away the ladders and machine-gunned everyone inside, there and then. These barges were still packed with women and children who had been shot. And on the beach itself were several hundred little children—little children with their heads caved in. They had been tied back to back with cords through their mouths and beaten to death. Their bodies lay right in front of us.

Later that afternoon the 5th Reconnaissance Regiment left Neustadt and stopped briefly at a small manor house several miles away. The German owner tried to be friendly. "Come and look at my books," he said. MacAuslan found it difficult to engage with him. "I wouldn't understand them," he replied. The German persisted: "I'll translate them for you—I've got Goethe and Dickens." MacAuslan struggled to comprehend a world where Goethe and Dickens co-existed alongside what he had just witnessed. "No," he said eventually.

Three days had passed since Hitler had committed suicide in the bunker in Berlin. Britain's Mass Observation Archive (where observers noted con-temporary reactions to events) recorded one of the comments made after his death: "I'm sorry in a way—it means that he will never be brought to trial. I would have liked to have heard his defense, because he must have had a defense, in his own mind, a certain aim, a feeling that he was right—some philosophy that made sense of it all. And now we shall never know."

On May 3 Soviet intelligence officer Elena Rzhevskaya moved into a makeshift office in Berlin's Reich Chancellery. On the desk in front of her were documents retrieved from the Führer Bunker. Much material had been destroyed, but as Rzhevskaya sifted through the fragments that remained—a pocket diary of Martin Bormann's that had been stuffed down the back of a chair, Goebbels' family manuscripts hastily crammed into a suitcase, then left forgotten and discarded—a picture began to emerge.

There was a fleeting hope of flight to the Berchtesgaden. The hope was dashed. Military reports were compiled on the state of fighting in the Reich's capital. Rzhevskaya sensed a growing isolation as communication with other parts of the front was lost. There were the Reuters news agency reports, typed up and prepared for Hitler—the last source of information for those trapped in the bunker. On one news report, on the death of Mussolini, Rzhevskaya noticed that Hitler had underscored in pencil the words "hung upside down." And then, the records showed a desperate, all-consuming search for gasoline. After his death, the Führer wanted his body burned with such intensity that no trace might be found of it.

The NKVD had identified the charred bodies of Joseph Goebbels and his wife, Magda, and General Hans Krebs. All had committed suicide on the early evening of May 1. They had interrogated surviving witnesses of the last days of the bunker. All the statements confirmed that Adolf Hitler committed suicide in the early afternoon of April 30. They had uncovered badly burned remains deep in a shell crater—the fragments contained parts of a jaw, and this was now being matched against Hitler's dental records. A positive identification seemed likely. The clearest piece of evidence left by the departed was the most chilling: the bodies of the six Goebbels children, murdered in the bunker on the orders of their mother.

Rzhevskaya turned to Magda Goebbels' papers. One item caused her wry amusement—an astrological prediction that had been drawn up for her. "In April 1945 Germany will achieve a dramatic turn-about of fortune on the Eastern front," it was forecast, "and fifteen months later will have finally conquered Russia . . . In the summer of 1946, all German U-Boats will be equipped with a terrible new weapon that will destroy the British and American navies."

There was Bormann's diary. It contained only brief jottings—on the increasing artillery fire as the Red Army drew nearer, the betrayal of the Führer by Göring and Himmler. It was all strangely insubstantial—fleeting glimpses, hard to grasp. On April 30, against the names of Hitler and Eva Braun, was the runic inscription of death.

As Soviet intelligence officers searched the Führer Bunker and the Reich Chancellery grounds, American troops were approaching Hitler's Bavarian mountain retreat, the Berchtesgaden. This was where the Führer had entertained heads of state, or relaxed with the closest members of his entourage. Its outlook was as lofty and spacious as the bunker had been cramped and claustrophobic. On May 2 Lieutenant Sherman Pratt and the 7th Regiment of the 3rd US Infantry Division had occupied Salzburg in western Austria. On the morning of the 4th they made a dash for the Berchtesgaden. Pratt felt a strange sense of apprehension. "The hills on either side of us became increasingly steep," he recalled, "and we were advancing along a narrow and restricted area." The troops were at risk of ambush—but their column proceeded safely. At 4:00 p.m. the Berchtesgaden came into view. "The houses were of Alpine architecture and design," Pratt said. "Some had gingerbread decorations. It looked like a village from a fairy tale."

It was all strangely innocuous. Some of the soldiers began exploring the town. There were German soldiers there, but they surrendered without a fight. Lieutenant Pratt took one of his platoons and advanced farther up the mountains, to the SS barracks and Hitler's house. "We were winding our way up a steep mountain road," Pratt continued. "The air was clear and crisp with almost unlimited visibility. We rounded a bend—and there before us, in a broad opening, lay the ruins of the Führer's residence." The entire complex had been heavily bombed by the RAF a week earlier. "Everyone in my group was struck into silence," Pratt said, "all too aware of the significance of time and place. After all the years of struggle and destruction, the killing, pain and suffering—here, surely, was the end of it."

5

LÜNEBURG HEATH

At the beginning of May Field Marshal Montgomery's TAC HQ had moved to its last site of the war, on windswept Lüneburg Heath in northwest Germany. There was nothing in modern warfare that quite resembled Montgomery's nomadic HQ—a Boer lager in the Zulu Wars or the wagon circles of the pioneers in the nineteenth-century American West were perhaps its closest parallels. On D-Day the whole camp consisted of 27 officers and 150 men. In May 1945 it was regimental size. But it kept advancing with the front—using jeeps, mobile caravans and even light aircraft to quickly move forward. Montgomery insisted on seeing for himself the conditions where the fighting was the most intense.

At its center was the radio caravan, an officers' mess, a map room and Montgomery's sleeping quarters, where lights went out at 9:30 p.m. sharp, whatever the military situation. The site was usually under the cover of trees and draped in a huge amount of camouflage netting. Despite its occupying a series of exposed positions, it was never once attacked during the entire war. The Lübeck campaign, where Montgomery had raced for the Baltic ports, had brought TAC HQ to its last outpost, to a bluff on the sandy, windswept heath of Lüneburg. The heather was brown, and cracked underfoot. The weather was freezing.

Montgomery had never forgotten his First World War fighting experience. During his four years of combat, he had seen his commander only on one occasion. In subsequent army training, Montgomery had developed the notion of a battlefield tactical headquarters—or TAC HQ—one completely separate from a main headquarters: a mobile communication center, often tented, from which the commander could easily visit his subordinate officers and soldiers. It was entirely typical of Montgomery's style of generalship—and was adopted by him in all his campaigns: North Africa, Italy and northwestern Europe.

Montgomery would summarize it as follows: "My system of command was from a tactical headquarters, located well forward in the battle area. TAC HQ was the headquarters from which I exercised personal command and control of the battle. It was small, highly efficient and completely mobile on its own transport. It consisted chiefly of signals, cipher, liaison staff, defense troops and a very small operations staff for keeping in touch with the battle situation."

Sergeant Norman Kirby, responsible for security and intelligence at TAC HQ, said:

> It seemed it was forever wedded to bracken and fir trees—and the idea of isolation, a strange paradox for a headquarters which, with its buzzing telephone wires, was one of the most vital nerve centers of the war, in constant touch with the British Prime Minister and other Allied war leaders. But perhaps it was its loneliness, its small size, its eccentricity—and the fact that it was the war-time home of General Montgomery—that gave its inhabitants the feeling of belonging to something unique.

Eccentric it certainly was. Albert Williams, a mechanic at TAC HQ, remembered how shortly after D-Day the mobile HQ arrived at the Norman chateau of Creully. The elderly couple who lived there were expecting to make way for the Allied commander—but they were told they could stay. Instead,

Montgomery parked his caravan in a far field. "Although popular with the troops, Montgomery was a rather quiet man," Williams recalled, "who enjoyed his own company. When we set up an HQ in each place, his caravans would be placed in a well-secured field, separate from the rest of the HQ. But he liked to have farm animals around him—I think he found their presence comforting. Petting a horse or a donkey could take his mind off the enormity of the situation he found himself in." When his stepson Dick Carver returned to TAC HQ in Italy in December 1943 he was given a tour that included Monty's collection of canaries and lovebirds; there had also been a peacock, but it had been given away to a local farmer after it had bitten two of his ADCs.

But at the heart of TAC HQ was an eerie silence. "His three caravans were usually in a separate field," Sergeant Kirby remembered, "and there was a reverential gap between the main camp and the hallowed ground of his enclosure. Even when called to report to the caravan I never lost the guilty feeling of being a trespasser. Everything about his living quarters contributed to the idea of seclusion: the tank by the entrance, the armored car, the immaculate jeep—and the three caravans themselves, veiled in camouflage netting as if entangled in some giant spider's web."

Field Marshal Montgomery was Britain's best-known Second World War military commander and immensely popular within the United Kingdom. A divisional commander during the battle for France in 1940, he took over the British 8th Army in the summer of 1942 and won a major victory against Rommel's Afrika Korps at El Alamein, a twelve-day attrition battle that began later that year, on October 23, and broke German power in North Africa.

The foundations of this memorable victory were not only tactical and logistical, but rested on Montgomery's clarity of thinking and remarkable gift for lifting morale. When Winston Churchill and General Sir Alan Brooke visited him in the desert on August 19, 1942, Brooke was moved to remark: "I knew Monty pretty well by then, but I must confess I was dumbfounded by the situation facing him, the rapidity with which he had grasped the essentials, the clarity of his plans and above all his unbounded self-confidence with which he inspired all those that he came into contact with."

Montgomery transformed the British 8th Army into a victory-winning force whose morale became legendary—there was virtually no sickness or absenteeism within its ranks: everyone wanted to fight. General Dwight Eisenhower paid his first visit to 8th Army HQ on April 1, 1943, and—much impressed by what he saw there—praised its commander: "It is obvious on all sides that a high degree of discipline, morale and battle efficiency characterizes the whole force. I congratulate you on the magnificent fighting machine that has been produced, whose excellence is proved by its long record of victories since last October."

The atmosphere of seclusion at the heart of the army headquarters captured by Sergeant Norman Kirby was a key feature of Montgomery's generalship. The British commander had a deep sense of spiritual responsibility for his soldiers, once remarking that "his chaplains were more important to him than his artillery"—and was always careful with the lives of his men. Well aware that these lives depended on the quality of his judgment, he created an atmosphere of calm and quiet in which to carry out his decisions.

This was a praiseworthy quality, although one frequently misunderstood by his American allies, and Montgomery was always a sound planner who placed great emphasis on proper training and refused to be rushed into a campaign before he was ready. He devised his war plans in seclusion but then shared them with his troops. His greatest gift was an ability to communicate the big military picture and what was required of his men with wonderful simplicity. He was a commander with a firm belief in being seen by his soldiers, who brought about a transformation of morale in every army that he led. He was also a natural showman, who understood the value of being a larger-than-life character in war. In the desert, these qualities were great strengths rather than weaknesses.

Montgomery led the invasion of Sicily and then fought in Italy before being recalled to plan the D-Day invasion. He was overall ground commander in the first six weeks of the invasion, but relinquished this post when General Eisenhower arrived in France to lead the war in person. Although this had been agreed in advance, when it actually happened Montgomery chose to take offense, clearly resenting the fact that he was commanded by a man with little battle experience. Although a measure of irritation was understandable, it was a sign of some pettiness and egocentricity that he allowed this grievance to consume him as much as it did. But Montgomery, now commander of the 21st Army Group, could still put in good battle performances, particularly during the German Ardennes offensive. He made mistakes militarily, however (the ill-fated Operation Market Garden), and also personally—the chief of these was his utter inability to get on with his American allies.

During the North African campaign Montgomery's "unbounded self-confidence" and his love of publicity and the media were considerable assets, allowing him to reach out and win the hearts and minds of his soldiers. In Europe they became a liability, one that reached its nadir with a disastrous press conference given during the Battle of the Bulge that succeeded in patronizing and offending almost every American commander present. In North Africa Montgomery primarily cared about his army; in Europe he came to be increasingly preoccupied by his own reputation and a belief that he had been denied a chance to exercise his full talents in the war's closing stages. In short, Monty had a point to prove—and at Lüneburg Heath he would play out that drama on a stage of his own choosing.

The result would be a bravura performance that delighted the assembled British officers, journalists and, most of all, Montgomery himself. The field marshal had top billing in a stand-out piece of theater that had everything— drama, pathos and knock-about comedy. The result was utterly beguiling— particularly as Montgomery not only had the surrender filmed, but in a notable first had a synchronized sound recording in place to accompany it.

Whereas Eisenhower's chief of staff, General Bedell Smith—or "Beetle" as he was nicknamed—managed the surrender at Rheims with a near-total aversion to publicity, became agitated if too many cameras were in the room and only with the greatest reluctance allowed one microphone to be present (as long as its wires were not showing), Montgomery preened himself before the assembled journalists and practiced the surrender with camera and sound crews as if he were choreographing a West End musical. And in a way, he was.

The German surrender at Lüneburg Heath was a spectacle to be enjoyed and savored, a *son et lumière* with a dash of George Formby thrown in. But as with most theater, it should not be taken at face value. In the script, Monty rode roughshod over the leering Hun; in reality, he wanted to strike a deal with the German military. In the script, Monty was always ahead of the game; in reality, he missed a trick (or two) that played into the hands of the Dönitz regime. But we should take our places. The lights are dimming, and so much entertainment at a military surrender, and an unconditional one at that, will rarely be seen again.

The curtain opens on three caravans, used by Montgomery as an office, map room and bedroom. It is the heart of a spider's web. Around it is a hub of activity. We are introduced to the unique features of Montgomery's command post. The first is a special liaison regiment, known as "Phantom." This is a secret intelligence and communication unit that gives the field marshal a constant, real-time picture of the battlefield. This is done by patrol—teams of special radio operators, drivers, dispatch riders—attached to the HQ of every division and corps that Montgomery commands. These patrols radio back to TAC HQ—a source of accurate, unembellished information about events on the ground.

Then Montgomery's liaison officers enter the stage. They are personally selected by the British commander and directed by him on a daily basis. They go out by jeep each morning with a list of tasks: people and HQs to visit, a tactical picture to construct—and return each evening to deliver a report to the field marshal in person.

On this occasion, a very special event is to occur—and Montgomery, informed of it well in advance, is making his plans. It is 11:30 a.m. on May 3, and a four-man German delegation is about to arrive at Montgomery's headquarters. It is led by Admiral Georg von Friedeburg, Dönitz's successor as head of the German navy, and also consists of General Eberhard Kinzel, chief of staff to Field Marshal Busch, Rear Admiral Gerhard Wagner and Major Jochen Friedel.

The delegation moves along the road to Montgomery's HQ sitting bolt upright in their cars, with long gray belted coats, jackboots and monocles. Friedeburg is cadaverous in his long leather greatcoat; Kinzel—a magnificent 6 foot 5 inches tall—the very epitome of Prussian arrogance. Friedel, according to Montgomery's ADC, Colonel Trumbull Warren, has "the cruelest face of any man I have ever seen." And as one war correspondent wrote, they are "accompanied by a general atmosphere of pent-up defiance." A British armored car escorts the column forward.

Let us pass the baton over to the great showman himself and allow Montgomery to describe what follows:

> They were brought to my caravan and were drawn up under the Union Jack, which was flying proudly in the breeze. I kept them waiting for a few minutes and then came out of my caravan and walked toward them. They all saluted under the flag. It was a great moment. I knew that the Germans had come to surrender and that the war was over.
>
> I then said to my interpreter: "Who are these men?" He told me.
>
> I then said, "What do they want?"
>
> Admiral von Friedeburg then read me a letter from Field Marshal Keitel offering to surrender to me the three German armies withdrawing in front of the Russians between Berlin and Rostock. I refused to consider this, saying that these armies should surrender to the Russians. Von Friedeburg said that this was unthinkable . . . I said that the Germans should have thought of all these things before they began the war—and particularly before they attacked the Russians.
>
> Von Friedeburg next said that they were anxious about the civilian population in Mecklenburg who were being overrun by the Russians. I replied that Mecklenburg was not in my area of responsibility.
>
> I then decided to spring something on them quickly. I said to von Friedeburg:
>
> Will you surrender to me all German forces on my western and northern flanks, including all forces in Holland, Schleswig-Holstein and Denmark?
>
> I added that if he could not agree to this, and if Germany refused to surrender in these areas unconditionally, I would order the fighting to continue and many more German soldiers would be killed, and civilians too from artillery fire and air attack.

I thought that an interval for lunch might be desirable, so that they could reflect on what I had said.

I sent them away to have lunch by themselves, with nobody else present except one of my officers. Von Friedeburg wept during lunch; the others did not say much.

Afterward Montgomery met the delegation again in his conference room, "with a map of the battle situation spread out on the table. I repeated my demand for unconditional surrender as a prelude to any discussion. They saw at once that I meant what I said."

"The Chief is putting on a pretty good act," Colonel Trumbull Warren whispered to Lieutenant Colonel Dawnay. "Shut up, you son of a bitch!" Dawnay replied good-humoredly. "He has been rehearsing it all his life."

Von Friedeburg then left to report to Dönitz. He was to return the following afternoon. Montgomery phoned Eisenhower at SHAEF headquarters at Rheims—and the supreme commander told the field marshal that if the German response the next day was favorable, he could accept it as a battle-field surrender on his behalf.

Montgomery phoned Rheims the following lunchtime, Friday, May 4. The surrender was on. "We've got everything in hand," he said. "The correspondents are all set." Among them was Alan Moorehead, who had already covered many of Montgomery's campaigns and now witnessed his final triumph:

Shortly after five o'clock on the 4th May, while the firing died along the front, the war correspondents gathered in a tent at Montgomery's headquarters. It was a wild hill-top on Lüneburg Heath, especially wild in those alternate gusts of cold rain and watery sunshine, and the lovely colors of the countryside spread away for miles, pools of dark green in the clumps of pine, purple in the heather.

Calmly, almost breezily, Montgomery began to tell us of the events . . . Half way through his talk Colonel Ewart came in to say that the German delegation had arrived back with their answer.

"Tell them to wait," Montgomery said, and he went on addressing us for the next half hour. He was finishing his war exactly as he had begun it—absolutely convinced that he was right and that things were going his way.

"And now," he said at last, "we will attend the last act. These German officers have arrived back. We will go and see what their answer is." He led the way to his caravan on the hill-top.

In the night, Montgomery's officers had managed to get hold of a copy of the surrender drawn up for Field Marshal Alexander in Italy. Based upon this, a similar instrument had been written up to meet the present situation. Friedeburg, cigarette in hand, slowly led his delegation across the heath to Montgomery's caravan, where he saluted, mounted the steps and went inside. There followed some discussion as to whether Dunkirk and the Channel Islands might be included in the surrender, but the subject was dropped as it might cause too much delay. The four other envoys, tight-waisted, rigid and silent, stood nervously in a semicircle at the steps of the caravan. Inside, Friedeburg had asked for a German copy of the terms, but he scarcely glanced at them.

Presently he came out, nodded to the others, said something along the lines of, "It's just as we thought," and the five men walked slowly past us to the conference tent. Its sides had been rolled up and six chairs had been placed at a trestle table covered with a plain army blanket. The Germans took their place at the table. Never have I seen Montgomery more sure of himself than at this moment. As he came past us he murmured pleasantly, "this is a great occasion," and he proceeded calmly to the tent, the terms of the surrender in his hand. He conducted proceedings rather like a schoolmaster taking an oral examination.

As he went into the tent the Germans rose and saluted. Then, sitting at the head of the table, spectacles on his nose, Montgomery read the terms slowly, precisely and deliberately in English. The Germans, who spoke hardly a syllable of English, sat there without a word, for the most part staring vacantly at the gray army blanket. Camera lights flicked on and off. The reading took a full three minutes.

At the end Montgomery picked up an unpainted post office pen, dipped it in the ink-pot and said: "You will now sign the document. First, Admiral Friedeburg . . . ," and he handed the pen across.

"Next, General Kinzel." Each man leaned over Montgomery's chair to affix his signature. "Next, Rear Admiral Wagner . . ."

And so it went on.

"Finally: 'I will now sign for General Eisenhower, the Commander-in-Chief of the Allied Forces,' and the Field Marshal added his own signature with the same pen."

Cameraman Paul Wyand and soundman Martin Grey recorded the ceremony. As the tent was only 20 feet square, Wyand had to film proceedings through a flap in the tent wall. "Lighting was my big problem," Wyand recalled. "I scrounged around for photoflood bulbs . . . borrowed an army generator and by 4:30 p.m. the tent was lit like a Hollywood film set."

Montgomery inspected the set-up and approved. He asked where he should stand and Wyand pointed out the ideal position. A flustered ADC said, "The Field Marshal cannot do that, he must meet them," but Montgomery was delighted. "Of course," he said, "they will come to me." When Wyand suggested a pause after the preliminaries, to allow him to change lenses, Monty replied: "There will be no preliminaries. If they don't sign we fight on."

An hour before the signing it began to pour with rain. Wyand started to shoot as the Germans came into the tent, met Montgomery and sat around the two tables covered with gray army blankets. "Crushed and defeated representatives of a crushed and defeated nation," Wyand wrote happily, "they took up the cheap pens and signed."

The instrument of surrender was signed with what Montgomery called "a post office pen that you could buy in a shop for two-pence." The document itself was typed on ordinary army foolscap and Montgomery defied orders to send it to Supreme Headquarters, adding it instead to his private archive; Eisenhower had to be content with a photostat copy.

Wyand continued:

Inside the tent was warmth, light and a moment of history, while outside my clothes clung to me as the rain beat down and the generator—exposed to the downpour—spluttered and spat as the sparking plugs shorted in the rain. I prayed that the generator would not fail and plunge the tent into darkness.

The signing over, the Germans stood up and filed from the tent. All save Friedeburg, who sat reading the terms over again, a picture of misery and despair. It made superb picture material. I had just finished shooting and was about to signal to Grey to pack up when one of the photoflood bulbs slipped from its socket, fell upon the Admiral's balding head, and exploded with a loud bang. The poor man jumped from his chair as though he had been shot.

The original surrender document showed that Montgomery had made a small slip, at first getting the date wrong; being forced to cross out the "fifth," the date the surrender took effect, and substitute it with that of the actual signing, the fourth.

Montgomery later recalled one other small incident at that historic ceremony. One of the Germans wanted to smoke to calm his nerves and took out a cigarette. "I looked at him," Montgomery related, "and he put the cigarette away."

After the signing, Montgomery spent the evening composing first a signal of thanks to his senior commanders and then "My last message to the armies," which ended on a characteristic note: "It has been a privilege and an honor to command this great British Empire team in Western Europe . . . Good luck to you all, wherever you may be." Finally, the field marshal drafted a piece for the following day's *Sunday Express*. With the crucial negotiations at Rheims still in progress, it was entitled simply "The German surrender."

It was Montgomery's triumph—and one that seemed to leave the hapless

Germans utterly routed. "He absolutely humiliated them," Colonel Trumbull Warren said. Captain Derek Knee, Montgomery's interpreter on the first day, remembered the look of schoolboy relish on the field marshal's face when he gave the following instructions to his staff: "The German delegation is to be lined up under the Union Jack [flying outside Monty's caravan] and kept waiting." "And when he barked out 'Who are you?' to the astonished Friedeburg," Knee continued, "I thought he was talking to a vacuum-cleaner salesman."

There was another moment to savor. Montgomery reeled off a list of demands. If they were not accepted, Montgomery said he would go on fighting. And then Captain Knee recalled, Montgomery returned to the phrase and embellished it, "and be *delighted* to go on fighting"—the relish of a master chef.

The Germans were to have lunch. But first they would be left alone, among the silver birch trees, observed from a distance. Then they would eat on their own.

Captain Knee remembered Monty's instruction: "a good lunch, with a glass of cognac." After lunch there was the map room. In the version fostered by Montgomery, and relayed to the waiting journalists the following day, the Germans were shocked to see how desperate their plight was. The intelligence summaries of the British 2nd Army reveal Friedeburg's response to be more sanguine: "I am well aware of the present battle situation," he responded tartly. In the Montgomery script a shaken Friedeburg shed a few more tears. The intelligence summary showed him impatient to get back to Flensburg. He knew a deal could be done.

That night General Eberhard Kinzel stayed on Lüneburg Heath as Montgomery's guest. The notes of Monty's chief of staff, General Freddie de Guingand, showed the conversation to be cordial and wide-ranging. They discussed the balance of power within the German military. Field Marshal Busch was the main player now, Kinzel said. The German general then gave Montgomery information on food stocks in Schleswig-Holstein. There was a little horse trading. The field marshal assured Kinzel that most of the German troops fleeing the Russians across the Mecklenburg Plain had already surrendered to British or American forces within his army group. The general suggested ways Montgomery's soldiers could speedily enter Denmark after the surrender had been signed.

The following day, General Kinzel was retained as a liaison officer at TAC HQ. He was to have a staff of twelve officers. The British supplied the rations for this group; the Germans the cooks. Kinzel was put in direct communication with Busch's Northwest Army Group. As administrative tasks were shared out with Busch's force, Kinzel asked whether German officers could remain armed "for disciplinary reasons" and German soldiers for sentry duty. "Agreed in principle," De Guingand noted.

Beneath the humor and theatrics, Field Marshal Montgomery had presided over a genuine triumph. He had retained his keen instinct for lifting the morale of his troops, making them feel part of the bigger picture—and used it to considerable effect. The massive surrender of German forces accelerated the end of the war and gave British soldiers and civilians an abiding pride in their achievement. In this, Montgomery understood both the mood of his army group and press and public at home. But—always political—he was also looking ahead, to the post of military governor of Germany. Montgomery had been told that Churchill was considering Field Marshal Alexander for the position. By proclaiming his achievement at Lüneburg and showing he could work well with the Germans, in a way in which his prime minister approved, Monty was hoping to land the job himself.

Montgomery's willingness to strike a deal with the German military commander in the region, Field Marshal Busch, held many practical advantages—but maintaining strong links with the Wehrmacht was not putting an unconditional surrender into effect. He did not take account of the politics of the Grand Alliance and the likely reaction of Russia. Nor did he consider how the Dönitz regime would portray the surrender to its soldiers still fighting in the east. He was not dishonest—but vanity blinded him to these possibilities. They would bequeath a most difficult situation to his supreme commander, General Dwight Eisenhower.

That Friday evening Kay Summersby, General Eisenhower's driver, described the atmosphere at Supreme Headquarters at Rheims:

All afternoon we waited tensely for Monty's call. Air-Chief-Marshal Tedder [the deputy supreme commander] joined the general in his tiny office; Butch [Eisenhower's naval aide, Captain Harry Butcher] joined me in my office. We waited and waited. Finally General Ike declared he was going home and could be reached there. Afraid of missing the big surrender, I succeeded in urging him to wait just another five minutes. The phone rang exactly five minutes later, at about 7:00 pm. I answered it—it was Monty. Butch and I eavesdropped shamelessly through the open door. The ceremony had gone through . . . Although dead tired, the General sat down and dictated a special message to the Prime Minister praising the courage and determination of the British people . . . Then he and Butch went off to dinner.

After dinner another message came in from Montgomery. "The Germans were flying to Rheims the following day, due in about noon, to discuss the general surrender of all German forces."

A Tory MP, Henry Channon, wrote in his diary that evening:

After dinner I went along the corridor of the Ritz, being, like everyone else, in a restless mood—all London had been on edge these last few days, waiting for the final announcement—and went to read the latest news on the tape machine. There I read that at 9:13 a communique had been issued at SHAEF that the Germans had capitulated in Holland, Western Germany and Denmark . . . We were all immensely relieved and celebrated with champagne.

Ordinary British families learned the news in a report following the nine o'clock BBC news bulletin. They were then able to hear the surrender as it had been recorded earlier that evening. It had a most powerful impact.

"I am listening now to the broadcast of Field Marshal Montgomery in Germany," wrote Maggie Blunt, a publicity officer from a metal factory in Slough. "My emotions at this moment are indescribable: enormous pride in the fact that I am British, wonder and excitement. Tomorrow morning the war in Europe will to all effect be over. It is a tremendous moment."

The following day units of the 21st Army Group began to enforce the surrender on the ground. Sometimes conditions were chaotic. According to the combat diary of the Canadian Argyll and Sutherlanders:

> Hundreds of German soldiers, some of them unarmed, were streaming along the roads, completely disorganized and without any sign of supervision. Some were going north and others south. Some were moving on foot, others on bicycles and horse carts. We now could see for ourselves that the once super-efficient German Wehrmacht was in a state of collapse. Every soldier in this procession seemed to belong to a different division and unit. Their parent formations had been cut to pieces and scattered over northern Germany. Their vehicles were either destroyed or out of fuel, their officers left for undisclosed destinations. The men are simply waiting for this nightmare to end.

The Canadian 8th Infantry Brigade tried to ascertain who the German commander of the area around Emden was. At first they were told it was Admiral Weyher, then a General Erich von Straube, who had his headquarters near Wilhelmshaven. After much confused telephoning and driving around, this officer was finally contacted and brought to the Canadian HQ in a jeep by the Infantry Brigade's commander, Brigadier Jim Roberts. In conditions of disorder, Von Straube complained vehemently that military protocol was not being followed and that he should have been met by a corps commander. "There was no time to cater to his whims," Roberts remarked, "we had to get him to headquarters immediately."

Once arrived, Von Straube said plaintively that he had only recently taken up his command. The Canadians recorded bluntly that he demonstrated a "noticeable ignorance of his force's composition, much to the embarrassment of his own staff officers, and seemed appalled by the number of detailed instructions involved in the surrender terms." The Canadians directed his attention to paragraph three of the surrender, which prescribed "strict and immediate execution of orders by the German command." They observed that such clear direction seemed to accord with the man's mind-set and that he "rallied magnificently"—after which all the documents were quickly signed.

General Erich von Straube was a career soldier, awarded the Iron Cross in the First World War, a divisional and then corps commander in the Second World War and a holder of the Knight's Cross to the Iron Cross with Oak Leaves. Von Straube seemed puzzled by Canadian informality. Before the war, Canada's army had been made up of about 5,000 regulars and about 50,000 militiamen. By the end of it the armed forces had swelled to over a million soldiers, sailors and airmen—mostly carpenters, farmers, teachers and factory workers, who had trained hard in their new profession and had fought well against the Germans in the last year of the war.

On the return journey, from the back of the jeep, Von Straube tapped Brigadier Roberts on the shoulder and asked him his pre-war profession. Before Roberts could reply, the German general added, in a hopeful tone of voice, that he expected he had been a soldier. Roberts was silent for a moment, recalling the jobs he had drifted through. "No, I wasn't a professional soldier," he said. "Very few Canadians were. In civilian life, I made ice cream."

The surrender at Lüneburg Heath meant that Denmark's war was now over. A token British and American force was flown into Copenhagen a day later, on May 5, drawn from Montgomery's army group and a SHAEF military mission, flying in on Dakota aircraft. War correspondent Alan Moorehead was among them:

While the cease-fire was still only a few hours old the aircraft took off—a dozen Dakotas, the fighter escort ranging high and wide on either side. Past Lübeck and Kiel and out over the Baltic. German ships seeing us coming ran up the white flag and turned apprehensively away. Then, one after another, the green Danish islands came into view. Every house on that liberation morning flew the national flag on a pole, the white cross on a red background, and from the air the effect was as if one were looking down on endless fields strewn with poppies.

Over the suburbs of Copenhagen there was at first not much movement in the streets . . . But then as we came lower they gathered confidence and poured out into the open. A thickening procession of cars and bicycles and pedestrians came careering down the road to the airfield. One after another the Dakotas slid into a landing between stationary German aircraft and drew up in line before the airport buildings. The airborne troops jumped down and with their guns ready advanced on the hangars. The scene did for a moment look slightly ominous, especially as none of us knew what to expect. Armed German guards were spaced along the runways. Two German officers stood stiffly in front of the central office and began to advance toward the landing aircraft. General Dewing, the leader of our mission, met them halfway. In two minutes it was clear: we would have no trouble in Denmark.

By the terms agreed at Lüneburg, the whole of Holland was also free. On Saturday, May 5, at 5:00 p.m., war correspondents were summoned to witness the surrender of the German commander in Holland, General Johannes Blaskowitz, to the Canadian lieutenant general Charles Foulkes. One of these, John Hodson, recalled:

"That afternoon we assembled in the empty bar and restaurant of a partly destroyed hotel at Wageningen where the surrender terms were to be formally ratified. The windows were out, brickwork near one window was precarious. Men were busy fixing up a BBC microphone and electric lamps for photographs. The room was dusty and dirty—and a litter of basket chairs were strewn about."

Both sides had gathered in the Hotel de Wereweld in the center of town. Trestle tables had been set up in the hotel dining room. Hodson continued:

Proceedings were brisk, but there was nothing grim, no attempt to humiliate . . . Indeed, at times the atmosphere was rather akin to a business board meeting. The terms held many interesting points. The Germans must accept further orders without argument or comment. The Dutch SS must be disarmed and the Germans be responsible for their behavior. The Germans would guard all the pumps at the dikes until Allied troops took over. Among General Foulkes' admirably blunt remarks was: "I want to make clear only one person will give orders and that is me."

Foulkes read out each condition, Blaskowitz showing his approval either by giving a nod or saying "Understood." Occasionally the wording of the text was amended or items within it changed. The agreement was signed at 4:04 p.m. and cooperation between victor and vanquished was quickly in evidence—even as Hodson left he noticed that already "the Canadian and German staff officers are getting their heads together over the practical details." Blaskowitz's chief of staff, Lieutenant General Paul Reichelt, produced a map showing the dispositions and strength of the Germans in western Holland. They numbered 120,000.

Under instructions from Montgomery's 21st Army Group, the Germans were told that they would now receive orders from either the Canadians or the German commander, Field Marshal Busch. Unconditional surrender meant that enemy troops straightaway became prisoners of war and were held in camps. That was how the Russians put the surrender into effect at Berlin. But the Lüneburg Heath agreement had created a dual chain of command.

Under the terms of the surrender agreement at Wageningen, which followed that of Lüneburg, General Blaskowitz remained "responsible for the maintenance and discipline of all German troops in western Holland." The Wehrmacht still retained a formidable presence and Dutch civilians were bewildered to see, in the first few days of liberation, "armed Canadian troops going up one side of the road and armed Germans going down the other side, neither interfering with each other."

There were a number of practical reasons for this. Locating German soldiers, guarding and escorting them and then disarming them was tedious and very unpopular work. The enormous numbers of surrendered Wehrmacht troops far exceeded Allied food and manpower resources. Keeping much of the German military structure intact kept the Wehrmacht self-sufficient and reliant on its own food stocks and meant that the Germans could support the Allies in maintaining law and order. And yet its risks were obvious.

To justify it, a rather uneasy legal formula was used. Following further instruction from Montgomery's 21st Army Group, the 1st Canadian Army announced that surrendering enemy soldiers "would not be classified as prisoners of war, but instead be given the status of capitulated troops." The position of these "capitulated troops" could then be decided through negotiation. Such negotiation could determine whether troop formations were disbanded—and in the intervening period how many of them remained armed.

Montgomery had drifted away from the unconditional surrender policy that was the bedrock of the Grand Alliance. Underlying the technical definitions was an unprecedented alteration of international law. Canadian troops did not now regard their adversaries as prisoners of war but as "Surrendered Enemy Personnel [SEP]," as the 1st Canadian Army made clear:

"In view of the very large number of German troops now surrendering, commanders are authorized to place such troops in the status of 'disarmed German forces.' These German forces will not be characterized as 'prisoners of war.' After disarmament these surrendered German units may be kept organizationally intact and to the extent deemed advisable by Allied Command required to administer and maintain themselves."

These arrangements worked well in practice. At the town of Julianadorp, the Germans marched in fully armed, wheeled into the airfield along one road and halted. Canadian soldiers merely collected and stacked German weapons. German war material was sorted, stored and guarded. Sometimes German formations moved unescorted into designated concentration areas; on other occasions they remained in their own barracks.

However, this situation created real problems internationally. The Soviet Union refused to allow surrendered Wehrmacht units to stay in being and automatically destroyed their equipment. They expected their Western allies to do the same. But the 1st Canadian Army now stated that "until further orders all German officers will be permitted to carry a personal weapon" and that German military police would also remain armed. Recognizing the sensitivity of such instructions, it was emphasized that "these weapons will NOT repeat NOT be displayed but will be carried in a pocket."

This was indeed a liberal interpretation of unconditional surrender. Article 1 of the 1929 Geneva Convention clearly conferred prisoner-of-war status on "all persons belonging to the armed forces of belligerent parties, captured by the enemy in the course of military operations." General Eisenhower was concerned enough to warn Canadian officials that "there should be no, repeat no, public declaration regarding the status of German armed forces or disarmed troops." The Russians got to hear of it anyway. The so-called "Stacking order," whereby Wehrmacht troops were kept in formation and their weapons merely stored rather than destroyed, and in some cases retained for use, would seriously damage relations between East and West in the last days of the war.

The surrender at Wageningen was complete. Throughout its proceedings Lieutenant General Reichelt (General Blaskowitz's chief of staff) had, in the words of one correspondent, "exuded a dignified gloom." But when one Canadian officer mentioned that the air force had been chasing his headquarters for a long time, the German chief of staff grinned broadly and replied: "I know—you got me out of bed twice!"

When Canadian troops finally inspected this headquarters, within the small Dutch town of Hilversum, it was indeed impressive. The command post was a 400-foot-square concrete bunker, with walls 10 feet thick. It was well camouflaged and appeared largely untouched, although the houses around it were smashed and crumbling. Inside were a dozen or so rooms, each with its own office space, a bed and some maps. They were air-conditioned, with fluorescent lighting—and adorned with masses of flowers and Dutch paintings.

With terms with the Germans agreed, on May 6 the Seaforth Highlanders (a regiment of the 1st Canadian Infantry Division) received orders to proceed forward. Although Wehrmacht troop formations were still in existence, the Canadians were now moving into western Holland as liberators. "We are now going into Amsterdam," the regimental combat journal noted, "and will be the first unit to travel into the newly liberated area." Over the next few days Canadian soldiers moved slowly toward their newly designated occupation zones, with enthusiastic Dutch crowds swamping their columns at almost every crossroads and roadside stop.

Lieutenant Colonel Harry Bell-Irving, commander of the Seaforth Highlanders, described their entry into Amsterdam: "The universal happiness amounted to an ecstasy which I have never seen or even approached in any crowd before. Before this, few of our men could have given a clear reason why they came. But here in Amsterdam, in one day, all that was changed.

Every life lost, every long day away from home, had been spent in a good and necessary endeavor."

Brigadier Geoffrey Hardy-Roberts, chief of staff to General Miles Dempsey, commander of the British 2nd Army, was in the Netherlands on May 6 with the Red Cross Commission. He wrote:

I heard the actual Dutch announcement, ending with the words "Nederland is frei!" Within ten minutes, the streets were full of people and flags with orange streamers were being hung out of all the windows. At first the crowds were quiet, but gradually they began to cheer and sing and as their numbers increased the excitement grew . . .

They sang for hours on end, the Dutch and British national anthems, Tipperary, marching songs, folk songs, everything that came into their heads. Meanwhile, along the main road to the north, a stream of heavy lorries was lumbering past, carrying food and other supplies, and it was thrilling to think that they would be arriving next morning in towns which it had been impossible to reach until the last few days.

There is absolutely no rowdy behavior or disorder. They are just irrepressibly happy and it is a joy to see.

Flares, like fairy lights, shimmer between the trees. Seeing liberation at first hand like this, one realizes something of what it means. It is the end of a nightmare. The future of Holland is full of problems . . . but nothing of this matters at the moment in comparison to the fact that they are free, their country is their own again—and the fear that has hung over them for five years is gone at last.

The German surrender at Lüneburg Heath, following swiftly after that in Italy, prompted a happy telegram from Winston Churchill to his foreign secretary, Anthony Eden, in San Francisco: "More than a quarter of a million Germans have surrendered to our British commanders on three successive days . . . quite a satisfactory incident in our military history."

On May 4 the world press announced: "Field Marshal Montgomery has won his greatest triumph. He reported to General Eisenhower last night that all the German forces in northwest Germany, Holland and Denmark have surrendered to the 21st Army Group." The surrender was to take effect at 8:00 a.m. the following morning. SHAEF had clarified that this was a battlefield surrender, involving the forces facing Montgomery's army group on its northern and western flanks. It was far more than that. German-occupied Holland and Denmark had also surrendered. More than a million men had been taken into custody.

The press delineated Montgomery's achievements. The Germans had failed in their plan to split the Allies by offering to the British the surrender of their troops facing the Russians. "This offer was resolutely refused by Field Marshal Montgomery." Because more than a million men were involved, it was the biggest surrender of the war. And that war was virtually at an end. It was added: "The present surrender means the war in Europe is almost over. There are now only two German-held pockets of any size—Western Czechoslovakia and Norway. The others are Dresden and Breslau inside Germany, four ports on the French coast, the Channel Islands, Latvia and a small group in East Prussia."

The sequence of events had occurred with breathless rapidity.

Montgomery was now looking to provide administrative stability. His ADC, Charles Sweeney, wrote of the chaotic conditions they were facing, and particularly those in the liberated concentration camps:

Everybody is sick of this bloody war. Europe is in a ghastly mess. There are millions of homeless, sick and wounded people, soldiers of all nationalities, lone women and children wandering the roads. Many of them are starving. I never expected victory to be glorious— except in the light of history—but the human misery in Europe is something ghastly. The concentration camps we liberate are much too awful to be described. The people in them are no longer human beings: they are animals devoid of any self-respect—cowed, tortured and starved. I never believed it possible to reduce humans to such a state. It is quite beyond the power of any reasonable thinking person to imagine these conditions . . .

In the process, Montgomery had usurped arrangements that Eisenhower wanted to oversee himself. On the evening of May 2, with a German surrender in the offing, General Freddie de Guingand, Montgomery's chief of staff, communicated with his counterpart at SHAEF, General Walter Bedell Smith. De Guingand described the situation as follows: "It is reported that General-Admiral Friedeburg, said to be representing Keitel, is expected at TAC Army Group HQ on May 3. It is not known on what basis he is going to negotiate." The following preliminary arrangement was made:

If negotiations brought up the issue of an overall surrender of German forces, or indeed of a surrender concerning anything outside the "tactical area" of 21st Army Group, SHAEF would issue instructions accordingly, and the German negotiators would meet with Eisenhower's representatives. Substantial territorial surrenders—and Denmark was specifically mentioned—were clearly defined as outside Montgomery's remit. Eisenhower had already decided that if it became a "major matter" he wanted it dealt with by SHAEF, and he would "bring the Russians into it"—in other words, he wanted the surrender of Denmark to be witnessed by the Russian representative, just as the surrender of northern Italy and parts of Austria had been earlier that day.

General Eisenhower, trusting the Russians, wanted them to be represented over Denmark. But here the attitude of the British prime minister became important. Winston Churchill remained suspicious about Soviet intentions—and feared they still might attempt to seize the country. Montgomery's drive to the Baltic on May 2 and his occupation of Lübeck and Wismar prevented a land advance by the Red Army. But Churchill began to imagine other scenarios—a seaborne invasion or even an airdrop of Russian paratroopers.

On May 3 Guy Liddell, the director of counterespionage at MI5, had briefed Churchill. "We talked quite a lot about the Russians," he noted in his diary. Churchill was already alarmed. "He thinks they are going to present us with tremendous problems," Liddell added, "and he is anxious to get ahead."

Liddell now saw an opportune moment to press his own concerns—believing that Russia wanted to build up a big navy, and control the narrows in the Mediterranean and the Baltic. Liddell then honed in on the Baltic, referring to intercepted German intelligence—albeit more than four years old—in which Nazi foreign minister Ribbentrop recalled Molotov stating (on his last visit to Berlin) that the control of Kattegat and Skagerrak was a crucial aim of Soviet foreign policy.

Churchill responded in kind. He told Guy Liddell that he had forgotten this—and found it extremely interesting, as he had been issuing strong warnings of his own about the urgency of getting to Lübeck and controlling the Kiel Canal. Liddell concluded: "Churchill had done this on the basis of reports that the Germans were desperately anxious for us to seal off Denmark, as they were expecting the Russians to drop parachutists in the area."

With this in mind, Churchill pressed Eisenhower for Denmark to be included in the tactical surrender at Lüneburg Heath. "Call from PM," Kay Summersby noted. "He is much disturbed over the fact that the Russians are landing in Denmark. There is supposed to be a large communist group in the country." The Russians were not landing in Denmark, but Eisenhower eventually agreed. Montgomery was then able to secure Denmark for his PM, ahead of any advancing Russians. The price to be paid for this was the exclusion of the Soviet Union from the surrender ceremony.

Relations between Britain and the Soviet Union had suddenly and dramatically taken a turn for the worse. On May 4 Churchill found out that the sixteen Poles he and America regarded as legitimate representatives of a more inclusive Polish government had in fact been arrested by Russia and branded as saboteurs. Two aspects of this deeply concerned Churchill: the charge of sabotage itself, which he believed was a pretext by Stalin to muzzle political opposition, and the delay in revealing what had happened (the Poles had disappeared in mid-March), which made the whole thing look even more suspicious.

Robert Boothby, in San Francisco as a journalist covering the conference, recalled the moment the Western Allies learned the news: "One evening [May 4], Molotov blandly told Stettinius and Eden in the corridor of our hotel that sixteen members of the Polish government in Warsaw, who had gone to Moscow at the request of the American and British governments, were all in prison. I was immediately behind them—and they were visibly shaken."

Michael Foot was another journalist in San Francisco. According to his report, the first inkling of the arrest of the Poles came "almost casually," in a throwaway remark by Molotov at the end of an otherwise cordial dinner. "He could hardly have caused a greater sensation," Foot continued, "if he had upset the whole table and thrown the soup into Mr. Stettinius's smiling face."

Michael Foot was sympathetic to the Soviet Union. But he was under no illusions about the effect this news would have on right-wing opinion in Britain and America: "The tragedy and the enigma," he commented, "is that the Soviet Union, which certainly appeared eager to play its full part in the world organization, has handed a weapon more powerful than any they themselves could fashion to the American enemies of international collaboration." Even from a left-wing perspective, Foot could find no justification for the way Russia had treated the Polish emissaries.

But Russia strongly countered such criticism. The following day Churchill received a fierce telegram from Stalin. The Soviet leader made it clear that if the British and Americans refused to accept the legitimacy of the Lublin government no further negotiation on Poland would be possible. The sixteen Poles were, in Stalin's view, linked to efforts by the Polish Resistance Army to begin a campaign of sabotage against Russian military installations. Their arrest was entirely justified. The Western Allies and the Soviet Union were now drifting far apart.

With such alarming international developments, an equitable enforcement of the surrender at Lüneburg was all-important. But something rather different was taking place. The English text of the surrender agreement signed at Montgomery's tactical headquarters contained a crucial clause. This clearly stated: "All German armed forces in Holland, northern Germany, Schleswig-Holstein and in Denmark to surrender unconditionally to the Commander-in-Chief 21st Army Group." But after talks between the British and German sides, a German text of the surrender was produced by the Dönitz government.

The Dönitz version—which was then widely circulated by the Flensburg regime—differed in a number of respects from the English one, which was supposedly the official text. Instead of an unconditional surrender, the German announcement spoke only of an "agreed truce between the British and German High Commands." The phrase in the English version referring to "the surrender to include all naval ships in the named areas" was revised in the German text to imply that only operations directed against Britain were meant; not those against the Soviet Union. And finally, according to the German version, the instrument of surrender did not apply to the area between the Bay of Kiel and the German-Danish border, where the Flensburg government of Dönitz was based.

In a supporting ordinance announcing the decision, on May 5, Field Marshal Keitel said bluntly: "When we lay down our weapons in Northwest Germany, Denmark and Holland, we do so because the struggle against the Western Powers has become pointless. In the East however, the struggle continues in order that we save as many Germans as possible from Sovietization and slavery."

Gottlob Bidermann, a German soldier in Courland, remembered that the agreement with Montgomery was portrayed as a truce with the West to allow soldiers and civilians to escape the Russians. In its aftermath, evacuation from the pocket was speeded up.

This worrying state of affairs played to a deep Russian fear that Britain, America and Germany might still negotiate a partial surrender, ending hostilities in the west but allowing fighting to continue in the east. On the evening of May 5, the Red Army had captured the town of Zobten, 30 miles southwest of Breslau. Field Marshal Schörner now organized a counterattack and regained it. It was the last German offensive in the war. The action had no real strategic significance—Army Group Center was retreating westward. But it made a powerful symbolic statement: the war in the east would go on. For how long remained to be seen.

SS lieutenant Heini Knauer described the action:

On the night of May 5, hellish fire from our artillery and flak rained down on the completely surprised Soviets. They had no longer expected this kind of firepower from us. Then at around 6:00 a.m. the artillery fell silent and the attack of our infantry on Zobten began. It came from three sides, from the assembly areas to the south, southeast and southwest of the town. The approach road looked ghastly. The Soviets suffered high casualties. Toward 11:00 a.m. came the report: Zobten in our hands!

Soviet lieutenant Evgenny Moniushko was inside the town: "We had passed through most of Zobten but when we reached its southern outskirts we were stopped by the heavy fire of the 'Fritzes' who had entrenched themselves in the last houses. Then, while we were trying to drive them out, other 'Fritzes' appeared, attacking on our flanks and entering the town from the east and west. Before my very eyes a heavy machine gun crew, trying to capture a German position, was destroyed by a direct hit. We received the order to pull out of the town."

Lüneburg Heath put Field Marshal Montgomery's prestige above the security of the Grand Alliance. General de Guingand's notes show that Monty was fascinated by the prisoner tally. The higher it rose, the more he would eclipse others: Field Marshal Alexander in Italy; his own chief, Eisenhower, at Rheims. To enlarge his haul, German armies that should have surrendered to the Red Army—including General Hasso von Manteuffel's 3rd Panzer Army and General Kurt von Tippelskirch's 21st Army—were brought into the fold. German senior commanders, army staff, officers and men mostly surrendered to the British 21st Army Group—despite the field marshal's protestations to the contrary at Lüneburg. Montgomery was prepared to accept German forces that had been fighting against the Russians. And whatever had actually been agreed between the two sides, an unconditional surrender that was then described as a truce would inevitably create problems.

After the cessation of hostilities on the evening of May 4 British troops were supposed to hold their positions. But on the morning of May 5 their special forces took possession of the German city of Kiel, 60 miles north of the halt line. The British gained possession of the dockyards and vital Walterwerke factory (with its technology for submarine propulsion systems)—relations with Russia deteriorated further.

At the beginning of May Major Tony Hibbert had been put in command of a T-Force (Target Force) instructed to seize the dockyards and factories of Kiel ahead of the Russians. T-Forces had been created by the Allied Supreme Command in the aftermath of the Normandy landings, to "identify, secure, guard and exploit valuable and special information including documents, equipment and persons of interest." T-Force units were lightly armed and highly mobile. Major Hibbert had recruited some two hundred men from 5 Kings Regiment and 30 Assault Unit, who would accompany a further fifty scientists in jeeps and armored cars. It is unclear whether the halt order after the Lüneburg surrender was disregarded or countermanded, but at 7:00 a.m. on May 5 the convoy headed off toward Kiel at speed.

The T-Force's own log book recorded:

The drive from Bad Segeberg onward was most eerie. We had left all signs of battle behind—there were no direction markers at the side of the roads, no traffic or sign of any traffic, no slit trenches and perhaps worst of all no white flags. One or two German soldiers, complete with kit, were struggling down the road, otherwise there were hardly any people about. Each wood that we passed might have contained the odd German platoon or company that had not yet received the ceasefire order. Our commander's jeep driver saw several Germans dart into the woods as we went through—this may have accounted for the erratic speed of our convoy.

The German armed guards at the barracks we passed seemed as unconcerned as we pretended to be. The roads were thronged by displaced persons who had just been freed from their camps. They waved and cheered and at times almost blocked the road in their excitement at seeing British troops.

At 10:00 a.m. the T-Force reached Kiel. It was now 60 miles into enemy territory and out of all radio contact with its own forces. The log book continued: "It was a very queer experience to stand in the center of Kiel on a wet Saturday morning and direct our mere handful of troops to their various targets. The civilians stared very hard at us—but we stared even harder when we saw that German soldiers, sailors, policemen and firemen were still armed."

One of those civilians was Margaret Engel. She recalled the moment the British entered Kiel:

"The downtown streets were deserted when a few vehicles approached over the Holsten Bridge and into the central square. They stopped directly in front of the Old Town Hall. I was struck by one thing. The British paused in their vehicle, relaxed a bit—as if they were sight-seeing—enjoyed a cigarette, then jumped from their car, ran up the town hall steps and demanded the surrender of the city!"

The T-Force log book then briefly stated: "Major Hibbert went to the Naval Academy and took charge there."

When Major Tony Hibbert's jeep pulled up at the Kiel Naval Academy his uniform was disheveled and his leg encased in a heavily stained plaster (the consequence of a car accident after the Rhine crossing). He had only his driver for back-up:

A very smart naval officer stood on the steps, looking at me with considerable disdain. I noticed he was pointing a gun at me. I was unarmed.

Because he was a naval captain and I was only an army major, I saluted him and said "Guten Morgen." I gestured toward his gun and told him in German that he should not shoot me. I then said in English:

"Sir, I have come to help you end this bloody war and if you would assist me up these damn steps and take me to your office we can get to work."

The German roared with laughter. He helped Hibbert up the steps and apologized that his office was on the first floor, so they would use a ground-floor one instead. He then phoned Flensburg and asked to be put through to Admiral Dönitz. Dönitz was taken aback that the British had suddenly appeared in Kiel, but seized the opportunity nonetheless. He confirmed the agreement at Lüneburg and now instructed that Kiel—its factories, docks, ships and U-boats—be entirely surrendered to Hibbert's tiny force. It was a wonderful swashbuckling adventure and it had won Kiel for the British, but further embroiled them with the Dönitz government.

None of this was known to the British press and people. They were simply delighted by Montgomery's triumph. It was a superbly orchestrated public relations exercise that seemed to bring the war tantalizingly close to an end.

But it was a triumph marred by personal tragedy. On May 5 Montgomery's ADC, Charles Sweeney, of whom he was enormously fond, was killed in a car crash escorting members of the German surrender delegation. Sweeney had been with Montgomery throughout the war. When the field marshal was visited by Winston Churchill and General Sir Alan Brooke for the Rhine crossing in March 1945 Sweeney remembered the last occasion they had all dined together, at a dinner party in Brighton in June 1940, only a few weeks after Dunkirk:

"The outlook was terribly black," Sweeney recalled. "We were almost afraid to look over the sea in case we should find the German invasion fleet darkening the horizon. I remember the Prime Minister saying, in a rasping voice bitter with hatred: 'They must never, never be allowed to put one foot upon British soil.' But we only had one fully equipped division and practically nothing else to offer them a fight. Now, five years later, we are crossing the Rhine."

Sweeney remembered a church service attended by Montgomery, Churchill and Brooke. "Winston made an extremely good address afterward," he said, "on the dark days when England stood alone against the Nazis. He believed that ever since those days, there was something more than simply our war efforts guiding us—it was the rightness of our cause. Churchill remarked that if anyone had asked him whether we could win in 1940, he would have had to admit he hadn't the faintest idea, but something would turn up! And something had turned up—Germany had invaded Russia."

On May 5, Sweeney left behind a half-finished letter to his wife—one that was full of hope:

> For the first time I can say where I am—Lüneburg Heath. It will be an historic spot in years to come, but as far as I am concerned it is just a damn cold windy place at the moment.
>
> Yesterday the surrender was signed at HQ. It is all too wonderful for words. The German Army is completely defeated. The last

few days have been terrific—German soldiers everywhere, pouring in countless thousands down the roads. We have contacted the Russians—6th Airborne did it first, and luckily for me I was liaising with them, so I arrived at the point of contact with the leading brigade. It was a thrilling moment. Yesterday I became involved in a party with 6 Airborne HQ and some Russian generals. A lot of whisky flowed very quickly . . .

It is a tonic to see the whole German Army completely finished: guns, transport, airfields, planes, ships—everything is in our hands. The Germans are terrified of the Russians and are surrendering to us to get away from them. I have been favorably impressed by what I have seen of the Red Army.

His widow was told: "Charles's grave is on Lüneburg Heath, very close to the spot where the armistice was signed and peace came to stricken Europe."

6

PRAGUE

By May 5 the remnants of the Third Reich had reached a crossroads. The Dönitz regime had surrendered territory to Field Marshal Montgomery at Lüneburg Heath, in the hope of being able to negotiate in the west and fight or retreat in the east. The city of Prague was vital to this policy. Held by a Wehrmacht garrison, its possession allowed Field Marshal Schörner to extricate his Army Group Center from the Red Army and move west to surrender to the Americans.

Prague was the last major European capital to be liberated, and the city lay between advancing American and Russian forces. On May 4 General George Patton's Third Army had been ordered into Czechoslovakia, although with strict instructions to go no farther east than Pilsen. The Soviet 4th Ukrainian Front was already fighting in southeastern Czechoslovakia near Olomouc. It was at present holding a static position, tying down the defenders in front of it—though it had the strength to increase this pressure and push farther west. Marshal Ivan Konev's 1st Ukrainian Front was planning to advance into the country from the north, liberate Prague and then pursue the retreating German Army Group Center. The 2nd Ukrainian Front would do the same from the south, trapping the Wehrmacht between these two Red Army pincers. It would be the last major Soviet effort of the war.

Czechoslovakia had suffered the longest period of German occupation in Europe and had paid a heavy price for it. The Nazis had dismembered the country, seizing the German-speaking Sudetenland, setting up an independent, pro-Fascist republic in Slovakia and renaming the remnant the Protectorate of Bohemia and Moravia. The Germans had butchered the Czech lands—and, after the assassination of Hitler's henchman Reinhard Heydrich (an SS general and the region's brutal Protector) by two Czech resistance fighters in Prague, butchered thousands of Czech people in reprisal.

The assassination had been prepared by the British Special Operations Executive with the approval of the Czech government-in-exile and further support from the fledgling underground resistance movement in Prague. On the morning of May 27, 1942, the chosen group readied themselves on Heydrich's route from his home to the city's castle, where he worked. Some acted as lookouts while the two assassins—Josef Gabcik and Jan Kubis—placed themselves on a sharp bend which would force his car to slow. It was a sign of the Protector's absolute self-confidence that he traveled to work in an open-topped Mercedes. At the crucial moment Gabcik's Sten gun jammed and instead Kubis threw a grenade into the car. Heydrich was only wounded in the attack but he died of those injuries just over a week later, on June 4.

The Nazis' revenge was terrible. More than 5,000 people were executed and two Czech villages burned to the ground. The two assassins—Gabcik and Kubis—and the remainder of their seven-man group were betrayed by an informer within the underground movement. On June 18 their hiding place, the Church of St. Cyril and St. Methodosius in Prague, was surrounded by the SS. Three of the men died in the main body of the church—the last four made a valiant stand in the crypt, holding off hundreds of SS soldiers for more than fourteen hours. With their ammunition about to run out, they killed themselves.

The assassination was a watershed moment. The British and French governments renounced the Munich treaty of September 1938 that had annexed the Sudetenland to Germany and promised to restore the region to Czechoslovakia at the end of the war. The SS—who regarded Heydrich as a martyr to their cause—accorded their fallen general a torchlit funeral procession in Berlin and never forgave Prague. And the Czechs—despite the savage reprisals—were shaken out of the paralysis of defeat and humiliation. Heydrich had remarked of them: "One must break them or humble them constantly." The killing of Heydrich roused this oppressed people into standing up to the Nazis and showed them that they were not a nation of slaves. The courage of the assassins, as they fought and died in the Church of St. Cyril and St. Methodosius in June 1942, became the courage of an entire city in May 1945.

The pride of a people determined to cast off German oppression and the ruthlessness of the SS, determined to eradicate the merest show of resistance, meant that Czechoslovakia could easily become a last bastion of Nazi resistance. A comment made by one British citizen in the aftermath of Hitler's death cast this warning clearly: "I fear the Nazis will continue to fight in Czechoslovakia and make a last stand there—to create the legend that they never gave up. If that is the case, I suspect that it will be down to the Russians to ensure that an unconditional surrender is imposed on these remaining forces."

There was a huge emotional desire among the Czechs to throw off the German yoke—in the capital and also the rest of the country—rather than wait to be liberated. There was some preparation by the Czech underground movement, but the popular uprising that began early in May 1945—in the capital and also in other towns and villages in the country—was largely spontaneous.

Shortly after midday on May 5 there was a scuffle for control of the Radio Building in the center of Prague and at 12:33 an appeal for help was dramatically made: "Calling all Czechs! Come to our aid immediately! Calling all Czechs!"

Aware that American troops were now in the country and could pick up Radio Prague on their transmitters, an appeal was also broadcast in English—made by Private William Greig, an escaped Scottish POW from a camp on the Czech border, who had made his way to Prague in early May and now wanted to help.

"Prague is in great danger," Greig warned. "We are urgently calling on our allies to assist us. Send immediately tanks and aircraft. Help us defend the city."

William Greig was one of the unsung heroes of the uprising. Later that afternoon, he and his friend Sergeant Tommy Vokes (another escaped POW) found themselves trapped in an old school building with a small group of resistance fighters. Ammunition was running out—and more than a hundred SS troops were outside. Greig and Vokes resorted to bluster. They dressed in their British uniforms, demanded to speak to the SS commander and told him that they were the vanguard of a British paratrooper unit and three Allied divisions would be arriving the next day. The SS officer was so bewildered that he agreed to a ceasefire. After this astonishing act of bravura Greig returned to the Radio Building and made more English broadcasts on behalf of the rebels. He was later awarded the Czech Military Cross for his efforts.

By the evening of May 5 nearly 30,000 citizens of Prague had joined the uprising and more than a thousand barricades had been thrown up. Prague was indeed in deadly danger. The British had intercepted a message from Field Marshal Schörner, ordering that the German troops in the vicinity suppress the rebellion with "exceptional brutality."

The Americans were in the best position to take Prague quickly, if they wanted to. US lieutenant George Pickett of the 64th Armored Battalion of the Third Army wrote: "Prague was the Paris of Czechoslovakia. All roads—political, cultural and historical—led to that city. Capturing it would have been a major success for our side."

The Third Army's commander, General George Patton, wrote in his diary on May 5: "General Bradley is going to let me know whether the stop line through Pilsen is mandatory. In view of the radio report about the Patriots having taken Prague, it seems desirable to me to push on and help them. Apparently, the Third Army is doing the last offensive of this war."

Eisenhower was being cautious. On May 4 he had communicated to General Alexei Antonov, chief of staff of the Red Army, that after the US Third Army occupied Pilsen it might be allowed to move to the western suburbs of Prague. Antonov rejected the plan, urging Eisenhower "not to move American forces in Czechoslovakia east of the originally intended line," to avoid, in his words, "a possible confusion of forces." After consideration,

Eisenhower agreed to Antonov's proposition. Patton was not to move east of Pilsen and Prague was not to be touched.

The capture of Prague had become a political issue. At the end of April 1945 Winston Churchill had raised the possibility of United States troops taking the city. There was no agreement with the Soviet Union that disallowed such a course of action and the British prime minister cabled President Truman directly:

"There can be little doubt that the liberation of Prague and as much as possible of the territory of western Czechoslovakia by your forces might make the whole difference to the post-war situation in this country," Churchill began, fully realizing that the Czech government-in-exile was pro-Soviet. "On the other hand," he continued, "if the western allies play no significant part in the liberation of the Czech lands that country will go the way of Yugoslavia."

Tito's communist partisans would form the new government in that country. Churchill was mindful of Yugoslav claims on Trieste and the uneasy standoff there between the forces of Field Marshal Alexander and Tito. He finished: "Of course, such a move by Eisenhower must not interfere with his main operations against the Germans, but I think the highly important political considerations mentioned above should be brought to his attention."

Churchill was right to raise this issue and here President Truman's lack of political experience told. Truman deferred to General George Marshall, General Marshall referred to General Eisenhower, and on May 1 Eisenhower stated:

The Soviet general staff now contemplates operations into the Vltava valley. My intention, as soon as current operations permit, is to proceed and destroy any remaining organized German forces.

If a move into Czechoslovakia is then desirable, and if conditions here allow it, our logical initial move would be on Pilsen and Karlsbad. I shall not attempt any action which I deem to be militarily unwise.

General Eisenhower was almost certainly being too careful. But after Eisenhower's brief report Truman had simply added the sentence: "This meets with my approval." As Churchill observed with wry humor: "This seemed to be decisive."

Churchill summarized the impact of this: "Eisenhower's plan was to halt his advance generally on the west bank of the Elbe and along the 1937 boundary of Czechoslovakia. If the situation warranted he would then cross it to the general line of Karlsbad-Pilsen-Budejovice. The Russians agreed to this."

Initially, neither Eisenhower nor Marshall had shown much enthusiasm for an attack on Prague. Both men, mindful that the war in the Pacific still needed to be won, wanted to minimize American casualties. And rather than secure a "political" objective—which was how Prague was seen—the Supreme Allied Commander wanted to destroy the remaining major concentrations of German troops and prevent the Nazis making a last stand. But here the chimera of the National Redoubt was still raising its head. The Americans still feared that the Nazis would make a last stand in a specially prepared chain of fortresses deep in the heart of the Alps.

In reality, the greatest concentration of SS and Wehrmacht troops was not in some Alpine fastness but in eastern Czechoslovakia. The capture of Prague would cut any escape route of these forces. And if Eisenhower had used a major river—the Elbe—as a clear demarcation line between US and Soviet troops in Germany, the Vltava, which ran through the Czech capital, offered him the same opportunity farther south—one that sadly would be missed.

A few days later, General Eisenhower became more positive. The National Redoubt was now revealed as largely a figment of the imagination and German resistance was collapsing. On the evening of May 4 Eisenhower authorized that an invasion of western Czechoslovakia take place the following day. He also proposed to the Soviet General Staff that the US Third Army, which would be conducting the operation, might continue to the line of the River Vltava. This expansion of the original remit would almost certainly deliver the Czech capital to the Americans.

But Eisenhower had been too tentative. The Soviets responded firmly the next day. They asked the Supreme Allied Commander to keep to the previously agreed halt line, the one that would not take American troops farther east than Pilsen. General Antonov cited the British incursion into the Soviet line of advance at Wismar—and said it was important to avoid battle confusion and possible friendly-fire incidents. Beneath this practical concern lay all the suspicions aroused by the German announcement of a truce at Lüneburg Heath that would enable the war to go on in the east. The Soviet Union now wanted to see whether the Western Allies would keep their word. Eisenhower, sensing more was at stake than a simple demarcation line, acceded to their request.

The future of Czechoslovakia had not really been discussed at the Yalta conference in February 1945—and no zones of influence, political or military, had been apportioned there. But Stalin had understood all along the importance of taking Prague. He saw it as the culmination of the Red Army's offensive in eastern Europe. He knew that such a campaign would gain him political capital and expand his influence, and would make it more likely that a pro-Soviet government would come to power in the country after the war. He was determined that the Red Army destroy the last major force opposing it on the Eastern Front, the German Army Group Center. And he was willing to pay the price in the blood of his soldiers to achieve these aims. This clarity—and ruthlessness—was lacking in the strategy of the Western Allies.

On May 5 General Omar Bradley, commander of the US 12th Army Group, had met Marshal Ivan Konev of the 1st Ukrainian Front at the latter's headquarters, some 30 miles northeast of Torgau. The meeting was amicable. General Bradley, anticipating the exchange of gifts, had brought with him a new jeep, just unloaded from Antwerp, with a painted greeting to Konev from the soldiers of his army group. "A holster was affixed to the side with a brightly polished new carbine inside," Bradley remembered, "and the tool compartment was stuffed with cigarettes."

Marshal Konev reciprocated. "I had prepared a personal present for Bradley," the Soviet commander said. "It was a horse which had followed me everywhere since the summer of 1943, when I assumed command of the Steppe Front. It was a handsome, well-trained Don stallion—and I presented it to Bradley with all its harness. It seemed that the American general was sincerely pleased with the gift."

There followed a lavish banquet with speeches and toasts. After the meal, in another room, the Song and Dance Company of the 1st Ukrainian Front sang the two national anthems followed by a performance of Russian folk dances and American music. Bradley honored Konev with an American decoration and received a Red Banner in return. Yet tension lay beneath the surface.

General Bradley also presented Konev with a map showing the disposition of every US division in Europe. The Soviet commander did not reciprocate. Instead, he pointed to Czechoslovakia and asked how far the US forces intended to go. Bradley told him they would stop at Pilsen. There was an awkward pause. Then the American general added that they would be willing to help the Red Army liberate Prague. Konev smiled. "No," he said, "that will not be necessary."

On hearing of the Prague uprising, Marshal Konev had moved forward his Czech offensive by a day, but realistically, Red Army troops would not reach the city until the early morning of May 9. In the meantime, the city would have to fend for itself.

The last Soviet offensive was a major operation involving armies stretching from Potsdam to the Danube. Although it involved three Ukrainian fronts (the 1st, 2nd and 4th) Stalin had given overall command of the offensive to Marshal Konev. If Zhukov had gained the honors for taking Berlin, the Soviet leader reasoned, Konev should receive the laurels for Prague. Konev had set out a directive for the attack on May 4. It involved three thrusts, and these would be staggered.

Konev would launch the offensive himself on May 6 from the area around the German town of Riesa, midway between Leipzig and Dresden. The first objective was to capture Dresden and gain access to the motor highway to Prague; the second was to take control of the Ore mountain passes, the main physical obstacle to reaching the Czech capital; the third would be a nonstop tank and motorized vehicle dash to Prague itself. The distance from Riesa to Prague was 134 miles. Konev reckoned that if all went well this last push could be made on the night of May 8.

In support of Konev's main offensive, two subsidiary attacks would be made on May 7. Marshal Fedor Tolbukhin's 4th Ukrainian Front would advance on German positions at Olomouc, some 174 miles east of Prague.

Marshal Rodion Malinovsky's 2nd Ukrainian Front would push forward from Brno, some 130 miles southeast of the Czech capital.

As these preparations unfolded, all were aware of an echo from the past. In August 1944 Red Army troops had suddenly experienced logistical difficulties as they approached the Polish capital. The supply problems may have been real, but it suited Stalin's political purposes to wait outside Warsaw while the Germans brutally crushed the popular uprising there, a revolt which had been organized by forces unsympathetic to the Soviet Union and its puppet Lublin regime. Once the Germans re-established control, the logistical issues were quickly resolved.

But Prague was no Warsaw. The uprising broke out independently of the Soviet-directed partisans, who had been active in harassing the Germans in the Bohemian countryside. But the Czech National Committee was pro-Soviet, and its vice-chairman, the communist Josef Smrkovsky, soon emerged as a key figure within it. And Stalin knew that if he hesitated the Americans might well take the city instead. Marshal Konev's orders to his troops made it clear that speed was of the essence: army formations needed to maintain a rate of advance of 20–30 miles a day, and tiredness and combat fatigue must be overcome. As Konev emphasized, in an address to Soviet officers after the war: "The success of the Prague operation consisted to a large degree in our ability to carry out actions calculated to prevent our [Western] allies from getting into the Czech capital. And the situation happened to be such that they could have made it. The drive to Prague was dictated by political and strategic objectives, to strengthen our ties with the Czech people and to create a more favorable position for us in post-war Europe."

The overall objective of this offensive, and these coordinated actions, was not, however, to take Prague but to ensure that Soviet armies reached western Czechoslovakia in force and prevented the German Army Group Center from surrendering to the Americans. The Czech capital was a means to that end—and as the 1st Ukrainian Front was strongest in tank and motorized formations, it was taking the main role in the attack. But once the uprising took place, the rebels would have to hold out for five days against the Wehrmacht and SS before the Red Army could reach them.

The main hope for the rebels was the Americans. Once they had invaded western Czechoslovakia, they were much closer to the Czech capital and German resistance to their forces was much weaker. General George Patton did want to take Prague—and he could have done so very rapidly. Patton was a swashbuckling, larger-than-life commander who reveled in fast-moving warfare. He and his Third Army had caught the public imagination by their dramatic breakout from Normandy in the summer of 1944. A natural showman, Patton cultivated a flashy, distinctive image—wearing an ivory-holstered, silver-plated revolver as if he was a gunslinger. General Patton was a maverick who possessed great military skill but was also reckless and impulsive.

One lieutenant in the Third Army stressed the positives, saying of his commander: "He never squandered the lives of his troops needlessly. Patton's sense of what was possible on the battlefield was unequaled . . . In the Third Army we knew what General Patton expected us to do, and we believed that if we did it we would win. That's what generalship is about."

Others, while admiring his courage, felt that Patton loved war a little too much. They nicknamed him "Old Blood and Guts," and said of him: "It's our blood and his guts!"

By the end of the war General Eisenhower had known George Patton as a friend and fellow soldier for twenty-six years. He had rescued his career after an incident at a hospital in Sicily in 1943 when Patton slapped two American soldiers suffering from combat shock. When news of this got out, it sent a wave of outrage across America—and many thought that Patton should never hold military office again. Eisenhower stuck by his friend and brought him back to army command. In return, Patton had repaid his supreme commander with victories on the battlefield. General Eisenhower wrote of him: "Patton was one of those men born to be a soldier, an ideal combat leader whose gallantry and dramatic personality inspired all he commanded to great deeds of valor. His presence gave me the certainty that the boldest plan would be even more daringly executed. It is no exaggeration to say that Patton's name struck terror at the hearts of the enemy."

This was a generous appreciation. The Germans certainly feared Patton, but within the US Army he remained a controversial figure. In Sicily in 1943 General Patton had deliberately disregarded the orders of his superiors.

General Bradley said of the slapping incident that if he had been in overall charge at the time he would have dismissed Patton and never had anything more to do with him. Patton's language to his troops was laden with expletives—and while his toughness and directness were often an advantage, he was also tactless and insensitive. In an address shortly before D-Day he created a furore by saying that Britain and America would dominate the post-war world, not Russia. Patton seemed to revel in such heedlessness.

Patton's charisma could certainly lift his men—and drive them forward. During the bitter German Ardennes offensive the American commander at Bastogne, Brigadier General Anthony McAuliffe, was summoned by the Germans to surrender. McAuliffe was heavily outnumbered, and yet it was vital that he hold on. His defiant response to the Wehrmacht was expressed in one word: "Nuts!" Patton—determined to relieve him—told his soldiers: "Any man as eloquent as that deserves to be rescued!"

And yet, his army group commander, General Omar Bradley, always quiet and methodical, and an excellent strategic planner, did not trust Patton's bravura style of generalship. He sensed the personal ambition—the thirst for glory—which drove it: "Canny a showman though George was, he failed to grasp the full psychology of the combat soldier," Bradley observed. "For a man who lives each day with death tugging him at the elbow inhabits a world of dread and fear. He becomes reproachful of those who flaunt the pageantry of command."

General Patton was a complex man. He was an inspirer and motivator of the ordinary American GI, but among the upper echelons of the US high command he was seen as a loose cannon and never promoted to higher office than army command. And while Eisenhower admired and liked Patton, although at times he was infuriated by his behavior, it was Bradley's opinion which he respected and listened to.

By May 1945 George Patton had grown increasingly mercurial and erratic. He had also become alarmingly anti-communist, referring to the Red Army as "Mongols" and making dark threats about the need to confront this new danger to America. He also professed sympathy for those "White Russians" who had been fighting with the Germans against the Bolshevik regime.

From a tactical point of view, George Patton was the ideal man to take Prague. From a political standpoint, he was an accident waiting to happen.

The extremity of General Patton's views was shown in an extraordinary discussion between him and Under Secretary for War Robert Patterson that took place in eastern Austria, close to the border with Czechoslovakia, on May 7. Patton began by raising concern over a perceived Soviet failure to respect demarcation lines and then moved on to American post-war plans for partial demobilization of the European Army: "Let us keep our boots polished, bayonets sharpened and present a picture of force and strength to the Red Army," Patton had told a surprised Patterson. "This is the only language they understand and respect."

Robert Patterson replied: "Oh George, you have been so close to this thing, for so long, you have lost sight of the big picture."

Patton would have none of it. "I understand the situation," he retorted. "Their [the Soviet] supply system is inadequate to maintain them in a serious action such as I could put to them. They have chicken in the coop and cattle on the hoof—that's their supply system. They could probably maintain themselves in the type of fighting I could give them for five days. After that it would make no difference how many million men they have, and if you wanted Moscow I could give it to you."

This was a quite staggering peroration—as if Patton were proposing to better Napoleon in 1812 and Hitler in 1941 and carve a unique niche for himself in the annals of military history. The Führer and many of his German generals had made similar bombastic claims at the onset of Operation Barbarossa. They had believed that the technical proficiency of their army would win them Moscow in months. They had never reached the Russian capital.

Patton continued: "They lived on the land coming down. There is insufficient left for them to maintain themselves going back. Let's not give them time to build up their supplies. If we do, then we have a victory over the Germans and have disarmed them, but have failed in the liberation of Europe: we will have lost the war!"

This was messianic rhetoric—and troublingly, it echoed the comments made by German generals and many of their officers and soldiers, for its logical corollary was that the Western Allies should unite with the Wehrmacht in common cause against the enemy from the east.

General Patton was tactically astute, with a superb instinct for war, and a courageous and brave leader. He was also an unpredictable general—and at times an utterly irresponsible one. He was at the head of an army whose morale was sky high. In the last months of the war its battle honors included four assault crossings of the Rhine, the capture of twenty-two major cities, the liberation of Ohrdruf and Buchenwald concentration camps, the seizure of a Nazi gold bullion hideaway at Merkers and taking some 280,600 Germans as prisoner. They had also managed to find and save the famed Lipizzaner stallions of the Viennese Riding School. Colonel Charles Reed of the 42nd Reconnaissance Squadron, who pulled off this exploit at the end of April, said: "We were so tired of death and destruction—we wanted to do something beautiful."

At 7:30 p.m. on the evening of May 4 Patton was given his last major assignment of the war, to invade western Czechoslovakia. Bradley had reinforced his Third Army, bringing it up to a total strength of nearly half a million men. "This gives us the biggest army we have ever had, 18 divisions in all," Patton wrote in his diary. His chief of staff, Major General Hobart Gay, concurred, recording: "This is probably one of the most powerful armies ever assembled in the history of war." And the green light was on for the attack on Czechoslovakia. Patton now made an observation both typical and frightening in its martial zeal. "Things like this are what is going to make the peace so terrible," he concluded. "Nothing exciting will ever happen."

General Patton had anticipated that such an opportunity might come his way. Earlier on May 4, before the order had been given, he had readied his armored units for the attack. Brigadier General John Pierce's 16th Armored Division was told to hand over its occupation zone around Nuremberg to units from the 4th Infantry Division and deploy at Waidhaus. Patton intended to use the 16th Armored to spearhead a drive on Pilsen. He put other units on combat alert. Characteristically, when the command finally came through, he was able to respond almost immediately.

The same day General Bradley had transferred Major General Clarence Huebner's V Corps from the US First Army to Patton's Third. Huebner had sat down with his staff officers for dinner that evening. He looked around the room and said: "Well, I'll give us just about twelve hours before General Patton calls up and tells us to attack something." Minutes later the telephone shrilled. When Huebner returned he added: "Well, I missed that one. Instead of twelve hours it was twelve minutes. We attack Czechoslovakia at daybreak."

General Eisenhower was counting on Patton's natural aggression to win him western Czechoslovakia quickly while trusting that Bradley would keep any further ambitions in check. On May 5 Patton's troops crossed the border. They were greeted coldly by the Sudeten Germans, but when they moved into the lands populated by the Czechs they were welcomed ecstatically. "We were totally unprepared for the scenes of celebration which greeted us in the first Czech town we liberated," Captain Charles MacDonald of the 23rd Infantry Regiment wrote. Captain Burton Smead of the 12th Field Artillery Battalion commented: "If you stop your vehicle, it is only with great difficulty that you can get moving again. People swarm all over it: laughing, shaking hands—and pressing food, wine, flowers and flags upon you."

By the late morning news of Patton's advance had reached Pilsen, and also Prague. In both cities the approach of the Americans—combined with the news of the major German surrender at Lüneburg Heath the previous evening—encouraged the local population to rise up and demand that the Wehrmacht immediately leave. By the evening the Third Army had taken up positions for an assault on Pilsen. And General Patton now knew there was an uprising in the Czech capital.

General Bradley, concerned about Patton's intentions, rang him that evening and reminded him to stop at the Karlsbad-Pilsen-Budejovice halt line. At the same time General Patton's chief of staff, Hobart Gay, told General Irwin of the US XII Corps that his mission was now to prepare to attack the Czech capital. He instructed Irwin to ready the 4th Armored and 5th and 90th Infantry for the assault. "We destroy the remaining enemy formations opposing us," Gay said, "and move on Prague." Patton and his soldiers were still looking to do something beautiful.

The US Third Army's advance units were now only some 40 miles southwest of Prague—and Patton wanted to move to help her. The Prague rising had been inspired by the arrival of the Americans in Czechoslovakia and US forces did not want to see the insurgents being abandoned to their fate.

The soldiers' paper, *The Armored Tribune*, brought out from recently liberated Strazny on May 5, caught the excitement. Leading with the exploits of the 4th and 16th Armored Divisions and the capture of Borova-Lada, Kvilda and Strazny itself—and featuring the surrender to the US Third Army of German Field Marshal Paul von Kleist, his anxious wife and twenty-five pieces of hand luggage—the paper closed with the exhortation: "Prague is within driving distance!"

Patton pleaded with Bradley for permission to advance beyond the Pilsen halt line. "For God's sake, Brad," he said, "those patriots in the city need our help. We have no time to lose." Patton even suggested a ruse that would get Bradley off the hook—he would remain incommunicado and report back to Bradley only when the Third Army was actually in Prague. But Bradley was not going to risk this without authorization from Eisenhower—and Eisenhower would not budge.

On May 6 Patton wrote in his diary: "General Bradley called up to state that the halt line through Pilsen was mandatory and that we should not do reconnaissance to a greater depth than 5 miles northeast of it due to the fact that General Eisenhower does not want, at this late date, to have any international complications. It seems to me that as great a nation as America is, it should let other people worry about complications." It was entirely typical of Patton to act first and think later—regardless of the consequences—and this made his generalship compelling but also dangerous. He concluded: "Personally, I would like to go to the line of the Moldau River and tell the Russians that is where I intend to stop."

After this frank declaration of intent, Patton voiced further dissatisfaction about kowtowing to the Soviets: "General Bradley also directed that we shall discontinue our advance east along the Danube to make contact with the Russians and let them make contact with us. We will remain in a position that is about 25 miles east of the agreed Russian-American line. Again I doubt the wisdom of this."

Finally, he recorded a pleasing military success: "As of 11:00 a.m. today, a combat command of the 16th Armored Division is reported to be in Pilsen."

At 4:30 a.m. that morning US advance forces were pushing forward toward this Czech city. Troop B, 23rd Cavalry Squadron, of the 16th Armored led the way. They found German troops surrendering in droves. The Wehrmacht defense of western Czechoslovakia lay in the hands of General Hans von Obstfelder's 7th Army. Badly mauled in the Normandy campaign, and again in the Ardennes offensive, this battered Wehrmacht formation consisted of two Panzer divisions (the 2nd and 11th), an engineer brigade and an officer cadet detachment. Desperately short of supplies and fuel and unable to mount a coherent defense along the Czech border, it could only hold roadblocks and set up strongholds against the advancing Americans.

On the morning of May 6 the German 7th Army's principal fighting unit, the 11th Panzer Division, surrendered to the US 26th Infantry Division after two days of secret negotiations. This tore open a hole in the already fragile German defense line, leaving the road to Pilsen wide open. The city was held by Lieutenant General Georg von Majewski and some 10,000 troops. On hearing of the 11th Panzer Division's surrender, Majewski made it clear that he also was willing to capitulate to American troops. His main preoccupation—like that of the vast majority of his compatriots—was to avoid being captured by the Russians. German resistance was collapsing like a house of cards.

At 7:00 a.m. Colonel Charles Noble's Troop B, 23rd Cavalry, was on the outskirts of Pilsen. The US commander had originally been ordered to seize and hold the high ground west of the city. But sensing the enemy no longer had the will to fight, he resolved to drive straight into the center of Pilsen. Noble had only 2,500 men—a quarter of the force that the Germans had—but his gamble proved absolutely correct. By 8:00 a.m. the first American troops had reached Pilsen's Republic Square, to be greeted by thousands of cheering Czechs, showering their liberators with flowers and gifts and offering them jugs of their famous Pilsner beer. US captain Howard Painter recalled: "No-one could ever forget the happiness shown by the population of Pilsen after being liberated from the Germans." The Wehrmacht's resistance was desultory.

The troops following Colonel Noble quickly secured Pilsen's airport and by 10:30 a.m. the last pockets of German resistance had been snuffed out. All eyes were now on Prague. Hearing the first radio appeal for assistance, Patton had boldly sent a US detachment under Captain Eugene Fodor to make contact with the rebels. Fodor managed to drive into the city unscathed, hold talks with the military and civil councils directing the uprising and then drive out again. On the morning of May 6 Fodor reported back to Patton. The German garrison would continue to fight against the Czech insurgents—but it would be willing to surrender to the Americans. It seemed a golden opportunity was opening up to capture Prague with little loss of life.

Even after his first request to move on Prague was refused, Patton began to push men forward, gambling that Generals Eisenhower and Bradley might still give him permission to take the city. On the afternoon of May 6, he disregarded orders to only conduct reconnaissance 5 miles from his front-line positions and told advance units of the 4th and 16th Armored Divisions to head straight for the Czech capital. General Patton wrote: "Reconnaissance elements of the US Third Army were now in the vicinity of Prague and by that act marked the furthest progress to the east of any western army." He was proud to claim this plaudit for his beloved Third Army. Typically for Patton, it was also an act that disregarded the clear orders of his Supreme Allied Commander.

Prague was almost within the Americans' grasp. Lieutenant Edward Krusheski of the 69th Armored Battalion recalled that his company was ordered to seize one of the bridges over the Vltava river for the use of follow-up troops in reaching Prague. "We got to within ten miles of the city," he said. One last armored push by Patton's men would link up with the Czech rebels and ensure the liberation of Prague.

Within Prague itself, the popular uprising had tapped into a powerful patriotism. Antonin Sticha was twenty-one years old at the time of the Prague uprising. In his teens, he had been sent to work as a slave laborer in a German factory, near the Buchenwald concentration camp. Conditions there were terrible, with regular executions, and the experience left him with an abiding hatred of the Germans and of the Nazi occupation of his country.

In the autumn of 1944 Sticha managed to escape from the factory and made his way back to Prague, where he was hidden by members of the Czech resistance. Sticha remembered that on the afternoon of May 4, 1945, unrest was already growing on the streets of the Czech capital. German posters and flags were being pulled down. And he was present at an incident in the late afternoon when inhabitants of Prague surrounded a Nazi prison train and attempted to release some of the people being held there. A German soldier attempted to fire on the crowd but was in turn gunned down by a Czech policeman. The crowd dispersed, fearing German reprisals.

By the evening of May 4 the mood in Prague was very volatile. Tram operators refused to accept Reichsmarks or to announce stops in German. The first Czech and Allied flags began to appear in apartment windows. Lone German soldiers were surrounded in the streets by Prague's citizens and disarmed. In the Vrsovice area of the city a crowd gathered, tore up a Nazi flag and began singing the Czech national anthem.

At 6:00 a.m. on May 5 Radio Prague came on the air and for the first time in the Nazi occupation began broadcasting in Czech. More Czech flags began to appear on buildings and German signs were pulled down. Shortly before midday a large crowd gathered on Wenceslas Square in the center of Prague. National flags started to be unfurled and scuffles broke out with German soldiers. The Underground Czech Military Council, which had been making preparations for an uprising for days, now decided to act. At midday a group of rebels drove a convoy of lorries toward the Radio Building and the Old Town Hall, opening fire on German soldiers in their path.

Sticha heard shooting on the streets of the capital. Realizing the uprising was about to begin, he went to the house of a friend whose father was a leading member of the Czech underground movement. German soldiers were attempting to force their way into the Radio Building—the staff barricaded themselves in. At 12:33 p.m. Sticha heard Radio Prague broadcast a dramatic appeal for help: "Calling all Czechs! Calling all Czechs! Come quickly to our aid. We appeal to all members of the police, army and government to join the patriots who are defending our radio station. Outside the building shots are already being fired. Prague must remain free!"

It was the signal for rebellion. Sticha heard that at the onset of the uprising a meeting of rebel leaders had been summoned—and he resolved to join it immediately. Small military units were being set up and barricades erected all over the city.

The insurgents quickly seized a number of key buildings in the center of

Prague: the Old Town Hall, the Radio Building, House No. 550 on the Old Town Hall Square (which became the headquarters of the military council directing the uprising) and the Credit Union Building on nearby St. Bartholomew Street, where the Czech National Committee (the new civil administration) met. At 2:00 p.m. this body announced that the Nazi Protectorate of Bohemia and Moravia had been overthrown—and that they were now the legitimate government. The Czech national flag was raised above the Old Town Hall.

The key military figure behind the uprising was fifty-five-year-old Czech general Karel Kutlvašr. A regimental commander in the Czech Legion in the First World War, he had received the award of the Holy Cross of St. George for conspicuous courage during the Battle of Zborova (July 2, 1917) after storming two Austrian machine-gun posts. In 1928 he became the youngest-ever general in the new Czechoslovakian state. During the German occupation he had been a leading figure in the Czech resistance. He was a brave and skillful soldier, and above all a patriot.

On May 5, 1945, Kutlvašr initiated a struggle for freedom on the Old Town Square. A little over twenty-five years earlier, on February 2, 1920, he had spoken on the same theme, with his soldiers lined up in the square, to the new Czech government of president Tomáš Masaryk and foreign minister Edvard Beneš. His words perhaps illuminate the spirit of the uprising:

> Thank you for the ceremonial welcome you have accorded to our soldiers of the Czechoslovak Legion. We have come to believe during all our years of fighting that a truly free nation can only be created if its citizens are honest, hardworking—and above all selfless.
>
> To all those who love our country, our precious new nation state, I make this appeal. Join with us in the fight to preserve its freedom, so that it will no longer be a sentiment fleetingly grasped by novelists and poets, but a living tribute to the heroes who fell in this struggle. It is they who have made this day a reality.

In the early afternoon of May 5 the Protectorate guard and remaining Czech police joined the uprising and the rebels then took the telephone exchange, the railway station and the main post office. At 3:00 p.m. the first German probing attempts to recapture these strongholds were beaten back. The main problem for the insurgents was weaponry. Rifles were in short supply and at the beginning of the rebellion the few available were given to former soldiers or members of the Czech police. The rebels had no tanks or artillery. And there were well-equipped SS units around the city.

By 4:00 p.m. fighting had spread all over Prague. General Kutlvašr directed the insurgents through the police communications system. A murderous battle took place for control of the Radio Building. The Germans sent reinforcements in, advancing along the rooftops. They broke into the upper stories and Kutlvašr sent a police battalion in to flush them out. The fighting took place in darkened corridors and stairwells and ended only when the remaining Germans were forced into the basement and explosives thrown in after them.

The insurgents had comradeship, patriotism and incredible bravery to unite them, but on May 5 many of them were unarmed. Antonin Sticha was sent out on a reconnaissance mission late that afternoon with other insurgents to a factory where it was known German soldiers had been garrisoned. There was hope that they could be overpowered through strength of numbers and their weaponry confiscated. But the Wehrmacht troops had pulled back to a stronger position. Sticha returned to the barricades.

"There was a surge of support for the uprising," Jan Svacina said. "But there were so few weapons. I was with a couple of friends and we wanted to join up. We moved from one rebel unit to another trying to find rifles. The main activity that evening was barricade building—everyone was pitching in to help."

By the evening of May 5, the several hundred Czech defenders of the Old Town Hall, the center of the uprising, were able to muster only twenty rifles, forty pistols and two light machine guns.

General Carl von Pückler-Burghaus was the commander of the Waffen SS in Bohemia and Moravia. He delivered his first action report that evening: "We have sustained a number of casualties—the insurgents are fighting unexpectedly well and with spirit." Pückler-Burghaus was determined to crush the uprising and began to assemble SS units to the north and south of the city. The afternoon had seen the first SS atrocity, when civilian hostages were shot on Prague's Mendel Bridge. Over the next few days a series of massacres took place by the main railway station, the castle and in the suburb of Pankrac. Czechs were dragged from air-raid shelters, slaughtered and their bodies mutilated. The victims included women and children.

That evening Pückler-Burghaus sent out for reinforcements. Part of the SS Division Das Reich was summoned from northern Bohemia. A battle group of sixty tanks and armored vehicles was brought in from Milovice (20 miles east of Prague). And the SS Division Wallenstein was mobilized at Benesov, 22 miles southeast of the Czech capital. During the first half of the night all was relatively quiet. At then, at 3:00 a.m. on May 6, Sticha and his fellow fighters heard the guttural sound of revving engines carrying in the night air from the south of the city. It was a column of tanks. The first armored SS units were moving toward Prague. General Pückler-Burghaus set out the following order: "Our attack begins at dawn. Swastikas are to be displayed on houses as visual markings for the Luftwaffe. We will use incendiary bombs. This nest of vipers will be exterminated."

At 8:50 a.m. on May 6 the Czech Military Council sent out urgent orders that more barricades be built, blocking off all access to the center of Prague. Support for the uprising was growing, and fresh combat groups were ordered to go underground and defend the system of sewers and tunnels that ran into Old Town Hall Square from German incursions. Ammunition was arriving—and boxes of Panzerfausts were distributed among the insurgents. But SS units were now converging on the city.

A makeshift hospital was set up in the basement of the Old Town Hall. It contained a small surgery and sixteen mattresses—and within a few hours more than 120 seriously wounded Czech fighters had been brought there. For later that morning SS forces had gathered in sufficient strength to start a major offensive against the rebels.

Shooting began again at about 10:30 a.m. The Czechs had no anti-tank weapons and despite determined resistance were steadily forced back. "We swore that we would hold on and keep Prague free," said Sticha. "There was an incredible resolve among our forces." But that afternoon groups of German tanks smashed through many of the outer barricades. By the early evening the rebels had been pushed on to a series of makeshift defenses in Prague's city center. Flames were rising from buildings and streets they had vacated.

"It was no longer possible to hold our positions," said Harak Bohumil. "The barricade we held at noon had to be abandoned hours later after three German tanks got behind it. That evening we were on our last defense line."

And that same evening, it was becoming clear that there would be no help from the Americans. General Omar Bradley sensed that Patton might be ignoring the new stop line. He rang him and did not mince his words, finishing with: "You hear me, George, goddammit, *halt!*" Patton was firmly told to withdraw his forward reconnaissance units and stay where he was. "We will probably never get the chance to do something like this again," he told his staff ruefully. His troops felt the same sense of disappointment. "After two hours holding the bridge over the Vltava, southwest of Prague, we expected at any moment to push on into the city," said Lieutenant Edward Krusheski of the 69th Armored Infantry Battalion. "And then, in the early evening, we were ordered back to Pilsen. It was an incredible let-down."

However, General Eisenhower's caution—misjudged earlier on—was now well founded. Early on May 5 the Reich Protector of Bohemia and Moravia, Karl Frank, had flown back into Prague after consultation with Admiral Dönitz at Flensburg. Dönitz and Frank had seen an opportunity to create further tension within the Grand Alliance. That morning Frank had radioed Dönitz—and the content of his message, decrypted by the ULTRA system, was then passed on to the Allied Supreme Commander: "I suggest to you that Czech Bohemia is the place where we can engineer a disagreement between the western allies and the Soviet Union even more serious than that of Poland."

At the end of April Karl Frank had threatened to drown any uprising in "a sea of blood." Frank, who succeeded to power in the aftermath of the assassination of Reinhard Heydrich, had shown the cruelty and ruthlessness necessary to carry out brutal intimidation of the Czech people, wiping the village of Lidice off the face of the earth (killing many of its inhabitants, transporting the rest to Ravensbrück concentration camp and burning the place to the ground) for its supposed connection with the assassins. But now Frank could see which way the wind was blowing. On the morning of May 5 he gained Dönitz's approval for a bold and surprising political maneuver. Frank proposed to dissolve the Protectorate of Bohemia and Moravia, hand power over to the collaborationist Czech government within Prague and invite General Patton's Third Army into the city. At 11:00 a.m. Frank presented this plan to a Czech delegation led by Richard Bienert, Minister for the Interior, at a meeting in the Cernin Palace.

The uprising brought these proceedings to a halt—and the insurgents arrested Bienert, who promptly swore an oath of allegiance to the exiled Czechoslovak government of President Edvard Beneš. At 9:00 p.m. talks resumed—through the mediation of the International Red Cross—between Frank and the Czech National Committee. They ended inconclusively. But the following morning—on his own authority—Frank sent a message to the US Third Army saying there would be no resistance if it entered the city. And at 2:40 p.m. Admiral Dönitz and Field Marshal Keitel issued orders that any American advance on Prague should not be opposed by Wehrmacht troops.

General Eisenhower was sitting on a powder keg. If he moved on the Czech capital he would not just be breaking an agreement over demarcation lines; it might also appear to the Soviet Union that he had entered into an illicit agreement with the Germans. And that would imperil the very future of the Grand Alliance. It was a risk he could not afford to take.

The terrible consequence was that Prague seemed now to be left to its fate. But in this desperate situation for the Czech insurgents, help now arrived from a most unexpected quarter—General Andrei Vlasov's Russian Liberation Army. For after days of secret negotiations with members of the Czech undergound, this army's 1st Division—a well-equipped force of over 15,000 men—was prepared to turn against its German masters and support the rebels in Prague. And it was stationed less than 20 miles from the Czech capital. The Vlasovites could join forces with the Czech insurgents in a matter of hours.

On November 14, 1944, Prague Castle had been chosen for the launch of General Andrei Vlasov's army. Himmler sent a letter of encouragement but excused himself from attending. Hitler acted as if he was entirely unaware that the event was happening at all. But most of the prominent civil and military figures in the Protectorate of Bohemia and Moravia were there. General

Vlasov made a speech to this assembly, setting out the patriotic manifesto of his new army, which was dedicated to the overthrow of Bolshevism. It had been decided that this anti-communist force was to start serious military training and would then fight alongside the Wehrmacht.

It was a supreme irony that a force created with such ceremony in Prague to reinforce the Wehrmacht would some six months later be fighting the Germans for possession of the Czech capital. Veterans of the Russian Liberation Army recalled the birth of their army with emotion and pride. And yet, General Vlasov had surrendered to the Germans in June 1942. It had taken his masters more than two years to respond to his invitation to raise an anti-Bolshevik army and they had only done so now—with the war going hopelessly against them—out of dire necessity.

The Wehrmacht did not really trust the formation of a Russian Liberation Army and allowed it only with reluctance. Vlasov was now forced to recruit his troops from Russian POWs or slave laborers held on German soil. Some of these men were motivated by genuine patriotism and a detestation of communism. But others were joining simply to ameliorate their squalid living conditions. And German atrocities against the Russian people were now common knowledge.

Nevertheless, two divisions were quickly formed. The first came into being on February 10, 1945, when it was reviewed by General Vlasov and its commander, General Sergei Bunyachenko, at Muensingen in Germany. By April it had taken up battle positions against Soviet troops on the Oder front. It would now have to fight against its own countrymen.

Things quickly went wrong for the Vlasov force. In the latter half of April Bunyachenko pulled his men out of combat on the Oder and withdrew them farther south. At the beginning of May the 1st Division of the Russian Liberation Army was at Beroun, 16 miles southwest of Prague. And it had become utterly disaffected with its German ally.

The reason for this lay in a bitter disagreement between General Bunyachenko and the German High Command. The Wehrmacht had insisted upon an attack plan despite Bunyachenko's strong opposition to it. On April 14, 1945, the Vlasov Division had been ordered to go into battle against an extremely well-defended Red Army position at Frankfurt-am-Oder. There were political reasons for this order, which was given only two days before the Red Army's own Berlin offensive—a desire to demonstrate the reliability of this new formation to the Wehrmacht by "blooding" them in combat against their compatriots. Bunyachenko vigorously protested—to no avail.

On one side was German unease at employing Russian troops as an independent fighting formation. On the other was Russian distaste at having to fight against their own countrymen. The planned battle engagement resulted in a dismal failure.

The Red Army defenses were held by Major General Likhov's 119th Armored Brigade. Likhov's bridgehead on the western bank of the Oder was strongly fortified, with machine guns and mortars covering all its approaches. It was further protected by the flooded fields in front of its position—which created a swamp about a mile wide and in places 6 feet deep. On the eastern bank of the river, Likhov had an artillery regiment ready to give supporting fire to the defenders.

Sigismund Diczbalis, a soldier with Bunyachenko's division, described the offensive: "A hail of bullets and mortar fragments swathed into our troops. Some sunk slowly into the marsh and drowned. A furious barrage of fire reduced the remaining force to platoon strength, with men being cut to pieces by eight machine guns from a Red Army reserve detachment that had appeared as if from nowhere. It was clear that the attack could go no further."

After five hours of senseless slaughter General Bunyachenko withdrew his troops and then shepherded them away from the German lines. He had lost more than 350 men; the Red Army a mere 13. The division moved south.

Bunyachenko's force was still nominally within the Wehrmacht command system but was now disregarding its orders. Nevertheless, at the end of April Field Marshal Ferdinand Schörner, the leader of the German Army Group Center, determined to take charge of the situation. He demanded that the Russians move to the vicinity of Prague, to rendezvous with his group, which was planning a westward retreat toward the city. Major Helmut Schwenninger, a German liaison officer with the Vlasov Division, was uncertain whether this would happen or not. "I suspect the plan is to wait in the wings," Schwenninger wrote in his journal on April 30, "until the time that a popular uprising breaks out in Czechoslovakia. I anticipate that the insurgents will try to make contact with Bunyachenko in the next couple of days."

The situation was poised on the edge of a knife. Schwenninger noted that General Vlasov had come to visit the division. Vlasov did not want a complete break with the Germans and on May 1 he persuaded Bunyachenko to stick with the Wehrmacht. Recognizing that his divisional commander disliked Schörner's fanaticism, he suggested that he open talks with more moderate German generals. At this late stage of the war, Vlasov was being pragmatic. He wanted to retain the Russian Liberation Army within the structure of the German armed forces and then negotiate a wholesale surrender to the Americans. He was gambling that this would be the best way of saving his soldiers.

But then Schörner intervened. Losing patience with Bunyachenko's division, and not really trusting it, on May 2 he ordered that it disband immediately. Bunyachenko was furious. He ignored this command and instead broke off contact with Schörner and all the other German generals too. The Vlasov troops were now on their own.

For Schwenninger, Field Marshal Schörner's heavy-handed intervention was the main reason the Vlasov Division turned against the Germans. "This blunder provoked the First Division of the Russian Liberation Army into joining the side of the insurgents in the Prague uprising," Schwenninger said. The German officer was a well-informed witness to these unfolding events. He added:

"It seemed to me that even at this stage Vlasov and Bunyachenko disagreed and that General Bunyachenko was the driving force behind the decision to support the uprising. Vlasov did not want to break his agreement with the Germans and felt what Bunyachenko was undertaking was too risky. Vlasov himself never renounced the treaty he made with Germany—what followed was confined to Bunyachenko and his own division."

Schwenninger's testimony was illuminating. It formed an important part of the story, but there was a further dimension to it.

Bunyachenko was disillusioned with the Germans, but still unsure about taking part in an uprising against them. He knew the rebels would be poorly armed and that they lacked political unity. On May 2, the same day as Schörner's ill-fated intervention, a communist group—parachute-dropped into the area a month earlier to encourage rebellion as the Red Army began fighting on Czech territory—opened communication with Bunyachenko's forces. These men had a number of contacts in the Czech underground in Prague and knew that an uprising was imminent—and they wanted Bunyachenko to join it.

This was a Soviet guerrilla group operating behind German lines. A key member of it, and the one who struck up a rapport with Bunyachenko, was a Czech—Francis Konecny. Over a number of days Konecny met first with Bunyachenko's chief of staff and then the general himself.

Twenty-six-year-old Konecny had a remarkable personal story. He had begun as a soldier on the side of the Germans, first in the invasion of France and later in the war in Russia, in the Wehrmacht's 28th Infantry Division. But he became disillusioned by the savagery of the conflict and the atrocities committed against the civilian population. He was captured by the Russians and spent a while in a prison camp, and then joined a force of Czech soldiers—the 1st Czechoslovak Brigade, who were now willing to fight with the Red Army.

Konecny had fought on both sides—and so had Bunyachenko. The two men understood each other.

Another German liaison officer, Lieutenant Colonel Hansen, had said of General Sergei Bunyachenko: "A troublesome but remarkably competent officer, who made his career in the Red Army, rising to Chief of Staff to Marshal Timoshenko. He deserted to us by flying over German lines and landing his plane in our rear."

There were two significant moments in Bunyachenko's military career in the Second World War. The first was at Mozdok, 50 miles west of Grozny, on August 31, 1942. Bunyachenko was fighting with the Red Army against the Germans. He was ordered to blow up a bridge before the majority of his soldiers had crossed it. He refused, was tried before a military tribunal and sentenced to death. This was commuted to ten years' penal labor, once the war had finished. Bunyachenko did not wait. Appalled at this willingness to sacrifice the lives of his soldiers, in a way he judged to be unnecessary, callous and incompetent, he deserted—and joined Vlasov's army as soon as he could.

The second, as has been related, was at Frankfurt-am-Oder on April 14, 1945. Bunyachenko was fighting with the Germans against the Red Army. After five hours of senseless combat, he refused to further endanger the lives of his men. These were two powerful stands on principle—but where could Bunyachenko go now?

Konecny persuaded Bunyachenko to make another brave and principled gesture nonetheless—to come to the aid of the Prague uprising. The general thought this offer over and then consulted with his men. They agreed with his decision. Sometimes in a demoralizing situation, a clear course of action can have a galvanizing effect, whatever the risks involved. Vlasov soldier Sigismund Diczbalis described the impact:

> At Beroun we learned that we were to advance on the Czech capital and help prevent the insurgents being crushed and the city destroyed by diehard SS units. Information reached us that an entire SS battle group—retreating from the Eastern Front—had been ordered to Prague to help reinforce the garrison. This news brought a surprisingly positive boost to the exhausted, dusty and foot-sore ranks of our soldiers . . . Not once did I hear any man suggest that this change of tactics was unacceptable. No-one opposed our First Division commander's decision. Everyone turned to checking their weapons, supplies of ammunition and equipment.

Faced with the threat of extermination by the SS, the Czech National Committee in Prague, although pro-Soviet, had taken the risk of inviting the Vlasov forces to their aid. On the evening of May 5 they had no other choice—it was a battle for survival. But now another dangerously unstable element had been added to the political mix. The Russian Liberation Army was strongly opposed to Bolshevism and had fought against the Red Army. And it had within its ranks the remnants of the notorious Kaminsky Brigade, Russian collaborators with the Wehrmacht who had conducted some of the most brutal anti-partisan operations ever seen within the German-occupied portion of the Soviet Union. For the advancing Red Army, a more incendiary choice of "ally" by the insurgents could hardly be imagined.

The die had been cast. And as General Bunyachenko began to prepare his troops, on the evening of May 5, he issued a defiant proclamation from his headquarters. It may have been at least partly motivated by expediency, but it carried desperate valor and idealism nonetheless:

> Brother Czechs and Russians, Germany is in its death throes. Prague has raised the flag of freedom against National Socialism. We Russian soldiers, inspired by our own nation's fight against the cruelties of Bolshevism, cannot ignore this rebellion against Nazi atrocity. I hereby order the First Division of our Russian Liberation Army to advance into Prague in support of the Czech forces there.
>
> The time has come for mankind to finally destroy the Nazi menace. I exhort you all—good Czechs and Russians—to fight for this cause.
>
> This is a battle for justice and independence. The cruelty of National Socialist Germany—which has raped nations and killed millions of innocent people—has followed the same path as the bloody consolidation of Bolshevik power in Russia.
>
> Let us wage war against the killers of mankind—Nazis and Bolsheviks alike. Let us fight for freedom!

The following day the 1st Division of the Russian Liberation Army marched on Prague. By the evening, General Bunyachenko had set up his battle headquarters just outside the city and made direct contact with the insurgents. One of his regimental commanders, Major Arkhipov, met with General Kutlvašr, head of the Czech Military Council, to discuss the best way to deploy the troops. And the Russian liberation force had twenty-two tanks and armored vehicles, which would make a vital difference in the city fighting. The division's advance units were already in the Czech capital gathering intelligence on German positions. Bunyachenko's soldiers were about to join the uprising.

7

THE DISPOSSESSED

On May 6 Major Hugh McLaren of the 10th British Casualty Clearing Station arrived at Sandbostel concentration camp in northern Germany, 35 miles northeast of Bremen. He wrote a memoir of his experiences, describing it as a "horror camp." Horror is not, perhaps, the most original word for the events of the time—the vast human displacement all over Europe, the death marches, the liberation of slave laborers and the uncovering of the Nazi policy of annihilating those considered undesirable to their new order—but it remains an apt description.

Allied troops who liberated the concentration and extermination camps were profoundly shocked and disturbed by what they encountered. The medical staff who accompanied or followed them had to then stay in these camps and attempt to transform the conditions there. McLaren knew, at the time of his posting, that Sandbostel had been liberated by the British troops of XXX Corps a week earlier, on April 29. Fighting was still going on and in the immediate aftermath of liberation resources were scarce. But in his first four days at the camp he was absolutely overwhelmed by what he encountered.

"My first view of Sandbostel was somehow what I had expected," McLaren began. "Miles of wire encircled each low hut, a further wire fence enclosing the whole compound. There were watch towers equipped with searchlights and machine guns were placed around the perimeter to cover all eleven exits. It was an ugly place to look at—but when you entered the main part of the camp you realized that it was built in a saucer shaped depression giving the prisoners a view of nothing but the sky and the wire wall."

Already McLaren was encountering a sense of alienation and deprivation. But he then described the camp in more detail: "The standard hut was about forty yards long, each having a dark central corridor. In the hospital where we worked, twenty small rooms led off the corridor. In the prisoner section, however, each hut was designed like a barn. There were a dozen shelves where the prisoners could lie down in close-packed rows; an occasional foul mattress was seen, but for the most part the prisoners lay on bare wooden shelves. There were between forty and sixty of them on each long wooden shelf. The most chaotic slum dwelling on the Clydeside was luxurious in comparison."

Sandbostel camp consisted of three sections. The first was for POWs from the Western Allies. Here conditions were basic. The second was for Russian prisoners. Here conditions were poor. The third was for political prisoners. Conditions here were appalling. It was this section which McLaren would be serving as a doctor. He was totally sickened by his first visit to the hospital. Each hut was crammed with about 350 patients. The latrines had been blocked for days. Most were too weak to rise from their beds. These skeletal patients—naked, unshaved and dirty—defecated where they stood or lay. In one of the huts six were found to be dead.

There had been 8,000 people left in the political prisoners' section of Sandbostel when the British arrived. Within days 1,500 had died; 2,500 were strong enough to be evacuated. The remaining 4,000 ended up in the hospital. They were first carried into a large marquee in which rows of trestles were placed, supporting stretchers. The camp survivors were washed and covered in anti-louse powder. They were then wrapped in a clean blanket, transferred to a fresh stretcher and delivered to the hospital by ambulance.

British forces—learning that there was a concentration camp at Sandbostel—had sent small medical units in with the troops—but these initial resources were limited. Hugh Johns, a member of one of the ambulance units accompanying the soldiers, recalled: "Behind barbed wire, thrusting their hands through in pleas for food, were human skeletons, skin and bone, half-dressed or naked." Ambulanceman Dennis Wickham wrote in his diary at the beginning of May:

> When we went over to the civilian compound, no words could adequately describe the horror. Typhus was rampant. Large pits were filled with corpses—bodies were piled in mounds about the yards. Others were lying virtually naked in rooms: grotesque figures, crouching in corners too weak to move—awaiting their turn to die. The stench was horrible—there was no sanitation whatsoever. The so-called rooms were far worse than a pig-sty. Within them were piles of skin and bones, with little or no clothing and of an ashen gray coloring. I would never have believed such a thing possible.

As at the camp at Bergen-Belsen, the survivors were of many nationalities. There were Canadians, a man from Jersey; all European countries were represented—there was even someone from Iran. The youngest of them were mere boys. Some had entered the camp at eleven years old. Others were Warsaw resistance fighters—captured almost a year earlier—who were now fourteen or fifteen. The most starved of the skeletal patients weighed only 39 pounds—he died two days after McLaren arrived at the camp.

It was hard to comprehend it all. Ambulanceman Clifford Barnard wrote home early in May: "I would rather see a soldier who had been killed in battle than the living dead who crawl around this place. You have probably read about these camps in newspapers and found the details hard to believe. I can tell you that they really do exist. I have seen things I shall never forget."

The state of the survivors deeply shocked McLaren and the other doctors and nurses—indeed, it was beyond anything that he had previously experienced. More than half the patients were totally apathetic.

"For the majority," McLaren said, "news of their liberation brought little or no emotional reaction. They were in a totally depressed state of mind. They just stared dully at us, or would mutter 'Water' or 'Nothing to eat.' I got the impression that they had descended into such a dark place that the past and the future had almost become blank."

In this underworld existence, the death of a neighbor was regarded with unnerving sangfroid. Often it was merely a signal to request the crusts or cigarettes under the dead man's pillow. After a while, McLaren began to find a macabre humor within this horror. One patient beckoned him over and, pointing to the bunk above him, asked whether the man was dead. McLaren examined the man and found that he had indeed just died. "Thank God!" said the patient with a trace of a smile, and he then proceeded to detach the groundsheet he had used to protect himself from the human droppings of his neighbor. Sometimes patients would predict their own death with an eerie calm. "Three days, Doctor, and I will be dead." They were invariably right.

The few victims who were less passive were usually mentally unbalanced. Sometimes they would be found wandering the corridors in a crazed fashion in search of food. Twice a Russian was found with his head and shoulders in the food pail. "He would not respond to our shouts," McLaren recalled. "A hard smack on his naked backside had some effect, and off he went to his bed streaming with soup. There was little laughter at these incidents; all eyes were on the food pail." The most terrifying incident involved a patient who—in a sudden surge of strength—drank his neighbor's entire blood transfusion.

For three to four days after McLaren's arrival there was no peace in the hospital at all. The medical staff could not cope with their patients' thirst. For each hut, McLaren reckoned they required 1,500 cupfuls of water a day— and some of the inmates needed help with their drinking. And practically all had "famine diarrhea." This would start after the resumption of a basic diet— and would last at least ten days. Finally, hundreds of inmates had typhoid fever. Work had to continue in these conditions—with a real danger to the medical staff and enormous and cumulative psychological distress.

"Capped and gowned in white, and well sprinkled with anti-louse powder, we looked more like bakers than doctors," McLaren wrote with wry humor. "Most of us wore a body belt on which hung drugs and a stethoscope. Diagnosis was made at speed and in the first week we had to give out such medicines that we had on the spot."

One of the deepest human urges in adversity is to strike up rapport. But the first conversations with those patients able to talk were halting and difficult. One man told McLaren how he had seen the SS push all Jews in the "over-60-years-old category" out of the second-floor window of the Lublin General Hospital. Stunned unconscious or dead, they were then carted away for burial. Another Polish Jew told the British doctor how he had seen the SS mow down his wife, mother, father and two sisters. "I soon learned not to inquire if their people at home had survived," McLaren wrote sadly of the Jewish inmates. "Strictly medical questions avoided an unbearable emotional pain."

Royal Ambulanceman Alan Walker tried to convey to his parents in Sheffield the horror of Bergen-Belsen camp in Lower Saxony, 11 miles north of Celle, liberated by the British 11th Armored Division on April 15, 1945. He was writing three weeks after the event, but the struggle with his own emotions was all too painfully evident:

"When we first entered the camp," Walker began, "I saw such terrible sights . . . the dead bodies lying all over the place—men, women and even little children." It was difficult to continue this description. He paused. "I can never describe the horrors of this concentration camp." Then he attempted to begin again: "They had been without food and water for ten days and they were so thin that their stomachs were touching their spine. We buried some of them . . ." It was too painful to hold this memory. "I cannot describe the picture of what I have seen in Belsen because it was so horrible," Walker reiterated. "How could the Germans have been so cruel?"

Slowly, more of his experiences came out—the sadism of the guards, the desperate, animal-like existence of the inmates, the mass deaths, the unbelievable suffering. "I know this letter will read like fiction," Walker concluded, "and people will say it's all exaggeration. But I swear it is the Gospel truth."

Captain Robert Barer wrote a series of letters to his wife about his experiences at Sandbostel. Brief sections of description of the camp were interspersed with attempts to find historical and literary parallels. Such parallels remained elusive—Barer was grasping at something he could not fully comprehend. "I am sure there has never been anything quite like this in the history of the world," he acknowledged toward the end of one letter. "The Middle Ages and Inquisition were probably humane by comparison." "I suppose people in England will not believe these things," he said in another. "They'll say the pictures are faked. But no picture on earth could convey one millionth of the real horror." And as for the horror itself: "No words of mine can ever really convey what I saw there. A combination of Charles Dickens and Edgar Allan Poe might have done so, but I doubt it."

Others across Germany and Austria were grappling with similar sentiments. On May 6 Private Harold Porter, a medical officer with the US 116th Evacuation Hospital, wrote to his parents about the liberation of Dachau, 10 miles northwest of Munich:

It is difficult to know how to begin. By now I have recovered from my first emotional shock and am able to write without seeming like a hysterical, gibbering idiot. But I know you will find it difficult to believe me, no matter how factual and objective I try to be. I even find myself trying to deny what I am looking at with my own eyes. Certainly, what I have seen in the past few days will affect my personality for the rest of my life.

We were briefed in advance that we were going to be working at Dachau and that it was one of the most notorious concentration camps. We expected things to be pretty ghastly but none of us had any real idea of what was coming. It is easy to read about atrocities—but they have to be seen before they can be really understood.

The trip to Dachau was disarmingly pleasant with neat cottages and country estates lining our route. The Alps were in the distance. It was almost as if we were passing through a tourist resort. And then we reached Dachau. In the center of the town was a train with a wrecked engine, about fifty cars [carriages] long. Every one of them was loaded with bodies—all starved to death.

Within the camp we came upon a huge stack of corpses, piled up like kindling next to a furnace house . . . One of the medical staff already present had performed autopsies the day before—wearing a gas mask—on ten bodies chosen at random. Eight of them had advanced tuberculosis and all of them showed extreme malnutrition. The victims included men, women and children.

I stood there looking at it all—but just couldn't believe it. The reality of this horror is only beginning to dawn on me . . .

"I could not immediately comprehend all that I saw," John McConally, a doctor with the US 90th Division, said of Flossenbürg concentration camp, in southern Bavaria.

Harold Porter began and ended his letter acknowledging that for people back in America, such descriptions would remain utterly unreal. At Gunskirchen Lager, a sub-camp of Mauthausen in northern Austria, Major General Willard Wyman, commander of the US 71st Infantry Division, was also struggling to convey to the wider world the reality of what they had just encountered. "The horror of Gunskirchen must not be repeated," Wyman wrote. On May 6 he ordered one of his soldiers, Norman Nichols—who had been an art student in Detroit before the war—on a roving assignment to sketch the conditions in the camp.

Nichols recalled:

The buildings, the roads and nearby woods, were choked with bodies. I first set up my easel in a stretch of woodland. It was a sunny May morning—but my surroundings stank of death. Bodies were everywhere—jumbled in grotesque postures. The half-dead and dying were being carried from one of the stinking huts to a truck for transportation to a hospital. We made the Germans do the burying. One group carried the bodies out to a clearing; the other dug the graves. As I sketched the scene, a young boy knelt by the holes, sobbing quietly, and asking that his dead brother be given an individual grave. Cynics disbelieve these episodes and put them down to "atrocity propaganda." But for me, "atrocity" is too mild a word for what I am witnessing here.

A terrible smell surrounded the camps. Captain John Pletcher of the US 71st Infantry Division said of Gunskirchen: "It was a smell I will never forget—completely different from anything else I have ever encountered. It could almost be seen—and hung over the camp like a fog of death." It was a fog of which local inhabitants were completely unaware.

On April 12, 1945, General Dwight Eisenhower—accompanied by Generals Omar Bradley and George Patton—had visited the concentration camp of Ohrdruf, 33 miles southwest of Weimar, liberated eight days earlier by troops of the US 4th Armored and 89th Infantry Divisions. Ohrdruf was the first German camp US troops had encountered.

"The things I saw beggared description," Eisenhower related. "The visual evidence and verbal testimony of starvation, cruelty and bestiality was so overpowering it left me physically sick. In one room were piled 30 naked men—all killed by starvation."

Significantly, Eisenhower then added: "I made the visit deliberately, in order to be in a position to give first-hand evidence of such things, if ever in future there develops a tendency to describe such incidents as mere 'propaganda.'"

Sergeant Eugene Schultz wrote to his sister on April 14 after a visit to the camp. "You will say nothing like this could ever happen," he began. Schultz confessed that he had always regarded Nazi atrocity stories as works of imaginative embellishment. His visit to Ohrdruf changed everything.

On April 19 inhabitants of Weimar were made to tour Ohrdruf camp in groups of a hundred. On the same day General Eisenhower contacted General George Marshall, the US Army chief of staff, and asked that members of Congress and groups of journalists be taken round the newly liberated camps. The request was approved by the secretary of war, Henry Stimson, and by President Harry Truman himself. And still the incredulity remained.

In October 1939 the British government had published a White Paper on the treatment of prisoners in German concentration camps. The White Paper contained reports of British consuls in various German cities on the Jewish pogroms of November 1938 and reports of escaped prisoners submitted to the Foreign Office between March 1938 and February 1939, including a statement from a former inmate at Buchenwald. The report had been suppressed for months—so as not to engender hatred between Britain and Germany, and perhaps because it was feared that many would not believe it. Now, as war began, it was released.

The White Paper had declared bluntly that neither the consolidation of the Nazi regime nor the passage of time had in any way mitigated its savagery. The attitude of the Nazis toward imprisoned Jews was that the biblical Pharaoh had not gone nearly far enough. "The National Socialist regime is taking a terrible revenge on all who oppose it," the report continued, before issuing the stark warning that what was happening in the concentration camps "was reminiscent of the darkest ages in the history of man."

And yet that warning went to a large extent unheeded—it was all too difficult to grasp. On July 23, 1944, Red Army soldiers liberated the death camp at Majdanek near Lublin in Poland. The SS had marched away most of its inmates, but had lacked time to destroy the infrastructure. It was the first functioning extermination camp captured intact by the Grand Alliance. What was found there stunned its liberators. Political commissar Vasily Yeremenko, with the Soviet 2nd Tank Army, said: "When we saw what it contained, we felt dangerously close to going insane."

Konstantin Simonov, the first Soviet war correspondent to visit the camp, warned his readers in an article for the army newspaper *Red Star* that his mind still refused to accept the reality of what his eyes and ears took in, and that they were about to uncover something immense, terrifying and incomprehensible. Russian soldiers could scarcely believe it all. "We had read about the existence of these camps, but to actually see one was completely different," said Captain Anatoly Mereshko of the Soviet 8th Guards Army. "We found warehouses full of belongings taken from the prisoners," Mereshko continued. "One of them was full of shoes, hundreds of thousands of them, piled up to the ceiling. We asked each other—'What has been going on here?'"

The killing had been done with clinical efficiency. It was the crematorium which had the greatest impact. Red Army troops filed past it in utter silence. "The ovens were still warm," Mereshko said bluntly.

Here was an opportunity to come to grips with what the Nazis had unleashed on Europe. British war reporter Paul Winterton had entered Majdanek with its Russian liberators. Profoundly shocked, he recorded a report for the BBC. "Here is the most horrible story I shall ever have to tell you," Winterton began. "I have just been down to Lublin in Poland to see the concentration camp at Majdanek . . ." Winterton tried to bring home the terrible reality of what he was seeing by avoiding sensationalism and relaying the information in a matter-of-fact way. "The furnaces are big enough to hold from four to six bodies," he continued. "Together, they are capable of dealing with some two thousand corpses a day."

The BBC was unable to relate to it all. "I was given a kind of reprimand," Winterton remembered. "They told me they didn't want this atrocity stuff. They seemed to think that it was Russian propaganda." Winterton's dispatch was broadcast only at the end of August 1944, over a month after it had been submitted. It was heavily edited and transmitted solely on the overseas service. The British Foreign Office dampened down reaction to the news even further. One official minuted that they should avoid responding directly to the news of Majdanek, adding: "The Russians will manage this more efficiently than us."

The Russians were in fact struggling to digest what they had uncovered. On November 27 a trial of the camp officials at Majdanek began. It received little publicity in the Western press. And on January 27, 1945, Red Army soldiers liberated Auschwitz, near the town of Oświęcim in Poland, the principal death camp of the Holocaust. "I had seen a lot in this war," said Captain Anatoly Shapiro of the Soviet 1085th "Tarnopol" Rifle Regiment. "I had seen many innocent people killed. I had seen hanged people. I had seen burned people. But I was still unprepared for Auschwitz."

The regimental combat journal stated: "The German leadership has turned Auschwitz into a death factory. Hundreds of thousands of prisoners of all nationalities have been held here. They are now trying to eradicate all evidence of their crime before they pull back." The 1085th Regiment, part of the Soviet 322nd Rifle Division, broke into Auschwitz I at about 2:00 p.m. Two hours later, Lieutenant Vasily Gromadsky's 472nd Regiment (of the Soviet 100th Rifle Division) fought its way into Auschwitz-Birkenau. At the end of January 27 Gromadsky wrote in his diary: "Battle for Auschwitz. Met with prisoners of this camp. Huge numbers of people were taken to this place, including children. Twelve train wagonloads of children's pushchairs were dispatched from here."

Soviet war correspondents were in the camp within days, and on February 2, 1945, one of their best-known journalists, Boris Polevoy, wrote a major piece on Auschwitz in *Pravda*, describing the camp as a "giant factory of death." "It was an enormous industrial plant," he related, "having its own special facilities . . . In one, the processing of arrivals took place—separating those who, before death, could be put to work for a while, while the elderly, the children and infirm were sentenced to immediate execution . . ."

However, Polevoy's report received little coverage in Western newspapers. And very quickly the Soviet authorities realized it contained serious inaccuracies. Polevoy had referred to an electric conveyor belt "on which hundreds of people were simultaneously killed" that was in fact non-existent—and he did not properly understand the function of the gas chambers either, and he placed them in the wrong part of the camp. Fellow war correspondent Sergei Krushinsky wrote of the difficulty of forging deeply disturbing information, of varying degrees of credibility, into a coherent narrative: "The wildest rumors are floating around here," he warned, "and most of the prisoners we talk to are more or less mentally ill." Rather than risk more inaccurate reports, the First Ukrainian Front set up a detailed commission at the beginning of February 1945 to examine a wide range of evidence on the working of the camp. Its findings were published a little over three months later, on May 6.

British and American troops were largely unaware of Majdanek and Auschwitz when they encountered the death camps of Germany and Austria, and the shock was all the greater. And yet the reactions of Soviet troops who liberated these camps or visited them afterward strongly echo those of the Western Allies. "We believed the Nazis had sullied humanity itself," exclaimed Lieutenant Vasily Gromadsky. "We resolved to finish the war as quickly as possible and send them all to hell."

Auschwitz had exacted the same toll on the Russian medical teams that had followed the soldiers into the camp. The new Soviet camp commander there, Colonel Georgi Elisavestsky, wrote: "We knew immediate action had to be taken to try and save the survivors—people who had been crippled physically and psychologically. It is impossible to describe how our doctors and nurses worked—without sleep or food—to try and help these unfortunates, how they fought for every life. Unfortunately, many were beyond help." The military hospital—mobile unit no. 2962—run by Dr. Maria Zhilinskaya, nevertheless managed to save 2,819 inmates. This was the shared bond endured by all the soldier-liberators of the Grand Alliance and the medical support teams which followed them.

The Soviet report on Auschwitz of May 6, 1945, represented a darkly symbolic moment. It was the most detailed study yet compiled on the functioning of a death camp. It was based on interviews with more than 2,000 camp survivors, a review of all the German documents found in the camp, inspection of its physical remains—including the crematoria and gas chambers—and autopsies performed on the bodies of the victims. And yet, even with the mass of information presented within it, there was an aspect that remained elusive.

Soviet war journalist Vasily Grossman had tried to describe the death camp at Treblinka, but the experience of writing about the camp had caused him to suffer a nervous breakdown. When he returned to the front he remained obsessed by its evil. Grossman was a writer who had lost his own mother in a massacre of Jews at Berdichev in the Ukraine. He felt that he was looking over the edge of an abyss. "Grossman was deeply shaken by the death camps," recalled Mark Slavin, editor of the 8th Guards Army newspaper, "and this worsened after the liberation of Auschwitz. He would refer to it all the time in conversation, saying 'The horror, the horror of these Fascist camps.' We all knew that they were terrible, but he felt another dimension to their evil, a dimension that we could not fully grasp."

Now that struggle was being replayed in the west. Richard Dimbleby had reported on Bergen-Belsen on April 19, 1945. Initially the BBC refused to transmit his report, then—uncertain of the reaction from the public—they heavily edited and shortened it. The boundaries of presenting the war's horror and deprivation were being challenged. Dimbleby spoke with the voice of someone profoundly changed by what he had witnessed:

"I wish with all my heart," Dimbleby had said, "that everyone fighting in this war and above all those whose duty is to direct it, from Britain and America, could have come with me through the barbed wire that leads to the inner compound of the camp . . . I passed through the barrier and found myself in the world of a nightmare."

It became clear that Bergen-Belsen would need to be fully filmed. British army cameramen worked in two-day shifts, such was the difficulty of the material they were dealing with. Many were physically sick during the filming.

At the war's end the British public was shown newsreel footage of the Nazi concentration camps liberated by the Allies. The so-called "atrocity films" produced stunned reactions in some of the audiences who saw them, but others seemed unable to engage.

One woman commented at the end of April 1945:

I saw the atrocity film at the New Gallery today. Of course, I expected it to be terrible—but it's worse than I imagined. Not because of the pile of corpses—after all, they're dead, but because of the survivors. They just aren't human anymore. I think the worst moment of all was when one of these almost skeletons tried to smile at an American soldier. You know his face couldn't express a smile any more. The audience were deathly quiet, not a whisper. Some of it was shown without a commentary, and I have never heard such a hush as there was all over the cinema.

But another reacted differently to a screening a few days later, on May 2: "The atrocity film was followed by a Walt Disney—Donald Duck—people are laughing again within a minute. And it's all mixed up with a propaganda film about noble London and how wonderful Londoners were during the Blitz. It felt as if the whole show was propaganda."

There was a huge difference, however, between the incredulity of some of the American and British public and the denial of the camps by many Germans. Private Ralph Dalton of the US 89th Infantry Division said of Ohrdruf: "I do not believe anyone could live close to such a place and not know what was going on." Staff Sergeant Paul Lenger questioned people living close to Ohrdruf: "When we talked to the inhabitants they told us they had no idea that there was a camp of this sort, despite the fact that when the inmates had to work in the nearby castle they actually walked through the outskirts of the town."

Allied soldiers and medical staff were left with searing images, of a kind never experienced before. Lieutenant William Loveday, who liberated Nordhausen with the US 3rd Armored Division, said: "When I entered the camp I saw a man who had died on his hands and knees in a praying position—apparently, he had been left there for days."

Amid such horror, any sign of humanity was greeted with joy and relief. At Sandbostel camp, a first indication of recovery was the desire to wear clothes again. Major McLaren remembered one incident: "A Russian amused us by tottering about the corridor quite naked but for an old hat. On being ordered away from the kitchen he would make an attempt at a smart salute." After a week of regular food and sleep, McLaren noted that signs of animal-like behavior among patients began to disappear. Human dignity was returning. "When pajamas arrived, the whole face of the camp changed," the doctor said. "Those who could walk were like schoolboys in their first long trousers. They made improvised cloth shoes and almost strutted with pride."

Another doctor at Sandbostel wrote:

A few days of hospital treatment and kindness could produce, in some at least, a dramatic change—although the men continued to hoard food. After every meal the nurses found bread or even bowls of soup hidden away under pillows or mattresses. The first issue of pajamas was always a great occasion. The men had not really been clean, shaved or had fresh clothing for several months. One of them, still too weak to stand alone, insisted on being helped by an orderly to stagger across the ward, to show himself off to others in his new pajamas.

He added: "When the Ward Sister brought a vase of flowers and green leaves into the room for the first time, it had to be placed in the center so everyone could see it. By next morning a number of the leaves were missing. Several of the patients had crawled out of bed and taken them, and put them on their pillows. The Sister asked a man why he had done this. 'They are so pretty—I wanted to have them close by me,' he replied."

McLaren would sometimes ask the German women who were recruited as auxiliary helpers whether they felt ashamed of the camp. The question was invariably deflected with "Well, what could we do?" But one—a Fräulein Bittner—proved more forthcoming. McLaren jotted down some of the questions and answers:

"Fraulein Bittner, you have helped us well at the camp—do you mind answering a few questions on political matters?"

"No."

Question 1: "Do you feel ashamed of this camp?"

"No—our Führer had good reason for doing this."

Question 2: "Do you approve of the starving of these camp inmates?"

"Our Führer has said: 'First I feed my soldiers, then my mothers and children.' The others will have to fend for themselves."

Question 3: "Do you condone Hitler's killing of three million Polish Jews?"

"Yes—the National Socialist Party had this policy carried out, and for good reason."

Question 4: "Do you really agree with the gassing of Jewish children?"

[Hesitation] "If they grow up they will come at us later—it is better that they die now."

The robotic utterances, the continued invocation of the dead Führer, seemed to create a mantra of death. There seemed no spark of compassion, of humanity—and only the hesitation before the last question revealed the slightest unease. McLaren was left aghast.

McLaren's interviewee was chilling because of her frankness. Lieutenant General Brian Horrocks, who ordered German women from surrounding towns and villages to help clean up Sandbostel and look after the surviving prisoners, was shocked to relate: "When the women arrived we expected some indication of horror or remorse when they saw what their fellow countrymen had been doing. Not a bit of it. I never saw a tear or heard one expression of pity from any of them." But Elfie Walther, a high-school girl from nearby Delmenhorst, also brought in to help clean the camp, had a very different reaction. She wrote in her diary on May 2:

"Nobody at home would believe us if we told them about it. I can't stop thinking about how we loved the Führer. Everything he told us was a lie. What is this thing that was called National Socialism? We always thought it was something beautiful and noble. Why is everything actually so cruel? Why do they kill innocent, helpless people?"

Allied soldiers and medical staff were grappling with this question every day. "I still shudder when I picture this wilderness of barbed wire," McLaren said. "Most of us had no doubt in our minds that Germany had to be beaten, but we did not realize the full savagery of the Nazis until we reached Sandbostel."

Yet a terrible vista was opening up for Elfie Walther. "I am dreadfully mixed up," she wrote. "Can this be true? If it is as the orderlies have told us, then the pictures of Bergen-Belsen are certainly true too. And what else might there be that we have no idea of? Is this what our soldiers were fighting for? I am terrified of tomorrow."

Trainee doctor Michael Hargrave had arrived at Bergen-Belsen at the beginning of May. Belsen had been liberated two weeks earlier than Sandbostel, but was a much larger camp and its medical staff were still struggling with conditions there. For Hargrave and ninety-four fellow medical students from Westminster Hospital it was an utterly harrowing experience.

"The first thing that struck me was the bleakness," Hargrave wrote in his diary on May 3. "Everything was gray or slate brown. The next thing was the dust . . ." It took a while for Hargrave to focus on his surroundings, as if the human eye could not adjust to what lay before it. And then he saw everything fully: "There were piles of dead everywhere, right up to the front gate."

Hargrave recalled a conversation with Brigadier Glyn-Hughes, deputy medical director for the British 2nd Army. Glyn-Hughes, accompanying the British 11th Armored Division, had been the first medical officer to enter the camp. He had immediately taken charge of the hospital, instituted measures for the control of typhus in the camp and the proper distribution of food. Although the SS had abandoned Bergen-Belsen days earlier, Glyn-Hughes found that the camp commandant and doctor had stayed on, for reasons he could not fathom. What struck him was that neither of the men was at all ashamed.

Around them were piles of dead everywhere—out in the open because the crematorium had broken down. A few of the inmates were leaning against these piles gnawing at scraps of food. Glyn-Hughes made the two assist in the burial of the bodies, but all the time they maintained an air of callous indifference.

It was unusual for German civilians to either openly acknowledge these atrocities, and their acceptance of them, or to show repentance. Most disengaged from the issue altogether. And so—for Allied troops—it became a powerful symbolic act to have Germans—soldiers and civilians alike—assist in the reburial of the camp dead. At the beginning of May General Eisenhower had ordered that Germans help in the reburial of all victims of atrocity "to serve as an object lesson for their participation in such crimes."

Lieutenant David Ichelson of the US 71st Infantry Division described an incident at Gunskirchen Lager: "The digging was done by ordinary German soldiers, who had no previous direct connection with the camp," Ichelson related. "A few feigned illness and complained in order to try and avoid their grisly task. One refused to work and was summarily shot and dumped into one of the mass graves. His horrified comrades thereafter completed their miserable job without a whimper."

At Dachau, Nordhausen, Buchenwald, Wöbbelin and Flossenbürg, American soldiers insisted that local Germans assume responsibility for burying the dead. Brigadier General Sherman Hasbrouck, artillery commander of the US 97th Division, wrote: "I was one of the first senior officers to visit Flossenbürg. I remember the heaps of the dead. It was a horrible sight . . . I gave orders to the burgermeister to turn out every able-bodied man and boy to dig graves and bury the dead."

At Wöbbelin concentration camp, 28 miles south of Schwerin on northwest Germany's Mecklenburg Plain, General James Gavin of the 82nd Airborne Division insisted that the local townspeople dig 400 individual graves and then transport the bodies in wheelbarrows. He refused to let them wear gloves.

Gavin forced every adult citizen of nearby Ludwigslust to dig these holes in the lawn of the town square in front of the palace of the Mecklenburg princes. Each body was afforded a private grave.

On the afternoon of May 3 the 82nd Airborne's chaplain, George Wood, presided over the reburial and then addressed the assembled Germans:

"Though you claim no knowledge of these acts, you are still individually and collectively responsible for these atrocities—for they were carried out by a government elected in 1933 and continued in office by your indifference to organized brutality. It should be the firm resolve of the German people that never again should any leader or party bring them to such moral degradation as is exhibited here."

Earlier that day General Gavin had received the surrender of about 150,000 soldiers from the German 21st Army. Noticing their commander, General Kurt von Tippelskirch, staring smugly at the procession of bodies, he struck him in the face and ordered him to take off his cap.

In Austria, the concentration camps at Mauthausen, Gusen and Ebensee were all situated in populated areas. Colonel Richard Seibel of the US 11th Armored Division took charge of Mauthausen—11 miles east of Linz—on May 6, a day after its liberation. He reported to SHAEF at Rheims: "The inhabitants of the town of Mauthausen and those in its general vicinity must have been aware of what was going on—and the conditions there. Some of the guards and their families lived close by . . . There was a standing order to the local population that they were to kill on sight any escaped residents of the camp."

Seibel pointed out that people given such an order could not have been unaware that prisoners were kept near by. He ordered the inhabitants of Mauthausen to assist in the burials at the camp dressed in their Sunday-best clothes.

Mauthausen was a massive slave labor complex that had contained around 60,000 people when the US 11th Armored Division liberated it on May 5. The thing that immediately struck Seibel and his American comrades was the terrible physical condition of the inmates. "I estimated the average weight of most of them was about eighty pounds," Seibel said. "Many had typhus, dysentery or pneumonia."

Prisoners were forced to work at a quarry at Mauthausen that contained 186 steps, dragging up this "stairway of death" rough-hewn stones, some as heavy as 110 pounds. One of the survivors, Edward Mosberg, said simply: "If you stopped for a moment, the SS either shot you or pushed you off the cliff to your death."

Survivor stories are utterly heart-rending. Some were told to the liberators in the immediate aftermath of gaining freedom, others took years to coax out. Many could be told here—but there is one that perhaps might speak for the others, in that it transcends physical and emotional cruelty and conjures the world of spiritual depravity and perversion that inhabited these camps.

Lubertus Shapelhouman, a Dutch resistance fighter, was nineteen years old when he was liberated from Mauthausen. He had entered the camp in November 1944 weighing 160 pounds but by May 1945 he had wasted away to 78 pounds and was close to death.

So many perished at Mauthausen and its numerous sub-camps, which operated a policy of *Vernichtung durch Arbeit*, "Extermination through labor," whereby malnourished inmates, living in overcrowded and disease-ridden conditions and subject to frequent beatings, were then killed when they became too weak to work. But Shapelhouman recalled one particular incident that surpassed even this horror, on Christmas Day 1944:

> There was a teenage boy—a Hungarian Jew—and both his parents had already been executed before he arrived at Mauthausen. He was in a bad way. A Belgian priest, who was also an inmate, took pity on him—because his suffering was so terrible, even in this place of great suffering. Seeking solace, he told the priest that he wanted to convert to Catholicism. All religious practices were forbidden in the camp. But on Christmas Eve a clandestine baptismal mass was held for the boy and for 28 other prisoners.

Shapelhouman was one of them. But the SS and camp guards found out about the ceremony from an informer: "The boy was weak, but he spoke of his desire to go to heaven," Shapelhouman continued. "But at the moment he was baptized the SS burst into the room and began to beat everyone. There was pandemonium—a storm of blows, punches and kicks rained down upon us."

One of these blows threw Shapelhouman's hip out of joint. Then they were all taken outside. It was minus 14 degrees Celsius.

"The priest and the boy were made to strip naked and embrace," Shapelhouman said. "Then the guards drenched them with a hose. They froze in that position and died in that position. And the next day—which was Christmas Day—the entire camp was marched out and made to look at them."

These two deaths are perhaps a symbol of hundreds of thousands of other stories. British and American troops found it inconceivable that Germans did not know about these atrocities. Across Germany and Austria—at concentration camps large and small—American troops now rounded up civilians and compelled them to view the camps, the mass pit graves and the cemeteries where bodies still lay uncovered. General James Gavin ordered that the entire population of Wöbbelin go around the camp. Troops of the US 71st Infantry Division at Gunskirchen Lager went into the nearby town of Lambach, knocked on doors and made everyone able to walk go and see it.

The concentration camps threw up a kaleidoscope of emotions among the liberators, the medical and support teams that followed them and those survivors who were able to recover from their ordeal. They were part of a cataclysm engulfing Europe. Vast numbers of freed POWs and slave laborers were swamping aid and medical organizations set up by the Allies.

British POW Bob Prouse had hoped that he and his fellow prisoners would be liberated from his work camp at Mühlhausen. But at the beginning of April they were abruptly woken and told to prepare to leave. They joined the chaos of thousands of other prisoners, German troops and civilians on the move. "It was a mad beehive of activity," Prouse recalled. "I felt certain that our guards had orders to march us in circles to avoid having us freed by the advancing British and Americans on one side, and the Russians on the other." After several days' marching, the prisoners ended up at another camp, Stalag IXC, at Bad Sulza. The sounds of fighting could now clearly be heard. When German guards ordered the British on again, they refused to move. The Germans threatened to shoot them.

"The prisoners held their ground and glared in defiance," Prouse remembered. "For a moment there was an ominous silence—suddenly broken by the unmistakable sound of approaching tanks. We knew this was our salvation and let out a thunderous cheer. The Germans took to their heels—rushing out of the main gate and disappearing in full flight."

The tanks of General George Patton's US Third Army arrived at the camp a few minutes later.

For the POWs, liberation by the American and British forces was a joyous occasion—but the arrival of the Red Army sometimes provoked unease. The transfer of prisoners in the recently liberated camps was a source of administrative tension between the Western Allies and Russia. And yet, the experience of liberation itself often brought East and West closer together. Soviet lieutenant Vasily Bezugly of the 144th Rifle Division never forgot freeing American and British POWs from Stalag Luft I, near the town of Barth on Germany's Baltic coast. "It was a very moving occasion," Bezugly said. "We shared rations, exchanged addresses—we even taught the POWs to sing our favorite war-time song, 'Katyusha.'" Bezugly and his comrades, masters of the larger-than-life gesture, rounded up several hundred cows and herded them into the camp in Wild West fashion for the hungry inmates to slaughter and eat.

The sheer number of "Displaced Persons" was overwhelming. By the end of March 1945 it had been reckoned at 350,000. On April 7 the figure had increased to 600,000. On April 16 it was estimated at 1,072,000; by early May the figure had nearly doubled to 2,002,000. There were fears that the organization put in place by the Allies, the United Nations Relief and Rehabilitation Administration (UNRRA), would simply be unable to cope.

UNRRA was struggling over issues of budget, bureaucratic inefficiency and the failure of its director general, Herbert Lehman, to get a grip of the situation. In September 1944 the British Foreign Office had warned: "Lehman has never shown a proper understanding of what is required by his organization, and as result UNRRA has not yet been put 'on the map.'" And yet, it was all there really was. In February 1945 General Eisenhower had signed an agreement with UNRRA to provide 450 teams to look after displaced persons in Germany. Whether it could cope with the influx remained to be seen.

Food supply officer Janet Finlayson remembered the assembly of Team 158 at Joux-la-Ville in France in late April 1945. It was a truly international gathering. The director—who was in charge of the team—was Dutch, the doctor, supply officer and nurse were French, the welfare officer Belgian. They drove through France and Belgium and into Germany in early May, through scenes of rubble and devastation, to a displaced persons camp at Minden.

Organization was chaotic. "We had no idea of who the Displaced Persons were, how many of them we were dealing with and where they went afterward," Finlayson acknowledged. "They tended to sort themselves out by nationality and eventually housing blocks were allocated on that basis. They knew where accommodation could be had and where the food was supplied. It was one meal a day—whatever was available. There was no way of checking who had eaten or for that matter who had eaten twice."

Kathryn Hulme remembered the displaced persons camp at Wildflecken. "In this camp," Hulme wrote, "our UNRRA team learned what it really meant to be displaced, to have been removed—abruptly and totally—from your homeland, not by the hand of God but by a human conqueror." Virtually everyone in the camp was Polish, and 1,428 of them were under twelve years old.

Displaced persons—who had often endured terrible hardship in an alien environment—suffered a range of emotional and psychological problems. These had been hard to anticipate, as an UNRRA report acknowledged:

"Implicit in our planning for care and control was the assumption that these individuals would be tractable, grateful and powerless after their domination under German slave labor policies," the report began. "They were none of these things. Their intractability took the form of what was repeatedly referred to by officers in contact with them as 'Liberation Complex.' This involved revenge, hunger and exaltation."

This was a state of mind without any inhibition. Captain John MacAuslan encountered recently freed Russians at Neustadt. "They were looting and burning the town—it was chaos." The report continued: "These qualities combined to make DPs, when newly liberated, a problem as to behavior and conduct, as well as for care, feeding, disinfection, registration and repatriation."

Marta Korwin, a Polish social worker attached to one team, said of the DPs she had encountered:

During their captivity, in conditions that were always extremely hard, and often sordid and horrible, they would counterbalance this reality by calling up daydreams of a past life. They became almost certain that the moment they were liberated they would find themselves in the same happy, beautiful world that they had known before the war. All past difficulties would be forgotten, freedom would take them back to a place where nothing had ever gone wrong.

But when liberation came, these people would be herded into camps and confronted by a reality that showed them "the ruin that had overtaken the world in the war years, that their hopes for a better future had been destroyed—and gave them time to reflect on it." Korwin noticed that for many, destroying things became a way of expressing their rage at what had happened to them: "Russians, especially, took special pleasure in ruining things and breaking them. On the first morning I went through part of the factory [adjoining the displaced persons' assembly center] filled with expensive machinery and was shocked when I saw a number of Russians smashing with meticulous precision one machine after another."

And yet, Korwin asked, "Could anyone be surprised by the license found in the camps, the escape into unruly behavior, drink or sex?" She added: "Fear of the future and the desire for revenge were the underlying factors responsible for most of the unbalanced behavior in the Displaced Persons that we encountered." Korwin became aware of their fragile state of mind, that they had to be handled very carefully if their cooperation was required, for example in keeping their living quarters clean. "It took much more time to convince people that things should be done in a certain way," she said, "but if we persisted, with sensitivity, it was worth the effort—we found we were working with friendly and helpful human beings again."

UNRRA was venturing into uncharted territory—with a host of issues thrown up by an entirely novel situation. And yet there was real optimism nonetheless. British relief worker Francesca Wilson, on her way to Germany, said: "It began to dawn on me what a great experiment UNRRA was—the first international body to try and do something concrete and constructive."

A remarkable example of the urge to do something "concrete and constructive" was found in Allied efforts to relieve famine in the Netherlands. By early April 1945 the 1st Canadian Army, part of Field Marshal Montgomery's 21st Army Group, had pushed the German occupiers under General Johannes Blaskowitz back into western Holland. These forces were now cut off from the rest of the Wehrmacht but their position could be strongly defended and flooding used as a weapon against the Allies.

On April 9 the British war cabinet focused on the famine in Holland. It was agreed it would be too dangerous to send the army into the western part of the country still held by the Germans—the fighting would only create further chaos and hardship. But they could not simply stand by while this tragedy was played out; 21 million people stood on the brink of starvation and many of them were already dying of hunger.

Field Marshal Montgomery—in the midst of his military build-up to cross the Rhine—had nevertheless allocated two divisions for feeding the Dutch people. He was also stockpiling rations for airborne food drops. The initial plan was to approach the German administration in Holland headed by Reich Commissar Arthur Seyss-Inquart, via Switzerland, and see whether food could be brought in via the Red Cross. Winston Churchill commented bluntly: "If they refuse, we shall hold all German troops left in Holland responsible for this."

On April 16 Seyss-Inquart responded. He made it clear that German forces would defend themselves as long as their government remained in place. And he added that if they were attacked, they were quite prepared to blow up the dikes and flood the land between themselves and the Allied forces. But Seyss-Inquart also made it clear that the administration was interested in allowing the Red Cross to bring in food, and also in pursuing a possible ceasefire or truce to enable this to happen. Seyss-Inquart was a devoted Nazi now looking to save his own skin through separate negotiations with the Allies. But his proposal could save lives.

Churchill and the Combined Chiefs of Staff now brought in the Americans and the Russians. It was not an easy decision to allow a truce, yet all parties agreed that negotiations should continue—and at the end of April a deal was hammered out. The Allies would halt military operations in occupied Holland. In return, the Germans would open up the country to immediate

The spell breaks: the Nazi eagle and swastika above the damaged grandstand of their rally site at Nuremberg.

East meets West: Lieutenants William Robertson and Alexander Sylvashko embrace at Torgau on the Elbe (April 25, 1945).

US infantrymen move down a street in Waldenburg, south-central Germany, April 1945.

Berlin falls to the Red Army: Marshal Georgi Zhukov on the steps of the Reichstag, May 2.

British tanks race toward Lübeck, May 2.

The horror: a sign erected by British forces outside
Bergen–Belsen concentration camp, May 1945.

The British arrive at Hamburg: a Cromwell tank
guards the bridge over the Elbe.

German soldiers—some using horse-drawn transport—make their
way toward British forces to surrender.

British and Russian troops meet at Wismar, May 3.

A Russian tanker and British sapper drink to victory.

Monty's triumph: the British field marshal receives the
German delegation at Lüneburg Heath, May 3.

A day later the formal surrender of Denmark, Holland and northwestern
Germany is signed in Montgomery's tent.

The American field command—seated (*left to right*) are Generals William Simpson, George Patton, Carl Spaatz, Dwight Eisenhower, Omar Bradley, Courtney Hodges and Leonard Gerow. Standing (*center*) is Eisenhower's chief of staff, General Walter Bedell Smith.

High-ranking American and Russian officers meet on the Elbe, May 5 (from the Soviet Third Guards Tank Corps and the US Third Army).

Confronting the truth: a German woman walks past bodies of murdered slave
workers exhumed by US troops near Nammering, Germany.

Prisoners of Mauthausen concentration camp (Austria) liberated by US soldiers on May 5.

The anguish: refugees on the road trying to return home.

"Displaced Persons"—one of the great humanitarian challenges faced by the Allies.

"Calling all Czechs!" Barricades go up in Prague at the beginning of the uprising, May 5.

US troops enter western Czechoslovakia, May 6.

Operation Manna: loading supplies to be airdropped to the starving Dutch population.

Unlikely rescuers: troops from the First Division Russian Liberation Army
(Vlasov Army) arrive outside the Militia HQ, Prague, May 6.

Field Marshal Montgomery meets his Russian counterpart, Field Marshal Rokossovsky, at Wismar on the Baltic.

General Alfred Jodl signs the first unconditional surrender at SHAEF headquarters, Rheims, on May 7.

"False alarms"—a special edition of *Stars and Stripes* prematurely announces "Germany Quits" on May 7.

VE-Day in London, May 8: a huge crowd gathers at Whitehall to hear Churchill's speech.

"The German war is . . . at an end": Churchill broadcasts to the nation.

"The day of death": SS units fight for the center of Prague with Czech insurgents, May 8.

The second signing at Karlshorst: the German delegation now headed by Field Marshal Keitel.

The Allied delegation now headed by Russia's supreme commander, Georgi Zhukov.

Russian troops liberate Prague.

VE-Day in Moscow, May 9.

The celebratory
fireworks that night.

food convoys by land, sea and air. To his great credit, General Eisenhower began the airdrops immediately. The British drops were codenamed Operation Manna; the American, Operation Chowhound.

These were two very different names—one emotionally engaged but invoking a higher cause, the other seeking to disengage from horror through humor. On April 25, 1945, Denis Thompson was in the rear gun turret of a Lancaster when his RAF unit, 170 Squadron, was sent to bomb the Berchtesgaden. Now he was involved in Operation Manna, dropping food supplies to the Dutch in the German-occupied zone of Holland. Denis and his fellow crewmen dropped off supplies over Vlaardingen:

"People were waving and shouting. The nurses were lying on the sloping roof of the hospital, waving and cheering us as we flew over. We were only about 600 feet in the air, and supplies were dropped in crates with no parachutes. People ran to gather the food—I was really worried a crate would land on their heads."

Between the end of April and May 7 British aircraft flew 3,928 sorties over Holland, delivering a total of 6,680 tons of food. The Americans flew a further 2,268 sorties, delivering another 4,000 tons.

It was an extraordinary experience for British and American bomber crews used to unleashing weapons of destruction as part of the Allied war strategy. They now knew that they were saving lives instead of ending them. Bob Upcott of RAF 115th Squadron recalled: "All our bombers were flying at low altitude so as not to damage the food parcels. On one of our Manna missions we flew over a hospital on our way back from the drop zone. We saw a nurse there unfold the largest Union Jack we had ever seen. It was a remarkable gesture—and a brave one. German soldiers looked on in bemusement."

Peace was signed in Holland on May 5. A day later, Captain Tom Stafford of the US 87th Infantry Division helped bring about a mass surrender of Wehrmacht and SS troops in southwest Germany, close to the border with Czechoslovakia. Stafford remembered casually drinking wine on the veranda of a beautiful house used as a divisional headquarters while German generals debated the protocol of surrender. One was unhappy to be negotiating with a young American captain. "I have been fighting this war since D-Day,"

Stafford said. "I have been a German officer for 30 years," the opposing major general replied. Both American and Russian troops were now in Czechoslovakia and Stafford pointed out that if the surrender was given immediately the Germans could avoid being captured by the Red Army. That carried the argument.

Colonel Jerry Tax of the US 71st Infantry Division would never forget the surrender that occurred in Wels in Austria:

"Drifting down into the town's great square, on foot, on hands and knees, came former inmates of Gunskirchen Camp," Tax recalled.

The news of our coming had reached the camp that morning—and all those who could move were en route to gaze upon their liberators. No more than one in a hundred walked upright; dozens were dragged into town on carts and others shuffled along, leaning on sticks, makeshift crutches and each other. Their garments came out of a wild costumier's hallucination: tattered uniforms that had been worn twenty-four hours a day for three or four years to wrappings of rags. None, obviously, had been washed in all that time. Lice and vermin of every sort crawled over their misshapen, emaciated bodies.

The hands that clutched at what scraps of food and candy we distributed—until we had no more—were skin and bone and blue-black nail. Skin and bone, filthy rags and vermin, row on row, endless, filling the square. And not a sound. Not one human sound came from these thousands of throats. Perhaps they hadn't the strength to speak, even in gratitude. Perhaps words of thanks were long-forgotten— forgotten under the lash and the pistol butt, the abysmal degradation.

It would be fine and thrilling to say that despite their pitiful condition, despite their rags, the years of torture, abject slavery and starvation, hope and joy shone from the eyes of these men. But it wasn't so. To be sure, their eyes were far from blank—but there was no joy or hope in them. These were not the eyes of men set free. Perhaps the gigantic, impossible fact of liberation was just too big, too miraculous to grasp. Perhaps, in their incredibly weakened physical condition, it was too big a shock to be assimilated. Whatever the reason, they were simply broken, beaten men—row upon row of them.

And in their eyes you read the story of the past four or five years. You didn't have to stare in helpless fascination at one of these walking skeletons to learn what systematic starvation can do to a man's body. From the depth of his soul that hunger came to you, from his eyes—blinding, insatiable hunger. Would it ever leave them?

For hours it seemed that we stared out on this sea of human misery. There was little that we could say and less we could do after all our food, candy and cigarettes were gone. But suddenly, we began to feel that something was happening out of our sight. The crowd before us had started to move toward one side of the square. And then, faintly at first, we heard the rhythmic step of marching soldiers echoing on the cobblestones. From one of the side streets leading into the square a column of German troops appeared and began filing into it. They were, we supposed, the garrisons who had surrendered earlier in the day. As they came in, they lined up in regular ranks in the space so recently left vacant, hundreds upon hundreds of them.

On one side of the square, in a neat, orderly formation, stood the would-be Herrenvolk. Their smart gray uniforms were pressed; chubby pink cheeks and an occasional paunch left no doubt they had fed well on their loot and what they could extract from the slave labor of their farms. In their eyes was still the arrogance of the conqueror.

Facing them, in disorder, in indescribable disarray, standing up in oxcarts, lying on their bellies, leaning on each other, were the free men of Russia, France, Poland and the Balkans . . . a heterogeneous collection of skin, bone and filth. About twenty yards separated the two groups—twenty yards and the whole world. And the square was as still as a tomb.

For half an hour—that dragged on interminably—the two groups stood there, immobile. Not a voice was raised, not a fist shaken—not a stir. Our Military Police were busy arranging for the Germans to be taken into captivity. That was all.

And yet I could have sworn something was taking place out there. I climbed out of the truck and walked slowly through the crowd. Was it my imagination? Was it wishful thinking? To this day I cannot answer these questions. But I saw, or thought I saw in those eyes, the faintest glimmer of what I had vainly looked for before. Perhaps the shock was wearing off. As they looked upon the Germans, waiting to be led away, a huge, impossible truth seemed to be dawning in their consciousness.

They had survived and to some extent would recover. The well-fed Germans had suffered a moral defeat and desolation from which there would be no return.

"Within another hour the square was empty. The Germans had been taken away. Every wheeled vehicle within miles had been commandeered to take the sick and starving ex-prisoners to places where they could be fed and cared for."

Compassion had awoken. "And that night—for the first time in the war—I began to sense the spirit of a new Europe coming into being."

8

RHEIMS

At Rheims, the weather on May 5 was poor. General Dwight Eisenhower's naval aide, Captain Harry Butcher, began to draw up contingency plans in case the German delegation had to be diverted to another airfield. Supreme Allied Headquarters was engaged in a waiting game. Eisenhower's driver, Kay Summersby, caught the atmosphere:

"There wasn't much work being done in our red schoolhouse when I arrived the following morning. Most of us sat around talking about the surrender ceremony . . . Just before noon we learned that the German party's plane had been diverted by bad weather and had landed at Brussels. They would come on to Rheims by car, arriving about five o'clock."

The place chosen for the surrender was the "War Room," where Eisenhower normally met with his top commanders and staff. Captain Butcher set the scene:

The room is about thirty feet square and has pale blue walls covered with battle maps showing the disposition of forces on all fronts. There are charts showing the current day's air operations, casualty lists, records of supplies landed, railway and communications systems and today's, tomorrow's and the next day's weather. On one wall there was a thermometer, mounted on a background of swastikas, showing the mounting thousands of German prisoners now in allied hands.

Now a mass of photographers had arrived and were waiting expectantly. But the arrival of the German delegation proved to be an anti-climax. Admiral Georg von Friedeburg claimed he had authority only to discuss terms and not to sign a final surrender document, adding that he had no means of communicating directly with Dönitz back in Flensburg.

The surrender document itself had been drawn up at speed—and purposely kept simple. John Counsell, serving in SHAEF's Historical Section, had been summoned to a meeting with General Bull, the American chief of operations, two days earlier. Counsell suggested that the existing Instrument of Surrender—drawn up after months of consultation by a committee representing Britain, America and Russia—not be used, as it existed only in draft form, and did not include alterations suggested by France. Instead he proposed that a simple act be drawn up to bring about an end to the fighting. The articles that followed were largely copied from the terms of surrender of the German armies in Italy. Counsell named it the "Act of Military Surrender." The Russians had never seen it before.

Now these terms were officially adopted by Allied Supreme Command. This was a surprising choice. General Walter Bedell Smith—in a response to the US State Department—claimed to have forgotten about the existence of the earlier draft surrender. The Allied Supreme Command was focusing on bringing about a surrender on the Western and Eastern Fronts as quickly as possible. When Friedeburg claimed he did not have the power to sign, Eisenhower's chief of staff, General Bedell Smith, suspected delaying tactics and was blunt:

"The Germans are our enemies and will remain our enemies until the surrender," he told Von Friedeburg, adding that "either he should straight away receive from Dönitz full and complete authority to make an unconditional surrender or someone else should be sent, a commander-in-chief, who held the necessary power to do so." A communication link was eventually raised to Flensburg and the assembled newsmen were told there would be a postponement.

A SHAEF report summarized the situation as follows:

Admiral Friedeburg arrived at Supreme Headquarters at 17:30 hours this evening. The stated object of his journey was to clarify a number of points. He was told that nothing less than unconditional surrender was acceptable. He replied that he had no power to sign any document of surrender.

The hopelessness of the German military situation was pointed out to him and he was urged to consider whether he should not obtain authority to sign. Admiral Friedeburg was then given the act of military surrender to study and he is now drafting a cable to Admiral Dönitz which we believe contains the suggestion that he should receive authorization to sign.

These diplomatic reports provide a vital backdrop to events—and are essential for an understanding of what was to happen over the surrender ceremony. This one concluded: "General Susloparov is being kept in touch."

Major General Ivan Susloparov, the commander of the Soviet liaison mission with the Allied Expeditionary Force and French government, was to play an important role in the surrender ceremony. Susloparov had fought with the Bolsheviks in the Russian civil war and graduated from the Kiev Military School in 1925 and the Artillery Section of the Dzherzhinsky Academy in 1938. The following year he was appointed Soviet military attaché in Paris, in charge of the Russian intelligence network in western Europe. After Germany's invasion of Russia he served as artillery commander of the Soviet 10th Army and in the summer of 1944, after the liberation of Paris, was transferred to the French capital as chief of the Soviet mission there.

George Bailey, who served in the SHAEF intelligence section at Rheims, recalled of Susloparov: "He was a major general of artillery and he talked a fine bombardment. And he did not neglect to lob in some politics:

'The communist system comes down to this—if you work well, you eat well.' Susloparov had obviously worked very well: he was a huge, round-faced, jovial man. In fact, he was one of the few really big Russian generals I have met."

Bailey first got to know Susloparov during discussions with the German occupation force in western Holland. A truce had come into effect—to which the Soviet Union had agreed—in order to allow Allied food drops to the starving Dutch population. Negotiations were carried out between the Nazi high commissioner, Arthur von Seyss-Inquart, and General Walter Bedell Smith, with Susloparov, General François Sevez (deputy chief of staff of the French army) and Prince Bernhard of the Netherlands. Bailey remembered that whenever Bernhard stepped out of the church building used for these proceedings, the assembled townsmen—wearing orange streamers, ribbons and sashes—would strike up the Dutch national anthem.

The main discussions were between Bedell Smith and Seyss-Inquart, although during the breaks Prince Bernhard took a lively interest in the Russian and, with Bailey acting as interpreter, quizzed him about the Soviet partisan movement. Bernhard grew quite animated and told Susloparov he would put his own plane at the Red Army's disposal to assist in supply drops. All Russian lands had long since been liberated from the Germans, but a bemused Susloparov thanked him nonetheless, expressing the view that the partisan movement was well organized and would be able to take care of itself. When the prince fled inside to escape another rendition of the national anthem, Susloparov turned to Bailey and said: "What's up with him—the war's almost over!"

From May 5, Bailey would carry messages from Bedell Smith, in SHAEF's red schoolhouse HQ, to Susloparov at the nearby Hôtel Lion d'Or. Eisenhower was determined that the German surrender would be unconditional—and wanted to reassure Russia that no partial surrender would ever be considered. Bailey recalled:

> Susloparov was in effect an intermediary in these matters—he could do nothing more than send and receive signals to and from Moscow on the radio transmitter the Russians always carried around with

them. Whenever I appeared at the Lion d'Or with questions or answers for Susloparov, he would begin by saying: "I have just sent a telegram to Moscow." But to the best of my recollection, he never once said that he had received a message from Moscow. I began to think that the receiver had broken down and that he was too proud to admit it.

Initially, all had seemed well with Susloparov's mandate. Eisenhower had kept General Antonov, chief of staff of the Soviet High Command, fully informed of developments. On May 4 he had briefed Antonov on the German surrender at Lüneburg Heath. He had also told him that representatives of Admiral Dönitz were proceeding to his headquarters the following day (the 5th) to arrange further surrenders. Eisenhower said he intended to inform the German delegation that surrenders on the Eastern and Western Fronts were to be made simultaneously, and asked, as a matter of urgency, whether this was satisfactory to the Russian High Command.

Eisenhower added that he felt it best if these happened as quickly as possible, in the interest of saving lives, but he would wait for a response from the Soviet High Command before proceeding with negotiations. He also said that Major General Susloparov would be invited to attend and if the Russians would like to send other representatives to his headquarters, fully empowered to act for them, he would be most happy to receive them.

General Antonov received this message—orally and in writing—late on May 4 and he responded immediately—stating shortly after midnight that Eisenhower's plan was in principle acceptable. He asked that should Dönitz refuse to accept the condition of a simultaneous German surrender on Western and Russian fronts, negotiations should be broken off. He also authorized Major General Susloparov to participate in the surrender negotiations, since there would not be time to send alternative representatives.

While there was a lull in surrender negotiations at Rheims, at Breslau General Hermann Niehoff had now resolved to give up the city to the Red Army. He had met with a group of Breslau's clergy—the Catholic bishop, Joseph Ferche, and his canon, Joseph Kramer, along with two Protestants, Joachim Konrad and Ernst Hornig. Niehoff and two of his staff officers received the delegation in the basement of the municipal library, which had been transformed into their army headquarters. Ferche introduced his colleagues and then addressed Niehoff directly.

"Herr General, we do not have the right to intervene in your decisions. But we regard it as our duty, before God and before our people, to ask you whether you can still take responsibility for continuing the struggle." Protestant clergyman Ernst Hornig then spoke. "The plight of the city's civilians is pitiful," he said. "Every day I am asked if everyone is supposed to die beneath the bombs and flames. And for what? Every day faith in the Party is waning. People no longer see any sense in defending Breslau. Perhaps in a few days they will no longer follow orders. In these circumstances, can you answer to God for continuing to defend the city?"

There was silence in the bunker. Niehoff lowered his head for a full minute. It was as if a spell was being broken. Then he looked up at the clergymen. "Your concerns are my concerns," he said.

The following day Niehoff broke off all telephone links with Field Marshal Schörner. Gauleiter [Regional Party Leader] Karl Hanke stormed into his command post and threatened to arrest him. Niehoff looked around at his soldiers and then said slowly: "If anyone is going to do any arresting, Gauleiter, it will be me." There was a long silence and Hanke, the party bully who had executed thousands of civilians for desertion, seemed to deflate before the general's eyes. "Forgive my threat," Hanke said eventually, "it was not meant as such. But what should I do?" Niehoff regarded him coldly: "Take your own life," he suggested. Hanke did not have the courage. He would flee the city that night by plane.

On May 6 General Niehoff summoned his staff. "It is time to end the struggle," he began.

> I have called you together for a final roll-call. What has been achieved by you, by our men and the civilian population, needs no words. One day history will pass judgment.
>
> Hitler is dead. Berlin has fallen. The eastern and western allies have shaken hands in the heart of Germany. There is no longer any reason to continue the struggle for Breslau. Any further sacrifice is a

crime. I have decided to end the fighting and offer to surrender the city and the garrison to the enemy on honorable terms. We have fired our last round. We have done our duty.

Every man agreed except Otto Herzog, commander of the *Volkssturm* and an inveterate Nazi. "In a few weeks the western allies and the Soviet Union will be at war, and the German army will be needed again," he exclaimed to Niehoff as he left the room. Herzog could not countenance surrender to the Red Army. An hour later he had shot himself.

At 3:00 p.m. on May 6 Niehoff received two Soviet negotiators in his command post. The discussions were amicable. Unsure whether they had proper authority to draw up surrender terms, he decided to seek out his opposite number, the Soviet commander of the 6th Army, General Vladimir Gluzdovski.

Hermann Niehoff was driven under Red Army escort to the southwestern edge of the city. Here, in the Villa Colonia, a smart detached house, Gluzdovski had made his headquarters. Staff officers stood smartly to attention as the German general passed them. He was shown into a room where a number of Soviet officers were standing around a large table, Gluzdovski among them. An orderly brought in a tray of glasses and schnapps, and Gluzdovski invited the German to drink. Niehoff refused. Gluzdovski looked at him quizzically, wondering whether Niehoff thought it was poisoned. The distrust between the two sides was deeply entrenched. He took the glass and drained it. Niehoff nodded and then emptied the fresh glass offered to him. Everyone smiled.

Gluzdovski's deputy, General Panov, brought in articles of surrender. The sick would receive medical assistance. Civilians would be protected. Soldiers would be fed, treated properly and allowed to keep personal possessions. The terms were reasonable. Niehoff looked through them and then signed. It was 6:00 p.m.

The terms were certainly reasonable, and may have been genuinely offered, but they were not kept. Red Army soldiers marched into Breslau on May 7 and the German garrison trudged out in the opposite direction. Most Wehrmacht soldiers were relieved of all their property. That night rapes began in the city. And yet the alternative—to carry on fighting—would have caused even more suffering.

At Rheims, Sunday, May 6, began uneventfully. In the afternoon Bedell Smith supervised the layout of microphones and cameras in the "War Room"—everything was kept simple. Bedell Smith and Susloparov haggled over two points in the surrender treaty: the definition of "property," the Russians plumping for the widest possible interpretation with an eye to reparations, and the question of whether Susloparov was able or could be empowered by Moscow to sign the articles on behalf of the Soviet High Command. George Bailey said: "The first point was settled pretty much in the Russians' favor, the second, to the best of my knowledge, was never cleared up."

By the 6th of May General Antonov had been fully informed of the course of the previous day's negotiations, in particular that General Eisenhower had flatly rejected Friedeburg's offer to surrender only the remaining German forces on the Western Front. That day, two documents were sent to Antonov. The first, entitled "An Agreement Between the Allied High Commands and German Emissaries," specified that the Germans were to appear at a time and place to be designated to sign an unconditional surrender. The second, named "Act of Military Surrender," gave the terms to be used for the surrender, providing for a simultaneous surrender on both Eastern and Western Fronts.

Eisenhower's behavior was both transparent and correct. Yet it contained a number of assumptions. The first was that—in the interests of speed and saving lives—the location of the surrender at the Supreme Allied Headquarters in Rheims would be acceptable to the Soviets. The second was that the text of the agreement, which the Russians had never seen before and had had no part in drawing up, would also be acceptable. The third was that as Major General Susloparov had been permitted to represent the Soviet High Command in the negotiations leading up to the surrender, it would also be permissible for him to sign for the Soviet Union in the actual ceremony itself. These were made in good faith—but would prove to be seriously flawed.

At 6:00 p.m. Dönitz's new emissary, General Alfred Jodl, chief of staff of the German armed forces, arrived at Supreme Headquarters.

That evening, a ninety-minute conference took place between the German delegation and Bedell Smith; then a meeting between Bedell Smith and Eisenhower, followed by further consultations with the Russian representative at Rheims, Major General Susloparov. Eisenhower remained firm that he would accept nothing less than a general capitulation. At 9:00 p.m. the Germans pleaded for another forty-eight hours to make up their minds. Eisenhower was having none of it. "You tell them," he ordered General Strong, his senior British staff officer, "that forty-eight hours from midnight tonight I will close my lines on the Western Front so no more Germans can get through, whether they sign or not." He then abruptly left the room.

General Eisenhower summarized the standoff in an important document:

> General Jodl appeared at my headquarters this evening and together with Admiral Friedeburg continued negotiating with my chief of staff and his assistants. It was obvious from the beginning of the discussion that the Germans are stalling for time, their purpose being to evacuate the largest number of German soldiers and civilians from the Russian front to within our lines.
>
> They continued the effort to surrender this front separately, even stating that no matter what my answer was, they were going to order all German forces remaining on the western front to cease firing and to refuse to fire against either British or American troops. They asked for a meeting on Tuesday morning [the 8th] for signing final surrender terms with a 48 hour interval thereafter in order to get the necessary instructions to all their outlying units. Their actual purpose was merely to gain time.
>
> I finally had to inform them that I would break off all negotiations and seal the western front, preventing by force any further westward movement of German soldiers and civilians unless they agreed to my terms of surrender. When faced with this ultimatum they immediately drafted a telegram to Dönitz asking for authority to make a full and complete surrender, but specifying that the actual fighting would cease 48 hours after the time of signing.
>
> Since this solution obviously placed the decision as to when the

fighting would cease in the hands of the Germans I refused to accept it and stated that the fighting would have to cease on both fronts in 48 hours from midnight tonight or I would carry out my threat. I repeat that their purpose is to continue to make a front against the Russians for as long as they possibly can, in order to evacuate the maximum numbers of Germans into our lines.

In any event, for all practical purposes fighting will cease almost immediately on this front, for the reason that with minor exceptions my troops are on the line I have directed them to occupy.

Eisenhower was clear, cogent and on top of his brief. He was going to have no nonsense from the Germans and they understood that. Count Schwerin von Krosigk said simply: "With our surrender to Montgomery we were able to call it a truce and get away with it. Those tactics didn't work with Eisenhower."

Finally, a suggestion was made that would have preserved a united VE-Day for all members of the Grand Alliance: "If the arrangement goes through as above indicated, I suggest that a proclamation should be made on Tuesday by the government naming Wednesday, May 9th as VE Day . . . We hope to have a formal signing by tomorrow."

Events, however, were to intervene. At 9:00 p.m that evening, when Bailey made another visit to the Lion d'Or, Susloparov had still not received an answer from Moscow to his request for empowerment.

The Germans realized the delaying tactics were not working. Jodl cabled Dönitz: "General Eisenhower insists we sign today . . . I see no alternative—it is either chaos or signature. I ask you to confirm to me immediately by wireless that I have full powers to sign capitulation."

At 1:30 a.m. on May 7 all was at last ready. A pool of seventeen pressmen had been chosen to cover the proceedings. General Bedell Smith would preside over the event—Eisenhower wished to remain aloof from the German delegation. George Bailey remembered: "I was the duty officer for General Bedell Smith that night. The long-awaited signal from Dönitz's headquarters had come in empowering Jodl to sign. But I was filled with apprehension because I was sure that Susloparov had still not heard from Moscow, and would be unable to sign, and was equally sure that the job of producing him in the War Room would fall to me. It did not. To my astonishment, in half an hour all the signatories—including Susloparov—were assembled in front of me."

Captain Butcher remembered how matter-of-fact everything was: "Major General Kenneth Strong placed the documents for signature in front of General Bedell Smith . . . Smith spoke briefly to the Germans (interpreted by Strong). It was merely that the surrender documents awaited signature. Were they ready and prepared to sign? Jodl indicated assent with a slight nod."

The signatories were General Jodl "on behalf of the German High Command," General Bedell Smith "on behalf of the commander of the Allied Expeditionary Force" and Major General Susloparov "on behalf of the Soviet High Command." Brigadier General François Sevez added his name as witness.

Butcher continued: "At the conclusion of the signing, General Jodl stood to attention, and said, in English: 'I want to say a word.' Then he lapsed into German, later translated as:

"With this signature the German people and the German armed forces are for better or worse delivered into the victor's hands. In this war, which has lasted more than five years, both have achieved and suffered more than perhaps any other people in the world. In this hour I can only express the hope that the victor will treat them with generosity."

The phrase "later translated" is significant, as George Bailey acknowledged:

> Jodl's speech was left in the air. Nobody translated his words or even moved to inquire whether a translation was desired. Major General Oxenius, Jodl's adjutant, who had been a schoolteacher in Wales before the war, did not do so: neither did General Strong, neither did George Reinhardt, the American interpreter in German, neither did I. For my part, the statement struck me as somehow improper, particularly the reference to the sufferings and achievements of the German armed forces. These, as the instruments of the Nazis, had inflicted and caused untellable suffering on hundreds of millions of non-Germans.

With the official ceremony over, General Eisenhower spoke briefly and privately to the German in his office. The supreme commander related:

"After the necessary papers had been signed . . . General Jodl was brought to my room. I asked him through the interpreter if he thoroughly understood all the provisions of the document he had signed. He said that he did. I told him: 'You will, officially and personally, be held responsible if the terms of this surrender are violated. That is all.' He saluted and left."

George Bailey recalled:

This was the only time I ever saw Eisenhower. Perhaps because of the drama and significance of the event, I experienced a kind of optical illusion. Eisenhower was seated at a table in an alcove, whose floor was a step higher than that of the room. He appeared to be of gigantic stature. The impression of massive size was increased when he turned his head and shoulders to face Jodl, who stood forward on the lower floor like a truant schoolboy about to be disciplined.

Eisenhower posed for photographers, holding up the signing pens in a "V for Victory." He then dictated a cable to the Combined Chiefs of Staff in the simple and direct manner that came naturally to him: "The mission of this allied force was fulfilled at 0241 local time, May 7, 1945." Joan Bernard, one of the junior staff at Allied Command, said: "It was the deliberate use of understatement that made the announcement so powerful." However, the drama of the day was just beginning.

George Bailey wondered about Susloparov and whether he had authority to sign. He speculated that "roused early in the morning by the call of history, and finding himself still without a reply from Moscow, he was overcome by the magnitude of the moment and decided to sign on the strength of his accreditation as the chief Soviet representative to SHAEF." Major General Susloparov was in an impossible situation. If he did not sign, he would be allowing Germany to make peace with Britain, America and France while leaving the Soviet Union at war. Importantly, he insisted on the insertion of a clause stating that a new surrender ceremony could take place elsewhere, as follow-up, if any of the Allies requested it.

Early on May 7 at Breslau, the surrender complete, German general Hermann Niehoff was invited to join his Soviet counterpart at the Villa Colonia in a banquet. "A sliding door was suddenly opened," Niehoff recalled, "flanked by two Red Army soldiers dressed in white. A decorated table filled the room—candles cast light on mountains of cold dishes, seafood, meat pies and bottles of vodka everywhere. The victor wanted to celebrate—and I was politely asked to join him."

Niehoff was exhausted and the scene unfolding before him appeared quite surreal. The battle for Breslau had been savage and uncompromising. But the German sensed genuine Russian respect for the way his soldiers had fought. Even in this most fanatical of wars, common ground between opposing soldiers could still sometimes be forged.

"Herr General, please have the best seat." Niehoff was placed next to Gluzdovski, flanked by an interpreter. The Soviet commander proposed a toast. "The fight is over. To the heroism of the Breslau garrison." Niehoff, inculcated with Nazi doctrine of a race war against the inferior Slavs, wondered whether he was dreaming.

At Rheims, it was now a question of timing. The formal announcement of the surrender would be dependent on an agreement jointly reached by the heads of the Grand Alliance, Truman, Churchill and Stalin.

But that morning it was clear something was very wrong. Kay Summersby remembered:

It was the worst day I ever put in at the Supreme Commander's office. One glance at the messages awaiting the General [Eisenhower] indicated that there would be no parties that day. Everything was in a muddle. One message stated that the Germans in Czechoslovakia refused to surrender to the Russians opposite their lines . . . A second message noted that the German radio had announced the Nazis had made a separate peace with the Western allies, not with the Russians. The latter not only complained bitterly at this report, but advised SHAEF they no longer felt General Susloparov had been an acceptable Soviet representative at the Rheims ceremony.

Around 3:00 p.m. the final blow fell. Beetle [Bedell Smith] roared into the office like a madman: Ed Kennedy of the Associated Press had smuggled into America a story of the Rheims surrender. The "scoop" already hummed over AP wires in the United States, leaving a pack of angry correspondents in France, a group of very upset gentlemen in the Kremlin, 10 Downing Street and the White House—and a very irate Supreme Commander in Rheims . . .

The rest of May 7 was all like that. Even the Prime Minister added to the general chaos in our office by telephoning a total of eight times from London . . . We all went home that night agreeing it was the most harrowing day SHAEF ever experienced.

The response from the Soviet High Command to Eisenhower was robust—and also, to Supreme Allied Headquarters, surprising and shocking. They now made clear their opposition to any agreement with Dönitz. Unfortunately their letter—dispatched early on the morning of May 7—arrived after the surrender at Rheims was actually signed.

The Soviet chief of staff, General Antonov, stressed the following:

In spite of the negotiations being conducted with the German command for the unconditional surrender of their troops in the west and also on the eastern fronts, Admiral Dönitz is continuing his announcements over the radio, calling upon German troops to continue the war against Soviet forces on the one hand, and not to resist the allied forces in the west on the other.

Dönitz made such an announcement on May 5, the same day that General Eisenhower was conducting negotiations with Admiral Friedeburg on all fronts. Such conduct creates public opinion that Dönitz already has a separate truce in the west and is continuing the war in the east.

The task is not to give public opinion in Europe the chance to claim that there is a separate truce between the allies and the Germans.

You of course understand that such a truce would be a violation of our allied relationship.

As is known, something like a truce was permitted with our

consent in Holland with the purpose of saving the Dutch population from flooding—which the Germans threatened to carry out—and hunger. This was permitted as an exception to the rule in view of extenuating circumstances.

As far as the remaining sectors of the western and southern fronts are concerned, what has to happen here is the surrender of German troops giving themselves up as prisoners. Without exception, this is what is happening on all sectors of the eastern front.

Then the Russians turned to the copy of the surrender document that Eisenhower had forwarded—the one that had now been signed at Rheims. They proposed a number of changes.

The first concerned an unfortunate slip in the drafting of the Rheims document naming the place and time of surrender, when the phrase "the truce" was used. John Counsell, involved in the drafting of this, admitted: "The Russians reacted violently to the word 'truce' which had been used in the 'Agreement with German emissaries,' reading in to it confirmation of their suspicions that we were preparing to end hostilities at their expense."

This mistake had been subsequently noticed and corrected, but given Russian sensitivity on this issue, and the deliberate use of this tactic by Dönitz (claiming a truce was in existence in the West to continue the struggle in the East), it was extremely unfortunate that it had cropped up in the first place.

Then the Soviet Union made it clear that it wanted nothing to do with the Dönitz administration:

In the message of Admiral Friedeburg to Admiral Dönitz the words appear: "New government," "German government" and "Head of State." Of course, these words of Friedeburg in no way obligate us. However, in the interest of clarity, the Soviet command considers it necessary to state that it prefers to do business with the German High Command, and not with the German government, which in reality does not exist, which is recognized by no-one as a government and in the opinion of the Soviet command should not figure in our documents.

And importantly, it made clear it wanted to add a strengthening clause around the actual surrender of German troops. After "cease active operations," the Russians wanted to insert the following: "And completely disarm, handing over their arms and equipment to the local allied commander or officers indicated by the allied representatives."

This was no cosmetic change. The Russians did not trust the Germans or Dönitz. They envisaged German units "ceasing active operations" (i.e. no longer fighting against them) but continuing to retreat away from them and toward the British and Americans in the west. The new clause was designed to preempt this—and would cause trouble in the second surrender signing at Karlshorst.

Finally, in blunt terms, the Soviet High Command expressed its wish that the signing of the act of military surrender should take place in Berlin, where it would be represented by Marshal Zhukov.

Two factors had powerfully changed the atmosphere between the Western Allies and Russia. The first was the way the Dönitz regime had portrayed the surrender at Lüneburg Heath as a truce with the West to enable the war in the East to continue. Russia now feared that the Germans would not honor a full unconditional surrender and began to imagine—with the failure to disarm some Wehrmacht troops in northwest Germany and Holland—that there might be those in the West willing to support such an outcome. The reference to "a violation of our allied relationship" conveyed in the strongest possible terms the pain and indignation felt by the Soviet side.

The second was a failure to anticipate. General Dwight Eisenhower, the Allied supreme commander, was a brilliant operational planner and an absolutely fair and straightforward negotiator. These were great strengths—and men trusted him. Where he had slipped was in a failure of imagination. Preoccupied with ending the conflict as quickly as possible (and in a way that would be fair to the Russians) to save unnecessary casualties, he failed to perceive how important the symbolic termination of the war would be to the Soviet Union.

Having sacrificed some 27 million soldiers and civilians to defeat the Germans, every Soviet citizen would have wanted and expected the surrender to take place in Berlin and for Russia to be represented by its foremost commander, Marshal Zhukov. This was neither political machination nor pedantry. No other alternative would have been acceptable to any Russian.

This risk had already struck one of Eisenhower's staff. Liaison officer at SHAEF Colonel Richard Wilberforce had noted in his diary, as negotiations commenced at Lüneburg Heath:

> It was thought that the Germans opposing 21 Army Group were about to surrender and their emissaries were expected on bigger business. It wasn't known who would come or what powers they would have, so we provided for three contingencies: Firstly, for a total [unconditional] surrender: But how about the Russians—surely they would want the document signed in Berlin? Here they only have a miserable liaison officer, a General Susloparov.

When they learned that the signing had gone ahead, the Russians were deeply shocked and angry. General Sergei Shtemenko was on the Soviet High Command. He recalled meeting with General Antonov just after the news of the Rheims signing had reached Moscow. "The western allies have forced this on us," Antonov said. "They want the world to picture the Nazi surrender in front of them, with our country relegated to a supporting role." Soon both men were summoned to an emergency meeting at the Kremlin. It took place in the Soviet leader's study and the atmosphere was grim. Stalin was pacing the carpet, thinking aloud.

> The western allies have negotiated this directly with Dönitz, and no good will come of it. It looks like some sort of shady deal—not a proper surrender agreement. None of our leading commanders or government officials were present. We have suffered most from Hitler's aggression and made the greatest contribution to our common victory. Russia broke the back of the Fascist beast. And now—at the very end of the war—this happens. No good will come from this supposed "capitulation."

Stalin gathered himself. "The surrender of Nazi Germany will become an important historical fact. It should not take place in France—the territory of one of the 'winners'—but in the place where all the aggression came from, the capital of the Nazi state, Berlin." He turned to those in the room. "The agreement signed at Rheims cannot be undone—but we cannot and will not accept it as it stands."

The Soviet leader asked that a new signing be set up. The Rheims surrender had allowed for the ceremony to be repeated, but Stalin did not want to publicly recognize the agreement of May 7 at all. Instead, for him the Berlin surrender would be definitive. The Soviet Union would be represented by Marshal Zhukov for the Soviet High Command and Andrei Vyshinsky, deputy foreign minister, on behalf of the Russian government.

Stalin looked at General Antonov: "Can suitable premises be found for the unconditional surrender of Nazi Germany in Berlin?" he asked. "The center of the city is badly damaged," Antonov replied, "but much of the suburbs are reasonably intact. I am sure we will be able to find an appropriate building there." Zhukov was delegated to make the choice. He decided on a military engineering school in one of Berlin's eastern suburbs, at Karlshorst.

Supreme Allied Command was told that the Soviet Union was not willing to ratify the Rheims agreement and Susloparov was summarily recalled to Moscow. "Who the hell is this famous Russian general?" Stalin had exclaimed angrily. John Counsell caught the moment:

"Major General Susloparov emerged from behind a screen. Gone was the jocund, upright figure with whom we had been exchanging toasts only minutes earlier. Instead, we saw an old man, sagging at the knees, his face drained of all color, his eyes expressionless. He passed us into the night and to a fate at which we could only guess."

The Soviets now proposed a compromise arrangement. The Rheims surrender—which they did not report to their own citizens—would be regarded as an initial or preliminary signing, with the conclusive signing taking place in Berlin. To his credit, Eisenhower now stepped into the breach—to limit the damage from this as much as possible—and went along with the Soviet proposal.

He sent the following clearly worded reply:

I feel sure you will understand that we have scrupulously adhered to the engagement of no separate truce on this front . . . We have consistently refused to discuss a separate truce with anyone and have proceeded exactly in accordance with our understanding of Russian desires.

While a brief instrument of unconditional military surrender, of which you have a copy, was signed here at 0240 hours this morning, before receipt of your message, that instrument provides that the German High Command is required to report at a time and place fixed for a more formal signing. I would be happy to come to Berlin tomorrow, at an hour specified by Marshal Zhukov, who I understand will be the Russian representative.

A bridge was being rebuilt between the Western Allies and Russia. But more was to happen on this fateful day. The hiatus meant that American and British forces on the ground now understood there to be a ceasefire, the Germans believed that a ceasefire was in place between them and the Western Allies but were not willing to surrender to the Russians, and the Russians—not knowing about the ceasefire or, in the case of the Soviet High Command, not choosing to accept it—were carrying on fighting.

At 7:45 a.m. on May 7 the US 803rd Tank Destroyer Battalion—part of General George Patton's Third Army—received orders to move along the road from Volary to Lenora in western Czechoslovakia and survey German positions. General Eisenhower's instructions to all US troops in the country made clear that any further advance was prohibited beyond limited reconnaissance missions up to 6 miles ahead of American lines. As the battalion moved forward it ran into a German ambush. Troops of the 11th Panzer Division, concealed in the woods on either side of the dirt road, let off a barrage of fire from Panzerfausts. These exploded around the lead American vehicle and the GIs driving in the jeep behind it were also hit. One of them—Charles Havlat—was killed instantly.

The US force returned fire, but a few minutes later the radio operator received word that a ceasefire had come into effect and they were to return to Volary. Havlat would be the last American soldier killed in Europe. Taken captive later, the German officer who led the ambush said he had known nothing of the ceasefire until thirty minutes after the engagement, but nevertheless apologized for the incident. The surrender was then scrupulously observed between the two sides.

But when Germans were faced by the advancing Red Army, it was an altogether different story. The urge to escape at any cost led to terrible scenes at the bridge over the Elbe at Tangermünde, 45 miles northwest of Magdeburg. The western side of the river was held by General William Simpson's US Ninth Army. Approaching from the east were the German troops of General Walter Wenck's 12th Army, the remnants of the 9th Army and a mass of civilians. The Russians were in hot pursuit.

General Wenck's army had been pulled from its position on the Elbe on April 23, with dramatic orders to rescue Hitler in Berlin. Wenck had got as far as Potsdam. Then, faced with strong Soviet opposition, he abandoned all plans to fight his way into the Reich's capital and instead concentrated on shepherding the German 9th Army, battered by the troops of Marshal Konev's 1st Ukrainian Front, back to the safety of American lines. The 9th Army was an Eastern Front formation, the 12th Army had become one—yet both had resolved never to surrender to the Russians. Nearly 100,000 Wehrmacht troops—and the same number of civilians—were fleeing toward American lines.

On May 4 Wenck had sent one of his corps commanders, General Baron von Edelsheim, ahead of his army to negotiate with his American counterpart, General Simpson. The discussions took place in the town hall at Stendal. Simpson was more circumspect than Field Marshal Montgomery at Lüneburg. He did not merely pay lip-service to the terms of unconditional surrender. He was aware of the humanitarian issue but also the United States' obligations to its Soviet ally—and also the practical problems of dealing with such a large influx of people. Simpson said he was willing to receive wounded and unarmed soldiers, but refused Edelsheim's request to help repair the bridge to speed the evacuation and made it clear that he could not accept civilian refugees.

On May 6 the crossing of the Elbe had begun. The Germans gave priority to the soldiers of the 9th Army, while the 12th held a shrinking bridgehead some 5 miles wide and 2 miles deep around Tangermünde. Beyond them were the Russians—and their artillery was now opening up on the German position.

On the morning of May 7 the perimeter of the bridgehead started to collapse. There was no longer time for an organized crossing of the Elbe—and German soldiers and civilians started to succumb to mass panic. Although civilians had been prohibited from crossing, they surged forward nonetheless. Only hours after the unconditional surrender had been signed at Rheims, detachments of the US 5th Armored and 102nd Divisions watched scenes of utter chaos unfold before them on the opposite bank. British journalist James Wellard was with the American troops:

> I have just witnessed the last battle on the western front, fought at Tangermünde on the Elbe, some 200 yards from me, between thousands of disorganized, hysterical, screaming Germans and the implacable, ruthless Russian tanks and infantry. From the top of an American tank, which if it had opened fire, could have slaughtered hundreds of Germans at point-blank range, I saw scenes so fantastic that they surpassed anything I had witnessed in four years of war.
>
> Russian mortar shells burst in the midst of German soldiers and civilians waiting to cross the bridge to the American side of the river and scores of women and children were killed or wounded. Wehrmacht soldiers pushed old women out of the boats in which they were trying to cross the river. Officers, stripped naked, paddled a rubber boat loaded with troops and three women, their baggage and bicycles. A girl drowned in mid-stream after screaming for help. Men swam the river in their vests, climbed up the west bank and were sent straight to the prisoners' cages, still in their vests.

At noon on May 7 Russian tanks broke through the screen of woods behind the German position. The Red Army was now less than a thousand yards from the riverbank. "I stood at the far-end of the broken bridge," Wellard continued, "and watched paratroopers, generals, high-ranking staff officers, nurses and tank-men run across it in a state of wild-eyed panic.

German soldiers fought with each other for planks, tubs and other pieces of debris to swim the river on." So ended the army Hitler imagined would save the fortunes of the Reich in Berlin.

At 2:30 p.m. the foreign minister of the Dönitz government, Schwerin von Krosigk, broadcast news of the surrender to the German people from Flensburg:

> German men and women, the high command of the Armed Forces has today, at the order of Admiral Dönitz, declared the unconditional surrender of all fighting troops . . . After a heroic struggle of almost six years of almost incomparable hardship Germany has succumbed to the overwhelming power of her enemies. To continue the war would only mean senseless bloodshed . . . We must now face our fate squarely and unquestioningly.

As he uttered these words, Von Krosigk knew that German army and SS units were battling to wipe out the insurgents in Prague and that fighting was still continuing on the Eastern Front.

The Soviet leadership chose to ignore this announcement. Having told the Western Allies that they regarded Rheims as a preliminary agreement, they relayed no news of it to the Russian people or its soldiers. The Prague offensive—the last major Red Army offensive of the war—had just been launched and would be continued until the Wehrmacht's Army Group Center surrendered to them or was destroyed. With this in mind, and aware that substantial bodies of German troops were still holding out in Courland and on the Hela Peninsula near Danzig, Stalin summoned General Antonov to another meeting. He wondered whether some advantage might be gleaned from the Rheims signing nonetheless.

Antonov was instructed to issue an appeal to the German formations still fighting against the Russians. In this communication, to be made by radio and leaflet drop, the Soviets would refer to the Rheims agreement as valid and in force. They would require the Wehrmacht to begin surrender preparations immediately and formally lay down their arms at one minute past midnight on May 8/9. This was the time designated at Rheims for the unconditional surrender to come into effect and would coincide with the second signing ceremony at Karlshorst, which was to be concluded at 2300 hours on May 8. The ploy was devised to save the lives of Russian soldiers but would have only a limited effect.

At Supreme Allied Headquarters at Rheims, the surrender was still under a news embargo. But at 3:00 p.m. Associated Press correspondent Ed Kennedy deliberately broke the agreement he had made. As the Dönitz government had already broadcast news of this, Kennedy decided there was no good military reason to delay his dispatch further. He phoned his agency in London: "This is Ed Kennedy," he told them. "Germany has surrendered unconditionally—that's official. Make the dateline Rheims, France and get it out." At 9:36 a.m. New York time (3:36 p.m. in London and Rheims) the message ran off the teleprinters all over the United States: "Germany surrendered unconditionally to the western allies and Russia 2:41am French time today."

The breach of a news embargo was an unprecedented action for an American war reporter to take and it would have very serious consequences. On hearing of the German broadcast, at 2:41 p.m. that afternoon, Ed Kennedy, increasingly frustrated at the delay, had asked to see Eisenhower's public relations officer, Brigadier General Frank Allen. "The absurdity of attempting to bottle up news of such magnitude was all too apparent," Kennedy would later write. But Allen made it clear to Kennedy that their hands were tied on the matter, as the timing of the announcement needed to be decided upon by Stalin, Churchill and Truman, and that a second signing was now to take place in Berlin.

This was too much for Kennedy. Hearing this, he came to the conclusion that the embargo was no longer about military security but was being determined by political factors. Suspecting the influence of the Soviet Union, he decided that Russia had no right to muzzle a story that was in the public interest. He found a back-channel telephone line and dictated 300 words to the Associated Press Bureau for immediate release before the line went dead.

Boyd DeWolf Lewis of the United Press was another of the fifteen reporters chosen by Supreme Allied Headquarters to witness the surrender at Rheims. On the flight from Paris all had solemnly pledged not to file their stories until permission was given. After the signing, the war correspondents were told that they could not be transmitted until the following afternoon (of May 8)—an embargo of eighteen hours. Lewis said: "We were all clear on the reason for this: it was to allow the Big Three to make the announcement and most importantly, in order for the Russians to make sure that the Germans were not just surrendering to the western allies but were surrendering on the Eastern Front also."

At dawn on May 7 the correspondents had flown back to Paris, their stories written on portable typewriters and cleared by the army censors. Upon landing, Lewis was the first to get to the Army Communications Center and was thus first in line for the transmission of his story over the radiotelegraph circuits once the embargo expired. Lewis said: "It was not simply about 'political censorship.' Kennedy also broke the embargo because it was the only way he could beat the United Press and get a scoop for his story."

Kennedy claimed that running the story would save lives. In fact, the last American soldier was killed in Europe seven hours before he breached the embargo. Lewis emphasized: "I must say that never at any time did it occur to me to try an unethical 'end run' with the story. Nor can I claim any struggle of conscience, weighing the danger of added war and death (if a breach of agreement blew up the surrender) against the value of a scoop."

Charles Kiley of the *Stars and Stripes* was also at the Rheims ceremony. He added: "As a reporter, I understood Kennedy's actions—but did not agree with them. For all the talk about 'political censorship' he wanted a scoop, plain and simple."

Kennedy was a "wire reporter"—and he was under constant pressure to beat his fellows. All war journalists understood the pressure he was under. But he chose not to include his editors in his decision to break the embargo— as he filed his dispatch by phone they naturally assumed he was in the clear to do so and that they could immediately publish. And yet Kennedy had always respected embargoes before. After a discussion with General Eisenhower, he had held back from reporting an incident in which General George Patton had slapped two invalided soldiers in a hospital in Sicily. By doing so, and sticking to his word, Kennedy had then seen another reporter break the story several weeks later.

There seems no reason to doubt Kennedy's own testimony that he believed the second surrender in Berlin to be merely "staged" for political reasons and found this no longer a justifiable reason for embargoing the story. In short it was anti-Russian sentiment—as well as the desire for a scoop—which propelled him to take this action. Kennedy—who had covered the war in Italy, France and Germany—was proud of the contribution made by American troops and deeply distrustful of the Soviet Union.

But this was a huge decision for a war correspondent to take—and one that would cause substantial international complications. Another reporter, Charles Kiley, who would be present at both the surrenders, at Rheims and Karlshorst, was more sympathetic to the Russian point of view. He believed that the embargo was justified and as all the press had signed up to it they should hold to their word. He realized that politics was involved in delaying the announcement—but also understood that the Soviet Union had suffered by far the highest casualty rate of all the allies in the war, some 27 million soldiers and civilians: "We knew that the Soviet high command was not present at Rheims," Kiley said, "and would not accept this ceasefire until the Germans surrendered in Berlin. And we felt that the Russians deserved to have their day."

The majority of Kennedy's fellow journalists were deeply angered by his action. "I am browned off, fed up, burned up and put out," wrote *New York Times* correspondent Drew Middleton. His paper wrote an editorial chastising the Associated Press for initially boasting of a historic "news beat." "If it was a 'beat,'" the *New York Times* wrote caustically, "it was only because Mr. Kennedy's colleagues chose to stand by their commitments."

SHAEF was determined to limit the damage of this disclosure, transmitting a carefully worded message to American news agencies and radio networks:

"Supreme Headquarters allows correspondents at 16:45 Paris time today to state that SHAEF has made nowhere any official statement for publication concerning the complete surrender of all German armed forces in Europe and that no story to this effect is authorized."

Alistair Cooke was reporting on the San Francisco World Conference:

"Within the hour the radio networks were spreading a harrowing turmoil of rumor. The city police, put on the alert at dawn, relaxed again. Before noon [San Francisco time] it was established that the Associated Press had unluckily announced VE Day too early. The American itch to 'jump the gun' has never been rewarded with such public humiliation."

At Supreme Allied Headquarters, British journalist David Walker—following the censorship rules, as all his colleagues had, with the exception of Kennedy—summed up the mood of frustration:

"This must be the greatest single press fiasco of all time," Walker wrote bitterly. "While the peace news has been broadcast all over the world, British and American newspapermen's copy still lies here pending the permission of officialdom. Even in their defeat, the Germans can laugh at us for our confusion, and for those of us who have been abroad on war stories since 1938 and 1939, this is the final humiliation."

Walker, not really comprehending the full situation, felt that once the story got out, Supreme Allied Command should have authorized it. "It is a pity that SHAEF lacked the courage of Lord Nelson," he continued, "who put his telescope to a blind eye; the only advantage they seem to have over Nelson is that they are more at sea."

The Associated Press subsequently apologized, its president, Robert McLean, saying the organization "profoundly regretted the distribution of the report of the total surrender in Europe, which investigation clearly disclosed was in advance of authorization by Supreme Allied Headquarters." The AP's general manager, Kent Cooper, added that Kennedy should have conferred with his editors about the decision to publish. He had violated a "cardinal principle" of journalism in breaking a pledge to keep the surrender confidential.

In New York celebrations were going on regardless:

"In Times Square thousands of people, yelling ceaselessly, packed the streets, stopping all the traffic as far as the eye could see. Milling crowds blocked all thoroughfares. Press photographers clambered on to windows to snap the fantastic scene of men and women going wild in the mid-morning sunshine."

All over the United States radio networks that had first mounted special victory programs later abandoned them and restored their normal schedules. At noon the CBS announcer began to address ordinary people's frustration:

"It's obviously a fact. But it's not official. Official is official is official. And there, for all the purposes of absolute definition, goes the day we thought ought to be called VE Day. If the objective of the supernatural powers had been to snarl up the actual end of the war in Europe, so as to save us all the waste of climactic hysteria, nothing could have worked out better."

For most of May 7 Britain had been starved of news. That morning the press had to remain non-committal. *The Times* predicted: "End of war in Europe at hand." The *Daily Telegraph* tried: "Germany's surrender imminent." "It may be today," hazarded the *Daily Mail.* The *Daily Express*, which had run the headline "No war this year" in 1939, played it safe with "The last hours."

People were puzzled and angry as the day went on, complaining at the lack of information, some saying the government had spoiled a chance to rejoice in victory. A *Manchester Guardian* reporter described the confusion:

All day people in London sensed that the end was near. In Piccadilly Circus, in Whitehall and in the Westminster area thousands gathered and waited for hours in the expectancy of hearing the great news. Most of the waiting people were Londoners, but servicemen and women of all nationalities mingled with them.

Buckingham Palace became the focal point. The area outside the massive railings and the royal parks around were thronged with waiting crowds, who seized on every movement within the Palace gates. They saw the red carpet being placed on the balcony on which the King and Queen were expected to appear. The Royal Standard fluttered from the roof of the Palace, the windows of which still carried black-out hoardings, some being bricked up.

When no announcement was made on the six o'clock news the crowds in Piccadilly Circus dispersed quietly, and at half-past six the crowds outside the Palace also began to disperse and by seven o'clock only a few people were left.

In Whitehall, where thousands of civil servants and others leaving their offices had added to the throng, the crowd waited on patiently until just before seven o'clock. Then a number of police inspectors walked along informing people that Mr. Churchill would not speak that night. Disappointed but in good humor the crowd gradually drifted away.

A young Auxiliary Territorial Services (ATS) clerk described the mood of excitement and impatience that had swept through her office: "The war is over—that's obvious—but when is Churchill going to say so? Everyone gives their opinion—'at nine'—'not until tomorrow'—'at midnight.' Normally the office is clear by 5:55, but tonight every single member of staff stays to hear the 6:00 p.m. news—and *still* it is the same."

BBC broadcaster Joseph Macleod blamed Churchill. The prime minister had, in his view, "a well-deserved reputation at Broadcasting House for complete disregard of people's arrangements, and that Monday [May 7] he surpassed himself, refusing up to the very last fifteen minutes to say whether he would broadcast at 6 o'clock." Macleod could not have been more wrong.

For relations between Britain, America and Russia now hinged on the timing of the victory announcement. They had all originally hoped to make a joint announcement and designate May 9 as VE-Day. After Eisenhower agreed to the second signing ceremony at Karlshorst, in Berlin, Stalin asked that this date be kept to. He stressed in his messages to Truman and Churchill that it was in his view essential that a clear commitment from the Germans to surrender on the Eastern Front be secured before VE-Day was officially proclaimed. He warned that in the east "German resistance is not slackening and, to judge from radio intercepts, an appreciable group is openly declaring its intention to continue the fight against us." The Soviet High Command, Stalin concluded, would like to hold up the announcement until the time that the agreement signed at Rheims "entered into force," namely one minute after midnight on May 8 (i.e. the first minute of May 9).

Here the Soviet leader was hoping both to strengthen the surrender arrangements themselves and to present them most advantageously to the Russian people. Stalin knew that the ordinary Soviet citizen expected the war to end as the result of a signing in Berlin rather than one at Rheims, and for it to be supervised by Russia's greatest war leader, Marshal Zhukov. The Soviet leader knew that if he was able to announce the surrender early on the morning of May 9 he need not mention the agreement at Rheims at all.

Stalin was used to a rigid system of state censorship and control of the press. This was a luxury not afforded to Western democracies. After the Associated Press announcement and the public clamor to know what was going on, it would be impossible for Britain and America to delay an official announcement until May 9, as had originally been hoped.

The best scenario for the Western Allies—after the breach of the news embargo—was to delay a formal announcement for one day. They would then celebrate VE-Day on May 8 and the Soviet Union on May 9. Two VE-Days rather than one would be far from ideal—but they could be linked by a declaration, in the West, of a two-day holiday to celebrate the end of the war. But this would require both Truman and Churchill to refrain from a victory announcement on May 7, despite the surrender at Rheims and hundreds of thousands of German soldiers laying down their arms on this day in the West.

Eisenhower saw the importance of delaying matters—to restore a measure of harmony with the Soviet Union—and General George Marshall agreed with him. Following Marshall's advice, President Truman said that he would also have to wait before making an announcement, "unless Stalin approves an earlier release." But Churchill was rapidly losing patience with the situation. He telegraphed the president saying he felt that it was "hopeless" to try to keep the German surrender secret until the following day. He asked the White House to phone him on the open line. He wanted a frank exchange of views. The British prime minister was frustrated that media reports were already carrying the news of the Rheims signing and he was out of sympathy with the Russian leader.

A rift was opening up in the Grand Alliance, particularly between Britain and the Soviet Union. For Churchill, the arrest of the sixteen Poles still rankled and seemed to him to embody Russian bad faith. In the subsequent days, he had grown more and more suspicious of Soviet ambitions within Europe, and even on May 7 continued to fret—or, as Montgomery put it in his diary, "bellyache"—about the situation in Denmark, trying to get more troops sent there in case the Red Army pushed its way into the country.

For Stalin and the Soviet leadership the fear that the West might conclude a separate peace with Germany had again reared its head.

The end of the war was about practical arrangements, but these were cloaked in a powerful symbolism. Churchill wanted to get on with things—making the victory announcement as quickly as possible. No more British or American troops would have to die in Europe. Stalin wanted to delay the announcement until as many of his soldiers as possible had finished fighting the Germans.

If VE-Day was announced in the West on May 7, as Churchill wished, Stalin might in turn refrain from announcing it in Russia until May 11 or even 12, when all the major fighting in the East had been concluded. The Grand Alliance would then appear disunited and in disarray—in quite devastating fashion, unable to properly celebrate its common victory over Nazi Germany. The frustration of journalists and ordinary people over the delay was understandable—but it would be a tragedy if this were to happen.

In the late afternoon, Truman's personal chief of staff, Admiral William Leahy, spoke to Winston Churchill by phone. Truman now accepted the need to work with the Soviet Union over the timing of the victory announcement. Churchill still wanted to make the announcement on May 7. Leahy asked him whether he had contacted Stalin. Churchill replied with some exasperation:

"The German Foreign Minister has given out an hour ago, on the radio, an address showing that they have declared the unconditional surrender. What is the use of me and the President looking to be the only two people in the world who don't know what is going on? The whole of this thing is leaking out in England and America . . . I feel it is absolutely necessary to go off at 6:00 pm."

After ascertaining that Churchill had not contacted Stalin, Leahy stressed that Truman would not make an announcement until the Soviet leader had been brought into the discussion.

Churchill showed his frustration: "I am very sorry about it because we fixed it all for six o'clock, and the king will go off at nine."

In the end, Churchill backed down.

The king's diary showed his own disappointment, as well as that of the government, at the delay:

"The PM wanted to announce it but President Truman and Marshal Stalin want the news to be broadcast tomorrow at 3:00 p.m. as arranged. The time fixed for Unconditional Surrender is Midnight May 8th. This came to me as a terrible anti-climax, having made my speech for recording purposes with cinema, photography—and with no broadcast at 9:00 p.m. today!"

Eisenhower had canvassed General George Marshall, and Marshall had persuaded President Truman to give the Russians the benefit of the doubt. For a few hours, Winston Churchill lost patience with Stalin and the Soviet Union altogether, but Admiral Leahy's firmness and tact and a reluctance to break ranks with America brought him round.

At 7:40 p.m. the Ministry of Information finally announced:

It is understood that, in accordance with arrangements between the three great powers, an official announcement will be broadcast by the Prime Minister at three o'clock tomorrow, Tuesday afternoon, May 8.

In view of this fact, tomorrow, Tuesday, will be treated as Victory-in-Europe day, and will be regarded as a holiday. The day following, Wednesday, May 9, will also be a holiday. His Majesty the King will broadcast to the people of the British Empire and Commonwealth tomorrow, Tuesday, at 9:00 p.m.

Churchill's prejudice against Bolshevism was understandable. It was a tribute to his statesmanship that he acceded to May 8 as Victory in Europe Day and to his generosity that he then announced that May 9, the second day of holiday, would be one on which to remember the sacrifices the Soviet Union had made in bringing about their common victory.

On May 7 Field Marshal Montgomery flew into Wismar to meet with his Russian counterpart, Marshal Konstantin Rokossovsky. Montgomery said of him: "Rokossovsky was an imposing figure, tall, very good-looking and well-dressed. I understand he was a bachelor and much admired by the ladies." General Eric Bols, commander of the British 6th Airborne Division, told an amusing anecdote around the contrast between the austere teetotal Montgomery and the very different Soviet marshal:

> I had been over to Rokossovsky's headquarters and had invited him to mine on a reciprocal visit. I arranged it so that Monty would be present. Rokossovsky, who spoke beautiful French, arrived and met Monty and was offered a drink. Rokossovsky also smoked and he noticed that Monty was abstaining, so he asked "Are you not having anything to drink?" Monty looked up at this tall great cavalryman and said "I neither drink nor smoke." That seemed as if it would end the matter, but the Russian—not to be rebuffed—continued: "Well, what do you do about women?" Monty failed to answer this inquiry—he decided to have a drink!

After inspecting an honor guard and then watching a nineteen-gun salute on an adjoining soccer field, the British and Russian parties had adjourned for lunch at the 6th Airborne Division headquarters, a requisitioned mansion on the town's Unruh-Strasse. There was some tension in the air: the British had suspected Russian intentions over Denmark; the Russians had noticed that British forces had moved across their own line of advance without giving them advance warning. But it was an invocation of the Battle of Stalingrad that thawed relations between the two sides.

General Pavel Batov, the commander of the Soviet 65th Army, who had accompanied Rokossovsky to Wismar, remembered Montgomery looking at his medals. "He saw that I had the Order of the British Empire," Batov related, "and overcome by curiosity, asked through an interpreter how I had received it. I explained that it had been granted to me after Stalingrad."

At the Teheran Conference in November 1943 Winston Churchill had presented Joseph Stalin with the Sword of Stalingrad as a token of the British people's appreciation of that remarkable triumph. The Russians were also given a number of the Order of the British Empire awards to present to generals who had distinguished themselves in that campaign. Batov—who had fought with Rokossovsky on the Don front—had received one.

"Montgomery looked at me for a moment," Batov continued, "and then said softly: 'Ah, the beginning of our victory!' He turned to Rokossovsky and spoke of British admiration for the heroism of the Red Army soldier and the Russian people, saying 'We are proud to have you as our allies.'"

El Alamein and Stalingrad were, in a way, kindred battles—although Stalingrad was fought on a much larger scale. They were both turning-points—one in North Africa, the other on the Eastern Front. In both, the tables were turned on the Wehrmacht in November 1942 (although Stalingrad finished, with a total German surrender, only on February 2, 1943). Rokossovsky reported afterward: "The meeting went particularly well. Field Marshal Montgomery would like to come to the Soviet Union—and visit Stalingrad." Heartfelt admiration for Russian courage had transcended the political difficulties.

On the ground, British and Russian forces manned roadblocks in Wismar some two hundred yards apart. On occasions there were problems with Soviet drunkenness. But soldiers from both sides managed to strike up a rapport despite the language barrier. "I was very proud to have met the Red Army," said Lance Corporal Ray Porter of the 6th Airborne. "We used each other's field kitchen facilities, swapped weapons and shared cigarettes. It became a happy occasion. We had an immense respect for Russia's performance in the war."

By the end of May 7 arrangements for the second signing at Karlshorst in Berlin's suburbs had been agreed between the two sides, after a flurry of communications between Rheims and Moscow. It was confirmed that it would take place the following day and that a high-powered Western delegation would attend.

The British public knew little of this frantic diplomacy. Yet as VE-Day approached, the wartime role of Britain's Russian ally provoked different reactions. Lady Catherine Ashburnham, last in line of the Ashburnham family near Battle in Sussex, wrote to a friend on May 7: "I shall be frightfully busy as I find my servants mean to celebrate VE Day and have hunted out the flags and stuff we made for the Coronation! I confess I don't feel much like it. There is so much horror left in the world still that I can't rejoice in the same way as after the last war. It is Russia that deters me. Two wrongs can't make a right."

Lady Catherine presided over a fine neo-Palladian house and extensive parkland. The family—ardent royalists—had built their present home and gained their aristocratic title as a reward from a grateful Charles II for the support they had given his father in the seventeenth-century Civil War. Then, they had been prepared to risk all against the forces of Parliament. Now, the twentieth-century Bolshevik onslaught was regarded with similar suspicion. What exactly was meant by "Two wrongs can't make a right" was revealed in an earlier letter, of January 22, 1945, as the Red Army was pushing its way into eastern Europe and was on the verge of capturing Budapest from Hitler's forces:

"I am as depressed by the advance of the Bolsheviks in to Hungary as most people are elated," Lady Catherine declared. "Austria and Hungary, two centers of Christian civilization, are overwhelmed by hordes of cruel barbarians as they were in the Middle Ages." After likening the invading Russians to the Ottoman Turks, who brought much of eastern Europe under their sway in the fifteenth century, Lady Catherine continued:

"Then the Christian monarchs pulled themselves together to drive back the invader. Now an Atheistic lot of Communists, Socialists and even Conservatives, all rejoice—blinded by the traitor press into the belief that it is 'liberation.' Words have lost their meaning since Hitler and Stalin took over. To exchange one tyranny for another and an even worse one, is NOT liberation."

Yet Ronald Horton, of Leek in Staffordshire, struck a very different tone in a letter to his mother. "The VE Day celebrations are set to go off quietly here," he began. He described the arrival of Russian POWs, flown into the area from liberated German camps and being held awaiting transportation home. Horton's sympathy for the Russians was as striking as Lady Ashburnham's deep suspicion of them. "Their faces are ravaged by suffering," he continued. "Last night one of them led with an accordion a fine spontaneous sing-song. It was good to see happiness in their faces after the terrible experiences they have suffered."

Horton had set up an Anglo-Soviet Friendship Society in Leek, a wartime achievement resonating with a certain quiet heroism of its own. "There are few here who have given much thought to the Soviet Union until the Germans moved against her," he declared, "or realize the immense losses suffered by the Russian people." Horton, who gallantly set up lectures, meetings and book-stalls to better inform those around him, had earlier written—on October 16, 1941—of the German onslaught on Moscow, when it appeared that the Russian capital might yet succumb to Hitler's blitzkrieg invasion of the East. He related to his mother with pained indignation:

> I can think of nothing but the fighting before Moscow and the lack of effective aid from our side. It looks like treachery to me. Many of those in high places want neither a Soviet nor a Nazi victory. They just want the two great armies to go on bleeding to death. The war will drag on indefinitely as a result. It is criminal, and one is furious when one thinks of the terrible sacrifices the Russians will have to make, after all they have been through, and the hopeful new society that they were building. But they will win in the end, and we over here will be put to shame.

These were extreme views, and the majority of British people, far less in-formed, charted their way between them—but their very extremity warned of the divide that existed in Allied opinion. In these circumstances, the second signing at Karlshorst represented a valuable compromise.

With the announcement made, Sir Montague Burton penned a letter to his son, stationed overseas. Burton's tailoring empire had made more than a quarter of British military uniforms in the Second World War. He now looked to the future:

> The unconditional surrender of Germany will soon be announced. The nightmare is almost over . . . Never has so much history been crowded into so few days: in fact, I do not think history has so exciting and sensational a parallel. Three important figures—two who have brought more sorrow than any other two men previously [Hitler and Mussolini] and one who has probably done more than any single indi-vidual for the survival of civilization in the hour of peril [Roosevelt]— have been moved from the world's stage within a few weeks.

And it was the loss of Roosevelt which preoccupied Burton. He continued: "We are living in unprecedented times. Most people feel deeply grieved that Roosevelt was not spared to help frame the peace: his guidance and wisdom will be sadly missed."

And then Burton wondered about the attitude of the Soviet leader: "There is hope that Stalin will permit Vladivostock to be used as a base to bomb Kobe and Tokyo and other Japanese towns—in that event, the war in the Far East might be over this year."

Stalin's continued cooperation with the West could not, however, be taken for granted. Within the Soviet Union, the surrender ceremony at Rheims was still not reported. Instead, *Izvestia* ran a long piece on the surrender at Breslau. "The long running, stubborn German resistance has finally been broken," the paper announced. "The garrison has raised the white flag. Eighty-two days have passed since our soldiers first surrounded Breslau . . . Where there was once a great, beautiful city there is now a shapeless mass of devastation . . . Civilians emerge from the cellars and basements. After the bitter, bloody fighting there is now peace and silence."

Soviet war correspondent Vasily Malinin, who had covered the siege in its entirety, wrote in his diary on May 7:

"In the streets there is an eerie calm. At the road junctions, surrendered weapons and ammunition are piled up. Columns of German soldiers are marching out of the city. Some keep their heads lowered; others smile at every Soviet soldier they see, calling out like chattering parrots: 'Hitler kaput, Breslau kaput, Krieg kaput.' Countless white flags hang from the windows. It dawns on us—the Fascists have finally surrendered."

In Breslau, Soviet troops now took up garrison positions in the city that had defied them for so long. "It may sound strange," Soviet soldier Alexander Fedotov wrote to his mother, "but what I have longed for most of all over the last few months is quiet—quiet from the sound of guns and falling shells." The others had gone on a "trophy-hunt," looking for pistols, field glasses and medals. "I went down to the river and for hours stared at the water running past me. And that evening, for the first time in my life, I heard the sound of nightingales singing in the bushes."

At 5:00 p.m. on May 7 Brigadier General Robert Stack of the US 36th

Infantry Division overtook a convoy of vehicles on the road near Kaufstein in Austria. It was the personal entourage of the former Nazi Reichsmarschall Hermann Göring, including his wife, daughter and sister-in-law, along with his chef, valet and butler—altogether about seventy-five persons. That morning Göring had made contact with the US division through an emissary. Stack now approached him and asked whether he was willing to surrender unconditionally. The man who had for so long been Hitler's designated successor meekly agreed.

The international tensions of this extraordinary day impacted most strongly on Czechoslovakia. Prague was caught between American troops who could have quickly reached the city but had been ordered not to out of fear of antagonizing the Russians, Red Army troops who genuinely wished to liberate the city but could not yet reach it, and Wehrmacht and SS troops bent on disregarding the ceasefire and crushing the uprising, either to secure a passage westward or simply out of defiance and spite.

In Britain, news of the Prague uprising had first been relayed with an optimistic hue. Basking in the success at Lüneburg Heath, the press first imagined that the Germans had simply surrendered and the Czechs were controlling the capital. Now very different stories were emerging. The *Daily Mail* reported: "In a final burst of fiendishness, SS troops in Prague are firing on helpless Czech civilians . . . The Wehrmacht commander does not accept what he describes as the 'armistice' [the surrender signing at Rheims] and will continue to fight until he has secured a free passage out of the country."

On the evening of May 6 the British had received decrypted ULTRA reports from the SS in Prague. "The tactics of terror are working and we will soon be in control of the city." On May 7 Churchill contacted Eisenhower directly.

"I am hoping that your plan does not inhibit you to advance to Prague," the British prime minister said, "if you have the troops and do not meet the Russians earlier. I thought you did not mean to tie yourself down if you had the strength and the country was empty."

However, it was now too risky for General Eisenhower to make any form of military intervention.

In the Czech capital, the rebels were clinging on to their last positions in the center of the city. The Germans, realizing the Vlasov troops were about to enter the fray, attacked at dawn in an effort to finish the insurgents off. At 5:00 a.m. they flung armored vehicles and infantry into the Old Town Square, breaching the last barricades and breaking into the Old Town Hall itself. The Wehrmacht and the rebels traded shots on the staircases and in the corridors, while the terrified wounded, women and children huddled in the basement. The Luftwaffe joined the battle, its planes flying low over the city, strafing and bombing rebel positions. A column of thirty tanks assembled outside the SS headquarters in the Law Faculty Building to deliver the *coup de grâce*. The uprising was about to collapse.

The 1st Division of the Russian Liberation Army now made a dramatic appearance. It was equipped with artillery and anti-tank weapons—and its soldiers, realizing what was at stake, immediately took the offensive against the SS. General Bunyachenko had planned his intervention with considerable skill. He sent one of his four regiments to seize the airport, to stop its planes bombing the city and prevent more reinforcements reaching the SS. Two more blocked the approach roads to Prague, from the north and south. His remaining regiment joined the rebels on the barricades and fought for control of the city center.

Sigismund Diczbalis was one of these soldiers. "Our men fought with desperate fervor, street by street, house by house," Diczbalis said. "They threw themselves at the Germans."

"I remember a platoon of Vlasov soldiers arrived at our barricade at around 7:00 a.m.," Antonin Sticha recalled. "We were very surprised, because these 'reinforcements' were wearing German uniforms, although with a distinctive arm patch. We were reassured by our commander that they were here to help us—and help us they did. They straight away pushed on past our barricade and began attacking a nearby German stronghold."

"We were afraid that German armor would simply roll over our position," Harak Bohumil added. "But early that morning we were reinforced with two companies of Vlasovites. They had two tanks, two self-propelled guns and a mounted machine gun. On May 7 we should have been destroyed. Instead, we were able to stop German tanks from getting through to the city from the south and even launched a counter attack."

Fighting for Prague's airport at Ruzne was particularly bloody. Bunya-chenko's men fought with the SS on the runways and brought up their artillery to open fire on the German planes. By evening the airport was in the Russian Liberation Army's hands. The Germans had been driven out of the Old Town Square and the barricades reinforced.

"Without the Vlasov forces we would not have held the city," said Antonin Sticha. The SS had flung more troops into the fray. But at the end of May 7—the hardest day of fighting in the uprising—the rebel position held. General Bunyachenko and his men had saved Prague.

9

KARLSHORST

S oviet Marshal Konev's 1st Ukrainian Front was moving south through Germany, in the last Russian military operation of the war, pushing toward Czechoslovakia. On May 8 Karl-Ludwig Hoch wrote:

> The Russians are marching into Dresden and the rule of the Bolsheviks is beginning. The Americans are on the motor highway near Chemnitz—but they are not going to come any further east. Someone has seen the first Russian soldiers. The sun comes up in a cloudless sky as though nothing were happening. In some of the neighboring houses looting is going on. In the front garden of a draper's shop, the owner lies dead: he had tried to stop it. Our teacher Pflugbeil's daughter was raped and murdered. We hid many girls in the three turrets of our large house and shoved furniture in front of the entrances.

But Hoch's own encounter with the Red Army would be rather different. "The first Soviet officer to find our out-of-the-way dwelling spoke to me in an almost friendly way," he recalled. "He wore the green cap of the GPU [Soviet security service]. He kept asking me: 'Where is Schiller?' It is unbelievable—

he turns out to be an Army Cultural Officer and he is looking for the Schiller House in Loschwitz, so he can safeguard its manuscripts. I show him the way."

In the Baltic states, fighting was still going on in Courland:

"On May 8 we made an adjustment to our frontline positions," Corporal Friedrich Kaufmann of the German 563rd Grenadier Division remembered. "We set up our heavy machine guns in a new emplacement and no sooner had we done this than an artillery barrage opened up from the Russian side and wave after wave of their troops charged toward us."

The Red Army was often profligate with the lives of its men. It had worked to overcome this fault but never fully succeeded in doing so. But it was ghastly to see soldiers' lives being needlessly endangered at the war's very end. Kaufmann described the unerring German response: "Our guns opened up and quickly found their range. All the Russians were killed. After a while there was another barrage from the enemy and another frontal attack, with the same predictable result." Three more charges followed—all of them were rebuffed in the same grim fashion. Then a Red Army officer called out to Kaufmann and his fellows, telling them that surrender negotiations were in progress. Soon this news was confirmed and all firing suddenly stopped.

"We could scarcely believe that the war might be over," Kaufmann said. "We had been fighting in this isolated place for over six months and it was hard to believe it was all drawing to a close. And yet, Russian and German soldiers were now clambering out of their trenches, crossing into no-man's-land and greeting each other and swapping cigarettes. Around this impromptu gathering lay the dead from the last Soviet attack, but this did not seem to dampen the bonhomie."

Then a Russian general appeared outside Kaufmann's command post. The Red Army considerably outnumbered the Germans on this section of the front and an entire Soviet division had been battering away against a company of Wehrmacht soldiers. The defenses had held firm. But there was no one of equal rank to the unexpected visitor, so Kaufmann greeted him instead. "How many troops do you have here?" he was asked. Kaufmann told him that the defenders numbered a little over a hundred. The Russian was markedly taken aback—he had expected several thousand.

Well-honed military coordination had triumphed over superior numbers. The Soviet general could hardly believe it. "He went round each individual foxhole," Kaufmann remembered, "calling out, asking how many were inside. After a while he turned to us in bewilderment, saying: 'How could you hold the line with so few people?'"

Kaufmann and his comrades had fought for a deeply corrupt ideology but at least they could take pride in their army's professionalism.

On the morning of May 8 General Bunyachenko's troops left Prague. A day earlier, they had saved the city from the SS and its local radio hailed them as heroes. But now the pro-communist National Council in Prague, aware the Red Army was rapidly approaching and that they loathed the Vlasov forces, panicked—and demanded that they leave.

"In a matter of hours our euphoria—a belief that we were engaged in a historic and important struggle, valued by the Czech people—changed to despondency," said Vlasov Army soldier Sigismund Diczbalis.

No longer were we liberators—we were now dubbed "collaborators" and "enemies of the people." At first our commander, General Bunyachenko, in the thick of directing us in the street fighting in the city, simply did not believe it. But after a while it sank in—and he comprehended the situation his men were now in. He ordered the immediate withdrawal of his troops from Prague.

We began to evacuate positions won in hard fighting the day before. I checked the house where I had stayed, filling my pockets with cigarettes, a piece of bread and two bags of field rations. None of us knew where we would go now—or what fate awaited us.

As Diczbalis and his fellow soldiers prepared to leave he noticed something, a small metal box by a bedside table. It was in the shape of the Holy Bible and it had a tiny figurine of the Virgin Mary inside it. The 1st Division of the Russian Liberation Army had renounced Bolshevism, but Diczbalis had been brought up an atheist and was a stranger to the Christian religion. He looked at the box briefly and then—realizing time was pressing—moved toward the door.

No sooner had I left than I felt something inexplicable, as if some force had turned me around and made me return against my will. Back in the room I took the little box in my hand to have another look at it. At that moment a stray artillery shell exploded behind the wall. Plaster from the ceiling collapsed over me as the door to the corridor was blown in. Coming to, I scrambled over the bricks and debris. It took me a while before I could stand up straight, gather myself and think clearly. Where I had been standing only a few minutes earlier—before I had returned to look at the little figurine— there was now a huge, gaping hole.

Sigismund Diczbalis took the little box and put it in his pocket. He would need all the help he could get. The Russian Liberation Army was now in a desperate situation. Its last hope was to head westward, in an attempt to reach the American lines.

Ordinary Czech civilians were bewildered and frightened that the Russian Liberation Army had been ordered to leave, and with good reason. As the Vlasov forces departed from Prague, the Germans launched a powerful new offensive against the rebels.

"At about 11:00 a.m. the SS attacked our area in force," Antonin Sticha recalled. "We slowly pulled back toward the town square—constantly shooting. It was a terrible day. Everything around us was ablaze. There was the constant din of artillery and tank fire. It seemed we would no longer be able to hold out."

Once more German troops broke through into the Old Town Square with tanks and artillery, this time in even greater strength. They began shelling the Old Town Hall and Radio Building. Soon the Town Hall was in flames and part of the structure collapsed completely. The Radio Building was hit by more than forty shells. The power lines were brought down and the transformer disabled. The main water pipe suffered a direct hit. The upper rooms were now ablaze, the lower ones flooded.

The SS, moving up in support of the Wehrmacht, began rounding up and shooting civilians. Women and children were herded in front of German armored vehicles and used as human shields. More and more troops pushed past the barricades and converged on the city center. They were closing in for the kill.

As Prague struggled for its very survival—dangerously short of tanks, armored vehicles and artillery after the departure of the Vlasov troops—two Czech armored units within the Grand Alliance were desperate to support their compatriots. One, a brigade of some 4,000 men, was fighting for the Western Allies (as part of Montgomery's 21st Army Group) and for the last six months had been besieging Dunkirk. On May 8 it received the surrender of the German garrison commander there, Admiral Frisius. It had been allowed by General Eisenhower and Field Marshal Montgomery to send a token force of some 150 men to General Patton's Third Army, so that it could participate in the American liberation of western Czechoslovakia. On May 8 this force, stationed close to Pilsen, in the village of Kysice on the road to Prague, was suffering terribly. Its commander, Lieutenant Colonel Alois Sitek, was now in touch with the Czech rebels by radio.

At 11:00 a.m. Sitek contacted the commander of the nearby US 2nd Division, General Robertson. He told him about the dire situation in the Czech capital. Sitek said: "The SS are now using civilians as human shields in front of their tanks to remove barricades. The situation is critical. In addition to my men, I have assembled a force of more than a thousand Czech partisans. We have the necessary transport and our intelligence indicates that there is a clear route into the city. I ask you to release my force immediately and allow it to proceed to Prague."

Robertson was sympathetic. He said he totally understood Sitek's wish to aid the uprising and would have gone there himself if he had not had direct orders to halt. But the American general was frank. He had been ordered to hold his present line and not take any offensive action beyond it. Permitting a body of armed men to cross over that line would be a breach of his orders and therefore he could not give his consent. However, he said he would try to get those orders reviewed in the light of what was now happening in Prague.

Robertson put a call through to the US Fifth Army Corps. The Fifth Army Corps called the headquarters of the US Third Army. The headquarters of the Third Army called Supreme Allied Command at Rheims and asked to speak to General Eisenhower himself. Eisenhower told them to stay put.

Vaclav Straka was with Sitek's force as a war correspondent. "It was ago-nizing for us," he said. "We were with the US troops advancing on Pilsen, and we heard the first Prague radio appeal [of May 5] 'Calling all Czechs! Calling all Czechs!' Every man in our unit wanted to help. Sitek told us 'Let's go to Pilsen—and then we'll go on to Prague.' We now begged the Amer-icans to release us. It was all to no avail."

On the morning of May 8 Radio Prague had sent out a last appeal for help in English, again broadcast by William Greig. US soldiers were now close enough to pick up the transmission: "Calling all Allied Armies. We need urgent help. Send your planes and tanks. The Germans are closing in on the city center. For the Lord's sake, please help us. Do not let them destroy our city." Sounds of fighting could now clearly be heard in the background.

"One of the most terrible days of my life was hearing the Czechs in Prague crying out for help on the radio," recalled Lieutenant Robert Gilbert of the US 2nd Infantry Division. "We could do absolutely nothing."

While the Czech and American troops around Pilsen waited in helpless frustration, another Czechoslovakian unit, the 1st Armored Corps com-manded by General Ludvik Svoboda, was advancing rapidly. It had been transferred to the 1st Ukrainian Front for the Prague offensive, assigned to the Soviet 38th Army and given a leading role as a "fast group," an armored formation ordered to bypass German formations—leaving them to the troops coming up behind—and keep moving. The Red Army and the Czech Armored Corps were also monitoring Radio Prague's appeals for help and every soldier realized the urgency of the situation. They were approaching the Czech capital as quickly as possible—there was little time left to save the city.

At 1:00 p.m. Prague's Military Council held an emergency meeting. The underground passages that ran from the Old Town Hall provided an escape route—but there was now a mass of wounded in the building and also many children. Reports were coming through of the SS rounding up groups of unarmed civilians and shooting them. The defenders resolved to fight to the death.

Small groups of insurgents, armed with bazookas, were sent out into the square to try to slow the advance of the German tanks.

"Our Panzerfausts were crucial," Jan Svacina remembered. "We did not have many of them, but they were easy to use and very effective in city fighting. On May 8 these weapons bought us precious time. I saw one nineteen-year-old standing behind the corner of a house. He let a German tank go right past him, then stepped out and blew it up with one bazooka shot."

The rebels were clinging on desperately. Some teenage boys were fighting the Germans. Others were being rounded up and shot. Twelve-year-old Jaroslav Oliverius said:

> May 8, 1945, was the worst birthday of my life. We were all huddled in the basement. The Germans had started to move along the street clearing each house of its occupants. All the men inside them were being shot. And then they reached our house. We suddenly heard blows on the door, hobnailed boots on the stairs and the chilling command: *Alle männer aus!*—"All the men out!" We were hauled on to the street and lined up. We all thought the end had come.

At 3:00 p.m. the Town Hall was completely in flames and its roof had collapsed. Fighting was going on in the building and the square outside it. "We were living by the hour, by the minute," Antonin Sticha said. "There was only one thought in our minds—to hold off the Germans."

The position of the insurgents was now hopeless. But at 4:15 p.m. a little miracle happened. Three German officers appeared at the Jan Hus Monument in the Old Square with white flags. General Toussaint, the Wehrmacht commander of Prague, had received reports of the rapid approach of the leading Red Army units. Russian artillery could be heard in the distance. The mood of the Germans changed. Toussaint decided to begin negotiations with the rebels. He offered to halt the fighting in return for safe passage out of the city.

Jaroslav Oliverius' birthday suddenly took a turn for the better. "Instead of being shot we were ordered to sit up on the front of their tanks," he recalled. "The Germans now knew that the Red Army was approaching—it was more important for them to evade their clutches than expend further time crushing the uprising." Oliverius and his fellows were being used as hostages, so that the Germans could pass through the Czech barricades and then leave the city as fast as possible, heading west toward the Americans.

As he sat on the tank, holding a white flag, Oliverius was stunned by his good fortune: Wehrmacht soldiers, who had been gunning down his compatriots only an hour earlier, were now cheerfully telling him they no longer wished to fight but only escape the Russians.

At 6:00 p.m. General Toussaint and the rebels reached an agreement. All German heavy weaponry would be surrendered on the outskirts of the city; light weapons would be handed over to the Czech National Army before Toussaint's troops reached American lines. All POWs held by the Wehrmacht would be transferred to the Czech police. Toussaint's troops were allowed to take out necessary food and supplies and were granted unhindered passage through Prague. Any German women and children remaining in the Czech capital would be protected by the International Red Cross. General Kutlvašr signed for the insurgents. The leading column of Wehrmacht troops—consisting of 27 tanks, 32 lorries and 3,000 infantrymen—left the city center fifteen minutes later. Some SS fanatics remained—but the crisis had passed. Against all odds, Prague had survived.

On the morning of May 8 Brigadier General Robert Stack was interviewing his new prisoner—Reichsmarschall Hermann Göring—at the headquarters of the US 36th Infantry Division at Kitzbühel in Austria. Stack had told the Reichsmarschall's aide that he wanted Göring in his room at 9:00 a.m. prompt. The man looked shocked, said that Hermann Göring always slept late—and that 11:00 a.m. would be a better hour. Stack—mindful that Göring was terrified of being captured by the Russians, the Austrian communists and even the German SS—simply repeated: "He will not sleep late tomorrow morning. I want him in my room at nine." Göring arrived punctually.

Stack started proceedings by questioning the Reichsmarschall about the National Redoubt. American military intelligence had made much of this supposed Alpine fastness, even believing that diehard Nazis had constructed underground factories, aircraft hangars and munitions depots and that they intended to conduct a last-ditch stand there. Göring looked surprised. "No," he said, "there had been some talk of such a plan—but nothing had been done to implement it."

Stack moved on to the last time Göring had seen Hitler—and what had happened subsequently. Göring told the brigadier general that he had met the Führer on his birthday, on April 20, 1945—and that the German leader was already very sick. The Reichsmarschall had then left Berlin and gone to the Berchtesgaden. Hitler had not followed him there. On April 23 he had found out that the Führer was surrounded by the Russians in Berlin and had had some form of breakdown. Göring then telegrammed Hitler—asking for the authority, as the Führer's successor, to assume authority over the Reich and negotiate a peace. Hitler had flown into a rage, accused him of treachery, dismissed him from his offices and placed him under arrest.

Göring told Stack that he had been guarded by an SS unit and that after the RAF had bombed the Berchtesgaden, he had been transferred to Salzburg. Here, a command had come through to shoot Göring and all of his family and staff. While the SS commander sought confirmation that this order was really from Hitler, two companies of Luftwaffe troops had rescued him. The Reichsmarschall and his entourage had then traveled northwest in an attempt to contact American troops.

It was all very dramatic—a mixture of truth and embellishment—but Stack felt an air of unreality about it all. Göring's influence within the Reich had waned considerably in the last year of the war. His prisoner now imagined a new role for himself. He carried a letter with him addressed to General Eisenhower, in which he offered his services to help rebuild Germany. Stack said: "He seemed to have no idea that he might be regarded as a war criminal."

In the early afternoon Göring was put on a plane to US Seventh Army headquarters at Augsburg, where he would be formally taken into custody. The Reichsmarschall's main concern seemed to be what uniform he should wear when he met the Supreme Allied Commander. Stack understood German well but had chosen to always speak to Göring through a sergeant-interpreter. The Reichsmarschall's last words to him, directed through the interpreter, were: "Ask General Stack whether I should wear a pistol or my ceremonial dagger when I appear before General Eisenhower." Stack, well aware that Göring would never meet the Allied commander, did not wait for the request to be translated but said abruptly: *"Das ist mir ganz wurst"*—German slang for "I don't give a damn." The Reichsmarschall looked so startled that he almost awoke from his reverie.

In Britain, VE-Day dawned brilliantly fine. Mollie Panter-Downes, writing for the *New Yorker* magazine, said: "When the day finally came, it was like no other that anyone could remember. It had a flavor of its own, an extemporaneousness which gave it something of the quality of a vast, happy village fete . . . The bells had begun to peal, and after the night's storm, London was having a perfect, hot, English summer's day."

Crowds were gathering in London from lunchtime onward. By 1:00 p.m. Whitehall was jammed with people. Many more were lining the pavements from Downing Street to the Ministry of Works. Police estimated the crowd to be 50,000 and growing. A bus passing down Whitehall had chalked across it: "Hitler missed this bus."

Harold Nicolson was at the scene:

The whole of Trafalgar Square and Whitehall was packed. Somebody had made a display with rosettes, flags, streamers and paper caps—and some of the Guardsmen, in full uniform, were wearing them. And through this cheerful but not exuberant crowd I pushed my way through to the House of Commons. The last few yards were very difficult, as the crowd was packed against the railings . . . Eventually I made my way through to Palace Yard, and as it was approaching the hour of 3 p.m. I decided to remain there and listen to Winston's broadcast, which was to be relayed through loudspeakers.

Big Ben struck three and silenced the vast crowd. Over the loudspeakers came the voice of the announcer—"the Prime Minister the Right Honorable Winston Churchill"—and the crowd sent up a mighty cheer. Then Churchill began to speak and for a few brief minutes his was the only voice to be heard in Whitehall:

Yesterday morning at 2:41 a.m. at Headquarters the representative of the German High Command and government, General Jodl, signed the act of unconditional surrender of all German land, sea and air forces in Europe to the Allied Expeditionary Force and simultaneously to the Soviet High Command. Today this agreement will be ratified and confirmed in Berlin . . . Hostilities will end officially at one minute after midnight tonight [Tuesday, May 8], but in the interests of saving lives the ceasefire began yesterday to be sounded all along the front . . . The German war is therefore at an end.

"Churchill made a very simple and impressive announcement," was one overheard comment. There were loud cheers when he said hostilities would cease from midnight. Churchill also spoke of the imminent liberation of the Channel Islands—and there were more cheers for that. But when he announced "The German war is therefore at an end" there were whoops of joy and all the flags were waved. The broadcast closed with the national anthem and one onlooker said: "Young and old sang 'God Save the King' with such fervor that the anthem sounded like a battle hymn."

A volunteer nurse remembered being at Paddington Green Hospital to hear Churchill's speech:

As the hands of the ward clock neared the hour, the nursing staff automatically moved apart. For once the ward was silent—the children stopped chattering and not one of them was crying. When the Prime Minister's voice came on the air I glanced at the women in uniform. Each stood quietly and you could tell by their eyes that their thoughts were far away from the hospital.

The announcement finished. I felt a tug at my hand, which was being held by the small girl in the cot I was standing by. A little face was gazing up at mine. "What does it mean?" she asked anxiously.

"The war has ended." I tried to reassure her with a smile.

"What does that mean?"

I hesitated for a moment, searching for something she would understand. "Well it means you will see lights in the streets and windows lit up." She looked dazed and I stumbled on. "It means you will never hear a siren again."

"Never hear a siren again?" she repeated in a voice of utter astonishment. And I could see by the look in her eyes that she did not believe one word I had told her.

In the Führer Bunker on April 30 Hitler had gathered his personal staff in the early afternoon and briefly bade them farewell. In a strange echo, shortly after 3:00 p.m. on May 8, the prime minister's aides at Downing Street gathered to acclaim him. One recalled:

> After his statement, we all rushed downstairs and into the garden to line the path when he came out to go on to the House of Commons, to make his statement there. We clapped and clapped and I think there were tears in his eyes as he beamed and said "Thank you all, thank you very much." Outside, through the Horse Guards Parade . . . the whole place was jammed with people waiting to welcome him. They cheered and shouted, "Good old Winnie," and some pressed forward to pat the car and jump on the running board, so that it was almost impossible to move . . .

At 3:23 p.m. in the House of Commons, Harold Nicolson observed: "A slight stir was observed behind the Speaker's chair and Winston, looking coy and cheerful, came in. The House rose as a man and yelled and waved their order papers. The Prime Minister responded, not with a bow exactly, but with an odd shy jerk of the head and a wide grin. Then he begged to move: 'That this House does now attend at the Church of St. Margaret, Westminster, to give humble thanks to Almighty God for our deliverance from the threat of German domination.'"

After Churchill's broadcast there was a lull in the streets outside. War correspondent John Hodson, walking back through Whitehall and Trafalgar Square in bright sunshine, found London "gay and densely thronged, but comparatively quiet":

"Streets were crowded and looked, from a short distance, impassable. But in the main one could move about. The crowd was lighthearted, wearing its red, white and blue rosettes as on a Cup Final Day—and wearing too, a host of comic hats . . . Girls had climbed on to various clumps of stone and turned themselves into living statues: the lions' heads in Trafalgar Square were being sat upon . . ."

The writer John Lehmann, walking across Hyde Park, was struck by the "not quite full-hearted nature of the celebrations." He felt that the crowds were aware that Japan had still to be conquered, at a cost no one could reckon, and were more dazed than excited. "It was a sober cheerfulness," another participant observed, "that was very different from Armistice Day in November 1918, when everything went completely crazy."

At Speakers' Corner in Hyde Park the merchants of doom were excelling themselves. Some were anti-government and anti-Churchill. Others predicted that the seeds of the next war were already sprouting in Poland and the Balkans. But they were a tiny minority. And real excitement did grow as the afternoon went on. Soon after 4:00 p.m. the royal family and Churchill appeared on the balcony at Buckingham Palace to greet everyone. "It was without doubt Churchill's day," Mollie Panter-Downes said. "When the crowd saw him there was a deep, full-throated, almost reverent roar."

Then word spread that Churchill would be making a second speech and crowds of people were soon jammed in front of the Ministry of Health building, calling out "We want Winnie." When he appeared, just before 6:00 p.m., complete with a cigar, and gave the "V" sign, another deafening roar went up.

People had waited for hours in the heat, chanting and singing. When Churchill appeared the crowd cheered itself hoarse. When he was eventually able to make himself heard he said: "This is your victory. It is the victory of the cause of freedom in every land. In all of living history we have never seen a greater day than this. Everyone, man or woman, has done their best. Everyone has tried. Neither the long years, nor the dangers, nor the fierce attacks of the enemy, have in any way weakened the deep resolve of the British nation. God bless you all."

Elizabeth Leighton, one of Churchill's private secretaries, was also on the balcony. She remembered: "At the end of his brief speech, Churchill gazed out at the seething mass of people. And then, quite spontaneously, he began to sing 'Land of Hope and Glory.' There was a roar of approval—and as one, the crowd joined in with him."

Mary Blythe, who had traveled up to London for the day, felt an intoxicating sense of happiness that evening. However, there was fragility amid the euphoria. Mollie Panter-Downes observed:

All day long, the deadly past was for most people just under the surface of the beautiful, safe present, so much so that the government decided against sounding the sirens in a triumphant "all clear" for fear that the noise would revive too many painful memories. For the same reason, there were no salutes of guns—only the pealing of bells, the whistles of tugs on the Thames and the roar of the planes, which swooped back and forth over the city, dropping red and green signals toward the blur of smiling, upturned faces.

And at 9:00 p.m. King George VI broadcast to the nation. For all who heard it, it was his best speech—delivered with sincerity and conviction:

Today we give thanks to Almighty God for a great deliverance. Speaking from our Empire's oldest capital city, war-battered, but never for one moment daunted or dismayed, speaking from London, I ask you to join with me in that act of thanksgiving . . . Let us remember those who will not come back, the men and women in all the services who laid down their lives . . . Then let us salute in proud gratitude the great host of the living who have brought us to victory . . . Let us think what has upheld us through nearly six years of suffering and peril . . . To that, let us on this day of just triumph and proud sorrow turn our thoughts, and then take up our work again, resolved as a people and then to do nothing unworthy of those who died for us and to make such a world as they would have desired, for their children and for ours.

Away from the massed crowds of London, England celebrated in its own way, with towns and villages across the country holding street parties, lighting bonfires, passing round beer and sandwiches. William Paton remembered the festivities in Stoneyburn in West Lothian, Scotland:

I heard Prime Minister Churchill speaking on the wireless at 3:00 p.m. when he gave his long-awaited and eagerly anticipated statement about the surrender of Germany. He announced that the war was over and that Germany had accepted unconditional surrender. It was a day of great rejoicing in every town and village of Britain. Stoneyburn was awash with flags, there was singing, dancing and a parade. Festivities were interrupted at 9:00 p.m. so that we could hear the King speaking. That night bonfires were lit at every street corner and crowds gathered round them and sang into the small hours.

Joan Strange wrote about the mood of celebration in Worthing:

It's come at last. I woke up at 7:00 a.m. to hear the sound of Mother wrestling with the flags (rather moth-eaten and patched). But we weren't the first in the road . . . the weather's been good for the first of the two VE Day holidays. There were church services at mid-day and in the afternoon we all listened to the thrilling broadcasts on the European victory. The highlights were the Prime Minister's short broadcast at 3:00 p.m. and the King's at 9:00 p.m.. Hostilities end officially at one minute past midnight tonight when it's hoped that any fighting against the Soviet Union will also cease. It's Russia's VE Day tomorrow.

It was the street parties which more than anything else caught the mood. A participant recalled:

Plate-loads disappeared, but no matter, they were filled again. Paper hats were worn by the ladies and aprons colored red, white and blue. A gramophone was brought out and we sang along to it. Chairs were placed near a wall, tables cleared and dishes washed—then races for the children. The women and children started dancing and the street was alive with record after record. Soon people were coming from other streets and joining in. When the pub closed at 10:00 p.m. an avalanche descended upon us. At 10:30 p.m. a bonfire was lit opposite my house. Hitler was on top of it—and how the crowd cheered when he came down in flames.

Irene Bain described events on her street in Mitcham:

A group of women in the street formed a committee to organize the party. On the actual day trestle tables were set up in the center of the road and covered in cloths. Chairs were brought out of the houses and arranged down each side. Use was now made of the precious items of food hoarded for such a purpose. Vases were filled with flowers picked from our gardens and set at intervals down the tables, which were soon laden with plates of food. All of us children went to the party with our brothers and sisters and the babies were carried along too. I wore my best dress and the recently-bought wooden soled sandals I was so proud of . . . At the end, one of only two car owners, a taxi driver, sat at a little table and handed out to each child in the road a sixpence.

The children were very much in people's minds. Some had suffered the terror of bombing and the V1 and V2 rockets. Some had been evacuated—and then later returned to their homes. Now they represented hope for the future. Shirley Cheves, who spent her childhood in wartime Lincoln, was also smartly dressed for the party she attended. "I wore my red parachute silk dress with the blue and white braid," she said proudly, "and we all had our picture taken together." A teacher in Thornaby-on-Tees observed: "People have gone to great trouble to give enjoyment to their children—red, white and blue dresses (I see three beautifully made from bunting). Decorated tricycles, toy motor cars . . ."

Mollie Panter-Downes wrote: "It was a day and night of no fixed plan—each group danced its own dance, sang its own song, and went its own way, as the spirit moved it. The most tolerant people on VE Day were the police, who simply stood by, smiling benignly, while soldiers swung by one arm from the lamp posts and laughing groups tore down hoardings to build the evening's bonfire."

Later that evening floodlights were switched on all over London. One woman, an office worker who lived on the Edgware Road, returned home that night after a party and wrote in her diary:

> I came back and went up on our flat roof, from which my husband and I had so often watched fires flaring up in a ring around London. We had seen explosions, listened to the sounds of bombs, planes and guns during the "Little Blitz" of spring 1944. We had watched the buzz bombs with their flaming tails careering over the houses before the final bang. And now there were floodlit flags and lights in the windows. It all seemed too good to be true.
>
> As I looked up at the sky, fireworks began to crackle around the horizon and the red glow of distant bonfires lit up the sky—peaceful joyous fires now, in place of the terrifying ones of last year. Toward midnight the fireworks reached a climax and there were more fires on the horizon. It was a warm, starlit night but just after midnight a streak of summer lightning joined the other illuminations and strangely enough, looked rather like a V sign flashing in the sky.

Yet not all Europe was peaceful. As Prague fought for its survival, uprisings had begun in other parts of the Czech lands. The country was awash with insurgents, retreating Germans and advancing Red Army troops. On May 8 South African POW Dave Brokensha was in a marching column in Czechoslovakia. Brokensha had been captured at Tobruk and then held in a prison camp near Dresden. As the Red Army approached the men had been evacuated south, across the border. The column of over 700 POWs—in a no-man's-land between US and Red Army forces—was mistakenly bombed and machine-gunned in three sorties by Russian dive bombers and fighters. Brokensha received a hand wound, but it was not serious. A small group— Brokensha among them—managed to escape the column and walked through a desolate landscape, littered with corpses and dead horses. The following day they at last managed to reach the safety of the American lines.

Supreme Allied Command was now honoring its commitment to the second surrender ceremony in Berlin. The delegation of Western Allies had reached Karlshorst in the early afternoon. It had been decided that Eisenhower would be represented by Air Chief Marshal Tedder. But before the delegation had set off, Eisenhower took further action to repair the breach with Russia. He sent an urgent recommendation to both the American and British governments:

> With reference to the message from the Russian High Command [the one objecting to the initial surrender] forwarded to both governments, referring to the possibility of the Germans continuing to fight against the Russians after the agreed upon hour for the cessation of hostilities, I recommend as a matter of urgency that both governments send a message along the following lines to the Russian High Command:
>
> The unconditional surrender of Germany was made jointly to Russia and to the Allied Forces and any continuation of hostilities, after the agreed upon hour for cessation, is an offense jointly against Russia and the western allies. Consequently, if any sizable bodies of German forces make any such attempt, they will no longer have the status of soldiers.
>
> You may be assured that General Eisenhower will, under such circumstances, continue to cooperate closely with the Red Army, looking toward the elimination of such bodies and operating along such lines as may be indicated to him as desirable by the Russian High Command. We do not accept that any German forces may continue to fight against the Red Army without in effect fighting our own troops also.
>
> I think that some such assurance as this would be beneficial— particularly in view of the fact that it seems inescapable that the announcement [of VE Day] must be made today by Britain and

America, and which the Russians feel should be postponed until tomorrow, the 9th.

This was Eisenhower at his best—proactive, clear, firm and generous. There is little doubt that this reassurance eased the tension between the Western Allies and the Soviet Union.

As Eisenhower took this precaution, Field Marshal Schörner was broadcasting his own response to the Rheims signing:

Soldiers of Army Group Center, false rumors are being spread that the Reich's government is willing to surrender to the Anglo-Americans and also the Soviet Union. This is an evil lie—and one that must never undermine our will to resist, which is directed implacably against the east. Loyal to the orders issued by Admiral Dönitz, the fight against the Bolsheviks will continue until all Germans are safe. The struggle in the west, however, is over. But there can be no question of surrender to the Bolsheviks—that would mean death to all of us.

With these false rumors about capitulation, the Red enemy is trying to undermine our resistance. It is all a propaganda trick. Standing proud and upright, we continue our sworn duty. Neither the few cowards and traitors in our own ranks, or the slogans of the enemy, can break our power.

The undefeated troops of Army Group Center will fight on heroically!

Still it was the same Nazi fanaticism, replete with the same dangerous lies. But this would be Schörner's last broadcast. A Red Army specialist unit had moved into Czechoslovakia and was tracking the movements of his headquarters. Colonel Vasily Buslaev's fast armored reconnaissance troops had located Schörner and his army staff in the town of Zatec by monitoring its transmissions. They wanted to disrupt Army Group Center's organization and, if possible, capture Schörner himself. Buslaev's men launched a surprise attack. They captured nine generals, a host of officers and documents and equipment, but there was no sign of Schörner. One of the German generals said contemptuously: "He slipped away with his Czech-speaking adjutant, changed into civilian clothes and went off to try and find the Americans. There will be no more heroic stands from him."

On May 8 President Truman celebrated his sixty-first birthday. He had made the American victory announcement from the Radio Room of the White House at 9:00 a.m. East Coast time.

"This is a solemn but glorious hour," Truman began. "I only wish that Franklin D. Roosevelt had lived to witness it. General Eisenhower informs me that the forces of Germany have surrendered . . . The flags of freedom fly all over Europe."

The president struck a somber tone. "Our rejoicing is sobered and subdued by a supreme consciousness of the terrible price we have paid to rid the world of Hitler and his evil band . . . We must work to finish the war. Our victory is but half-won. The West is free, but the East is still in bondage to the treacherous tyranny of the Japanese. When the last Japanese division has surrendered unconditionally, only then will our fighting job be done."

Nevertheless, the mood in Washington was a happy one. Major Keith Wakefield of the Australian Military Mission remembered that "the lawns around the Washington, Lincoln and Jefferson monuments were teeming with joyous people." In New York there were scenes of celebration in Times Square throughout the day—and ticker tape came down on the crowd. In Louisiana, Anne Ralph recalled being on a train "and hearing bells ringing as we went through the little towns . . . I didn't know what was going on until the train stopped and someone told us the war in Europe had ended. In New Orleans people were literally dancing in the streets. They were singing, dancing, jumping in and out of fountains. It was like the Mardi Gras—and just this incredible sense of relief that part of our war, anyway, was finished."

In San Francisco a young journalist named John F. Kennedy filed a dispatch on VE-Day to the *New York Journal*. The paper noted that as a navy lieutenant in the Pacific he had been decorated for bravery against the Japanese and that he was the son of former ambassador to Britain Joseph Kennedy. In "A Serviceman's View," John Kennedy noted that San Francisco had taken VE-Day in its stride.

"This city overlooks the Pacific and to the people here 'the war' has always been the war against the Japanese," Kennedy began. "The servicemen who crowd the streets have taken it calmly. The war in the Pacific is the only war that most of them have ever known—and when you have just come home from long months of fighting and are returning to the war zones in a few days, it is difficult to become excited about 'the end of the war.' Victory for them is a long way off."

But then Kennedy addressed the United Nations conference. Here, he believed, news of the end of the war in Europe would act as a stimulant to all the delegates convened there. And he spoke perceptively about Russia:

The question of the Soviet Union had dominated the conference. Molotov's work was about done. He leaves the other delegates divided in their attitude toward him and the entire Russian policy. Some are extremely suspicious, while on the other hand, there is a group which has great confidence that the Russians in their own strange and inexplicable way really want peace.

The arguments of these delegates boil down to this: It starts with an assumption that a nation can usually be depended upon to act in its own best interests. In this case, Russia needs peace more than anything else. To get this peace, she feels she needs security. No-one must be able to invade her again. The Russians have a far greater fear of a German come-back than we do. They are therefore going to make their western defenses secure. No governments hostile to Russia will be permitted in the countries along her borders. They feel they have earned this right to security. They mean to have it, come what may.

At Allied Supreme Headquarters, General Dwight Eisenhower sensed that he had mastered the storm. Others would have lacked his patience, humility and integrity. Eisenhower confided his inner thoughts about this sudden crisis in the Grand Alliance to his friend and patron General George Marshall, chief of staff of the US Army:

A group of my representatives, headed by my deputy supreme commander, have just departed for Berlin to sign, in company with Marshal Zhukov, the formal instrument of military surrender. The meeting, completely concurred with by the Russians, finally relieves my mind of the anxiety that I have had due to the danger of misunderstanding and trouble at the last meeting [the Rheims surrender signing].

This anxiety has been intensified by very skillful German propaganda that was inspired by the German desire to surrender to us instead of the Russians. All the evidence shows that the Germans in the east are being paid back in the same coin that they used in their Russian campaigns of 1941 and 1942 and they are now completely terrified—individually and collectively—of Russian vengeance.

If it is true, as alleged, that the head of the Associated Press Bureau here broke the pledge of secrecy under which he was permitted to witness negotiations, and in addition, used commercial lines out of Paris merely to get a scoop for his company, then he was guilty of something that might have had the most unfortunate repercussions, involving additional loss of American lives.

To be perfectly frank, the last four days just passed have taken more out of me and my staff than the past eleven months of this campaign. However, as noted above, I am at last reasonably certain that in so far as hostilities are concerned, the Russians and ourselves are now in complete understanding and the meeting today should be marked by cordiality.

But there was one last problem—the alteration of the original treaty (signed at Rheims) by the provision of an additional clause concerning the immediate surrender of German weapons and troops. The Germans were justified in asserting that the original text was the one binding under international law. When Field Marshal Keitel was given a copy of the new surrender text, at Berlin's Tempelhof Airport, this crucial interpolation was heavily underscored and a note in the margin stated "New!"

Keitel made it clear to Zhukov that he would not sign the revised surrender terms unless further clarification was provided. He stated:

> The basic modification was the interpolation of a clause threatening to punish troops who failed to cease fire and surrender at the time provided. I told the interpreter that I demanded to speak to a representative from Marshal Zhukov, as I would not sign such an interpolation unconditionally.
>
> I explained that I was objecting because I could not guarantee that our cease fire orders would be received in time, with the result that the troops' commanders might feel justified in failing to comply with any demands to that effect. I demanded that a [further] clause be written in that the surrender would only come into force twenty-four hours after the orders had been received by our troops; only then would the penalty clause take effect.
>
> About an hour later Zhukov's representative was back with the news that the Marshal had agreed to twelve hours' grace being given.

Behind this last round of negotiating was the very real fear—on the part of the Russians—that Germany would still not abide by the terms of unconditional surrender. On the German side was a wish to continue to play for time—which might allow, even at this late stage, more of their troops to surrender to the Western Allies. As the moment of signing drew closer the issue raised its head once more. Keitel noticed that Zhukov had not inserted the "12 hour" clause into the surrender document as agreed. There was another delay.

After the postponement, everyone assembled for the surrender ceremony at 10:30 p.m. that night. It was staged in a plain, concrete-built former German engineering works simply because most of its buildings were still intact. The room itself was much larger than the one at Rheims, about 60 feet long and 40 feet wide, with two levels and a small balcony running along one side. The delegation from the Western Allies consisted of Air Chief Marshal Sir Arthur Tedder (Eisenhower's deputy), General Jean de Lattre de Tassigny (commander of the 1st French Army) and General Carl Spaatz (head of the United States 8th Air Force).

Eisenhower's driver, Kay Summersby, recalled the scene:

The huge room was banked with klieg lights—quite blinding as we stepped in from the dim hallway. Inside were the Russian press, who numbered about a hundred, and movie cameras were placed in almost every conceivable spot. Microphones hung from the ceiling and sprouted from the floor creating a spider's web of wires and cables.

A long table at one end of the room commanded all the attention. From it stretched three other tables, for the press and smaller fry. Set apart, under the balcony, was a small table—apparently reserved for the surrendering Germans. There was a momentary silence as Marshal Zhukov, a short stocky officer with a stern expression, entered the room. Everyone stood up. As we sat again, he called proceedings to order.

Summersby was struck by the commanding influence of Soviet Deputy Commissar for Foreign Affairs Andrei Vyshinsky, who seemed to hover over the entire proceedings. Even Zhukov deferred to him. At this moment of military victory, the Kremlin was once more reasserting its authority over the army.

Then the signal was given for the enemy's entrance. As the door opened just behind the empty table, silence smothered the babble. Every pair of eyes in the room focused on a tall German officer in smart blue-gray field marshal's uniform, his chest covered with decorations and medals, his head poised high. He stepped stiffly to the table, jerked up his silver-headed baton in curt salute and sat down.

The noise rose again. No-one seemed to notice the other two Germans who took their places beside Keitel [Admiral Georg von Friedeburg and Luftwaffe colonel general Hans-Jürgen Stumpff].

But German concerns over the clause inserted by the Russians were brought forward again. American war correspondent Charles Kiley, writing for *Stars and Stripes*, recalled: "Keitel, tall and erect, was a model of Prussian arrogance to the end. After he had been called from the German delegates' table to the one occupied by the Allied officers, to sign, he returned to his seat and bitterly argued a point in the surrender." Again, he wanted more time to inform German units of the new provision. And the "12 hour" clause promised by Zhukov was still not in the official document. It was now two minutes to eleven at night (central European time).

A further round of argument continued in the surrender hall. The ceasefire was formally to take effect at one minute past midnight. As that time was reached, both sides remained deadlocked. The impasse was broken only when Marshal Zhukov yelled across the room: "I give you my word as a soldier!"

It was already several minutes past midnight. Kiley's account continued: "The three principal German delegates then took their seats on the opposite side of the Allied table. Air Marshal Tedder addressed them: 'I ask you— have you read this document on unconditional surrender and are you prepared to sign it?' The Germans nodded."

Marshal Zhukov and Air Chief Marshal Tedder signed as representatives of the Allies, followed by Generals Spaatz and De Tassigny as witnesses.

Kiley recalled: "While Stumpff was signing, and the documents were being passed to Zhukov, Tedder, Spaatz and de Lattre, Keitel first became annoyed by the photographers darting around the room and then called the Russian interpreter, to once more discuss the possibility of having the 'end of hostilities' clause removed."

The reluctance of the Germans to surrender to the Russians was mirrored by the interminable delays to the signing ceremony itself. Finally, Keitel conceded. Kay Summersby remembered the moment: "The Field Marshal carefully pulled off one gray glove before taking the pen. He looked up contemptuously at the boisterous newsmen, then scribbled his signature, as though anxious to dispense with a dirty job . . ."

Then Zhukov gave an order of dismissal. "The Nazis arose as at a parade-ground command. Keitel again jerked his baton in brief salute. They left the room with an exit as dramatic as their entrance . . . Now, even for the Russians, VE-Day was official."

However, Field Marshal Keitel's reluctance to accept the additional clause had further aroused Soviet suspicions. In a private room at 1:00 a.m. on May 9 the Russians now interrogated Keitel on German good faith over the military surrender.

Proceedings were led by Colonel General Ivan Serov, chief of logistics in the 1st Belorussian Front. He emphasized primarily that the Red Army would not accept any delay in implementing surrender.

Keitel offered to send, on the afternoon of May 9, an officer of the Army General Staff, with maps showing the full deployment of German forces in the east and their commanders. The next day, May 10, he believed liaison officers would be in place to resolve any outstanding issues.

Serov turned to the matter of the so-called Dönitz government—saying it was acting as a legitimate administration when such a situation did not really exist in Flensburg. Keitel temporized, saying more time was needed to set up an alternative government that could work with the Allies. Serov asked on what authority Dönitz called himself head of state. Keitel referred back to Hitler's will. Serov remained unconvinced.

At 1:30 a.m. the victors reassembled in the place of surrender, now converted into a banqueting hall, complete with orchestra in the balcony, to celebrate their victory. The meal lasted four hours. Summersby wisely drank water:

By five o'clock in the morning, even the expert interpreter couldn't understand the toasts. The majority of the banquet guests were drunk. Several Russians literally went under the table. Songs bubbled up in four languages. The orchestra, which had struck chords for each and every toast, began to lose its way as the vodka cloud permeated the balcony. As the party broke up just before dawn it was reckoned there had been twenty-nine individual toasts, each requiring five to ten minutes for translation, plus the musical chord. We all agreed we had been in on the VE party to end all VE parties.

Marshal Zhukov wrote of this occasion: "After the signing I congratulated everyone present. Then an incredible commotion broke out in the hall. Everyone was congratulating one another and shaking hands. Many had tears of joy in their eyes. I was surrounded by my comrades-in-arms."

The second toast Marshal Zhukov made, after the obligatory one to Stalin, was to General Eisenhower. The Soviet commander praised him as a great general "and one of America's outstanding sons." And of the banquet, and the singing and dancing that followed, Zhukov added:

> The Soviet generals were unrivaled as far as dancing went. Even I could not restrain myself, and remembering my youth, did the Russkaya dance. We left the banquet hall to the accompaniment of a cannonade from all types of weapons on the occasion of the victory. The shooting went on in all parts of Berlin and its suburbs. Although shots were fired into the air, fragments from mines, shells and bullets fell to the ground and it was not completely safe to walk in the open. But how different it was from the danger to which we had grown accustomed during the long years of the war!

For Zhukov, the Soviet Union's most gifted and ruthless commander, it was a powerful moment of relaxation, happiness and deep pride. "Where Zhukov goes, victory will follow," Red Army soldiers would say. That victorious road, one that had begun at Leningrad and Moscow in 1941, had now reached Berlin. It was right that Zhukov led the signing at Karlshorst—for the Soviet Union and for the world. It was Russia which had ripped the guts out of the German war machine—and paid the price in the blood of 27 million of its soldiers and civilians.

Zhukov evoked a universal bond of military comradeship. He had celebrated the war's end in Berlin. Private John Frost of the British 11th Armored Division wrote home at the end of that day from Lübeck:

> It is VE Day and fighting has ceased—we have much to be thankful for. This afternoon we all listened to Churchill broadcast over the radio—it put the official touch to things that it was all over. At nine

we shall be hearing a speech from the King. From the radio news we have all learned of the wild celebrations going on in London and other cities. I wish I could see all the flags flying and hear the bells pealing.

This morning on parade we had three special Orders of the Day read out to us. They were congratulatory messages from Army commanders on our achievements in Germany. One, from General Dempsey, was for our division only—he congratulated the 11th Armored on their recent capture of Lübeck and advance to the Baltic Sea.

General Miles Dempsey, commander of the British 2nd Army, had every reason to be pleased with the 11th Armored Division, which had fulfilled its last combat mission so effectively, preventing the German 3rd Panzer Army from reaching Schleswig-Holstein and ensuring that Red Army troops did not enter Denmark. "Along this road today are passing thousands more German soldiers," Frost continued. "They look battle-worn and completely tired. Also on the road, making their own escape from the Russians, are hundreds of civilians. Those that have carts have household belongings piled up in them; most are walking—women and children too. VE-Day is very different in Germany."

For some, the sight of the Wehrmacht prostrate brought out feelings of compassion. Red Cross welfare worker Nancy Wilson was stationed at a hospital in the Scharnhorst Barracks in Lüneburg. The sense of relief and congratulation on VE-Day was tempered by images of the beaten army. She recalled: "The sight of the bedraggled remnants of the German Army slowly trudging toward our line of lorries was terrible. They had been disarmed and told to get home as best they could. They stumbled past, limping, bandaged, some supported by their comrades, totally broken and beaten. The sight reminded me of the painting of the French retreat from Moscow in 1812."

And yet, in the Italian theater of war, which had concluded with a triumphant campaign in the Po valley and the signing of the first unconditional surrender of German troops at Caserta on May 2, Sergeant Major Harry Dutka of the Royal Army Service Corps was able to take a Victory Day excursion to Venice. He remembered:

We left on a truck early in the morning, [and] passing through war-damaged Padua arrived in Venice. It seemed we were the first soldiers—and there were still gondolas in abundance waiting for clients. It was still quite cool and the water was smooth like a mirror. It seemed unbelievable to admire the wonders of this fantasy city, unmarked by war, just hours after the fighting had ended. On returning to camp we were pleasantly surprised to hear that VE Day had been prolonged to include the 9th May as well.

Field Marshal Alexander, the Supreme Allied Commander in the Mediterranean, broadcast to his men: "Some of you will be going home," he said. "Others will go to defeat the last remaining aggressor, the Japanese, who are already in a sorry way and know what is coming to them. We and our Allies, by means of the same united strength which has at last brought us victory in Europe, shall now proceed to clean up the Japanese once and for all."

On VE-Day Peter Haddington of the British 21st Army Group's Kinematograph Service dispensed with war newsreels and rigged up his screen, amplifier and projection equipment in the market square of the Dutch town of Zevenaar. The grateful populace, most of whom had not seen a film for five years, erupted in gales of laughter at the cartoon antics of Popeye and Mickey Mouse.

One of Haddington's tasks had been to show film of the newly liberated concentration camps to Allied soldiers. On May 8 British soldier Noel Mander was stationed in the Royal Army Pay Corps headquarters on the outskirts of Rome. "We were given the day off," Mander recalled. "The city was throbbing with excitement and jubilation, drinks were pressed on everyone and bands were playing." Yet Mander left the celebrations early. It was not only the unfinished war with Japan which was on his mind. He had also seen pictures of the concentration camps on the cinema screen just days earlier.

There were surges of exhilaration. In Paris, Corporal William Dryer of the US Air Force wrote to his fiancée: "The people went mad. Mad with laughter, mad with happiness, mad with anything and everything. All up and down the streets the cheering populace let it be known that Hitler was kaput."

Ferdinand Picard was also in Paris that day:

I was immersed in a Parisian crowd drunk with the joy of victory. From the Saint-Lazare train station to the Place de la Republique I followed a river of people spread along the entire width of the boulevard. All generations mingled in this tide of humanity. Women carried babies in their arms, which they sometimes held aloft to show to the Allied soldiers. White-haired, thin old men rediscovered the enthusiasm of their youth. Teenage boys and girls, in colorful clothes and wearing ribbons and brocades, thronged around the American jeeps and trucks. They screamed—and were beside themselves with joy.

But Canadian gunner James Brady, who was in the town of Marx in Germany when the war ended, struck a more reflective tone. He wrote in his diary on May 8: "At last the wondrous day—Victory in Europe. Our crew, however, are silent and thoughtful: anti-climax. There is no feeling of exaltation, nothing but a quiet satisfaction that the job has been done and we can see home again."

Brady remembered his artillery regiment's commemorative service:

"We assembled and paraded before our commanding officer, Colonel Gagnon. Then we marched to a memorial service in a little rural church nearby. The Colonel began to read the thirty-six names of the fallen. Tears were in his eyes. He faltered—then handed the list to an adjutant, who calmly folded the paper and put it in his pocket. Then, quietly, he said: 'It is not necessary. They were our comrades. We remember.'"

The war had left more than 42,000 Canadian servicemen dead: 23,000 in the army, 17,000 in the Royal Canadian Air Force and 2,000 in the navy. More than 54,000 had been wounded—and 9,000 taken prisoner. Total casualties among the Western Allies from D-Day to the end of the war numbered 186,000 dead, 545,700 wounded and 109,600 missing in action.

Some were numbed by it all. Major Harry Jolley of the 5th Canadian Armored Division wrote to his sister that his own and his comrades' reaction to the Nazi surrender had almost been a disappointment: "I imagined it would be a day of unforgettable scenes. Not so. I saw a few men gathered around our signals wagon as I went over to listen but none of us shouted, threw hats in the air or anything of that sort. I remember I shouted to a friend 'It's all over now!' He barely acknowledged what I had said."

Lieutenant William Preston with the US 65th Infantry Division (part of General Patton's Third Army) wrote to his brother about VE-Day:

The war in Europe is over. I can hardly believe it, for it seems only yesterday that we were seeing our first action on the Siegfried Line.

On VE Day I sat by an open window and listened and watched as German soldiers, thousands of them, passed by me on their way to a POW camp.

I don't know what the reaction is like in the States as a whole. Over a patched-up radio we heard that ticker tape and paper floated down from New York buildings. We heard that there were wild celebrations in the streets of London by civilians and British and American soldiers. But the front-line troops didn't celebrate. Most of the men merely read the story from the division bulletin sent to the troops, said something like "I'm glad" and walked away. Perhaps it was a different story in their hearts, or perhaps they were too tired or thinking about home or their buddies who didn't see the victory to do too much celebrating or merry making. But I'm sure of one thing—the troops were glad they wouldn't have to fight anymore.

Corporal Tom Renouf of the Black Watch Infantry Regiment (51st Highland Division) had fought from the Normandy beaches to Bremerhaven in Germany. He had been wounded crossing the Seine—and awarded the Military Medal for Gallantry at the crossing of the Rhine. "We were told the war was over—and at first it just didn't sink in," Renouf said. "We had been living from day to day, just trying to survive. And then I began to realize that I was one of the lucky ones—and how fortunate I was to have survived."

General Sir Alan Brooke, Chief of the British General Staff, said of the 51st Highland Division: "During the war I had the opportunity to see most of the British and Dominion Divisions, many of the American Divisions and some of the French and Belgian Divisions. I can assure you that among all these the 51st unquestionably takes its place alongside the very few which, through their valor and fighting record, stand in a category of their own."

In North Africa, Sicily and northwest Europe the 51st had lost 3,084 men killed, 12,047 wounded and 1,457 missing in action.

Field Marshal Montgomery commented: "It is both a humiliation and an honor to have had such a Division under my command. I shall always remember the Highland Division with admiration and high regard."

At the end of the war, the 51st had been opposed by its old rival from North Africa, the German 15th Panzer Grenadier Division, a formation that had kept its cohesion and discipline to the last. Now the fighting had stopped. Corporal Renouf continued:

And then other things started to happen. I was no longer listening for bullets and mortars coming in my direction. I was no longer looking for enemy strongholds that would be sniping at us. I was no longer smelling the cordite from exploding shells. It was all gone.

And instead, I was listening to the birds, smelling the flowers, enjoying the scenery—just looking at the beauty of the world. What a contrast it was—from one extreme to the other. And I felt that I had been born all over again.

And I vowed from then onward that I would lead a proper life. I would not waste my time. I would try to make full use of everything that lay ahead of me.

A Royal Canadian naval officer on convoy escort duty on VE-Day recalled how startling it was to see the lights go on at sea: "The sight of 60-odd ships, in formation and fully illuminated, was a truly remarkable one," he said, "and after five and a half years of darkness a little frightening to behold."

The darkness over Europe was ending.

Lee Dickman of the 11th Field Company South African Engineer Corps was near Klagenfurt in Austria on the night of May 8. He wrote:

Some God, somewhere, said "Let there be again light" and there was light.

Searchlights swept magic wands from side to side, parachute flares, brilliant white, floated slowly down. Star shells plucked bursts of flame out of the sky. Verey lights formed arcs of red, green and orange in pale glimmers near the horizon; tracers dropped red necklaces into the cupped hands of the night. Everybody threw anything that exploded into the sky in an outpouring of joy, of relief, of hope.

I walked slowly through the dark of this small Austrian town. Golden droplets of light spilled across my feet as black-out curtains were swept aside, shutters burst open and street lights sputtered, flickered, then burned strong.

I remembered comrades who had died next to me. The horror of falling bombs. The sullen surrender of a disillusioned German soldier.

And I thanked that anonymous God for the fact that I, however minutely, had helped cast aside the evil that had shrouded Europe for so long.

It was VE Day. The killing had stopped. I could go home.

10

MOSCOW

MAY 9, 1945

Moscow journalist Lazarus Brontman—who wrote for *Pravda*—had heard about the Eisenhower signing at Rheims, but was unsure whether or not they should celebrate it. The news had been embargoed. Then, on May 8, it emerged that Marshal Zhukov was to host a second signing at Karlshorst with Field Marshal Keitel—once the pictures of this came through they could run the story; May 9 would be Russia's "holiday of victory."

The last few days had been worrying ones for the Russian people. "The Eisenhower treaty at Rheims was not reported," said Grigory Klimov, "but instead we heard rumors that the western allies and representatives of the German High Command were involved in secret negotiations. Nobody knew anything exactly, but the uneasiness increased. It was a time of strained expectation." Now Russia could properly celebrate its triumph.

In the Courland Pocket, the sustaining Nazi propaganda image of a breakwater, forever shoring up the defenses of the Reich, had finally cracked asunder. There would be no sudden turnaround of fortunes. Fortress Courland had repelled countless Red Army attacks but a total surrender was now coming into force. "The order to lay down our arms took me completely by surprise," Corporal Günther Klinge of the 563rd Grenadier Division confessed. "I still believed that new 'miracle weapons' would bring us final victory." The Germans began to realize they were not just giving up their weapons—all traces of their presence in Courland were being expunged.

Sergeant Wilfried Ohrts of the 14th Panzer Division wrote in his diary on May 9:

> The outcome that we had resisted for so long has now come to pass— the war is over and we have been defeated. Our homeland has been ravaged and occupied by the enemy. And here in Courland we have submitted to captivity and a future of misery, hardship and hunger. As we began our march, as prisoners of the Red Army, we passed former battle sites and saw that our military cemeteries had been desecrated by the Russians. The ground where our comrades lay buried had been plowed up and the marker crosses smashed to pieces. I had a sudden, terrible realization. Across all the land east of the rivers Oder and Neisse, land now held by the Soviet Union, it will no longer be possible for a German grave to remain intact. The Bolsheviks want revenge, and they will take it not only on the living but also on the memory of the dead.

The last evacuation of German troops had been taking place at the Latvian port of Libau. Lieutenant Gerhard Anger had been struck by the discipline of his soldiers. There were only a few boats remaining—and thousands waited on the quayside. The Red Army had put the port under an artillery and aerial bombardment of growing intensity. "If a panic had broken out it would have led to a disaster," Anger said. "The ships would have been stampeded and swamped." Yet the men waited calmly and in silence. A steamer docked at the harbor and its captain told Anger he could take fifty men. The lieutenant found places for all his soldiers. And then an officer came on board and asked whether there was space for another forty wounded German soldiers. The captain replied that there was no more room and it would not be safe. Anger remarked: "I do not even have to give an order—all my soldiers immediately left the boat to make way for the wounded."

Now it had all ended. "The morning of May 9 was our first day of peace at Courland," said Captain Sergei Isachenko of the Soviet 198th Rifle Division. "German weapons were gathered at agreed collection points—the soldiers formed long columns as they moved off to designated camps. All along the front our guns fired victory salvoes into the air." The Russian soldiers had heard about the German unconditional surrender at Karlshorst. And in Courland it was being enforced within the agreed twelve-hour period from the actual signing—although a small minority of Wehrmacht soldiers and Latvians refused to accept it, vowing to carry on fighting in the forests.

On May 9 Red Army lieutenant Pavel Elkinson was in Hungary. He had witnessed much loss of life in the bitter fighting in eastern Europe. His unit heard about the German surrender that morning. "It's unbelievable," he wrote in his diary. "The silence is piercing my ears. Not a single shot—it's wonderful."

Soviet lieutenant Nikolai Inozemtsev was in Stettin on Germany's Baltic coast. He found out what was happening at 2:00 a.m. when a long burst of anti-aircraft fire was followed by flares and staccato gunshot. The gunshot continued in regular bursts—a signal of victory. Inozemtsev was immensely proud of the Red Army's achievement. "We have shown the world what we can do," he wrote in his diary, "and how much grief and suffering we can bear. Our victory has been won by iron determination and a selfless love of our motherland. Now we must rebuild our country."

Inozemtsev paused for a moment and thought of the comrades he had lost. "How many lives have been given in the name of our victory," he reflected. "How many smart, capable, talented people have died, so that we might enjoy a happy and secure future. We must never forget their sacrifice."

But elsewhere, the war continued. Sergeant Alexei Nemchinsky's 207th mine-clearing battalion was crossing into Czechoslovakia across the Ore mountains with the Soviet 21st Army. The troops, part of Marshal Konev's 1st Ukrainian Front, had advanced over 60 miles in three days. The men heard about Germany's capitulation in the early hours of May 9. They pulled off the road, shooting their rifles in the air and letting off flares to celebrate the victory. But then they were on the move again, following Field Marshal Schörner's army group. Although it was now without its commander, they had been warned that these men were not accepting the ceasefire but retreating westward toward the Americans.

Later that night Nemchinsky's unit suffered casualties in a clash with German troops. They would be fighting for a further three days. "Holding a funeral for a fallen comrade after victory has been declared is particularly painful," Nemchinsky said.

Captain Vasily Zaitsev's Soviet 4th Tank Army was also pushing through the Ore mountains toward Prague. The men were driving hard. "We kept hearing the desperate radio appeals of the rebels," Zaitsev remembered.

On May 8 it seemed that Prague was dying. The insurgents were running out of ammunition—and we feared that the Nazis would completely eradicate the city in one last act of hate. They kept saying to us: "Russian brothers—help Prague!"

Early on May 9 we heard on the radio about the unconditional surrender of the German armed forces. Our entire staff embraced each other. But later that night we found the behavior of the enemy had not changed. They knew about the signing. They had ceased attacking operations—but they were not going to surrender to us. Whenever we met them on the road we had to fight.

Red Army troops had liberated the first concentration camp at Majdanek in Poland on July 23, 1944. Early in the morning of May 9 they would liberate the last, at Theresienstadt, 39 miles northeast of Prague.

Theresienstadt had been a Jewish ghetto and then a deportation camp, sending trainloads of prisoners directly to Auschwitz. With the Germans preoccupied in quelling the Prague uprising, the administration of Theresienstadt had been handed over to the International Red Cross. But conditions there remained unstable and dangerous. On the evening of May 8, one of the camp inmates, Erich Kessler, remembered, SS troops passed through the ghetto. "They lobbed hand grenades into the camp," Kessler said, "then opened up with machine gun fire. Everyone had to run for cover."

Early the following morning Kessler was awakened by a commotion just outside the camp's perimeter fence. He heard the sound of tanks—and cries of jubilation. It was the Russians. "I ran across the hospital courtyard," Kessler said. "Their armored vehicles were already tearing the fencing down. A procession of tanks was moving steadily past us on their way to Prague. It was pitch dark, but the light of their headlights lit up the road. We cheered them on and all sang the 'Internationale'—each as well as he could, German, Czech, Polish, Hungarian—all mixed together, but every version rendered with grateful enthusiasm."

Other Red Army soldiers followed up behind. Halina Reingold remembered: "A Russian officer shouted out to us: 'The war is over, you are free, you will get bread and you will never be hungry again.' It sunk in—we were free—and as it did so, people seemed to form into three groups: those who cried for joy and embraced each other, those who immediately ran to the food depots and those who started rounding up Germans and beating them."

The beating was not just of SS guards. Ben Helfgort had left the camp and walked to the nearby town of Leitmeritz. Theresienstadt was on the border of the Sudetenland—and the Sudeten Germans were now being expelled from their homes by the Czechs. They had become scapegoats for Czechoslovakia's misfortunes. The cycle of violence and revenge would continue—and others joined it. Helfgort was horrified to find a German woman and her two children—already chased out of their home—being beaten by two Jewish women survivors of the camp. "I told them to stop it. They said: 'But she's German. The Germans beat us—so now we will beat her.' I pushed them away."

Helfgort did not experience joy at liberation—but a kind of sickness. And Halina Reingold also felt a painful mix of emotions on being freed from Theresienstadt: "I was left wondering about my sick mother and the whereabouts of my father," Reingold said. "An unexpected, deep sadness came over me."

The very first Russian units arrived in the Czech capital at around 6:00 a.m. on May 9. Captain Zaitsev and his comrades reached Prague at about 10:00 a.m. They were warmly greeted by the city's inhabitants. The Czechs were now making Sudeten Germans dismantle the barricades. In victory, there would be a settling of old scores. The Germans were forced to lie prostrate on the ground as the Red Army soldiers approached. "They are not worthy to see you," one of the Czechs told Zaitsev. There was something ominous about this scene.

The German garrison had pulled out of Prague on the evening of May 8—but diehard SS units were still holding out there. However, the main threat to the city had passed. "We knew that our capital was now safe," Antonin Sticha said. "Early on May 9 advance units of the Red Army had reached Prague's outskirts. And at about 10:00 a.m. a column of their tanks rumbled past us. I remember a Russian soldier, sitting atop one of the vehicles, machine gunning a German sniper position. I was struck by his presence of mind—to him, it was a simple reflex action."

Jaroslav Oliverius recalled:

On the morning of May 9 we heard on Prague Radio that Red Army troops were approaching. The sense of relief was extraordinary—people began to shout, hug and cry. A group of us rushed to one of the main thoroughfares and began to pick sprigs of lilac, which had just come into bloom. And then a line of Russian tanks and lorries could be seen. The soldiers were grubby and covered in dust—they had clearly been on the move for days—but were smiling at us. One tank stopped right by our group. We presented the driver with lilac—and he offered us a ride. A day earlier, I had been carried to Prague's outskirts by the German tank; now I was being brought back to the city-center on a Russian one.

The Red Army soldiers entering Prague were welcomed as liberators. It was a moment of profound joy for the inhabitants, but Russian troops were still fighting the Germans to the east and west of the Czech capital and Marshal Konev ordered that celebrations in the city be cut short so that his men could push on and surround the remnants of Army Group Center.

At Deutsch-Brod (Nemecky-Brod), in the Bohemian mountains 70 miles southeast of Prague, a mass of German divisions were now trapped by the Red Army. Deutsch-Brod was the main headquarters of Army Group Center. The troops had abandoned the town in the early hours of May 9 and began moving westward toward the American lines, desperate to avoid surrendering to the Russians. But the US positions were simply too far away.

Czech partisans put the German columns under rifle and machine-gun fire, slowing their progress.

German soldier Joachim Halfpap remembered:

We were under constant bombardment. Our convoy stopped, started, and then stopped again. Shortly after dawn on May 9 our escape bid had slowed to a walking pace. We were in a valley and all around us were lightly wooded hills. The road ahead of us rose up and as the light grew stronger I saw that it was blocked by Russian tanks.

The soldiers behind me were pushing and shoving. They did not understand why we had come to a stop. There was a sense of rising panic—with men jostling and colliding into each other. But as the sun rose the reason for our halt became only too clear. In the fields around us, the hills, woodlands, everywhere were Soviet tanks and armored vehicles.

The Russians began to move down the road. Their machine guns were trained on us, their rifle bayonets fixed. They fired their rifles into the air and yelled at us to put our hands up. I had never seen a more menacing sight.

The Red Army had surrounded a considerable number of Wehrmacht troops, including most of the 253rd and 304th Infantry Divisions, the 78th and 320th Volks Grenadier Divisions and part of the 19th and Brandenburg Panzer Divisions. Other German soldiers were still on the move.

Gustav Lombard's 31st SS Division had swung north of Prague in an effort to reach the Americans at Pilsen. At Neu-Paka the road was blocked by Czech insurgents. They told Lombard of the surrender agreement made by General Toussaint and added that if the men laid down their arms, they would be allowed safe passage to the Americans. But it was a trap. The treaty with Toussaint had been honored but after the events of the uprising the Czechs had a score to settle with the SS. The troops surrendered their weapons and continued along the road—only to run straight into an ambush. Lombard and the other lead vehicles managed to accelerate, drive through their assailants and escape. Those following them were overwhelmed and almost certainly murdered.

Although the Wehrmacht's chain of command had broken down and most of these German soldiers were now fending for themselves, they were united in a desire to escape the Red Army. Few in Czechoslovakia intended to honor the Karlshorst surrender, even with the twelve-hour period of grace that Field Marshal Keitel had obtained in his negotiations with Marshal Zhukov.

This reaction was in part a result of race propaganda and a fear of the Slav, along with knowledge of the atrocities the Red Army had committed on German territory. But it ran deeper than that. Hitler had launched his predatory war on the Soviet Union after both sides had signed a non-aggression pact. And in the brutal struggle that followed, German soldiers were instruments of the Führer's belief in the racial superiority of his people over the Slavs. They were perpetrators—not victims. As General Eisenhower had remarked to General George Marshall, the German fear of the Russians primarily stemmed from the crimes that they themselves had committed or were complicit in within the Soviet Union. "They are being repaid in the same coin," Eisenhower said.

In the winter of 1941/42 alone, more than 2 million Red Army POWs had been starved to death—and most Wehrmacht soldiers knew about this. By 1944 their front-line units had been involved in anti-partisan operations in Belorussia so brutal and indiscriminate that they amounted to genocide. The soldiers knew or sensed their collective guilt—and it manifested as collective terror. In the words of German liaison officer Captain Wilhelm Hosenfeld: "We carry too much blood-guilt on our hands to receive a shred of sympathy from our opponent."

The Red Army had been propelled into Germany on a tide of "revenge propaganda." Some Russian soldiers found it hard to let go of that outlook; others began to change their attitude to the German people. But now, that revenge policy had, officially at least, been disavowed. Instead, the Russians wanted to make their German captives work—work to rebuild the swathes of Russia and the Ukraine that their armed forces had earlier laid to waste. They regarded this as their moral right after all the destruction that had been inflicted on their country by the German invasion—and they were determined to enforce it. If German soldiers chose not to honor the Karlshorst surrender, and tried to evade the Soviet forces, they would be pursued and surrender imposed on them at the barrel of a gun.

Many Westerners, unaware of the full military situation, were bewildered by what they saw as Russian intransigence. The day after VE-Day in the West, Britain was enjoying its second public holiday.

"Another day of meals in the street and bonfires at night," wrote Frank Lockwood of Acocks Green, Birmingham. "Celebrations continued," recorded Mary Derrick in Bristol. "Everyone was marching around—there were lights, and excitement. I shall never forget this day—it was just complete joy. There was no vandalism—everyone was so happy." Mary Derrick closed her diary entry with a simple yet heartfelt comment: "War is terrible—I hope it never happens again."

The surrender of the Channel Islands was received with overwhelming happiness. It had been the only part of the United Kingdom to fall under German occupation—and now the Nazi yoke was lifted.

Guernsey had been occupied on June 30, 1940, followed by Jersey on July 1. Alderney and Sark were occupied two days later. The islanders had not been allowed to communicate with relatives or friends overseas, except by a closely scrutinized twenty-five-word British Red Cross message once a month. They could not travel outside the Islands, run a car or listen to the radio. On December 20, 1941, the death penalty was announced for anyone keeping pigeons. More than a thousand British-born islanders were deported to Germany and hundreds more were sent to camps across Europe. Those who remained were forced to live side by side with the occupation forces. They endured curfews, censorship and a host of other restrictions—including growing shortages of food and clothing.

In the summer of 1944 the British armed forces had prepared a military unit—known as Force 135—with responsibility for recapturing the Channel Islands. On May 9 a small contingent of this force, led by its commander, Brigadier Snow, left for the islands on board two destroyers, HMS *Bulldog* and HMS *Beagle*. At 7:15 a.m., on the quarterdeck of the *Beagle*, General Siegfried Heine signed the instrument of surrender on behalf of the entire German command of the Channel Islands.

Within an hour, a British advance party had arrived in St. Peter Port, Guernsey. A British war correspondent described what followed:

Behind the dock gates was a seething, cheering crowd of men, women and children. The church bells were clanging tumultuously. The crowd pushed their way through the gates and engulfed the small British force. "We have waited so long for you," one woman said. Two girls with great Union Jacks led the little procession through the town, with more and more people joining it. At the Old Court House the soldiers formed up on each side of the steps, at the top stood the Bailiff of Guernsey. A command rang out, the halyard was pulled and the Union Jack floated out in the soft, sunlit breeze. One could hear a sob from the crowd, then, rising to a great volume of sound, "God Save the King."

"Oh what a day of days this is," Guernsey resident Violet Carey confided to her diary. "The town is crowded. The banks are changing Reichsmarks into good money again and the queues are enormous. The Post office is taking masses of letters and stamping them . . . At about 1:30 p.m. we heard the sound of [RAF] engines over the island. The planes! The planes! Another moment of pure bliss. They have been flying over every ten minutes since. I really think I shall blow up with emotion!" Dorothy Higgs wrote simply: "We are alive and well and BRITISH again."

Molly Bihet said: "It is difficult for me to put into words all the emotion I felt. I never dreamed I could feel such happiness and exhilaration." Hans von Aufsess, head of civil affairs within the German administration, recorded the actual transfer of power: "I performed a last official duty, in making the formal return of the island to the States [Legislative Assembly] of Guernsey. This was brought into effect briefly, in a single sentence spoken in English: 'The war is over—we herewith hand back the island to you.' All members of the States were present. We faced each other with polite but wordless bows—like so many Chinese mummers."

Shortly afterward, a second group departed for Jersey. There followed another series of joyful ceremonies. One resident of the island remembered:

Amidst roar after roar of delirious cheering, the welcome visitors at length reached a waiting car and, as it crawled at a snail's pace through the masses of excited people who pressed up to and even mounted the running boards, the occupants were compelled to shake dozens of hands through the windows. Soon, however, the car was forced to a standstill . . . and finally the officers were plucked forcibly from it and, showered with flowers, carried shoulder high to the office of the Harbor Master.

"Everyone just stopped what they were doing and ran out to greet the liberating force," Elaine Langley recalled. "Shops were left unattended—their entire staffs ran out leaving the doors wide open behind them." At 2:00 p.m., the commander of Jersey, Major General Wulf, signed a separate surrender for the island at the Liberation HQ, the Pomme d'Or Hotel. At 3:40 p.m. the swastika flag was lowered from the hotel balcony, signaling the end of the occupation, and the Union Jack hoisted—after which the crowd once again broke into a spirited rendition of the national anthem.

In the west, the German army appeared submissive and cooperative. On Crete on May 9, a handful of British soldiers and administrators received the surrender of four Wehrmacht divisions. A small British force was preparing to fly to Norway—in Operation Doomsday—to oversee the implementation of the ceasefire and the disarming of hundreds of thousands of German troops. And with a prevailing mood of happiness and relief, for some the Russians, in contrast, appeared obdurate and unyielding. They did not understand the Soviet insistence that peace could not begin until the Germans capitulated to them, at a place and time of their choosing. They thought that the signing at Rheims should have been enough. And yet, it is possible to see a different view.

In May 1945 Winston Churchill's wife, Clementine, was in the Soviet Union representing the British Red Cross Aid to Russia Fund. She had founded this organization in October 1941 and within a year it had raised nearly £2 million to buy clothes and medical supplies. Donations had poured in from every corner of the British Empire—and from every level of British society, from the king and queen, who each donated £1,000 in the first days of the fund, to ordinary factory workers, who contributed to the penny-a-week subscription. Hundreds of community groups undertook fund-raising activities. By January 1945 more than £4 million worth of goods had been shipped to the Soviet Union, some 11,600 tons of medical aid and clothing, 2,000 tons of powdered medicines, countless sterilizers, syringes, X-ray installations and blood transfusion sets. Two hospitals had by then been equipped in war-devastated Rostov-on-Don as a permanent memorial to the fund.

Clementine Churchill wrote that the fund "provided an outlet for the feelings of sympathy and admiration, respect and gratitude which swept over our people as the noble struggle of the Russians to defend their country grew through bitterness and agony to strength and power." A similar sense of indebtedness was carried through the letters of donors to the fund, praising the Russians and the Red Army as "heroic," "valiant," "brave," "patriotic" and "deserving."

Yet Mrs. Churchill also experienced the harsh, critical face of Soviet bureaucracy. Her organization was chided for its failure to meet quotas. The production rates at a British syringe factory were "too low," and when she managed to acquire some twenty kilograms of a rare drug, she was told in no uncertain terms that this was only a fraction of what was needed.

And yet, as the war drew to a close, it was the Russian generosity of spirit which prevailed. Mrs. Churchill was invited to pay a six-week-long visit to the Soviet Union to see how the money was being spent. This was to be an official thank-you from the Soviet leadership, but also a way for ordinary Russian people to show their gratitude for the British aid.

At the beginning of her trip, in late March 1945, she had an audience with Stalin in the Kremlin. The Soviet leader received her with considerable courtesy—but a telling moment occurred when Clementine Churchill presented Stalin with a gift from her husband, a gold fountain pen. This was an aristocratic gift—and she relayed the message that the British prime minister hoped the Soviet leader "would write him many friendly messages with it." Stalin accepted the present with a genial smile but observed, in true Bolshevik fashion: "I only write with a pencil."

Mrs. Churchill traveled all over Russia. She exclaimed of Leningrad, despite its war damage: "I think it is the most beautiful city I have ever seen."

And on April 11 she wrote movingly to her husband of the aftermath of the 900-day German siege of the city: "Yesterday we visited a scientific institute. Attached to it is a hospital where we saw many children still being nursed back to health from the effects of prolonged starvation during the Blockade."

The siege of Leningrad had been lifted on January 27, 1944. By then, more than a million of its civilians had perished from hunger and cold. German policy had been to deliberately starve the city's inhabitants to death.

Clementine Churchill was even more deeply moved at Stalingrad, which she reached four days later. She wrote: "What an appalling scene of destruction met our eyes. My first thought was how like the center of Coventry or the devastation around St. Paul's, except that the havoc and obliteration seem to have spread out endlessly."

Coventry had a special bond with Stalingrad. Its inhabitants, and particularly its women, had encouraged the Soviet city during the battle and this had forged a special bond of friendship. The two cities had twinned in 1944—the first places in the world to do so. Mrs. Churchill continued:

> One building that caught my eye was a wreck that had been ingeniously patched and shored up. I learned that it was the building in whose cellar the Russians had captured Von Paulus, the German commander [the Univermag Department Store]. It was characteristic of them, I thought, to make every effort to preserve this ruin because of its symbolic value. It represented the final overthrow of the enemy after one of the most savage struggles in all human history. Stalingrad was the turning-point of the war—and that will be remembered by the Russians for centuries to come.

Winston Churchill—also inspired by the heroism of Stalingrad—had asked Clementine to pass on his personal appreciation, and Dmitry Pigalev, the chairman of the local soviet there, thanked him for it, adding that they would rebuild their city. Mrs. Churchill saw this work in progress, telling her husband: "Two great factories have been reconstructed and are making steel and tractors . . . They are rebuilding their city with the same spirit of determination with which they fought the Germans."

The British prime minister was uplifted by Clementine's descriptions of Russian perseverance against the odds. He told her in return of the emerging horror of the concentration camps, and reflecting on this, that he felt the real hope for the future of the world lay in a friendship between the British and Soviet peoples. And such a friendship was offered to Mrs. Churchill time and time again on her travels.

"Last night we attended the local theater," she wrote after one visit. "The audience was rapturous in its welcome and threw bunches of violets from the gallery . . . The whole town turns out to greet us everywhere we go and I am continually amazed and moved by so much enthusiasm . . . *I want you to know that this tremendously warm feeling seems universal*" (emphasis added).

The visit was developing into a resounding success and it was to Clementine Churchill's considerable credit that when her husband cabled her twice, on May 5, when Anglo-Soviet relations had dropped to a new low, and asked her to return home early, she refused.

"You seem to have had a triumphant tour," he wrote to her, "and I only wish matters could be settled between you and the Russian common people. However there are many other aspects of this problem than those you have seen on the spot." Churchill added: "The Ambassador has my authority to show you the telegrams about the position," and spoke of "poisonous politics and deadly international rivalries."

Winston Churchill had asked his wife to return on May 7, before VE-Day. Clementine replied, courteously but firmly, that now she was back in Moscow a detailed program of events had been drawn up for the remainder of her stay and it might appear rude to leave in a hurry. She would not be able to leave before May 11. Clementine realized that an unexpected and premature departure from the Russian capital would only make matters worse.

To his credit, Churchill accepted his wife's desire to stay for the duration of her visit. With two Victory Days in existence, on May 8 and 9—one for the West, the other for the East—the presence of Mrs. Churchill in Russia for both became a huge diplomatic asset. Churchill came round to embracing its possibilities, suggesting that Clementine broadcast a message on his behalf to the Russian people on May 9, "congratulating Marshal Stalin, the Red Army and the Russian people on their splendid victories."

Mrs. Churchill herself was aware how different the Rheims signing of May 7 appeared from a Russian view: "On Victory Day I remember being struck by astonishment that the surrender was signed in Rheims and only as an afterthought in Berlin," she said. "This was rather incomprehensible to the Russians—and I must confess, to me."

Foreign correspondent Alexander Werth was concerned that the Victory Day announcements had not coincided: "The one day difference between VE Day in the west and VE Day in the east made an unpleasant impression," he remarked. It would have been ideal if the dates had been the same. But in the circumstances, it was a considerable achievement to have them only one day apart.

In Moscow May 8 was an ordinary working day. In the evening, Mrs. Churchill spoke to a group of journalists in the British embassy there. "Unless," she told them, "the friendship that has been established between the Soviet Union and the English-speaking people during the war continues, increases and deepens, there will be very little happiness in the immediate future for the world and in the lives of our children and great-grandchildren. I hope that, in a small way, my visit will help."

Also doing his best to promote this cause was another British visitor to Moscow, Dr. Hewlett Johnson of Canterbury Cathedral, known to his countrymen—from his extreme left-wing opinions—as the "Red Dean." Hewlett Johnson was undertaking a separate tour from Mrs. Churchill, but for a similar reason, having founded his own Anglo-Soviet Medical Aid Fund. He had a naive enthusiasm for the Bolshevik cause, seeing Stalin as "a man of kindly geniality . . . leading his people down new paths to democracy." Hugh Lunghi said with wry amusement: "Three years living in Russia had given me a very different view of the Soviet leader." It was the fact that Mrs. Churchill was in Moscow on May 9 which was politically and symbolically important. Frank Roberts, an attaché at the British embassy, cabled the Foreign Office: "The presence of Clementine Churchill in Moscow for both VE Days is making a valuable contribution toward future relations between the United Kingdom and the Soviet Union."

The Russian people learned that the war was finally over through an announcement made on the radio early on the morning of May 9 by their most famous broadcaster, Yuri Levitan, who was regularly employed to read out the Orders of the Day and other state declarations. Stalin had even made a rare joke about him. When asked when the war would be over, he replied: "Don't worry—Levitan will tell us."

When journalist Lazarus Brontman inquired when *Pravda* would run the story of the unconditional surrender at Karlshorst, he was told simply: "After Levitan's announcement." At 1:10 a.m. on May 9, Levitan's voice duly intoned: "Attention, this is Moscow. Germany has capitulated." Russia now learned of the signing concluded in Berlin's outskirts and Moscow Radio announced that "in honor of the victorious conclusion of the great patriotic war" this day, May 9, would be a "festival," with flags hoisted on all public buildings, and a general holiday. Then, in a mark of respect not followed by the other Allied powers when making similar announcements, the national anthems of Britain, America and France were played after the "Internationale."

Pravda's leading article duly appeared: "The capitulation of Germany carried through the Moscow night like the wind. The people had waited four years for this moment . . . A nationwide celebration began. On the streets were more and more people. There is a crowd at the Kremlin walls. People are embracing, kissing. Today there are no strangers." Valentin Berezhkov, who had interpreted at some of the wartime conferences, wrote: "It is hard to describe the joy of thousands of people in Red Square and around the country. The pride that victory was finally won over a treacherous and foul enemy, the grief for the fallen, hopes for a lasting peace and continued cooperation with our wartime allies—all this created a very special feeling of relief and hope."

That morning, Svetlana Stalin phoned her father in the Kremlin. She was the youngest child and only daughter of the Soviet leader. Her father had doted on her when she was a child, calling Svetlana his "little sparrow." In the war years, they had drifted apart. Stalin had reluctantly given permission for Svetlana, aged seventeen, to marry a fellow Moscow University student, Grigory Morozov, but chose never to meet her husband. Now the couple were expecting their first child. Overcome with emotion, Svetlana struggled to speak, but finally blurted out: "Father, congratulations on the victory."

There was a pause. "Yes, the victory," said Stalin distantly. And then his voice warmed. "Thank you. I congratulate you too. How are you?"

"I felt wonderful," Svetlana said, "like everyone in Moscow on this special day. My husband and I invited our friends round. The room was full. We drank champagne, danced and sang. The streets outside were overflowing with people."

When Nikita Khrushchev phoned the Kremlin to add his victory congratulations he found the Soviet leader in a less expansive mood. "I'm busy," Stalin said abruptly. "Please do not interrupt me when I am working."

That morning saw a spontaneous expression of joy that surprised experienced foreign journalists. "The weather was chilly," Hugh Lunghi recalled, "but the gathering crowd was radiant as the fitful sunshine picked out the many colors of its kerchiefs." The correspondent of *The Times* clambered to the top of a building to gain a rooftop view of the festivities. He wrote:

> Hundreds of thousands of people have been streaming into the center of Moscow since early morning. The crowds fill the broad street, two or three times the width of Whitehall that runs below the western walls of the Kremlin, past the university and on to the Moskva River. They line the river bank below the terrace. They are packing Red Square. Crowds sweep each side of St. Basil's Cathedral toward the bridge over the Moskva, away toward the theater square, where a bandstand has been erected for street dancing. It is a homely, democratic crowd, in which generals and soldiers, commissars and workers, mingle.

"Everyone was polite," recalled Lazarus Brontman. "There was no swearing or scuffling—just a crowd of happy people, everyone laughing."

Military correspondent Alexander Ustinov ran out on to the street. "People were pouring out of their homes," Ustinov remembered, "congratulating each other on the long-awaited victory. Red banners appeared—a spontaneous celebration began. Joyful people sang and danced to the accordion."

"The sun shone down graciously on jubilant Moscow," Grigory Klimov said. "People embraced and kissed each other on the street. Strangers invited one another into their homes. Life had been difficult but now it was all over.

We had held out and won." Klimov described some episodes that happened spontaneously among the crowd:

> As we walked along, a group of girls in bright spring clothes came toward us, happy and excited. They had flowers in their hands. Just in front of us a group of airmen were chatting animatedly—they were obviously members of the Moscow air defense force. One of them was in civilian clothes; his right sleeve was empty.
>
> The left side of his jacket was studded with military orders and above the pocket shone two five-cornered gold stars: the stars of a "Hero of the Soviet Union."
>
> One of the girls thrust her flowers into the wounded man's hand and he awkwardly pressed them against his chest. The girl embraced him—and did not want to release him. They did not say a word to each other and yet this gesture said everything: "Thank you for defending our city."
>
> We saw an old woman in a white kerchief, peering about her uncertainly, as though looking for someone in this seething torrent of human beings. She was not accustomed to the bustle of the city—just a homely Russian mother.
>
> We had come across hundreds of such mothers as we entered villages evacuated by the retreating Germans. And hardly had we taken one step across the thresholds of their cottages than we were calling them "mother." Without a word they would thrust a hunk of bread into our greatcoat pockets and surreptitiously sign the cross over us as we turned away.
>
> Two elderly soldiers in ragged frontline uniforms were leaning against a house-wall. Their faces were unshaven; packs hung over their shoulders. You could see that they had either come straight from the front or were on their way back to it. But they were in no hurry; today they had no reason to fear the military police patrols.
>
> They warmed themselves peacefully in the sun and rolled themselves cigarettes. What more does a soldier need than a piece of bread in his pack, some tobacco in his pocket and the sun shining?

The old woman in a kerchief pushed uncertainly through the crowd and went up to the two soldiers. She spoke to them in an agitated voice and tried to pull them by the sleeves. The soldiers looked at each other and nodded.

How many sons had she given for the sake of this sunny morning? The sons who were to have been her comfort and support in her old age had been taken from her. Her son Kolya had been killed at Poltava; Peter the sailor had died in a sea-fight. All through the war she had held on to an expensive bottle of vodka, not exchanging it even for bread. She had suffered hunger and cold, but that bottle of vodka was sacred. And now her heart was no longer suffering. She had gone into the street to find her "sons," to invite the first soldiers she met to celebrate the victory with her.

As the afternoon went on, more and more people appeared. In terms of turnout, it was without doubt the biggest anywhere in the world that week. The *Manchester Guardian* correspondent was struck by this, explaining: "The victory celebrations are popularly regarded as the greatest moment in the history of this country since the Revolution. Never has Moscow seen such crowds, and never before during this war have the Soviet people shown their whole-hearted appreciation of allied help so freely and emphatically."

These comments were important, because the Russians had often been accused in the Western press—with some justification—of being ungrateful for the sacrifices made on their behalf and suspicious of—and determined to stay aloof from—Western influence. But on Victory Day it was very different. "It was sufficient to look like a foreigner," continued the *Manchester Guardian* reporter, "to be kissed, hugged and generally feted. In Red Square all foreign cars were stopped and their occupants dragged out, embraced and sometimes even tossed in the air."

Among those to suffer this boisterous treatment was Hewlett Johnson, the "Red Dean." Leaving the British embassy after the victory service that morning, Johnson saw "a dense crowd, enthusiastic and genial, [which] released at last from the long strain of war, blocked our road and engulfed us—cheering every Englishman or American. They seized General Younger, a British officer in full uniform, and tossing him in the air, caught him as gently as if he were a babe. My turn came next."

A crowd gathered outside a big hotel where many British and Americans stayed, and pounced on anyone leaving, demanding a speech. Carrying a Briton shoulder high was another popular tribute. Bob Dunbar was the Moscow editor of *British Ally*, a Russian-language weekly that informed its readers about the British way of life. Toward the end of the war, demand for it had grown and grown. Dunbar received one faded copy, returned by front-line Red Army soldiers, with a simple accompanying message: "Send us more!" Such was the interest in British culture that Dunbar took a subtitled version of Sir Laurence Olivier's *Henry V* (produced, with the encouragement of Winston Churchill, a year earlier to coincide with the D-Day landings) to Leningrad to show to audiences there.

"The atmosphere in Red Square was amazing," Dunbar recalled. "The Russians were singing all the songs they knew the British sang. As they struck up 'Tipperary' we were all flung high into the air. We had defeated Fascism together—and for an extraordinary moment it seemed that our peoples had forged an enduring friendship."

The United States was equally popular. A large crowd gathered outside the American embassy, where the correspondent of the *New York Herald* heard repeated shouts of "Long live America!," "Long live Truman!," "Long live the memory of Roosevelt!" and "Long live the American people!"

Robert Tucker was one of the staff in the American embassy. He recalled:

Our embassy stood just across the square from the Kremlin. And when the news reached the Muscovites that the war was over, the surrender had taken place and that the long-awaited day of victory had come, hundreds, then thousands, then many thousands gathered in front of our embassy. It was a five-story building, with an American flag out in front, and it seemed that all these people were just standing there, looking up at us. It was something unthinkable in Stalin's Russia—a spontaneous demonstration. All these Russians had gathered to say thank you for being with us, for sending us the munitions, the trucks, the jeeps, the tinned food. Thank you for being in the same war that we were in—for all these terrible years, for fighting with us as allies. Thank you, America. These were the words that nobody spoke, but everybody, by their presence there, communicated to us.

Tucker remembered how George Kennan—the chargé d'affaires in the absence of Ambassador Harriman—sent for someone to get a Soviet flag, and he hung it side by side with the American one. "There was a huge roar of approval. Then he stepped out on a balcony in front of one of the lower windows of the embassy and spoke in flawless Russian in a loud voice. He congratulated everyone—all Russians—on our common victory. The mood was euphoric. And whenever anyone left the building, they were hoisted onto the shoulders of those in the crowd and carried into Red Square, which was the center of all the jubilation."

George Kennan had earlier written: "News had reached us of terrible atrocities committed against the German civilian population in East Prussia. Not so much by the frontline troops, it seemed, as those following behind. Many of these stories had been told by Red Army soldiers themselves, disgusted at the behavior of their comrades. And yet it left me thinking: 'Is this the kind of victory we have strived for?'"

Now Kennan, like all the others, was caught up in the emotion of the day. Russia's triumph against Nazi Germany had its flaws, most certainly, but it was a triumph nonetheless.

These expressions of appreciation were striking, for it was known, from the Orders of the Day, that Russian soldiers were still fighting the Germans, whereas all actions involving the Americans and British had ceased. Military communiqués of May 9 reported that there was still fighting in Czechoslovakia between the Red Army and the Wehrmacht—and this would continue for several more days. The joy transcended this.

Grigory Klimov recollected:

I had witnessed many Moscow parades and celebrations. The strongest impression I got from them was that the people would rather have really enjoyed themselves than be forced to demonstrate their merriment and joy. They were simply puppet shows and one could not rid oneself of a sense of hypocrisy. Most of the participants tried not to acknowledge their reason for being there—corrosive fear of being put on a list, of giving offense by being absent.

May 9, 1945, was completely different. There was no organized demonstration, nor was it necessary to have one. The streets of Moscow were packed with people everywhere, on the pavements, in the roads, at the windows, on the roofs. In the city center the streets were so crowded that all traffic came to a standstill. All the population had taken to its feet.

Aircraft navigator Nikolai Kryuchkov said simply: "It is impossible to describe everything that happened that day. Everybody, young and old, rejoiced. It was difficult to even walk past all the people who wanted to enthusiastically greet and kiss the soldiers. We drank to the victory—and remembered all those who were killed. We prayed we would never see such a loss of life again."

Alexander Werth added: "The spontaneous joy of the two to three million people who thronged the Red Square that evening, from the Moskva River embankments all the way up to Gorky Street, had a quality and depth that I had never seen in Moscow before. The crowds were so happy that they did not even have to get drunk."

On the evening of May 9 Clementine Churchill broadcast her husband's message "to Marshal Stalin, to the Red Army and to the Russian people":

From the British nation I send you heartfelt greetings on the splendid victories you have won in driving the invader from your soil and laying the Nazi tyrant low. It is my firm belief that on the friendship and understanding of the British and Russian peoples depends the future of mankind. Here in our island home we are thinking today about you all. We send you—from the bottom of our hearts—our wishes for your happiness and well-being and that, after all the sacrifices and sufferings of the Dark Valley through which we have marched together, we may also, in loyal comradeship and sympathy, walk in the sunshine of victorious peace.

One senses a measure of strain in Churchill's use of language. He wanted to reach out to Russia but was also fearful of her. Later that night, Stalin's own message to his people was dignified yet cautious:

Comrades, fellow countrymen and-women, the great day of victory over Germany has come. Fascist Germany has been forced to her knees by the Red Army and by the troops of her allies . . . Being well aware of the subterfuges of the German leaders, who consider their treaties as mere scraps of paper, we had no reason to accept their word. Nevertheless, this morning German troops have begun to surrender en masse to our Soviet armies. This fact is no longer a scrap of paper but what is happening on the ground. It is the actual capitulation of their armed forces. It is true that one of their army groups, in Czechoslovakia, is still trying to avoid surrender. But I trust that the Red Army will bring it to its senses. . . . The age-old struggle of the Slav peoples for their existence and independence has ended in victory over the German invaders and their tyranny. . . . The Great Patriotic War has ended with our complete victory. . . . Glory to our heroic Red Army. Glory to our great people. Eternal glory to the heroes who fell in the struggle. . . .

This was a candid acknowledgment of the untrustworthy Dönitz regime. The Soviet Union had not been able to win a complete surrender from its foe. That afternoon, at 4:00 p.m., General Alexei Antonov, chief of the Red Army general staff, had sent General Eisenhower a concerned message:

The German forces of Army Group Center and a southern group of troops [those in Yugoslavia] did not cease resistance at 2301, May 8, 1945, the time fixed by the act of military surrender, did not remain in their places and did not lay down their arms—and thus have violated that agreement. It is now 1600 on May 9 and these forces are not capitulating.

The central and southern groups, while resisting the Red Army, are moving off to the west, evidently with the purpose of giving themselves up to the Americans.

In connection with this, please issue an order to your troops not to take prisoner these forces and kindly advise what measures you consider it necessary to take against them for breaking the agreement.

General Eisenhower ordered his commanders to block the way. In western Czechoslovakia, General George Patton wrote in his diary: "General Bradley called up and told me to be prepared to place road blocks on all roads leading southeast or northeast. We are to put signs in front of them saying that in accordance with the terms of surrender all German military personnel will remain beyond that point—that is east of this line. The message was immediately passed on to Corps commanders."

There was a renewed spirit of cooperation between Russia and the West. And this spirit resolved a potential flashpoint in their relations, the Danish island of Bornholm, in the Baltic, 92 miles east of Copenhagen and 155 miles west of Danzig. General Dietrich von Saucken's Army Group of East Prussia was continuing to use the island as an evacuation point for its soldiers, even though such actions breached the terms of surrender at Lüneburg Heath (which included all Danish possessions) and the subsequent surrenders at Rheims and Karlshorst.

German-occupied Denmark had been surrendered to Field Marshal Montgomery on May 4, the capitulation to come into effect at 8:00 a.m. the following day. From this date and time onward the Germans were bound to refrain from any further military activity in the country. But on the island of Bornholm this was ignored. The island had a German governor and a token contingent of troops. It was in radio contact with Copenhagen, but the British forces—overstretched as they were—did not have the strength to occupy it, even with a small supervisory group.

On May 6 General Dietrich von Saucken, whose German troops were stationed along the Hela Peninsula west of Danzig, breached the unconditional surrender agreement and sent substantial reinforcements to Bornholm. He dispatched General Rolf Wuthmann, with a Panzer grenadier regiment of 800 men, to take control there. Wuthmann was directed "to defend Bornholm, so the island can be used during the Army Group's evacuation to the west."

The Russians, aware that the Germans were evacuating their army, demanded that Bornholm surrender to Marshal Rokossovsky's 2nd Belorussian Front. On May 8 Soviet planes flew over the island, dropping leaflets warning that if these military activities continued they would occupy the island by force. Wuthmann replied that he would surrender only to British troops—deliberate delaying tactics that were sanctioned by Admiral Dönitz and Field Marshal Keitel.

Early on the morning of May 9, Dönitz had sent General von Saucken the award of Diamonds to his Knight's Cross in recognition of his efforts in evacuating soldiers and civilians from the Russians. A handwritten note accompanying the award urged him to carry on doing this for as long as feasibly possible.

On the morning of May 9 Corporal Alfred Pröbstle and his men were waiting on a jetty on the Hela Peninsula for a ship to take them to Bornholm. He remembered:

> From the evening of May 8 Russian artillery fire from the other side of the lagoon had come close and closer. Everyone around me was saying: "We have to get out of here now, we have to get to Bornholm." Our commanding officer told us that he had to wait for orders—but we continued to pressure him. Shortly after midnight he told us: "Save yourselves—in any way that you can."
>
> At about 4:00 a.m. we marched down to the port. About 20,000 people—soldiers and civilians—were waiting there. We had just taken our places when a fresh artillery bombardment began—sending up spumes of water as shells landed in the harbor basin.

Pröbstle and his men managed to find room in a patrol boat. The evacuations continued. Twelve hours after the Karlshorst signing—with the Germans still disregarding its terms and moving their troops out from Hela—the Russians lost patience and sent a force by sea to take over the island.

At 2:30 p.m. Russian torpedo boats appeared outside Bornholm's main port at Ronne. But aware of the political sensitivity of their action, and trusting Allied Supreme Command enough after the Karlshorst agreement and the honoring of the American pledge not to enter Prague, they sought the sanction of SHAEF rather than acting unilaterally. The British—still suspicious of Soviet intentions—had inquired of Eisenhower whether it might be possible to put a US force on the island. The Russians sought his permission to occupy Bornholm as it was within their military zone of influence. General Eisenhower approved the Red Army's request.

At 3:00 p.m. the Supreme Allied Commander received an urgent telegram from the German Army High Command, still operating in Flensburg as part of the Dönitz government:

> The commander of the Bornholm garrison has reported that five Russian torpedo boats have arrived outside Ronne harbor. According to their orders, the new Soviet commander of the island will arrive at 1730 to accept the capitulation of the German garrison.
>
> Russian occupation forces are on their way. But Bornholm is Danish territory—and the surrender of the island is clearly covered in the capitulation agreement signed with Field Marshal Montgomery. We request immediate clarification from Allied Supreme Command whether Russian claims to Bornholm are justified. We consider ourselves legally bound by the agreement with Montgomery.

This was a last delaying tactic from the Dönitz government—and a last attempt to sow discord within the Grand Alliance. General Eisenhower promptly scotched it, replying clearly and firmly: "In accordance with arrangements for military capitulation, German commanders are required to follow the orders of the Allied Expeditionary Force or the Red Army. You remain bound by the ceasefire agreement with Montgomery, but due to the aforementioned reason you must take orders from the local Russian commander."

The British continued to view developments with concern. Sir Orme Sargent warned Churchill later that day: "The Russians have reached Bornholm first." But in fact the Red Army's behavior was scrupulously correct.

Colonel Ivan Yusman, chief of staff of the Soviet 18th Rifle Division, reported on the Russian occupation of the island later that day. The division had set up its headquarters at Ronne and began disarming the German garrison and also those units scattered around the island who had come from the Hela Peninsula. Yusman drew attention to the fact that the divisional commander, Colonel Strebkov, had received inquiries from representatives of the governments of Britain and Denmark, who wanted clarification concerning the Red Army's longer-term intentions for the island. This was immediately passed on to Marshal Rokossovsky, who in turn requested that a clear statement be delivered by the Soviet High Command. One was made later that evening.

The Soviets informed the Danish government that Bornholm was clearly recognized as part of Denmark and was being garrisoned only as it lay behind the Russian occupation zone. The Red Army would not interfere in Danish administrative matters but would refer them back to Copenhagen. The Danes found this a satisfactory resolution of the issue. The Grand Alliance had dealt with the matter in a proper fashion. The Red Army made a complete withdrawal from Bornholm the following year.

The British were right not to drop their guard. Real problems remained. On the evening of May 9 Field Marshal Montgomery wrote to Eisenhower: "I motored today for about twenty miles into the Russian zone, and it is a dead zone—with not one single German civilian about. There are some awkward issues ahead—and I consider it essential to keep a very firm front facing east."

But enough goodwill and trust had been restored to celebrate both VE-Days with a genuine sense of pride in the Alliance's joint achievement. And that was how the end of the war in Europe deserved to be commemorated.

On May 9 President Truman had cabled his congratulations to Winston

Churchill. Churchill had responded with a generous appreciation of the American contribution to the war. And in response to the British prime minister's praise of the Soviet leader and the heroism of his country, Stalin had replied:

> I send my personal greetings to you, the stout-hearted British Armed Forces and the whole British people—and I congratulate you with all my heart on the great victory over our common enemy. This historic victory has been achieved by the joint struggle of the Soviet, British and American Armies for the liberation of Europe.
>
> I express my confidence in the further successful and happy development in the post-war period of the friendly relations which have developed between our countries during the war.

This hope would not be realized. The "awkward issues" would come to dominate the post-war international landscape. Yet it would be a mistake to assume that these sentiments were insincere. Whatever the problems, goodwill was there also.

Although for some Red Army soldiers the war would carry on, the end was now in sight, if not yet fully realized. The official celebrations in Moscow on the night of May 9 were on a far greater scale than in any other capital. For the American correspondent of the *New York Herald* it was a magnificent spectacle. Red Air Force planes swooped over the city letting off multicolored flares. A thousand guns, lined wheel to wheel along the river embankment, fired off thirty salvoes. The sky blazed with searchlight rays. A thousand feet above the crowd these searchlights played upon a gigantic red banner, held aloft by cords from balloons, invisible in the night sky. And then the victory fireworks were let off. Moscow was *en fête*.

Grigory Klimov said:

> That night we made our way slowly to Red Square. Soon the guns would be firing their salutes—and the Square gave the best view. No official demonstration had ever drawn such an enormous crowd

outside the Kremlin walls. It was impossible to do anything other than let the torrent of people take charge and move you as it wished.

Amidst this human ferment the Kremlin stood silent and lifeless, like a legendary castle fallen into an enchanted sleep. More and more people poured into that vast open space. What was drawing them there?

The silvery firs stood on guard along the ancient walls. The pointed pinnacles of the towers pierced the darkened sky. Their ruby-red stars gleamed.

From the mist of the past, another Red Square emerged in my memory. The morning of November 7, 1941, was leaden and dull. A flurry of falling snow blurred the face of Moscow. The troops marched past the Lenin Mausoleum and straight to the front. The enemy was at the gates!

On November 7, 1941, Stalin had resolved to hold the traditional parade on Red Square with German troops less than 30 miles from the capital. It was gesture of defiance—and belief that Moscow would not fall to Hitler's Wehrmacht. Now the war had been won.

The earth began to thunder. Above the black silhouette of the Kremlin, the sky turned crimson with gunfire. The fire streamed higher and higher, hung motionless for a moment at its zenith, then burst downward in sparkling, multi-colored little stars. Then the air was shattered by a gun salvo. It was the first salute to a glorious victory.

For a moment it seemed possible to open your eyes, open your heart and imprint these few seconds forever. The earth shuddered again, the crimson fire lit up the Kremlin walls, the night sky and the soul of the people. Once more the little stars burst forth like messengers of hope, then faded. This was victory captured in a point of light. And in those precious seconds you saw it—and felt its breath on your face.

11

———

THE WAR THAT DID NOT END

At midnight on May 8 Major Jan Tabortowski and 200 men from the Polish Resistance Army moved into position in front of the jailhouse at Grajewo, 124 miles northeast of Warsaw. The operation had been carefully planned and the ground reconnoitered with the assistance of informers within the town. The men had assembled over a two-day period, gathering at a farm a short distance away. Their objective was to seize Grajewo's prison and release members of the Polish underground movement held there. Other units drew up in front of the town's militia headquarters and NKVD building. Before the attack, Tabortowski spoke briefly to his soldiers: "For us, the fight continues," he said. "The Soviet Union wants to annex Poland and to turn our country into its next socialist republic. We must show the world that we will never accept this."

The attack was deliberately timed to span both VE-Days—and it intended to make a simple, symbolic statement. For the Polish Resistance Movement, the war continued.

On February 27, 1945, the Polish Underground Government had formally responded to the Yalta agreement. It stated: "We wish to express our opposition to the provisions set out at the Yalta Conference, which were resolved without our participation or agreement but rather imposed upon us. Poland was the first country to begin armed resistance against the Nazis. It is now the victim of fresh burdens and injustices."

A month later, the Soviet Union decided upon an apparently conciliatory gesture, offering to hold talks with sixteen members of the Underground Government. When these talks actually took place, they promptly arrested the delegates. Stefan Korbonski—who had avoided the meeting, fearing a trap—reported back to the Polish government-in-exile in London at the end of March: "Not one of our sixteen delegates has returned from the NKVD building where these 'talks' were held. Draw your own conclusions."

A new Polish Underground Government was formed a month later. One of its first acts was to appeal to the San Francisco Conference, on May 3, over "Russia's capture of sixteen members of our Polish Underground State with malicious intent." This appeal forced the Soviet Union to formally acknowledge that these men had indeed been arrested—a belated admission that plunged relations between the Western Allies and the Soviet Union into a crisis. It had been temporarily resolved, but on May 8 Stefan Korbonski cabled the Polish government-in-exile: "The end of the war has been met with indifference in Warsaw. It does not change anything for us."

The Polish Underground Government did not advocate violent resistance against the Soviet Union and its puppet Lublin regime—and instead continued to work for a diplomatic solution. Others now chose to fight the Red Army, the NKVD and the Lublin government's militia. They formed a loose coalition, the National Military Alliance—also known as the Polish Resistance Army. On the night of May 6/7, while the first unconditional surrender was being signed at Rheims, the Polish Resistance Army demonstrated its defiance of the settlement by fighting a pitched battle with the Soviet 2nd Border Regiment of the NKVD at Kurylowka in southeast Poland. At midnight on May 8, as the Grand Alliance prepared for its second surrender agreement at Karlshorst, Major Tabortowski's soldiers readied themselves for the assault on Grajewo.

The attack was sudden and took its opponents completely by surprise. Tabortowski and his followers opened fire on surprised members of the Red Army garrison and Polish militia, killing a number of them and forcing the rest to take cover. The resistance fighters then stormed the prison building, freeing members of the Polish underground movement held there, seizing police documents and the radio transmitter. At 4:00 a.m. a green flare signaled the operation's complete success and all resistance units pulled out of the town.

The Polish Resistance Army's struggle continued. Later on May 9 another prison was stormed at Bialystok. On May 21 a large NKVD camp at Rembertow, on the eastern outskirts of Warsaw, was attacked and more than 300 political prisoners released. And on May 27 units of the Polish resistance joined forces with the Ukrainian Insurgent Army, which was fighting for the Ukraine's independence from the Soviet Union, stormed the town of Hrubieszow, burned down the prison and killed all the NKVD troops stationed there.

For many Poles, the end of the Second World War had failed to provide a just settlement of their cause. Edward Szczepanik was a Polish officer who served with General Władysław Anders' Polish II Corps alongside British troops in Italy. These soldiers were fighting for the Polish government-in-exile in London and had no truck with the Soviet-sponsored Lublin regime set up as the Red Army "liberated" their country from the Germans. The word "liberated" remained contentious—the Soviet Union had invaded the eastern half of the country in 1939 and on its return had taken the whole of Poland under its effective control. In the meantime, Szczepanik fought for the Western powers at Monte Cassino and Ancona and his were some of the first Allied troops to enter Bologna in April 1945.

He said:

When VE Day arrived, it came at a price for the Polish people. The Yalta agreement left very little opportunity for us . . . I did not in any way celebrate the 8th May 1945. What was the point? Poland, and my people, were not free. Poland had already been occupied by Russia. It had not been liberated, like many of the western European nations—it had been annexed, purely because of its position between Russia and Germany. The Yalta agreement had done nothing to protect us from that, dragging us from one occupation to another, with no respite in between.

There was real truth in Szczepanik's comments about the Yalta agreement—it was a view shared by many exiled Poles. Augustyn Buczek, a member of a Polish Air Force squadron based near London, said: "VE Day found us depressed—we did not celebrate at all. Yalta had left us high and dry and now the future of our country was highly uncertain." Tadeusz Krzystek, another Polish Air Force man stationed in Britain, added: "We had seen in Churchill a guarantor of our future. After Yalta such hope had faded away. On VE Day I felt sad and empty inside. The end of the war gave nothing to us. Rather, we feared it marked the end of the struggle to secure a free Poland."

Winston Churchill chose to believe that a fair settlement for Poland had been achieved at Yalta, but the Soviet Union had subsequently reneged upon it. When President Truman first came into office he had strongly supported Churchill on this issue, but by May he had become more cautious. A number of his advisers warned him that the Yalta accord had been left with vague wording over Poland—wording that could be subject to very different interpretations. And some had added that although the Soviet Union could be difficult and suspicious in its conduct of international diplomacy, once it gave a firm and clear commitment it did not usually break it. The broader question of trust between East and West remained the paramount issue.

General Anders cabled Churchill on May 8, 1945. The Polish commander congratulated the British prime minister on the victory against Germany, adding pointedly that he hoped for a peace "where justice would prevail." For Anders, and many other Poles who yearned for self-determination for their country, it would be a long wait.

Britain and France went to war on behalf of Poland and Polish servicemen subsequently fought and died in Britain's navy, air force and army. They sacrificed their lives for the cause of their country's freedom. In the desperate battle at Monte Cassino, Polish troops had stormed the summit, displaying incredible bravery.

Field Marshal Harold Alexander, commander-in-chief of the Allied forces in Italy, paid General Anders and his troops a heartfelt tribute in the battle's aftermath. He conferred the Order of the Bath upon the Polish general (on behalf of the British sovereign, King George VI), and then said: "It was a day of great glory for Poland when you took a stronghold that the Germans considered impregnable . . . I sincerely and frankly tell you all— men of the Polish II Corps, that if I had a choice of the soldiers I would like to command it would have been the Poles. I honor you all."

At the end of the war, this heartfelt tribute was left suspended in the air. In the second week of May, the uneasy specter of Poland hovered over the Grand Alliance. In the aftermath of VE-Day, Churchill spoke bullishly to General Sir Alan Brooke and Field Marshal Montgomery about the need to square up to the Soviet Union in order to ensure that a democratic government was installed in Poland. Brooke wrote after a war cabinet meeting of May 13: "Winston . . . gave me the feeling of already longing for another war—even if it entailed fighting against the Russians!"

This was inflammatory stuff. General Anders believed that a fresh war between Russia and the Western powers was the only way to restore an independent Poland. It was a noble aspiration, but General Sir Alan Brooke said of the Polish commander: "He wishes to take part in the occupation of Germany and then has wild hopes of fighting his way home to Poland through the Russians! A pretty desperate problem the Polish Army is going to present us with."

Churchill himself briefly got caught up in these "wild hopes." He commissioned "Operation Unthinkable," a top-secret war plan drawn up by the Combined Chiefs of Staff to explore using military force against Russia to secure a free Poland. The British prime minister instructed them that "with the Russian bear sprawled all over Europe" they should consider the possibility of pushing the Red Army back eastward and "impos[ing] upon Russia the will of the United States and British Empire" in order to secure "a square deal for Poland."

In reply, the chiefs of staff made it absolutely clear that such a course of action would be almost impossible to execute militarily and an utter disaster politically. Churchill rapidly backtracked from this fantastical scenario, reassuring his military advisers that "by retaining the code-word 'Unthinkable' the staffs will realize that this remains a precautionary study of what, I hope, is still a purely hypothetical contingency." General Sir Alan Brooke had discouraged his political master from one of his wildest schemes. Even as a hypothesis, it was a most dangerous one, founded on a deep fear of Russian intentions in Europe.

Churchill confided in President Truman on May 13: "I have always worked for friendship with Russia but, like you, I feel a deep anxiety because of their misinterpretation of the Yalta decisions and their attitude toward Poland . . ."

Harold Macmillan, the British Minister Resident in the Mediterranean, amplified Churchill's concerns: "We had already seen the terrible blow to Poland implicit in the Yalta decisions, even with its minor concessions," Macmillan remarked. "We had little expectation of the Russians carrying out either the letter or the spirit of the bargain. My meetings with Władysław Anders, commander of the Polish forces in Italy, convinced me that any more hopeful view was mere wishful thinking."

Macmillan believed that "Russian statesmen cannot be cajoled; but being strong realists they can be dealt with on the basis of frankness and truth." And yet, it was uncertain how such a diplomatic formula would work in practice, for one side's "frankness and truth" might not coincide with the other's. South Africa's Jan Smuts, whose father had been appointed president of the General Assembly at the San Francisco Conference, took a more belligerent view, observing of the Soviet Union's international role:

> Russia will make little attempt to cooperate, in fact the opposite appears more likely at present . . . her part in the Polish dispute and the fact that she has already gone against her Yalta word and that she is actively fomenting trouble cannot be doubted. Our request to be permitted to send observers there to see for themselves has been flatly refused. Likewise our wish to send observers to Czechoslovakia and Vienna (both in the Russian zones) has been flatly turned down . . . Is that trust and goodwill?

Smuts concluded bluntly: "Appeasement will never pay with the Russians. They understand only one thing—straight angry talk, with military might in the background to back it up if necessary."

As Smuts himself acknowledged, these were strange words to be writing during a conference dedicated to securing world peace.

However, underneath the bullish rhetoric Winston Churchill was tired and frequently downcast. He had once told his private secretary, John Colville, that he would fight for a free Poland even if it meant going to the brink of war with the Soviet Union. But on reaching that brink, Churchill confessed to feeling overwhelmed by "the dark cloud of Russian imponderability."

At the beginning of May 1940—with British operations in defense of Norway collapsing—Churchill had confided to Colville that he believed May to be an unlucky month for him. At the start of May 1944 an abrupt and surly telegram from Soviet foreign minister Vyacheslav Molotov, claiming that Britain was plotting behind the Soviet Union's back in Romania, caused the British prime minister to "set off on gloomy forebodings about future tendencies of Russia, adding 'I have always disliked the month of May.'"

On May 1, 1945, with the news of the death of Hitler, and the end of the war imminent, the dark cloud had lifted. A week later, VE-Day had been a personal triumph for Winston Churchill. But now the cloud seemed to have returned. "Russia shows no willingness to compromise over Poland," Churchill lamented. He wondered whether he had the strength to carry on. The prospect of having to negotiate directly with Stalin over the issue left the prime minister feeling "overpowered by it all."

Over 200,000 Poles fought within the British armed forces during the war. The hard-won military achievements of these men and women deserved a better reward. And yet, the only way for Britain and America to secure stronger negotiating leverage over Poland would have been to open the second front in northwestern Europe a year earlier and push their forces deeper into Europe. This was not a realistic option for the Western Allies—Germany was too strong at this stage of the war. Even if the initial landings were successful they would then have sustained massive casualties as they moved inland—a cost that democracies could not easily bear. In the event, the Red

Army carried the main burden of fighting against the Nazi state—and its successes earned the Soviet Union its power over Poland's fate.

"I have done all I can for Poland at this time," President Roosevelt admitted to the American ambassador to the Soviet Union, Averell Harriman, at the end of the Yalta Conference. Charles Bohlen, the State Department Russian expert who translated for Roosevelt at Yalta, and thus heard every word uttered by the American president and Stalin, said simply: "Stalin held all the cards and played them well. Eventually we had to throw in our hand."

On matters of trust, and keeping to agreements, the Soviet Union behaved very differently over Greece, as Churchill himself acknowledged. Stalin and Churchill had apportioned areas of influence in eastern Europe— and the Soviet leader conceded to the prime minister a predominant role in overseeing the future of Greece. When Britain crushed a communist uprising—led by the Greek partisan movement and enjoying widespread popular support—Russia did not interfere. Churchill reported to the British war cabinet on February 12, 1945: "As regards Greece the Russian attitude could not have been more satisfactory . . . Stalin has most scrupulously respected his acceptance of our position . . . the conduct of the Soviet Union in this matter has strengthened my view *that when they make a bargain they desire to keep it*" (emphasis added).

The impasse over Poland might show something rather different: a Soviet world-view of cynical realpolitik, where Russia kept to smaller agreements but was ready to break the important ones if they endangered her interests. Alternatively, the Soviet Union and the Western Allies might have very different understandings of what the Yalta accord on Poland actually meant.

A British ATS clerk wrote in her diary on May 17:

It is little more than a week since VE Day, but already the reaction is setting in. I find the news extremely depressing. Britain and America seem at loggerheads with the USSR over nearly every controversial point, and the US isolationist press, in its usual unhelpful way, is fomenting this state of affairs . . . There seems to be nothing but strife and confusion ahead when we should be seeing the bright skies of peace—and we are all feeling tired and hardly capable of coping with it.

However, in military affairs there was a new-found spirit of cooperation where only days earlier there had been suspicion and mistrust. When the Red Army approached the Czech capital, General Eisenhower did not pre-empt it—and instead kept to the agreed halt line. As Soviet troops moved into Prague, SS general Carl Pückler-Burghaus led the last German soldiers out of the city. Pückler-Bíurghaus and his men hoped to escape Russian captivity. Czech partisans forced him away from the direct road to Pilsen and he turned southwest, toward Písek. He was hoping to reach the US demarcation line and surrender to the Americans, but the Red Army was in fast pursuit.

A few days earlier, the Soviet High Command had insisted that American troops should not cross the halt line. Now they asked for help. Marshal Malinovsky's 2nd Ukrainian Front was ordered to overtake Pückler-Burghaus and the Soviets asked American forces to move across the demarcation line and assist them, closing the escape route west. General Eisenhower agreed. The Germans were overhauled at the small town of Minin-Slivice, 40 miles southeast of Pilsen. On May 11 American units from the US 4th Armored Division (part of General Patton's Third Army) blocked Pückler-Burghaus' path, insisting that he honor the unconditional surrender and capitulate to the Russians. The SS general refused. With troops of the Soviet 25th Guards Rifle Corps rapidly approaching from the east, his men took up a fortified position in a stretch of woodland between Minin-Slivice and Cimelice and prepared to fight it out.

This was a desperate last stand. Pückler-Burghaus had about 6,000 men under his command, mostly experienced troops from the SS Das Reich and Wallenstein Divisions. But they were heavily outnumbered—and had nowhere to go. Yet on the evening of May 11 they beat off the first Russian assault. The Soviets—confident of success—launched a Katyusha rocket barrage and sent in their infantry troops. But they were beaten back.

Red Army soldier Alexei Kuchikov remembered: "We were advancing into a forest of spruce trees and visibility was poor. The Germans cleverly exploited the terrain—using the irrigation channels from disused water mills and transforming them into a line of trenches. We were taken aback by the ferocity of their resistance."

Russians and Americans now worked together on a concerted plan of attack. Major General Sergei Seryogin of the Soviet 104th Guards Rifle Division and Lieutenant Colonel William Allison of the US 4th Armored Division met in the Old Mill House in Cimelice. It was decided that just before dawn the Americans would bring down an artillery barrage on General Pückler-Burghaus's stronghold from the west and the Russians would do the same from the east. Then Soviet infantry would storm the German position.

The sheer strength of Allied firepower now told. Early on May 12 Russian soldiers overwhelmed the first line of German defenses. "We jumped into their trenches, throwing grenades and firing our machine guns," Alexei Kuchikov recalled. "We shot everyone we encountered, whether they were resisting or trying to surrender. Panic broke out among the enemy."

Within hours it was clear that the German position was hopeless. At 9:00 a.m. Pückler-Burghaus signed terms of unconditional surrender in the upper room of Cimelice's Old Mill House. His men would at last capitulate to the Russians. The terms were witnessed by Major General Seryogin and Lieutenant Colonel Allison: the success had been a joint Allied effort. The SS general—aware that he would be tried in the Soviet Union for war crimes—chose to commit suicide shortly after signing the agreement.

Remaining Wehrmacht and SS units in western Czechoslovakia were rounded up later that day. "We surrounded a last group of Germans near Besenov on the evening of May 12," Soviet artilleryman Petr Mikhin—fighting with the 52nd Rifle Division—recalled. "We only properly celebrated VE Day on May 13. Our moment of triumph was bitter-sweet—several of our comrades had been killed after the unconditional surrender had supposedly brought the war to an end."

But the war in the East was not yet over.

In Yugoslavia, Colonel General Alexander Löhr, the German commander-in-chief in southeast Europe, also defied the unconditional surrender agreements. Löhr had about 13,000 German soldiers under his authority, along with Croatian and Chetnik soldiers who had supported the Wehrmacht in its war against Tito's Yugoslav communist partisans. He attempted to escape with these troops to British-controlled Austria.

Events intervened. On May 9 General Löhr was captured by the 14th Slovenian Division, a formation allied to Tito's partisan army, at Topolšica in northern Yugoslavia. In talks with his Yugoslav opponents he offered to exchange all his weapons and supplies in return for safe conduct to Austria. This was refused outright. Löhr was then prevailed upon to agree to a ceasefire—but his men refused to obey these instructions. Löhr then managed to escape, countermanded his orders and opened contact with the British. His troops continued to move north toward Austria.

Tito's forces now gathered in strength and blocked Löhr's escape route at Poljana, close to the Austrian border. Field Marshal Alexander, the Allied commander in the region, was jointly occupying the Italian city of Trieste with Tito's Yugoslav forces. Churchill and Truman wanted the Yugoslavs to leave Trieste and also move out of the Austrian province of Carinthia. This had become a political problem, with the Soviet Union, still looking for a resolution of the Polish issue, cautious in its support of its Yugoslav communist ally.

On the ground, Great Britain realized it was vital to implement the unconditional surrender agreement. In a goodwill gesture, Field Marshal Alexander sent twenty British tanks to reinforce the Yugoslavs at Poljana. In two days of bitter fighting, on May 13 and 14 the German and Croatian troops were defeated, Löhr was captured and the surrender terms were imposed by force.

On May 15 the clashes in Yugoslavia ceased and Tito sent his troops a communiqué congratulating them on defeating the remnants of the Wehrmacht. On the same day, the Soviet Information Bureau reported that all military action against the Germans had ended. In the West, fighting against Germany concluded on May 7, and the announcement of this, and the declaration of VE-Day, was awaited with impatience for a matter of hours. In the East, VE-Day was announced on May 9 and fighting then continued for another week.

Milovan Djilas, fighting with Tito's partisans in Yugoslavia, expressed a sense of grievance over this: "On May 9th we greeted the unconditional surrender of Germany—Victory Day—in bitter loneliness. It was as if that joy was not meant for us. No-one invited us to the feast, even though—both as a government and as a people—we had helped prepare it through the most terrible suffering and losses."

However, fulfilling the unconditional surrender terms required British troops in Austria to return to Tito those soldiers—of Germany's ally Croatia, and Chetniks who had fought with Wehrmacht divisions in Yugoslavia—who crossed the border after May 9. Some of these men had been involved in bloody anti-partisan operations, but Tito had promised that all would nevertheless receive trial by military tribunal. This commitment was not kept—and the violence continued. Some Croatian and Chetnik units, disarmed and returned to the Yugoslav army, were brutally massacred. British 8th Army soldiers, who had fought an honorable war in North Africa and Italy, were appalled at having to practice deception or resort to force to return these soldiers to Yugoslavia against their wishes.

The troops of Germany's allies met with very different fates. The Latvian SS Legion was formed of two divisions—the 15th and 19th. Both had fought on the Eastern Front. But in April 1945 the German High Command ordered the 15th to help defend Berlin—and the Kriegsmarine transported it to Germany, while the 19th remained in the Courland Pocket. The men of the 15th were subsequently able to escape to American lines; the 19th went into Soviet captivity on May 9.

The Galician SS Division, formed of troops from the Ukraine, managed to reach Rimini in northern Italy, where it was sheltered by General Anders' Polish II Corps. Anders did not witness the creation of a free Poland but was able to protect these men from deportation to Russia, arguing that the area they were recruited from should be seen historically as part of a greater Poland, not the Soviet Union. This did not correspond to the agreement made between the Allies at Yalta, where Britain and America promised to return to the Russians all those who belonged within the 1939 frontiers of the Soviet Union—but Britain accepted Anders' plan and more than 7,100 Ukrainians were secretly repatriated within the United Kingdom.

The very last of the fighting—on the Dutch island of Texel—did not come to an end until May 20. Texel's garrison force included regular Wehrmacht troops but also a brigade of Georgians from the Soviet Union—men who had been recruited from POW camps and were now willing to fight for the Nazi state.

The Georgians were initially deployed by the Germans to guard supply depots and perform sentry duty. But in April 1945, as Canadian troops made inroads in Wehrmacht positions in northwestern Holland, the German High Command instructed this force—the 822nd Battalion of the Georgian Legion—to move to the mainland and engage with the soldiers of the Western Allies. The Georgians balked at this and their commander—in an uncanny echo of the volte-face of the Vlasov troops—disobeyed these orders and launched an uprising against his German masters.

The Georgian Legion knew that Stalin would not take kindly to soldiers from his home republic collaborating with the Germans—and was particularly fearful of its fate. On April 5, 1945, the men of the 822nd Battalion—realizing that active combat against the Western Allies would ensure they were handed back to the Soviet Union as POWs—attacked the Germans instead and took over most of the island. However, they were unable to capture the two largest gun batteries there and the Germans responded quickly, landing several thousand more troops on Texel.

The Wehrmacht was incensed by this betrayal on the part of soldiers formerly under its command. Combat was savage and neither side took prisoners. After several weeks of bloody fighting the Georgians were forced back into their last stronghold, the island's lighthouse. They resisted defiantly—but the Germans brought up engineering units, blasted holes in the base of the building and forced their way in. Some fifty Georgians were captured there, forced to dig their own graves and then executed.

However, the remaining Georgians—supported by members of the Dutch underground—went into hiding, and as the Germans sought them out, sporadic fighting continued. Neither side recognized the ceasefire signed at Rheims and Karlshorst and a Canadian reconnaissance team reported that clashes were still occurring on Texel on May 17. Only when the main body of Canadian troops arrived on the island three days later—on May 20—were hostilities eventually brought to an end.

The Canadians were impressed by the Georgians' desperate resistance and attempted to intercede on their behalf with the Soviet Union. The Canadian 1st Army commander, Lieutenant General Charles Foulkes, wrote a letter of commendation praising the Georgians as "valiant allies" whose continued resistance had led to more than 4,000 German troops being committed to the island, men who otherwise would have impeded the Canadians' advance. The 226 Georgian survivors were handed over to the Russians at Wilhelmshaven only after Foulkes' staff officer, Lieutenant Colonel Lord Tweedsmuir, held talks with Red Army liaison officers and each Georgian had been awarded a certificate of bravery.

The Soviet Union was implacable in pursuit of those of its nationals who had collaborated with the Germans, but whether as a result of the Canadian intervention, or the sensing of a propaganda opportunity, the Georgians enjoyed a near-miraculous escape from the firing squad. Most were briefly held in camps, undertook additional service in the Red Army, and were then allowed to return to their homes—on the strict condition they did not speak about their wartime role. *Pravda* then published an article portraying the men as heroes. No mention was made of their collaboration with the Germans.

Some of the Georgian fighters were even offered bit-parts in a film made of their exploits, *The Crucified Island*. Only these exploits had now been liberally revised. Instead of forming part of the Georgian Legion, the men were recast as POWs kept in a camp on Texel. The film showed them staging an intrepid breakout and then waging war on all the Germans on the island. This became the "official" Soviet version of the fighting on Texel—with the heroism of the Georgians offered as a paean of cinematic praise to the Soviet leader. It was—even by Russian standards—an astonishing re-creation of historical events. The men of the Georgian 822nd Battalion had won a most fortunate reprieve.

However, there was little hope for the Vlasov Army, despite its heroic role in the Prague uprising.

On May 7, with relations between East and West under strain, Soviet marshal Ivan Konev formed a special operations unit, recruited from the Soviet 25th Tank Corps, and provided it with secret instructions. Konev anticipated that as his soldiers approached Prague the Vlasov Army would retreat westward and try to surrender to the Americans. If they did so, the special Soviet force was ordered to cross the American lines and seize Generals Andrei Vlasov and Sergei Bunyachenko, regardless of the consequences. The Soviet Union was determined to bring these men before a Russian military court and put them on trial as traitors, whatever the ramifications of this for the Grand Alliance.

It was hard for Westerners to understand the deep hatred Russians felt for General Vlasov and all that he represented. In Britain, the most famous turncoat, William Joyce—nicknamed Lord Haw-Haw—had gained notoriety through his radio broadcasts, which always began "Germany calling!" and derided Churchill and the war effort in sarcastic, mocking tones. The British public was discouraged but not actually prohibited from listening to him—and by the end of the war Joyce's commentary had become the butt of humor. His last broadcast, from Hamburg on April 30, 1945, extolled the heroic defense of Berlin and warned of the menace of Bolshevism—but was delivered with Joyce quite plainly drunk. William Joyce was captured near Flensburg on May 28 after making an unsuccessful attempt to escape to Denmark. He would be tried and executed as a traitor—but the small band of British Fascists who had extolled Nazi Germany's virtues now became an object of ridicule.

Vlasov symbolized something rather different. He had attempted to portray himself as a patriot, offering the Soviet Union an alternative ideology. But Stalin was astute enough to broaden the appeal of the nation's struggle into a genuine patriotic war, and Vlasov's message was strongly contaminated by his collaboration with the Nazi state. Few within Russia were sympathetic to it; on the contrary, his urging of Russians to fight against their fellow countrymen was seen as unnatural and abhorrent. Those who gathered under his banner were viewed with revulsion.

On May 11 the Red Army gained intelligence of Vlasov's whereabouts. He was at the small town of Lnare, 30 miles southeast of Pilsen, with General Bunyachenko and the 1st Division of the Russian Liberation Army, negotiating with an advance force of the American 90th Infantry Division (part of General Patton's US Third Army). The commander of the Soviet 25th Tank

Corps, Major General Fominykh, now ordered a rapid response unit—Captain Ivan Yakushev's motorized battalion (attached to the 162nd Tank Brigade)—to capture Vlasov and Bunyachenko at all costs.

Soviet lieutenant Grigory Sukhorukov was Captain Yakushev's second-in-command. He recalled:

> On the 9th May we had fought our way into Prague, with our tanks garlanded with flowers and young Czech girls sitting on top of them. On the 10th our soldiers were invited as guests of honor to a local wedding. On the 11th we were given a new military mission. The surrender may have been signed in Berlin and the end of the war announced in Moscow, but we were now to carry on fighting. We were ordered to advance with all speed to the area around Nepomuk [24 miles southeast of Pilsen] and capture the Vlasovites.

On the evening of May 11 Yakushev's motorized force sped out of Prague. Generals Vlasov and Bunyachenko remained locked in fruitless negotiations with the local American commander, Captain Donahue. The discussions took place in the genteel surroundings of Lnare's seventeenth-century castle, but were far from cordial. Donahue made it clear that he could not accept the surrender of the 1st Division of the Russian Liberation Army. He added that Lnare was to be included in a designated Soviet zone and that his troops would very shortly evacuate the town and hand it over to the Red Army. In Austria, the Americans had already returned General Mikhail Meandrov and the remnants of the 2nd Division of the Russian Liberation Army to the Soviets, so the omens were scarcely promising. The US commander concluded bluntly: he had received strict instructions not to let the Vlasov forces cross over the agreed demarcation line, whatever the circumstances.

As Vlasov and Bunyachenko received this dispiriting news, Captain Yakushev's Soviet motorized battalion was rapidly approaching. Lieutenant Grigory Sukhorukov, sent on an advanced reconnaissance mission, drove straight into a body of US troops stationed near by. He greeted the commanding officer, introduced himself—and asked whether his American counterpart had any news of the Vlasov Army. The American spread out a map and showed Sukhorukov the exact location of all the United States, German and Vlasov forces in the vicinity. Marshal Konev had made his dispositions fearful of American intentions; in reality, his Western ally could not have been more helpful.

"I was amazed at the accuracy of the intelligence," Sukhorukov related, "and very grateful." The Soviet troops were closing in on their prey. He continued: "Our soldiers were invited to stay for dinner—but I politely declined." His parting words were wonderfully understated: "We are rather pressed for time," he told his American hosts.

Early on the morning of May 12 Captain Donahue summoned Vlasov and Bunyachenko to a final meeting. He informed them that the Soviet 25th Tank Corps was approaching from the east and Lnare would be handed over to the Russians later that day. The Vlasov Army would have to fend for itself.

General Bunyachenko drove to his divisional headquarters at Jezbyre, a mile north of Lnare. A week earlier, he had drafted a rousing exhortation to his men to come to the rescue of beleaguered Prague. His last command to his soldiers ended not with a martial bang but a despairing whimper: "The division is to disband immediately," Bunyachenko stated. "Form up into small groups and avoid major roads and populated places. Try to reach southern Germany. Look for me there."

More than 15,000 Vlasov troops were left utterly leaderless. Some burned documents and buried their weapons. Others changed into civilian clothes provided by the civilian population. Thousands lay listlessly on the ground. They were too tired to undertake another march. All the fight had been knocked out of them.

Captain Yakushev's Soviet soldiers were now advancing cautiously into the woodland around Lnare. The main body of Major General Fominykh's 25th Tank Corps was moving up close behind. These men would take care of the majority of the Vlasov troops. Yakushev was focused on one objective—to find and arrest their commanders.

And then there was a breakthrough. The Soviet motorized battalion found a group of Vlasov soldiers. Their commanding officer—disillusioned at being abandoned in such peremptory fashion and hoping to save his own skin—turned informer. He told the Red Army troops that Generals Vlasov and Bunyachenko were about to leave Lnare in a convoy of four vehicles. There was no time to lose. "Yakushev took an armored car—and I jumped in beside him, with a couple of other officers and the Vlasovite turncoat," Lieutenant Sukhorukov recalled. "Which road are they leaving from?" he yelled at the informer. "They were heading south, toward Horazdovic. Our driver put his foot hard on the accelerator."

At 2:00 p.m. Vlasov and Bunyachenko left Lnare. Bunyachenko had changed into civilian clothes. Vlasov—more elaborately—had ordered a false floor to be constructed in his car, and was hiding beneath it. Two miles out of the town their convoy of vehicles slowed for a railway crossing. And then a military vehicle sped past them, swerved and blocked the road ahead. Soviet soldiers jumped out of it, machine guns at the ready. The informer had identified General Vlasov's car.

Captain Yakushev had cornered the Russian Liberation Army's leaders in the no-man's-land between the US and Russian demarcation lines. These commanders were regarded with loathing by Red Army soldiers and emotions were running high. But when Yakushev pulled open the door of General Vlasov's car he found two frightened women huddled together on the rear passenger seat. "Is this some kind of joke?" he exclaimed indignantly. But then Yakushev noticed the vehicle's red-carpeted floor was unusually high. Ripping away the fabric, he found General Vlasov cowering underneath it. He hauled him out, yelling to his comrades: "We've got the bastard!"

General Bunyachenko, traveling in the car behind, chose to surrender in a more straightforward fashion. Both men were taken to the Soviet 25th Tank Corps headquarters at Nepomuk for initial interrogation. When asked for his identification, Vlasov fumbled in his tunic for what seemed an age, at length unearthing papers identifying him as a general of the Soviet 2nd Shock Army. He stood to attention and presented himself in this fashion. This had been Vlasov's command when he surrendered to the Germans in the summer of 1942. A lot had happened in the intervening three years. For a moment, Vlasov may have imagined his creation of an anti-Bolshevik army to be a bad dream. If so, he soon received a rude awakening.

Major General Fominykh regarded his counterpart contemptuously. "Issue surrender instructions to the remainder of your troops," he spat out, "or we will round up your gang of bandits and shoot them on the spot." Vlasov issued the necessary orders. Three days later he and Bunyachenko were transferred to Moscow's Lubyanka Prison, along with many of the high-ranking officers who had followed them. They were joined there by General Mikhail Meandrov and other Vlasov commanders. They were all tried the following year and hanged for treason on August 1, 1946.

The thousands of ordinary soldiers of the Russian Liberation Army presented a dismal picture. Most would be tried by military tribunal and either shot or sentenced to years of hard labor. Sigismund Diczbalis was one of the few fortunate ones—he managed to escape from his captors and cross over to the American zone. He was not forced to return. The majority of Vlasovites were not so lucky. Looking at the assembled prisoners, Lieutenant Sukhorukov initially felt little sympathy for them. "They are traitors to our country," he thought, "and they deserve their fate." But over time, he would gain a different perspective.

Some of the prisoners, possessing useful technical expertise, were briefly allocated to the Soviet 25th Tank Corps, before being sent on to special camps. Over a number of weeks Sukhorukov got to know a former lieutenant of the Vlasov Army who briefly served with them as a mechanic. He had graduated from technical school, joined the Red Army—and then had been captured by the Germans in the autumn of 1941. There followed three years of hell in a POW camp. Thousands of his fellow prisoners had died of beatings or starvation. And then a representative of General Vlasov arrived.

After a long period of physical hardship and emotional disorientation, the blandishments offered by the Vlasov officer gave this man hope: he possessed little news from the outside world, and was told that Germany and the Red Army would wear themselves out in a long struggle—leaving the way open for the Russian Liberation Army to carve a new future for the Soviet people. By the autumn of 1944 there was scant prospect of that—but three years in a POW camp were scarcely conducive to lucid thinking. The man was offered freedom from the camp and decent food. That was enough. His decision was an opportunist one, but as he said to Sukhorukov: "I no longer believed I had any real future in this world. I threw myself upon the mercy of fate."

Fate would not be merciful. This Vlasovite would shortly be sent to a camp and a long sentence of hard labor followed. Sukhorukov hated the Vlasov Army—but could not help but feel sympathy for him.

The period of European history after Hitler's fall was unique—with soldiers and civilians traversing a desolate landscape. Red Army lieutenant Boris Komsky and his men were now marching home from Berlin. As they passed through Poland, Komsky was struck by the terrible war damage in Warsaw, writing in his diary:

> House by house, street by street, the wide central roads have been cleared of bricks. Only the pavements give this enormous cemetery the barest resemblance to a city and allow one to imagine its past beauty. Not a single building is intact—it is a staggering panorama of lifelessness. The ruins of Pompeii do not come close to this massive flattening of the land.
>
> Some of the mutilated remains preserve traces of beautiful architecture. How many thousands of people died beneath these ruins? How many corpses are buried beneath these colossal brick pyramids? Trees stand, charred and splintered by shell fragments—witnesses of the death of Warsaw. Of 2.5 million people living here before the war only 50,000 survived.

These were chilling statistics—the result of the brutal suppression of the Warsaw uprising in August 1944. And Komsky was now to encounter the grim evidence of the Holocaust. He recalled:

> In Kutno in Poland we had a day's rest. The regiment settled in the fields outside the city. The weather was warm and it was nice to be outside. Officers were allowed to go and find a private apartment where they could stay. My friend and I found some accommodation— we would sleep there and during the day go back and work with our soldiers. One evening, as I was walking back to where I was living, a man came up to me. He looked at me and said: Comrade Lieutenant, are you Jewish? I answered "Yes, I'm a Jew." He pointed to two young

women standing on a balcony and revealed that they were the only Jews left in the city. Previously half the population had been Jewish.

These women had looked at Komsky only for a matter of seconds but felt a deep sense of kinship with him. On some instinctive level, they knew that he was Jewish as well.

Komsky met the women—they lived on the second floor of an apartment—and they laid out a table of food to share with him. Two Jews left, out of the thousands who had once lived in the town. In such terrible circumstances, the feast seemed like a celebration of being alive.

Komsky's experience was very much a personal one, but it also spoke for many others—soldiers and civilians—trying to make sense of the war's aftermath.

And yet, amid the horror and the loss, there was also hope. The relics of Hitler's Nazi state were being jettisoned. Two weeks after VE-Day the Dönitz government in Flensburg was finally arrested. This course of action had been suggested to Winston Churchill considerably earlier by Foreign Office under-secretary Sir Orme Sargent—but the prime minister objected to it, fearing that such an action would raise "grave constitutional issues."

Churchill wrote to Orme Sargent on May 14:

I neither know nor care about Dönitz . . . The question for me is has he any power to get the Germans to surrender quickly, without further loss of life. We cannot go running around into every German slum and argue with every German there that it is his duty to surrender or we will shoot him.

Do you want to have a handle with which to manipulate this conquered people, or just have to thrust your hands into an agitated ant heap?

But there were no actual constitutional issues involved—this administration had never received formal recognition by the Allies and the instructions in Hitler's will were scarcely binding on his victorious opponents. The removal of the so-called Dönitz government was long overdue, whatever Churchill's concerns. American diplomat Robert Murphy, political adviser to the Supreme Allied Headquarters, described Dönitz's administration rather differently: "They are a motley array of individuals who, under Admiral Dönitz, nevertheless style themselves as the 'Acting government of the Reich.' Dönitz shows no remorse for Germany's acts, but instead refers to Hitler's achievement in maintaining excellent discipline within the Reich—as if the Führer was still standing by his side."

SHAEF liaison officer Colonel Richard Wilberforce wrote scathingly of the Flensburg government: "They try to present themselves as indispensable to the allies—but there are little grounds for such assertions." Wilberforce visited Flensburg and took the opportunity to explore the Naval Academy at Mürwik. "I went down a long corridor," he remembered. "The rooms had impressive designations—offices to a variety of supposed ministries. I opened one door and found it was in fact a bicycle storeroom. Another contained a bed, with a woman fast asleep on it."

The Dönitz regime held "cabinet meetings" every morning at 10:00 a.m. It set up an "information service," placing an old radio set in one of the lecture rooms of the Naval Academy. A minister of food was appointed—although his only responsibility was to fetch the whiskey by which the meetings were enlivened. Dönitz was provided with a Mercedes to take him the 500 yards from his home to the Academy. Official pictures were taken of "the new government at work."

The Soviet Union had by now lost patience with the situation. On May 20 *Pravda* referred to the Dönitz administration as a "gang," writing caustically: "Discussion of the status of the Fascist gang around Dönitz continues. Some in allied circles clearly deem it necessary to make use of the 'services' of Dönitz and his Nazi collaborators."

The following day the Supreme Allied Command and the Soviet High Command took a joint decision to dispense with the administration entirely. On May 23 British tanks and soldiers appeared on the streets of Flensburg and the Dönitz regime was escorted aboard the ship *Patria*. In front of American major general Lowell Rooks, British brigadier Edward Foord and

Soviet major general Nikolai Trusov the so-called government was formally dissolved. Admiral von Friedeburg committed suicide shortly afterward; Dönitz, Jodl, Speer and the others went into captivity.

On the same day a disheveled fugitive was captured by British soldiers on the bridge at Bremervörde in northern Germany. He had shaved off his mustache and was clumsily disguised with an eye patch. The man was taken into custody and his real identity became apparent. He was Heinrich Himmler. He killed himself during a medical examination by biting into a cyanide capsule embedded in one of his teeth. One of the most powerful men in Hitler's Third Reich, the head of the SS and the architect of the Holocaust, he had spent his last few days sleeping rough in local railway stations.

In the twilight of Hitler's rule, Himmler had tried unsuccessfully to divide the Grand Alliance, offering peace terms to the West but not to the East. His overtures had been spurned. But after the arrest of the entire Flensburg administration on May 23, Sir Orme Sargent wrote: "We bungled the Dönitz business . . . By first playing with the Dönitz government we only aroused suspicion in Moscow."

The Dönitz regime did indeed come close to creating a rift between the Western Allies and the Soviet Union in the last days of the war. But now its divisive influence was finally removed.

In the weeks after VE-Day President Truman's attention firmly turned toward the Pacific. American forces were now in the midst of a bloody battle for the island of Okinawa, and he wanted to ensure that the Soviet Union joined the war against Japan—and that the difficulties at the San Francisco Conference were resolved. As a result, he was prepared to be more accommodating toward Russia.

Winston Churchill admired the courage of the Russian people but also saw the cruelty inherent in the Soviet system. He remained deeply concerned over eastern Europe's political future. "An iron curtain is drawn down upon their front. We do not know what is going on behind it," the British prime minister had warned in a telegram to President Truman. Churchill was captivated by the phrase "iron curtain," but should have thought more about its origins. He felt deeply for the fate of Poland—but was caught up in his own prejudices over Bolshevism.

Stalin was enmeshed in a web of prejudices of his own. In a reception given to honor the Red Army on May 24 the Soviet leader proposed a toast to the Russian people in which he fleetingly acknowledged the mistakes he and his government had made at the beginning of the war. A month later a magnificent Victory Parade was held on Moscow's Red Square—where captured Nazi banners and standards were triumphantly cast at the foot of Lenin's Mausoleum. But the repression of independent thinking—at home and in those countries under Soviet influence—intensified. Stalin ruled through fear—and at the war's end he would not loosen his control over his own people or those in the states around him.

The Soviet leader did not trust the West—but nevertheless genuinely hoped that the hard-won spirit of cooperation would outlast the war. Russia had its own suspicions about Western intentions for post-war Europe. The chief of intelligence for the 2nd Belorussian Front had reported to the Soviet High Command:

Rumors abound about an upcoming clash between Britain and the Soviet Union. It is spoken about openly in German POW camps and also among the several thousand Poles in the area around Lübeck who are now enrolling in the Anders Army. At Neustadt—where a lot of Wehrmacht troops have surrendered—some German officers have not even been confined. One British captain remarked that soon the Allies would be using Germans to fight against Russia.

After VE-Day the Main Intelligence Directorate of the Soviet General Staff (the GRU) intercepted Churchill's instructions to Field Marshal Montgomery to collect and store captured German weapons for a possible rearming of Wehrmacht troops surrendering to the Western Allies. These were passed on directly to Stalin. According to a GRU senior official, General Mikhail Milstein, the report created a mood of deep suspicion within the Kremlin.

That suspicion could, however, be thawed.

At the end of May, on President Truman's urging, the American Harry Hopkins paid a special visit to Moscow. Hopkins was a remarkable figure. An architect of the New Deal and a brilliant administrator, from the late

1930s—after an operation for stomach cancer—he suffered from constant ill-health. And yet he remained a gregarious and charismatic figure and during the war worked—at considerable cost to himself—as a tireless diplomat. He had held no official position within the administration of Franklin D. Roosevelt during the war years but his influence with the late president was enormous. And he won the respect of Winston Churchill. The British prime minister said of their first meeting:

> Thus I met Harry Hopkins, an extraordinary man, who played, and was to play, a sometimes decisive part in the whole movement of the war. His was a soul that flamed out of a frail and failing body. He was a crumbling lighthouse from which there shone the beams that led great fleets to harbor. He also had a gift of sardonic humor. I enjoyed his company, especially when things went ill . . . Hopkins always went to the heart of the matter.

Harry Hopkins' practicality was praised by the acerbic US chief of naval operations, Admiral Ernest King: "Hopkins did a lot to keep the President [Roosevelt] on beam," King said. "I've seldom seen a man whose head was screwed on so tight." And US Army chief of staff General George Marshall even wrote to Hopkins' future wife (his third marriage, to Lucy Macy, a former editor of *Harper's Bazaar*, which took place in 1942) expressing his concerns: "To be frank, I am intensely interested in Harry's happiness, and therefore in your impending marriage," Marshall confided, "as he is of great importance to our national interests and he is one of the most imprudent people regarding his health that I have ever known. I express the hope that you will find it possible to see he takes the necessary rest."

Marshall's concern was well founded. On his return from one visit to Russia, Hopkins had to be given a blood transfusion and eighteen hours' forced convalescence. His digestive tract was in such bad shape that he could hardly absorb nutrients—and he seemed to exist on a diet of whiskey and cigarettes. And still he continued to work. General Sir Alan Brooke, the British Army chief of staff, wrote of his unorthodox yet highly effective style:

I met with Hopkins, expecting to be taken into his office. Instead, we went to his bedroom where we sat on the edge of his bed looking at his shaving brush and tooth paste, whilst he let me into some of the President's inner thoughts. I mention this meeting as it was so typical of this strange man with no official position, and yet one of the most influential people with the President [Roosevelt]. A man who played a great and nebulous part in the war. A great part, that did him all the more credit when his miserable health was taken into account.

Throughout the war, Hopkins had been the top American dealing with the Soviet Union. He regularly met with Anastas Mikoyan, the Soviet trade secretary, over the administration of Lend-Lease. He had often explained Roosevelt's plans to Stalin and other top Soviet officials, in order to enlist Russian support for American objectives, and in turn explained Stalin's goals and needs to Roosevelt. He was the foremost decision-maker in Lend-Lease, and he gave priority to supplying the Soviet Union because they were bearing the brunt of the war. And of all the Americans involved in the relations between the two countries, Hopkins was the man the Russians most trusted.

On the death of Roosevelt, Hopkins attempted to retire because of his ill-health, but at the end of May 1945 President Truman persuaded him to make a last visit to Moscow. Truman wanted to achieve some sort of resolution over the issue of Poland. If anyone could do this, it was Hopkins. The American president wrote directly to Stalin. "I am sure you are as aware as I am of the difficulty in dealing by exchange of messages with the complicated and important questions with which we are faced," Truman stated, suggesting that Hopkins be sent to Russia to discuss matters personally with the Soviet leader. "I readily accept your proposal," Stalin responded warmly. Hopkins was given carte blanche at the negotiating table by the American president, Truman adding that "he was free to use diplomatic language or a baseball bat—whichever he felt was right."

Hopkins preferred diplomatic language, but he was frank with Joseph Stalin and the Soviet leader was frank with him. Their discussions were forthright—but cordial and constructive. Averell Harriman, the American ambassador to Moscow, accompanied Hopkins, and he found proceedings far more positive than he had expected. Numerous misunderstandings were resolved.

At the beginning, there was a revealing interchange. Hopkins spoke of perceptions in the Western press about Poland. Stalin was irritated by this remark, and said in return that he would not cloak his own concerns behind a screen of "so-called public opinion." The Soviet leader took little heed of public opinion within the Soviet Union and initially saw this as a negotiating ploy by the American. But when Hopkins visibly flinched he reconsidered his stance. In subsequent remarks, Stalin added that he had not meant to deride Hopkins' observations.

The Bolshevik state had evolved in isolation from the international community and remained deeply suspicious of it. And yet it was willing to learn—and if it considered its attitudes unjustified, was prepared to correct them. Harry Hopkins was such an effective negotiator with the Russians because he dispensed with ideological differences as much as possible and focused on the issues themselves.

At the end of three days of meetings, from May 26 to 28, a compromise over Poland was reached. The Lublin government would be recognized by the Western Allies. In return, four ministerial posts in the new Polish government would be offered to non-communists. It was a far cry from free and fair elections, but in the circumstances it was probably the best deal that could be obtained and Hopkins—"who always went to the heart of the matter"—had pulled it off.

In a personal meeting with Stalin, Hopkins also raised the issue of the sixteen arrested Poles. The Soviet leader insisted that they would have to stand trial. Hopkins made it clear how badly this would come across in Western public opinion. Again, a compromise was reached. The majority of Poles would receive light sentences—a promise that was kept by the Russians.

Britain and America now cut off relations with the Polish government-in-exile. For many Poles, this was a most unpalatable solution. Even with the ministerial posts for non-communists, a government "friendly to the Soviet people" had largely been imposed upon the country. The arrangements for

Poland's future were nevertheless ratified when the Big Three met for the last time at the Potsdam Conference, from July 17 to August 2, 1945.

Potsdam was only 26 miles southwest of Berlin. At the beginning of the conference President Truman and Prime Minister Winston Churchill took the opportunity to visit the war-damaged German capital. Truman arrived at the ruined Reich Chancellery first. He surveyed the seat of Hitler's regime, commented on the scale of destruction and the plight of the city's inhabitants, but remained in his military jeep and was soon driven off again. Churchill's reaction was rather different. He clambered out of his vehicle, and accompanied by an escort of British and Russian soldiers proceeded to explore the depths of the Führer Bunker. Churchill wished to make a connection with Hitler's last stand in Berlin—and he concluded his visit in the courtyard next to the bunker, where the corpses of the Führer and Eva Braun were carried out and cremated.

Stalin chose not to visit Berlin at all. The Soviet leader appeared to show no interest in the city his soldiers had fought so hard to win or the bunker where his great foe had met his end. Stalin was always disengaged from the human dimension but his nonchalance may have been a front. In the summer of 1941 Hitler's surprise attack on Russia had left his country teetering on the brink of destruction and for a period of several days plunged the Soviet leader into total despair. He had then rallied—but that dark moment was something he probably wanted to avoid recalling. The ruined Reich Chancellery may well have been a painful reminder to him.

Now the brutal war had finally been won. Harry Hopkins understood how to deal with Russia better than any other Westerner. Nevertheless, on his return from Moscow, he expressed "serious doubts over long-term collaboration with the Soviet Union." He realized that the two countries' outlooks were very different, and predicted that "the American belief in freedom might well lead to insuperable differences between them."

The world was moving on. The atomic bomb had been tested by the Americans and would shortly be used on the Japanese cities of Hiroshima and Nagasaki. At Potsdam President Truman acknowledged the existence of the bomb and his plans for it to Stalin only obliquely. In an interval between sessions he told the Soviet leader that America had discovered "a weapon of unusual destructive force," without disclosing further details. The United States had chosen not to share this new technology with Russia.

It was a watershed moment. The Western Allies now held a powerful military advantage although the Soviets would obtain much of the information anyway, through their espionage system within the United States. In private, Soviet foreign minister Molotov told Stalin: "The Americans have been doing all this work on the atom bomb without telling us." "We were supposed to be allies," the Soviet leader retorted. Mistrust between East and West was growing. There would be no more meetings between Britain, America and the Soviet Union. The Cold War era was approaching.

And yet, in May 1945 Britain, America and the Soviet Union had held their wartime coalition together. Harry Hopkins had pulled off a notable success in Moscow, but it was the fairness and straight dealing of General Dwight Eisenhower which, more than anything else, had kept the Grand Alliance in being. Hopkins and Eisenhower shared similar qualities—clarity of expression, straight talking and a readiness to honor their commitments. They were willing to trust the Russians and that trust was reciprocated. When Hopkins began his discussions with Joseph Stalin on May 26, 1945, the Soviet leader told him that Eisenhower's actions in Czechoslovakia at the beginning of that month had restored the Soviet Union's faith in its Western Allies.

Nikita Khrushchev enlarged upon this, recalling: "I remember how Stalin on a number of occasions talked of Eisenhower's personality. He remarked on his chivalrous attitude toward an ally—saying what a decent man he was."

Stalin held General Eisenhower in high regard but had a low opinion of Field Marshal Montgomery. This was a reflection of the events of early May 1945. The Soviet leader believed that "Eisenhower and Montgomery were both representatives of the capitalist system, but they differed in the way they observed the principles of partnership, treaty agreements and their word of honor," and attributed Montgomery's agreement with the Germans at Lüneburg Heath to the British field marshal's vanity—and the resentment he felt toward his supreme commander. "It was Eisenhower who set up the conditions to defeat the Germans in the west," the Soviet leader said. "Montgomery wanted to reap the fruits of that victory for himself."

When General Eisenhower visited Moscow in August 1945, Stalin invited the American to stand on the rostrum above Lenin's Mausoleum with him and watch a parade in Red Square—an unprecedented mark of recognition for a Westerner—and conferred the highest military honor of the Soviet Union upon him, the Order of Victory.

In his telegram to President Truman on May 9 Winston Churchill also paid generous tribute to General Eisenhower: "In him we have had a man who set the unity of Allied Armies above all nationalistic thoughts," Churchill said. "In his headquarters unity and strategy were the only reigning spirits . . . At no time has the principle of alliances between different races been carried and maintained at so high a pitch."

Churchill respected Eisenhower's intrinsic sense of fairness and his personal integrity—qualities that allowed the Allied commander to mend the rift between East and West at the very end of the war, a period referred to by Eisenhower himself "as having taken more out of me and my staff than the previous eleven months of our campaign."

Toward the end of May General Eisenhower paid a brief, impromptu visit to London. He went to see a revue at the Prince of Wales Theatre, where, as Kay Summersby remembered, "the entire audience rose to its feet and almost shouted the roof off . . . they cheered, whistled, stamped and applauded." In response to cries of "Speech!" the Supreme Allied Commander made one of those spontaneous replies at which he excelled: "It's nice," Eisenhower said, "to be back in a country where I can *almost* speak the language."

Churchill's British coalition government ended on July 26 when the general election results were announced as a Labour landslide victory. Looking to the future, the issues of jobs, homes, health and education were now uppermost in people's minds. Most were well aware that peacetime life would not bring a speedy end to wartime austerity—and the international situation remained uncertain. "A whirl of Victory celebrations," Royal Navy captain Andrew Yates wrote, "but there was not the wild relief of 1918—and we still had not forged a post-war understanding with Russia."

At the end of the First World War on November 11, 1918, there had been a sense of euphoria—a short-lived belief that war itself was defeated and that living conditions "fit for heroes" would soon be created for Britain's returning soldiers. But after a brief boom the economy had slumped and the country then descended into mass unemployment. Now the mood was more realistic. There was still little meat in the shops—and many of the cinema and theater lights, which had dazzled onlookers on the night of May 8, had been switched off again to save fuel. The process of rebuilding and recovery would be long and hard.

And yet, surveying the broader sweep of events, it was remarkable that the Grand Alliance had achieved so much. The threat of fascism within Europe was destroyed. A devastating war was brought to a close. Talks were held to create a new structure for world peace—the United Nations.

If the ten days after the death of Adolf Hitler saw a major crisis within the Alliance, one largely hidden from public view, it was a crisis successfully mastered. In the days after Hitler's death, goodwill triumphed over suspicion—an achievement that can be celebrated on the anniversaries of the two VE-Days on May 8 and 9. After Hitler, a malignancy had been incised from our history.

After VE-Day Lieutenant Robert Frank and several other officers of the US 87th Division spent several days with the Russians, crossing over the demarcation line at Marienberg in Germany. They had a memorable time. Frank never forgot the attempts of a Russian band to strike up "The Star-Spangled Banner," the rounds of festivities and dancing and the efforts of American GIs to teach Red Army soldiers the hip-hop. And Frank was honest enough to admit that throughout it all "we didn't trust them—and they didn't trust us."

The ten days after the death of Hitler heralded a flawed triumph for post-war Europe. For some, suffering and injustice continued. Others struggled to make sense of what they had experienced. The war had been a catastrophe for millions—and many survivors would be permanently scarred by it.

And yet flowers were blossoming over Europe in the May sunshine. Prague was covered in lilac bloom—and the city was now free after years of

Nazi occupation. "We were proud of our uprising and the part that we played in driving the Germans out of our capital," Antonin Sticha said. "It was just recompense for all the humiliation and the suffering we had endured." Amid the political uncertainties, and the desolation left in the war's wake, many would have agreed with him. Defeating the Nazi menace was a victory worth achieving.

NOTES

CHAPTER 1 | THE FUNERAL PYRE

Mohnke's morning meeting with Hitler, Holzwark's diary entry and Mongrovius's account of the Vlasov Army commander Mikhail Meandrov are from Kempowski, *Das Echolot*. For the general background, I have used Beevor, *Berlin: The Downfall* and Moorhouse, *Berlin at War*. On the end in the bunker, Trevor-Roper, *Last Days of Hitler* remains important, alongside the more recent Fest, *Inside Hitler's Bunker*. On the chronology of events and the reliability of the various sources, Kershaw, *Hitler, 1936–45: Nemesis* and *The End* have been particularly valuable. As late as April 21, Hitler's staff were still expecting him to leave Berlin and fly out to the Berchtesgaden: Musmanno Collection, Duquesne University, Pittsburgh (Christian, Herrgeswell). On the fitness of the Führer to lead a defense of Berlin, the Soviet interrogation of Wolf Heisendorf is particularly interesting. It is found in *Russian Archives: Great Patriotic War* (vol. XV), as is General Helmuth Weidling's account of the defense of the city. The Goebbels diary extracts are from Trevor-Roper (ed.), *Final Entries 1945*. On Churchill and Hitler, see Roberts, *Masters and Commanders*, and Hastings, *Churchill as Warlord*. For the decision to allow the Red Army to take Berlin, particularly helpful have been Oleg Rzheshevsky, "The race for Berlin," *Journal of Slavic Studies*, 8 (1995); Donald Shepardson, "The fall of Berlin and the rise of a myth," *Journal of Military History*, 62 (1998). On SS general Steiner's secret talks in Berlin in April 1945: Norman Goda, "Report on the Otto Ohlendorf file": www.archives.gov/research-papers/ohlendorf. Armin Lehmann supplied additional information on the last days of the German capital; also see his and Tim Carroll's *In Hitler's Bunker*. The German LVI Panzer Corps' role in infecting Russian civilians with typhus in 1944 is discussed in Michael Jones, *Total War*. For the deployment of Hitler Youth in Berlin, as couriers and fighters, see the interview with Artur Axmann in Musmanno Collection (Axmann). British sergeant Trevor Greenwood's letters are from "The War Archive of Trevor Greenwood" at www.trevorgreenwood.co.uk. I am grateful for permission to use this material in some detail. Franz Kuhlmann's account is from "Der Endkampf um den Führerbunker in Berlin," *Marineforum*, 70 (1995). Gellermann, *Die Armee Wenck*, shows that the German 12th Army never intended to plunge into Berlin—Wenck's intention, influenced by General Gotthard Heinrici, was to rescue the remnants of Busse's 9th Army and German refugees, and bring them safely to American lines on the Elbe. This is corroborated by Musmanno's interview with Gerhard Engel, although Engel tries to take sole credit for the decision: Musmanno Collection (Engel). The Joint Intelligence Committee's paper on "Hitler's last days," drawn up on July 21, 1945, is in The National Archives (TNA), KV 4/466. It stresses the effect the Führer's breakdown had on his overall health and capability. Wilberforce's diary extract is from the Imperial War Museum (IWM), 12931. Erich Mende's account is from his *Das Verdammte Gewissen*. General Weidling's comments on the defense of the German capital are from his "Der Endkampf in Berlin," *Wehrwissenschaftliche Rundschau*, 1–3 (1962). Traudl Junge's account of the last days in the bunker is found in her *Bis zur Letzten Stunde*. Felix Sparks' recollections of Dachau are at www.remember.org/witness/sparks2. Donald Jackson's "The 40th Combat Engineer Regiment at Dachau" is from www.scrapbookpages.com/dachauliberation. Kuhlmann's concluding description is from his "Der Endkampf."

CHAPTER 2 | MAY DAY IN BERLIN

This chapter follows the version of events supplied by Chuikov, *End of the Third Reich*, and, in more detail, Vishnevsky, *Diaries of the War Years*. Vishnevsky transcribed the negotiations for Chuikov on May 1/2; a full summary of them—without subsequent editing—is found in *Russian Archives: Great Patriotic War* (vol. XV), as is Yachenin's report and the post-surrender interrogation of Berlin garrison commander General Weidling. Further information—from the combat records of Red Army units involved—is drawn from Igor Venkov, "How the Berlin garrison surrendered," *Army History*, 17 (1990). I owe the body of the narrative to Red Army veterans present at the surrender, particularly Andrei Eshpai, the interpreter who escorted Krebs to Chuikov's HQ, Anatoly Mereshko, present throughout on Chuikov's staff, Mark Slavin, covering the event for the 8th Guards Army newspaper, Anatoly Smriga, and Stepan Doernberg, who typed up the final surrender documents. For the private comments and letters of Chuikov, my thanks are to his son, Alexander. On the broader diplomatic background, I am grateful to Hugh Lunghi and Zoya Zarubina—present as interpreters, on the British and Soviet sides, at the Big Three summits at Teheran, Yalta and Potsdam—and to Dr. Martin Folly, whose *Churchill, Whitehall and the Soviet Union* has been particularly valuable. Also helpful were Rees, *Behind Closed Doors* and Birse, *Memoirs of an Interpreter.* Schwanenflügel's diary extract is from her *Laughter Wasn't Rationed.* On the general course of the fighting in Berlin, and the storming of the Reichstag, I have particularly benefited from information supplied by Vasily Ustygov; see also Abyzov, *The Final Assault.* On Stalin, the Polish Army and Berlin, Antonin Jablonski's recollections are on the Axis History Forum, under "Polish victory flag in Berlin'": www.forum. axishistory.com. Combat orders and records of the Polish forces are reproduced with acknowledgment to "The Polish Army in Berlin": www.Berlin -1945.com. Accounts of Filin, Kalinin, Koshova, Krichevsky, Martschenko, Romanova and Sebeljov are from Kempowski, *Das Echolot*; Drabkin, Makarov, Sampson and Vasilenko from Schultz-Naumann, *Mecklenburg 1945.* Comments of Genkin and Uspensky are from Jones, *Total War*; Inozemtsev's from his *Frontline Diary.* Additional material has been drawn from the combat records of the 129th Rifle Division (70th Army) and 385th Rifle Division (49th Army) Russian Defense Archive, Podolsk. For the contrasting fate of Demmin and Greifswald, see Buske, *Kriegsende in Demmin*, and Meyer and Seils, *1945: Kampflose Ubergabe der Hansestadt Greifswald*—the diary of university rector Karl Engel. On incidents of rape committed by American and British soldiers: Omar White, *Conqueror's Road* and Cullingford's comments, in Jordan (ed.), *Conditions of Surrender.* Stalin's remark is found in Djilas, *Wartime.* The insinuation that Red Army commanders licensed two days of plunder in Demmin is strongly contradicted by Elke

Scherstjanoi in "Die Einnahme der Stadt Demmin durch die Rote Armee am 30 April 1945," in Petra Clemens (ed.), *Das Kriegsende in Demmin 1945: Umgang mit Einem Schwierigen Thema*, which draws on the combat records and war diary of the Soviet 65th Army. For the arrival of Red Army troops in the bunker, see Musmanno Collection (Messerer). Comments on the death of Hitler are from Kempowski (ed.), *Das Echolot*, Hargreaves, *Breslau 1945*, Jordan (ed.), *Conditions of Surrender*, and Colville, *Fringes of Power*. Additional reaction—from the British public—can be found in the Mass Observation Archive, now held at the East Sussex Record Office, SxMOA1/2/49/1/D/3 (henceforth Mass Observation Archive). The unconditional surrender of Berlin was to come into effect at noon. At 1:00 p.m. it was countermanded by Dönitz, who—in a broadcast direct to the Berlin garrison—ordered them to carry on fighting. As a result, the struggle flared up anew, and the Red Army engaged in piecemeal negotiations throughout the afternoon and evening to try to persuade the last strongholds to surrender. This important sequence of events—reported in *Russian Archives: Great Patriotic War* (vol. XV)—is not widely known, and had a major impact on the Soviet view of the Dönitz government.

CHAPTER 3 | EAST MEETS WEST

McFadden's experience is from Horn and Wyczynski, *Paras Versus the Reich*; Derek Thomas' account is from his unpublished memoir, kindly made available to me by his daughter Amanda Helm. For the American side, see NARA (World War Two Operations Report) RG407; Karel Margry, "The US-Soviet Linkup," *After the Battle*, 88 (1995); Krasilshchik and Scott (eds.), *Yanks Meet Reds*; Dobbs, *Six Months in 1945*. For the Russian side, the account of SMERSH counterintelligence officer Vladimir Bogolov, and ancillary documents, in *My Life*, are supplemented by the reminiscences in *Yanks Meet Reds*. The comments of Churkin, Odintsov and Sokolov are from *Russian Archives: Great Patriotic War* (vol. XV). On the broader political context Spalding, *Truman*, and Henry Ryan, "Anglo-American relations during the Polish crisis of 1945," *Australian Journal of Politics and History*, 30 (1984) have been particularly helpful. Yuri Eltekov's testimony is from an interview with me. I am grateful to the Russian Council of Veterans in Moscow for arranging this meeting. Accounts of Jary, Lawrenson and Close are from Buckley, *Monty's Men*. Ronald Mallabar's testimony is in IWM/11211. Vaughan-Thomas's report is from Delaforce, *Invasion of the Third Reich*. Marcosovitch's story is from www.69th-infantry-division.com/Marcosovitch. The US doctor's letters from Nordhausen are cited with acknowledgment to www.wwii.letters-to-wilma. US First Army material is drawn from John Greenwood (ed.), *The War Diary of General Courtney J. Hodges*. All references to British war cabinet meetings from March to May 1945 are from TNA, CAB 195/3, part 1. For the British-Soviet meeting, Karel Margry, "The British-Soviet link-up, May 2, 1945," *After the Battle*, 88 (1995). The background to the German decision not to defend Lübeck is drawn from Liddell Hart Archives, De Guingand, 2/4/1 (report that Field Marshal Busch was ready to surrender the city without resistance to prevent it falling into the hands of the Russians), and City of Lübeck Archives, HS 1099/13 (for which I owe thanks to Richard Hargreaves). These latter records show that Busch's chief of staff, General Eberhard Kinzel, discouraged any organized resistance to the British advance on Lübeck and Wismar. Eisenhower's view of the Soviets is from his *Crusade in Europe*. Henry Swan's letter is from the US National Library of Medicine (Swan Papers), reproduced at www.profiles.nilm.nih.gov. Andy Anderson's diary of May 2 and the dash for Wismar are from Gary Boegel, *Boys of the Clouds*. William Knowlton's account, "Your mission is to contact the Russians," is from the *Reader's Digest*, 47 (August 1945). I am grateful for permission to cite extracts from this. Background information is from the US 7th Armored Division After-Action Report, May 1945, transcribed by Wesley Johnston from NARA, 407/15545, folder 14.

CHAPTER 4 | A SHADOW REALM

Comments of Böhm-Tettelbach, Becheim and Kretschner are from the ZDF TV program *Karl Dönitz—the Successor*; material on Ohlendorf is at NARA, RG319, box 165A. On the setting up of the new government, see

Lüdde-Neurath, *Unconditional Surrender*; Steinert, *Capitulation*; Padfield, *Dönitz* and Dönitz's own *Memoirs*. Particularly insightful comments on Dönitz and his relationship with Hitler can be found in Grier, *Hitler, Dönitz and the Baltic Sea*. Von Krosigk's elevation to foreign minister (he was named as finance minister in Hitler's will) had an immediate impact. On his policy—which was to nominally adhere to unconditional surrender, but in fact to delay surrendering to the Russians for as long as possible—see Musmanno Collection (Von Krosigk). Statements in these retrospective interviews are sometimes self-serving, but Von Krosigk's fits well with his broadcast against Bolshevism on May 2, which strikingly used the phrase "iron curtain" about Soviet-occupied Europe (the full text is given in Jordan [ed.], *Conditions of Surrender*). This was a Nazi anti-Bolshevik slogan—first coined by Goebbels in February 1945. Churchill, who made it famous, was seduced by the power of the imagery, but perhaps should have thought more about its antecedents. John MacAuslan witnessing the sinking of the *Cap Arcona* and the massacre at Neustadt is from IWM/8225. Background material is from Darlow, *Victory Fighters*. The Hamburg negotiations and the reaction of Crozier are from Jordan (ed.), *Conditions of Surrender*. For General von Saucken's outpost on the Hela Peninsula, see Schäufler, *Panzer Warfare* and information provided by Phil Curme in "The evacuation of Pillau, East Prussia (1945)," available at www.walkingthebattlefields.com. The testimonies of Khukhrikov and Roth-kirch are from Jones, *Total War*. Kaltenegger's view of Schörner (*Feldmarschall der Letzten Stunde*) stresses his "iron determination'; Bidermann (*In Deadly Combat*)—who fought under him—emphasizes his unnecessary cruelty. On Breslau, see Hargreaves, *Breslau 1945*, and Gleiss, *Breslauer Apokalypse*. The accounts of Hartnung and Seifert are from Kempowski, *Das Echolot*. On the Courland Pocket, the comments of Kaese, Willbrand and Meyer are taken from www.kurland-kessel.de. Useful background material is provided in Buttar, *Between Giants*; Bagramian, *We Went on to Victory*; Bidermann, *In Deadly Combat*; Isachenko, *Somewhere in Courland*. Elena Rzhevskaya's account is from her *Berlin, May 1945*. Sherman Pratt's testimony is drawn from John McManus, "The race to seize the Berchtesgaden," *World War Two* (May 2005).

CHAPTER 5 | LÜNEBURG HEATH

For TAC HQ, see: Dallas, *1945: The War That Never Ended*; Kirby, *1100 Miles with Monty*; and Caddick-Adams, *Monty and Rommel: Parallel Lives*. Albert Williams's recollections are courtesy of *Bristol Evening Post* journalist David Clensy and his "Old soldiers" archive. The character sketch of Montgomery is drawn from Horne, *Lonely Leader*. For the theatrical element, see John Keegan, "The German surrender to Montgomery at Lüneburg Heath, May 1945," in Byron Hollinshead and Theodore Rabb (eds.), *I Wish I'd Been There, Book Two* (New York, 2009). The British commander's gift for transforming morale is noted in Danchev and Todman (eds.), *Alanbrooke: War Diaries*. Eisenhower's initial praise for Montgomery is from a recently discovered letter auctioned at Bonhams, Lot 320 (Nov. 12, 2013). The accepted narrative of the surrender is provided by Montgomery, *Memoirs*, and Moorehead, *Eclipse*. The background to the negotiations is found in General Dempsey's war diary: TNA, WO 285/12. The initial report, on May 3, on the purpose of the German delegation—to surrender the three armies retreating from the Russians and now in the Mecklenburg pocket—is from Churchill College Archives Center (henceforth CCA), PJGG/9/9/31. The testimony of Captain Derek Knee, Montgomery's interpreter, is drawn from IWM/Sound Interviews/14881. The comments of Trumbull Warren are from the TV documentary *Monty in Love and War* and Warren's personal papers, IWM/1864. The solicitor's letter about Montgomery keeping the original treaty, and the field marshal's reply, is IWM/14881. The British prime minister's response to the surrender—"quite a satisfactory incident in our military history"—is found in Churchill, *Triumph and Tragedy*. For the shock of Belsen, see Hargrave, *Bergen-Belsen 1945*, and Shephard, *After Daybreak*. Sweeney's letter is IWM/19536. De Guingand's notes on the German surrender are from the Liddell Hart Archives, De Guingand, 2/4/1–7. The British 2nd Army Intelligence Summaries are at TNA, WO 285/8. I am grateful to Terry Gallacher for permission to use his article "Movietone at war: filming the surrender at Lüneburg Heath," at www.terencegallacher.wordpress.com. Additional information is drawn from Wyand, *Useless if Delayed*. For the vital differences in the surrender texts, see Kurt Jürgensen, "Toward occupation: first encounters in North Germany," in Jordan (ed.), *Conditions of Surrender*. Liddell's meeting with Churchill is from West (ed.), *Guy Liddell Diaries*, Volume II. For Churchill pressuring Eisenhower on accepting Denmark as part of the "tactical surrender" at Lüneburg Heath on May 4, see CCA, CHAR 20/217/69, and Summersby, *Eisenhower Was My Boss*. The reaction of Channon is from his *Diaries*. Maggie Blunt's comments are from the Mass Observation Archive. Keitel's ordinance is from Lüdde-Neurath, *Unconditional Surrender*. Schörner's Order of the Day to the troops of German Army Group Center is found in Kaltenegger, *Schörner: Feldmarschall der Letzten Stunde*. On the Canadian occupation of western Holland, see "The German surrender May 1945," *Canadian Military Headquarters Report*, 56 (1958); Zuehlke, *On to Victory*; and background information in Hodson, *Sea and the Land* and Chris Madsen, "Victims of circumstance: the execution of German deserters by surrendered German troops under Canadian control in Amsterdam, May 1945," *Canadian Military History*, 2 (1993). Hardy-Roberts' account is taken from Liddell Hart Archives, GB0099. I owe the Brigadier Jim Roberts story to Hastings, *Armageddon*. For the spite counterattack on Zobten—the last German offensive in the war—see Pencz, *For the Homeland!*, and Moniushko, *From Leningrad to Hungary*. On the orders to the Courland Pocket, that after the surrender to Montgomery all military evacuations by sea would continue, see Bidermann, *Deadly Combat*. T-Force operations in Kiel are sourced from TNA, FO 1031/49. Background information is drawn from Dopheide, *Kiel May 1945*. Tony Hibbert's account is from www.paradata.org.uk. Charles Sweeney's unfinished letter of May 5, 1945, is found in IWM/19536.

CHAPTER 6 | PRAGUE

For the American advance into Czechoslovakia two articles by Bryan Dickerson have been particularly helpful: "The US 9th Armored Division in the liberation of western Czechoslovakia 1945," at www.global.com/articles, and "The liberation of western Czechoslovakia 1945," at www.militaryhistoryonline.com. All extended quotations from General George Patton's diary are from British Online Archives, Papers Related to the Allied Command

1943–45 (full transcript of General Patton's Diary, Jan. 26–Sept. 1, 1945). The crucial communication between Eisenhower and Antonov is also drawn from Papers Related to the Allied Command, Records of the Supreme Command, and is supplemented by *Russian Archives: Great Patriotic War* (vol. XV). For the personal dimension of the American command dynamic, Jonathan Jordan's *Eisenhower, Patton, Bradley* has been very useful, alongside Carlo d'Este's *Patton: A Genius for War.* Patton's conversation with Patterson is found in Blumenson, *Patton Papers.* Marshal Konev's dispositions for the Prague campaign are taken from *Russian Archives: Great Patriotic War* (vol. XV). His meeting with Bradley is described in Margry, "US-Soviet linkup." On the crucial German surrender by General von Wietersheim as the invasion got under way, see "The end of the 11th Panzer Division" on the US 90th Division's website: www.90thdivisionassoc.org. For Reed's "We wanted to do something beautiful," see Karen Jensen, "How General Patton and some unlikely allies saved the prized Lipizzaner Stallions," *World War Two* (November 2009). Churchill's urgings to Eisenhower and Truman on an advance to Prague are from his *Triumph and Tragedy.* Additional material on the advance to Pilsen is taken from the Pilsen Liberation Festival's "Pilsen—from D-Day to VE-Day," available at www.ddayvday.eu. For Charles Noble's *coup de main*: Bryan Dickerson, "There at the end: the US 16th Armored Division's liberation of Pilsen," www.globeatwar.com/articles. Krusheski's remarkable testimony is from Dickerson, "Western Czechoslovakia." Much of the material on the Prague uprising has been provided by Tomas Jakl from his exhibition in the Prague Military Institute, "The Czech Uprising in May 1945." Jakl's *May 1945 in the Czech Lands* is also an essential point of reference. I am also grateful to Antonin Sticha, both for providing a strong eyewitness narrative of the uprising and for arranging additional veteran interviews. Two useful articles on the Radio Prague website are "'Calling all Czechs!': the Prague uprising begins" and (on Greig's role) "A Scottish hero of the Prague uprising": www.radio.cz. And particularly helpful, on the same site, is David Vaughan's "Do not let Prague be destroyed!," drawing on material in the Prague City Archives. ULTRA decrypts on the progress of the revolt, and the role of Frank, are from TNA, HW 1/3754-8. For the formation and role of the Vlasov Army, see Andreyev, *Russian Liberation*

Movement, Hoffman, *Wlassow-Armee* and Ausky, *Vojska Generala Vlasova*.
The diary of the German liaison officer Major Helmut Schwenniger, which
records the progress of the Vlasov Army's 1st Division in support of the
Prague uprising, is printed in Pavel Zacek, "Vlasovci nemeckym pohledem,"
Securitas Imperii, 18 (2011). On reaction within the Vlasov Army, see
Diczbalis, *Russian Patriot*. Material on Francis Konecny's meeting with
Bunyachenko is taken from www.fronta.cz. Bunyachenko's proclamation is
from the Prague City Archives.

CHAPTER 7 | THE DISPOSSESSED

For general background, particularly valuable are Shephard, *Long Road Home*
and Hitchcock, *Bitter Road to Freedom*. The key source I have used for Sandbostel, Major McLaren's memoir "Sandbostel horror camp, Germany 1945,"
is in the Archive of the Royal College of Obstetricians and Gynecologists,
GB/1538/S56; see also IWM/11147. McLaren arrived at Sandbostel on May
6, 1945. Also useful was Barnard, *Two Weeks in May 1945*. Lieutenant
General Horrock's impression of the camp and the response of German civilians from nearby villages is from his *A Full Life*. Elfie Walther's diary extracts are found in Jordan (ed.), *Conditions of Surrender*. On Bergen-Belsen see
Shephard, *After Daybreak* and Hargrave, *Bergen-Belsen 1945*. Captain Robert
Barer's letter to his wife is from Jordan (ed.), *Conditions of Surrender*. On the
experiences of the US Army, I have found Ast, *American Soldiers Enter Concentration Camps* particularly helpful. The reaction of Soviet soldiers to Majdanek and Auschwitz is sourced from Jones, *Total War*. Paul Winterton's
rebuff, and the background to it, is cited with acknowledgment to the BBC's
What Aunty Did in the War. Dimbleby's broadcast on Belsen is at www.bbc
.co.uk/archives/holocaust. The reaction of the British public to films of
the camps is taken from the Mass Observation Archive. For the liberation
of Gunskirchen I have used "The 71st Infantry at Gunskirchen Lager,"
www.remember.org/mooney/gunskirchen. Reactions to the reburial of bodies
from Wöbbelin are found in Mrozek, *82nd Airborne Division*. Extracts from
Harold Porter's "Letter to his parents describing Dachau concentration camp"

and Alan Walker's "Letter to Sheffield from Germany, May 1945" are reproduced with permission from www.fold3.com and www.chrishobbs.com/
belsen1945. Seibert's report on Mauthausen and reaction to Flossenbürg is
from Ast, *American Soldiers*. Lubertus Shapelhouman's testimony is drawn
from Jaime O'Neill, "The way to Mauthausen," *Sacramento News and Review*
(August 2, 2007). Vasily Bezugly's account of the liberation of Stalag Luft 1
is sourced from www.merkki.com/russians. Finlayson's "From Edinburgh to
UNRRA" is used with thanks to the BBC's "People's War" and acknowledgment to Janet Finlayson. Kathryn Hulme's impressions of Wildflecken
are from her *The Wild Place*. Marta Korwin's comments are from Hitchcock,
Liberation. For Bob Prouse, see Rollings, *Prisoner of War*. On the Dutch
famine, Eric Heijink's website is valuable: www.operationmanna.second
worldwar.nl. Also see Onderwater, *Operation Manna/Chowhound*. For Denis
Thompson and Operation Manna, I owe the information to the RAF Cosford
Oral History Project. The initial discussions on the Dutch famine are from
TNA, CAB 195/3, part 1. Tom Stafford's account is from "The mass surrender
of German troops to the 367th Infantry Regiment on May 6, 1945," available
at www.87thinfantrydivision.com. Jerry Tax's remarkable description is from
his "And afterward," at www.remember.org/mooney/gunskirchen. I am
grateful to John Mooney of the US 71st Division website for permission to
quote at length from this piece.

CHAPTER 8 | RHEIMS

Diplomatic material on the Rheims signing is primarily from the British
Online Archive, Papers Related to the Allied High Command 1943–45
(Eisenhower Correspondence, Records of the Supreme Allied Command).
George Bailey's reminiscences of Susloparov are from *The Reporter* (May 20,
1965). On the hurried drafting of the text, see Counsell, *Counsell's Opinion*.
For Richard Wilberforce's perception of the flaws in the surrender treaty
drawn up at Rheims, see IWM/12931. The narrative, derived from Butcher,
My Three Years with Eisenhower and Summersby, *Eisenhower Was My Boss*,
alongside Eisenhower's own *Crusade in Europe*, is most recently supplemented

by Crosswell, *Bedell Smith*. Bernard's comments are from IWM/18001. For the Russian response, particularly revealing is Sergei Shtemenko, *Memoirs*. On Ed Kennedy, see Cochran (ed.), *Ed Kennedy's War*. The alternative view is put in Boyd Lewis, *Not Always a Spectator*. For Charles Kiley's view I am indebted to his son, David Kiley, "My father and Edward Kennedy": www.huff ingtonpost.com/2012/05/07. The reactions of Cooke and Walker are from Longmate, *When We Won the War*. Von Krosigk's broadcast to the German people is found in Lüdde-Neurath, *Unconditional Surrender*. The course of the surrender negotiations in Breslau is drawn from Gleiss, *Breslauer Apokalypse* and Hargreaves, *Hitler's Final Fortress: Breslau 1945*. For Churchill's continued concern about Denmark, see CCA, CHAR/20/217/110 and Buckley, *Monty's Men*. Reaction in San Francisco to the news of the Soviet arrest of sixteen Poles is taken from Gilbert, *Day the War Ended*. Charles Havlat's death at Volary is recounted at www.737thtankbattalion.org/Volary/Havlat. On the clash at Tangermünde, see Gellermann, *Die Armee Wenck* and Gilbert, *Day the War Ended*. Macleod's comments are from his *A Job at the BBC*. A full transcript of the crucial phone call between Leahy and Churchill is provided in Records of the Supreme Command; see also Leahy, *I Was There*. The letters of Lady Ashburnham and Ronald Horton are from the East Sussex Record Office, AMS 6375/1/13 and AMS 6732/1/25. West Lothian miner William Paton's diary entry is from the National Records of Scotland, NRAS 4107/6. Montague Burton's letter is from Ian Whitehead, "Victory! VE Day celebrations on the British Home Front," *Everyone's War*, 11 (2005), as are the reactions of the ATS clerk to the continuing delay. Brigadier Stack's recollections of the capture of Göring are at www.kwanah.com/36division/ps0277. For Rokossovsky's meeting with Montgomery, see Batov, *Campaigns and Battles* and Margry, "British-Soviet link-up." The subsequent report of the 2nd Belorussian Front, noting Montgomery's wish to visit Stalingrad, is from *Russian Archives: Great Patriotic War* (vol. XV). For the situation on the ground in Wismar, Roy Porter's recollections have kindly been shared with me by Russell Porter. Antonin Sticha has generously provided me with an overview of the events in the Czech capital on May 7. Further references are from the Prague City Archives and Jakl, *May 1945 in the Czech Lands*. Additional material on the Vlasov forces is from Diczbalis, *Russian Patriot* and Tomas Jakl's article "Armor of the First Division of the ROA" at www.konr.webz.cz /ROA. Harak Bohumil's account is taken from www.pametnaroda.cz/story /harak-bohumil.

CHAPTER 9 | KARLSHORST

For general background, see Gilbert, *Day the War Ended*, Miller, *VE Day: The People's Story* and Longmate, *When We Won the War*. Karl-Ludwig Hoch's account of the Russian entry into Dresden is from Clayton and Russell (eds.), *Dresden: A City Reborn*. Diczbalis' account is from his *A Russian Patriot*. Jaroslav Oliverius' experiences in Prague are sourced from www.pametnaroda .cz/story/oliverius-jaroslav. I owe my interviews with veterans Straka and Svacina to Antonin Sticha. See also www.pametnaroda.cz/story/svacina-jan. For additional material, I am grateful to Richard Gaskell for his thorough study "The Czech token force" on his website www.webring.com/people/fc /czechandslovakthings. See also, for Straka, the interview on www.memory ofnations.eu/index.php/witness. The surrender treaty between General Toussaint and the Czech rebels is in the Prague City Archives. The draft text of the German capitulation—to be signed at Karlshorst—was presented to Keitel on his arrival at Berlin Tempelhof. The changes to the text of the original Rheims treaty were underscored in red, along with the passage newly added by the Russians. In the margin, in blue, was written "new!": Bundesarchiv, RW 44-1/37. For the proceedings at Karlshorst, Zhukov, *Memoirs*, and Keitel, *Memoirs* have been helpful, alongside the impressions of Kiley, "This is how Germany Gave Up!" *Stars and Stripes* (May 10, 1945), and Summersby, *Eisenhower Was My Boss*. Serov's interrogation of Keitel is from *Russian Archives: Great Patriotic War* (vol. XV). Brokensha's experience of May 8 is drawn from Vercoe, *Survival at Stalag Luft IVB* and www.pegasusarchives .org. For Schörner's "last stand," see Kaltenegger, *Schörner* (for the rehetoric) and Lelyushenko, *Notes of a Commander* (for the reality). Mollie Panter-Downes's description is from www.eyewitnesstohistory.com/londonveday. Harold Nicolson's account is from *Diaries: 1907–1964*. John Lehmann's comments are found in Miller, *VE Day*. Elaine Leighton's recollections are from

IWM/16175. Paton's diary entry is from National Records of Scotland, NRAS 4107/6. Mary Blythe's letter about the VE-Day celebrations in London is in the Surrey History Center Archives, Z/439/3. Irene Bain's recollections of her street party are found in Ian Whitehead, "Victory!" Other reactions are from the Mass Observation Archive. The final operations of the 51st Highland Division are at www.51hd.co.uk/accounts/final_op; those of their opponents—the 15th Panzer Grenadier Division—at www.ww2talk .com/forum/487168-post23. John F. Kennedy's report is from Gilbert, *Day the War Ended*. Picard's recollections are from Kempowski, *Das Echolot*. Reactions in Italy are from Gilbert, *Day the War Ended*. Friedrich Kaufmann's account, "Mein letzter einsatz in Kurland," is from www.kurland-kessel.de. William Preston's letter is from Andrew Carroll, "An Infantryman recalls VE Day," at www.historynet.com. For Brady and Jolley, see J. L. Granatstein, "The end of darkness," *Legion Magazine* (May 1, 2005). Tom Renouf's experiences are taken from www.51hd.co.uk/accounts. Lee Dickman's are found at www.wartimememories.co.uk.

CHAPTER 10 | MOSCOW

Lazarus Brontman's recollections of May 9 are taken from his *Diaries 1932–1947*. The diary entry of Wilfried Orts is from www.kurland-kessel.de. For the Russian view of the Courland surrender, see Isachenko, *Somewhere in Courland*. Nikolai Inozemtsev's account is from his *Frontline Diary*. Red Army soldier Pavel Elkinson's description of the end of the fighting in Hungary is from the Blavatnik Archive, New York. Kessler on the liberation of Theresienstadt is found in Kempowski, *Das Echolot*. The testimonies of Reingold and Helfgort are from Gilbert, *Day the War Ended*. On the continuing Prague offensive: Nemchinsky, *Warning—Mines!* and Zaitsev, *Memoirs*. Joachim Halfpap's account of the surrender at Deutsch-Brod (also known by its Czech name of Nemecky-Brod) is from Kempowski, *Das Echolot* with additional information supplied by Richard Hargreaves. German troop strength at the time of the surrender is sourced from www.forum .axishistory.com. Gustav Lambard's recollections are from *For the Homeland*.

On Bornholm, Bent Jensen, "Soviet occupation of a new type: the long liberation of the Danish island of Bornholm," *Scandinavian Journal of History*, 25 (2000) is supplemented by the recollections of Pröbstle (Kempowski, *Das Echolot*) and the combat report of the Soviet 18th Rifle Division: Russian Ministry of Defense Archives, Podolsk. The key SHAEF documents are printed in Hornemann (ed.), *Bornholm Mellem Ost Og West*. Orme Sargent's message to Churchill is from TNA, FO 954/23B. Hans Schäufler remembered General von Saucken instructing his troops on May 7 that "military operations would continue," with the justification that "it was imperative that no German soldier fell into Russian hands": Schäufler, *Panzer Warfare*. For Von Saucken's garrisoning of Bornholm after the Rheims surrender, see "Bornholm May 1945" on www.forum.axishistory.com. The award to him of the Diamonds and Oakleaves to the Knight's Cross on the early morning of May 9, with handwritten note praising his evacuation of soldiers and civilians and urging him to continue this for as long as feasible, is Catalogue Entry 0273 at www.liveauctioneers.com/item/445848. The diary extract of Frank Lockwood is reproduced with acknowledgment to the Acocks Green Historical Society, Birmingham; with thanks to the BBC's "People's War" and acknowledgment to Mary Derrick. For the liberation of the Channel Islands I have drawn from Bunting, *Model Occupation*; Nowlan, *Von Aufsess Occupation Diary*; Evans, *War Diaries of Violet Carey*; and Bihet, *Child's War*. I am grateful to Molly Bihet for discussing her recollections of May 9 with me. Clementine Churchill's contemporary journal, "My visit to Russia," is in IWM/16175. Additional material is from Soames, *Speaking for Themselves*. Frank Roberts's May 8 assessment that "her presence here is making a valuable contribution toward future relations between the United Kingdom and the Soviet Union" is from CCA, CHAR20/204B/121. The May 5 exchange of telgrams between Winston Churchill and Clementine is found in CCA, CHAR20/204B/103–5. For Stalin's reaction to VE-Day, the contrasting responses are from Svetlana Alliluyeva, *Twenty Letters to a Friend* and Nikita Khrushchev, *Memoirs*. The Soviet leader's message to the British people is from Churchill, *Triumph and Tragedy*. Alexander Werth's comments are from his *Russia at War*. The quotations from *The Times* and *Manchester Guardian* are found in Longmate, *When We Won the War*. For Bob Dunbar's experiences of May 9 in Moscow, see IWM/17386. Hewlett Johnson's description is from his *Searching for Light*. Robert Tucker's memories are at www.gwu.edu/nsarchiv/coldwar/interviews. Accounts of Alexander Ustinov and Nikolai Kryuchkov are from the RIA Novosti Archive (for which I owe thanks to Ralph Gibson). Grigory Klimov's remarkable description is from *The Terror Machine*.

CHAPTER 11 | THE WAR THAT DID NOT END

Material from "VE Day in Grajewo, Poland" is used with acknowledgment to www.doomedsoldiers.com. The biography of Stefan Korbonski is drawn from www.en.korbonski.ipn.gov.pl. The accounts of Buczek and Krzystek are from IWM/10618, 16626. Szczepanik's comments are from Cabell and Richards, *VE Day*. On Churchill, Poland and the end of the war, see Hastings, *Finest Years* and Colville, *Downing Street Diaries*. General Anders' May 8 telegram to the British Prime Minister, hoping for a peace "where justice will prevail," is CCA, CHAR20/227A/10. Alanbrooke's comments are from Danchev and Todman (eds.), *Field Marshal Lord Alanbrooke: War Diaries*. Reactions of Macmillan and Smuts are from *Tides of Fortune* and *Jan Christian Smuts*. For Churchill's telegrams to Truman, appreciating the efforts of Eisenhower but also warning that "an iron curtain is drawn down upon their front": Churchill, *Triumph and Tragedy*. On Russia keeping her word: TNA, CAB 195/3, part 1; Folly, *Churchill, Whitehall and the Soviet Union*; and Ryan, "Polish crisis." Also see Rees, *Behind Closed Doors*. Bohlen's comments are from his *Witness to History*. Broader context is found in Mastny, *Russia's Road to the Cold War* (critical of the Soviet Union) and Roberts, *Stalin's Wars* (more positive). Fresh information on the battle for Slivice is provided in Jaroslav Cvancara, "The end of the Second World War in Europe in May 1945," *Loyalty Is Our Honor*, 4 (2010). Alexei Kuchikov's account is from an interview with me. For the combat at Benesov, see Mikhin, *Guns Against the Reich*. On the surrender of General Lohr, see Tomasevich, *War and Revolution in Yugoslavia*. The Yugoslav reaction to VE-Day is from Djilas, *Wartime*. For the last stand of the Georgians on Texel, material in Dick van Reewijk,

Sondermeldung Texel has been supplemented by the work of Alan Newark, "The Texel Island Battle," set out on the Axis History Forum: www.forum. axishistory.com. Marshal Konev's secret plans for the capture of Vlasov are from *Russian Archives: Great Patriotic War* (vol. XV). I am grateful to Artem Drabkin for the testimony of Grigory Sukhorukov, from his "I Remember" website. Wilberforce's visit to Flensburg is from IWM/12931. The end of the Dönitz regime is drawn from Marlis Steinert, "The allied decision to arrest the Dönitz government," *Historical Journal*, 31 (1988); see also Longerich, *Himmler.* Boris Komsky's account of the Red Army's return march through East Prussia and Poland is from the Blavatnik Archive. Captain Andrew Yates' comments are from IWM/10525. For "rumors abound about an upcoming clash between Britain and the Soviet Union," the Intelligence Report of the 2nd Belorussian Front, May 1945, is to be found in *Russian Archives: Great Patriotic War* (vol. XV). General Milstein's comments on the interception of the "Stacking Order" are from Zubok, *Failed Empire.* On Hopkins and his May mission to Moscow, see Roll, *Hopkins Touch* and archive information from "Harry Hopkins: a Glimpse into the Russian Records" at www.documentstalk.com/wp/harry-hopkins and "The Hopkins mission to Moscow" at www.digicoll.library.wisc.edu. Stalin's contrasting opinions of Eisenhower and Montgomery are related in Khrushchev, *Memoirs.* For Robert Frank's account I am grateful to the US 87th Infantry Division Legacy Association: www.87thinfantrydivision.com.

BIBLIOGRAPHY

Abramson, Ruby, *Spanning the Century: The Life of W. Averell Harriman, 1896–1986* (New York, 1992)

Abyzov, Vladimir, *The Final Assault* (Moscow, 1985)

Alliluyeva, Svetlana, *Twenty Letters to a Friend* (New York, 1967)

Ambrose, Stephen, *Eisenhower and Berlin, 1945* (New York, 1967)

——, *The Supreme Commander* (New York, 1970)

Andreyev, Catherine, *Vlasov and the Russian Liberation Movement* (Cambridge, 1987)

Arthur, Max, *Forgotten Voices of the Second World War* (London, 2004)

Ast, Theresa, *Confronting the Holocaust: American Soldiers Enter Concentration Camps* (Atlanta, 2013)

Ausky, Stanislav, *Vojska Generala Vlasova V Cechach* (Toronto, 1980)

Bagramian, Ivan, *We Went on to Victory* (Moscow, 1977)

Barnard, Clifford, *Two Weeks in May 1945: Sandbostel Concentration Camp and the Friends Ambulance Unit* (London, 1999)

Batov, Pavel, *In Campaigns and Battles* (Moscow, 1974)

Beevor, Antony, *Berlin: The Downfall 1945* (London, 2002)

Beevor, Antony and Luba Vinogradova, *Writer at War: Vasily Grossman with the Red Army, 1941–1945* (London, 2005)

Bellamy, Chris, *Absolute War: Soviet Russia in the Second World War* (London, 2007)

Bessel, Richard, *Germany 1945: From War to Peace* (London, 2009)

Best, Nicholas, *Five Days That Shocked the World: Eyewitness Accounts of Europe at the End of World War Two* (Oxford, 2012)

Bidermann, Gottlob, *In Deadly Combat: A German Soldier's Memoir of the Eastern Front* (Lawrence, Kansas, 2000)

Bihet, Molly, *A Child's War* (Stroud, 1985)

Birse, Arthur, *Memoirs of an Interpreter* (London, 1967)

Blumenson, Martin (ed.), *The Patton Papers, 1940–1945* (New York, 1996)

Boegel, Gary, *Boys of the Clouds: An Oral History of the First Canadian Parachute Battalion, 1942–45* (Victoria, British Columbia, 2005)

Bogolov, Vladimir, *My Life* (Moscow, 1996)

Bohlen, Charles, *Witness to History, 1929–1969* (New York, 1973)

Botting, Douglas, *In the Ruins of the Reich* (York, 2012)

Bradley, Omar, *A Soldier's Story* (New York, 1999)

Brontman, Lazarus, *Diaries 1932–1947* (Moscow, 2004)

Bryn, Günter de, *Zwischenbilanz: Ein Jugend in Berlin* (Frankfurt, 1994)

Buckley, John, *Monty's Men: The British Army and the Liberation of Europe* (London, 2013)

Bunting, Madeleine, *The Model Occupation: The Channel Islands Under German Rule* (London, 1995)

Buruma, Ian, *Year Zero: A History of 1945* (London, 2013)

Buske, Norbert, *Das Kriegsende in Demmin 1945: Berichte, Erinnerungen, Dokumente* (Schwerin, 1995)

Butcher, Harry, *My Three Years with Eisenhower* (New York, 1946)

Buttar, Prit, *Between Giants: The Battle for the Baltics in World War II* (Oxford, 2013)

Cabell, Craig, and Allan Richards, *VE Day: A Day to Remember* (Barnsley, 2005)

Caddick-Adams, Peter, *Monty and Rommel: Parallel Lives* (London, 2011)

Carver, Tom, *Where the Hell Have You Been? Monty, Italy and One Man's Incredible Escape* (London, 2009)

Chandler, Alfred (ed.), *The Papers of Dwight D. Eisenhower* (Baltimore, Maryland, 1970)

Channon, Henry, and Robert James, *"Chips": The Diaries of Sir Henry Channon* (London, 1967)

Chuikov, Vasily, *The End of the Third Reich* (London, 1967)

Churchill, Winston, *The Second World War*, Volume VI, *Triumph and Tragedy* (London, 1954)

Clayton, Anthony, and Alan Russell (eds.), *Dresden: A City Reborn* (London, 2001)

Clemens, Petra (ed.), *Das Kriegsende in Demmin 1945: Umgang mit Einem Schwierigen Thema* (Demmin, 2013)

Cochran, Julia Kennedy (ed.), *Ed Kennedy's War: VE-Day, Censorship and the Associated Press* (Baton Rouge, Louisiana, 2012)

Colville, John, *The Fringes of Power: Downing Street Diaries 1939–1955* (London, 1985)

Counsell, John, *Counsell's Opinion* (London, 1963)

Crosswell, Daniel, *Beetle: The Life of General Walter Bedell Smith* (Lexington, Kentucky, 2010)

Dallas, Gregor, *1945: The War That Never Ended* (London, 2005)

Danchev, Alex, and Dan Todman (eds.), *Field Marshal Lord Alanbrooke: War Diaries, 1939–1945* (London, 2001)

Darlow, Stephen, *Victory Fighters—The Veterans' Story: Winning the Battle for Supremacy of the Skies over Western Europe, 1941–1945* (London, 2005)

De Guingand, Freddie, *Operation Victory* (London, 1947)

Deane, John, *The Strange Alliance: The Story of American Efforts at Wartime Cooperation with Russia* (London, 1947)

Delaforce, Patrick, *Invasion of the Third Reich: War and Peace* (Stroud, 2011)

D'Este, Carlo, *Patton: A Genius for War* (New York, 1995)

Diczbalis, Sigismund, *The Russian Patriot* (Stroud, 2008)

Djilas, Milovan, *Wartime: With Tito and the Partisans* (London, 1977)

Dobbs, Michael, *Six Months in 1945: From World War to Cold War* (London, 2012)

Dönitz, Karl, *Memoirs: Ten Years and Twenty Days* (London, 1990)

Dopheide, Renate, *Kiel May 1945: Britische Truppen Besetzen die Kriegsmarine-stadt* (Kiel, 2007)

Duffy, Christopher, *Red Storm on the Reich: The Soviet March on Germany, 1945* (New York, 1991)

Eisenhower, Dwight, *Crusade in Europe* (London, 1948)

Evans, Alice (ed.), *Guernsey Under Occupation: The Second World War Diaries of Violet Carey* (Chichester, 2009)

Evans, Richard, *The Third Reich at War* (London, 2008)

Fest, Joachim, *Inside Hitler's Bunker: The Last Days of the Third Reich* (London, 2004)

Folly, Martin, *Churchill, Whitehall and the Soviet Union, 1940–45* (Basingstoke, 2000)

Fritz, Stephen, *Endkampf: Soldiers, Civilians and the Death of the Third Reich* (Lexington, Kentucky, 2011)

Geckeler, Christa (ed.), *Erinnerungen der Kieler Kriegsgeneration* (Husum, 2003)

Gelfand, Vladimir, *Deutschland Tagebuch 1945–1946* (Berlin, 2008)

Gellermann, Günther, *Die Armee Wenck: Hitlers Letzte Hoffnung* (Bonn, 2007)

Gilbert, Adrian, *POW: Allied Prisoners in Europe, 1939–45* (London, 2006)

Gilbert, Martin, *The Day the War Ended* (London, 1995)

Glantz, David, and Jonathan House, *When Titans Clashed* (Lawrence, Kansas, 1995)

Gleiss, Horst, *Breslauer Apokalypse 1945* (Wedel, 1988)

Gorlitz, Walter (ed.), *The Memoirs of Field Marshal Keitel* (New York, 2000)

Greenwood, John (ed.), *From Normandy to Victory: The War Diary of General Courtney J. Hodges and the US First Army* (Lexington, Kentucky, 2008)

Grier, Howard, *Hitler, Dönitz and the Baltic Sea: The Third Reich's Last Hope, 1944–1945* (Annapolis, Maryland, 2007)

Hamilton, Nigel, *Monty: The Making of a General, 1887–1942* (London, 1981)

——, *Monty: The Master of the Battlefield, 1942–1944* (London, 1984)

——, *Monty: The Field Marshal, 1944–1976* (London, 1986)

Hamilton, A. Stephan, *Bloody Streets: The Soviet Assault on Berlin, April 1945* (Solihull, 2008)

——, *The Oder Front 1945: Generaloberst Gotthard Heinrici, Heeresgruppe Weichsel and Germany's Final Defense in the East, March 20–May 4, 1945* (Solihull, 2011)

Harding, Stephen, *The Last Battle* (Boston, Massachusetts, 2013)

Hargrave, Michael, *Bergen-Belsen 1945: A Medical Student's Journal* (London, 2013)

Hargreaves, Richard, *Hitler's Final Fortress: Breslau 1945* (Barnsley, 2011)

Hart, Stephen, *Colossal Cracks: Montgomery's 21st Army Group in Northwest Europe, 1944–45* (Mechanicsburg, Pennsylvania, 2007)

Hastings, Max, *Armageddon: The Battle for Germany, 1944–45* (London, 2004)

——, *Finest Years: Churchill as Warlord, 1940–45* (London, 2009)

Hills, Stuart, *By Tank into Normandy* (London, 2002)

Hitchcock, William, *Liberation: The Bitter Road to Freedom, Europe 1944–1945* (London, 2009)

Hodson, John, *The Sea and the Land* (London, 1951)

Hoffmann, Joachim, *Die Geschichte der Wlassow-Armee* (Freiburg, 1984)

Horn, Bernd, and Michel Wyczynski, *Paras Versus the Reich: Canada's Paratroopers at War, 1942–45* (Oxford, 2003)

Horne, Alistair, *The Lonely Leader: Monty 1944–1945* (London, 1995)

Hornemann, Jacob (ed.), *Bornholm Mellem Ost Og West* (Ronne, 2006)

Horrocks, Brian, *A Full Life* (London, 1960)

Hulme, Kathryn, *The Wild Place* (London, 1953)

Inozemtsev, Nikolai, *Frontline Diary* (Moscow, 2005)

Isachenko, Sergei, *Somewhere in Courland* (Moscow, 1977)

Jakl, Tomas, *May 1945 in the Czech Lands* (Prague, 2004)

Johnson, Hewlett, *Searching for Light* (London, 1968)

Jones, Michael, *Total War: From Stalingrad to Berlin* (London, 2011)

Jordan, Jonathan, *Brothers, Rivals, Victors: Eisenhower, Patton, Bradley and the Partnership That Drove the Allied Conquest in Europe* (New York, 2011)

Jordan, Ulrike (ed.), *Conditions of Surrender: Britons and Germans Witness the End of the War* (London, 1997)

Junge, Traudl, *Bis zur Letzten Stunde* (Berlin, 2002)

Kaltenegger, Roland, *Schörner: Feldmarschall der Letzten Stunde* (Munich, 1994)

Kempka, Erich, *I Was Hitler's Chauffeur* (Barnsley, 2010)

Kempowski, Walter, *Das Echolot: Abgesang '45* (Munich, 2005)

Kennan, George, *Memoirs 1925–1950* (Boston, Massachusetts, 1950)

Kershaw, Ian, *Hitler 1936–1945: Nemesis* (London, 2011)

——, *The End: Hitler's Germany 1944–45* (London, 2011)

Kesselring, Albert, *Memoirs* (London, 1974)

Khrushchev, Nikita, *Memoirs: Commissar (1918–1945)* (Philadelphia, Pennsylvania, 2005)

Kirby, Norman, *1100 Miles with Monty: Security and Intelligence at TAC HQ* (Stroud, 2003)

Klimov, Grigory, *The Terror Machine* (New York, 1953)

Knappe, Siegfried, *Soldat* (London, 1993)

Koskodan, Kenneth, *No Greater Ally: The Untold Story of Poland's Forces in World War II* (Oxford, 2011)

Krasilschchik, Semyon, and Mark Scott (eds.), *Yanks Meet Reds: Recollections of*

US and Soviet Vets from the Linkup in World War Two (Santa Barbara, California, 1988)

Le Tissier, Tony, *Marshal Zhukov at the Oder* (Stroud, 2008)

——, *Race for the Reichstag: The 1945 Battle for Berlin* (London, 1999)

Leahy, William, *I Was There* (Toronto, 1950)

Lehmann, Armin, with Tim Carroll, *In Hitler's Bunker* (Edinburgh, 2003)

Lelyushenko, Dmitry, *Notes of a Commander: Moscow—Stalingrad—Berlin—Prague* (Moscow, 1987)

Lewis, Boyd, *Not Always a Spectator: A Newsman's Story* (Vienna, Virginia, 1981)

Linge, Heinz, *With Hitler to the End* (Barnsley, 2013)

Longerich, Peter, *Heinrich Himmler* (Oxford, 2012)

Longmate, Norman, *When We Won the War: The Story of Victory in Europe, 1945* (London, 1977)

Lüdde-Neurath, Walter, *Unconditional Surrender: A Memoir of the Last Days of the Third Reich and the Dönitz Administration* (London, 2010)

MacDonald, Charles, *The US Army in World War Two: The Last Offensive* (Honolulu, Hawaii, 2005)

Macleod, Joseph, *A Job at the BBC* (London, 1946)

Macmillan, Harold, *Tides of Fortune, 1945–1955* (London, 1969)

Mastny, Vojtech, *Russia's Road to the Cold War: Diplomacy, Warfare and the Politics of Communism, 1941–1945* (New York, 1979)

Melvin, Mungo, *Manstein: Hitler's Greatest General* (London, 2010)

Mende, Erich, *Das Verdammte Gewissen* (Munich, 1986)

Meyer, Thomas, and Gustav Seils, *1945: Kampflose Ubergabe der Hansestadt Greifswald* (Greifswald, 1995)

Mikhin, Petr, *Guns Against the Reich* (Barnsley, 2010)

Miller, Russell and Renate, *VE Day: The People's Story* (Stroud, 2007)

Minott, Rodney, *The Fortress That Never Was: The Myth of Hitler's Bavarian Stronghold* (New York, 1964)

Moniushko, Evgenny, *From Leningrad to Hungary: Notes of a Red Army Soldier* (Oxford, 2005)

Montgomery, Bernard, *The Memoirs of Field Marshal Montgomery of Alamein* (London, 1958)

Moorehead, Alan, *Eclipse* (London, 1945)

Moorhouse, Roger, *Berlin at War* (London, 2010)

Mrozek, Steven, *82nd Airborne Division* (Nashville, Tennessee, 2000)

Nadeau, Remi, *Stalin, Churchill and Roosevelt Divide Europe* (New York, 1990)

Naimark, Norman, *The Russians in Germany: A History of the Soviet Zone of Occupation, 1945–1949* (London, 1995)

Nemchinsky, Alexei, *Warning—Mines!* (Moscow, 1973)

Nicolson, Nigel (ed.), *The Harold Nicolson Diaries: 1907–1964* (London, 2005)

Nolan, Kathleen (ed.), *The Von Aufsess Occupation Diary* (Worcester, 1985)

O'Donnell, James, *The Bunker: The History of the Reich Chancellery Group* (New York, 1978)

Offner, Arnold, and Theodore Wilson (eds.), *Victory in Europe 1945: From World War to Cold War* (Lawrence, Kansas, 2000)

Onderwater, Hans, *Operation Manna/Chowhound* (Hinckley, 1991)

Overy, Richard, *The Bombing War: Europe 1939–1945* (London, 2013)

——, *Why the Allies Won* (London, 2006)

Padfield, Peter, *Dönitz: The Last Führer* (London, 1984)

Panov, Mikhail, *In the Direction of the Main Strike: A History of the First Don Guards Tank Corps in Battle* (Moscow, 1995)

Pencz, Rudolf, *For the Homeland! The History of the 31st Waffen-SS Volunteer Grenadier Division* (Solihull, 2002)

Pogue, Forrest, *George C. Marshall: Organizer of Victory* (New York, 1973)

——, *The Supreme Command* (Washington, 1954)

Rees, Laurence, *World War Two: Behind Closed Doors—Stalin, the Nazis and the West* (London, 2008)

Reewijk, Dick van, *Sondermeldung Texel: Opstand der Georgiers* (Texel, 2002)

Reynolds, David, *In Command of History: Churchill Fighting and Writing the Second World War* (London, 2004)

Roberts, Andrew, *Masters and Commanders: The Military Geniuses Who Led the West to Victory in World War Two* (London, 2008)

——, *The Storm of War: A New History of World War Two* (London, 2010)

Roberts, Geoffrey, *Stalin's General: The Life of Georgy Zhukov* (London, 2012)

——, *Stalin's Wars: From World War to Cold War, 1939–53* (New Haven, Connecticut, 2008)

Rokossovsky, Konstantin, *A Soldier's Duty* (Moscow, 1988)

Roll, David, *The Hopkins Touch: Harry Hopkins and the Forging of the Alliance to Defeat Hitler* (Oxford, 2013)

Rollings, Charles, *Prisoner of War: Voices from Captivity During the Second World War* (London, 2007)

Russian Archives of the Great Patriotic War, Volume XV, *The Battle for Berlin—Documents and Materials* (Moscow, 1995)

Ryan, Cornelius, *The Last Battle* (New York, 1966)

Rzhevskaya, Elena, *Berlin, May 1945: Notes of a Military Translator* (Moscow, 1986)

Sagan, Günter, *Kriegsende 1945* (Petersberg, 2008)

Schäufler, Hans, *Panzer Warfare on the Eastern Front* (Mechanicsburg, Pennsylvania, 2012)

Scherstjanoi, Elke, *Rotarmisten Schrieben aus Deutschland: Briefe von der Front 1945* (Munich, 2004)

——, *Wege in die Kriegsgefangenschaft: Erinnerungen und Erfahrungen Deutscher Soldaten* (Berlin, 2011)

Schwanenflügel, Dorothea von, *Laughter Wasn't Rationed* (Medford, Oregon, 2000)

Service, Robert, *Stalin: A Biography* (London, 2010)

Shephard, Ben, *After Daybreak: The Liberation of Bergen-Belsen 1945* (London, 2005)

——, *The Long Road Home: The Aftermath of the Second World War* (London, 2010)

Shtemenko, Sergei, *Memoirs* (Moscow, 1989)

Schultz-Naumann, Joachim, *Mecklenburg 1945* (Munich, 1989)

Sluga, Glenda, *The Problem of Trieste and the Italo-Yugoslav Border* (Albany, New York, 2001)

Smith, Walter Bedell, *Eisenhower's Six Great Decisions* (New York, 1966)

Smuts, Jan, *Jan Christian Smuts* (London, 1949)

Snyder, Timothy, *Bloodlands: Europe Between Hitler and Stalin* (New York, 2010)

Soames, Mary (ed.), *Speaking for Themselves: The Personal Letters of Winston and Clementine Churchill* (London, 1999)

Spalding, Elizabeth, *The First Cold Warrior: Harry Truman, Containment and the Remaking of Liberal Internationalism* (Lexington, Kentucky, 2006)

Speer, Albert, *Inside the Third Reich* (London, 1970)

Stafford, David, *Endgame 1945: Victory, Retribution, Liberation* (London, 2007)

Steinert, Marlis, *Capitulation 1945: The Story of the Dönitz Regime* (London, 1969)

Stettinius, Edward, *Roosevelt and the Russians: The Yalta Conference* (New York, 1949)

Stimson, Henry, *On Active Service in Peace and War* (New York, 1948)

Summersby, Kay, *Eisenhower Was My Boss* (New York, 1948)

Sweeney, Michael, *Secrets of Victory: The Office of Censorship and the American Press and Radio in World War Two* (Chapel Hill, North Carolina, 2001)

Trevor-Roper, Hugh, *The Last Days of Hitler* (London, 1962)

—— (ed.), *Final Entries 1945: The Diaries of Joseph Goebbels* (Barnsley, 2008)

Tomasevich, Jozo, *War and Revolution in Yugoslavia, 1941–1945* (Redwood City, California, 2002)

Vercoe, Tony, *Survival at Stalag IVB: Soldiers and Airmen Remember Germany's Largest POW Camp of World War Two* (Jefferson, North Carolina, 2006)

Vishnevsky, Vsevolod, *Diaries of the War Years* (Moscow, 1974)

Walker, Jonathan, *Poland Alone: Britain, SOE and the Collapse of the Polish Resistance, 1944* (Stroud, 2008)

Weigley, Russell, *Eisenhower's Lieutenants: The Campaigns of France and Germany 1944–45* (Bloomington, Indiana, 1981)

Werth, Alexander, *Russia at War, 1941–1945* (New York, 1964)

West, Nigel (ed.), *The Guy Liddell Diaries, Volume II, 1942–1945* (Abingdon, 2005)

White, Osmar, *Conqueror's Road: An Eyewitness Report of Germany 1945* (Cambridge, 2003)

Whiting, Charles, *The Last Battle: Montgomery's Campaign April–May 1945* (Marlborough, 1989)

Williamson, David, *The Polish Underground, 1939–1947* (Barnsley, 2012)

Wilmot, Chester, *The Struggle for Europe* (London, 1952)

Wyand, Paul, *Useless if Delayed* (London, 1959)

Yeremenko, Andrei, *A Time of Retribution, 1943–45* (Moscow, 1985)

Zaitsev, Vasily, *Memoirs* (Sverdlovsk, 1989)

Zhukov, Georgy, *Reminiscences and Reflections* (Moscow, 2002)

Zubok, Vladislav, *A Failed Empire: The Soviet Union in the Cold War* (Chapel Hill, North Carolina, 2009)

Zuehlke, Mark, *On to Victory: The Canadian Liberation of the Netherlands, March 23–May 5, 1945* (Vancouver, 2011)

INDEX